## TAKING SIDES

Clashing Views on Controversial

# Issues in Drugs and Society

FIFTH EDITION

Clashing Views on Controversial

# Issues in Drugs and Society

### FIFTH EDITION

Selected, Edited, and with Introductions by

**Raymond Goldberg**
*State University of New York College at Cortland*

McGraw-Hill/Dushkin
A Division of The McGraw-Hill Companies

*To Norma, Tara, and Greta*

Cover image: © 2002 by PhotoDisc, Inc.

Cover Art Acknowledgment
Charles Vitelli

Manufactured in the United States of America

Fifth Edition

23456789BAHBAH5432

Library of Congress Cataloging-in-Publication Data
Main entry under title:
Taking sides: clashing views on controversial issues in drugs and society/selected, edited, and with introductions by Raymond Goldberg.—5th ed.
Includes bibliographical references and index.
1. Drug abuse—Social aspects. I. Goldberg, Raymond, *comp.*
362.29
0-07-248416-0
ISSN: 1094-7566

Printed on Recycled Paper

# Preface

One of the hallmarks of a democratic society is the freedom of its citizens to disagree. This is no more evident than on the topic of drugs. The purpose of this fifth edition of *Taking Sides: Clashing Views on Controversial Issues in Drugs and Society* is to introduce drug-related issues that (1) are pertinent to the reader and (2) have no clear resolution. In the area of drug abuse, there is much difference of opinion regarding drug prevention, causation, and treatment. For example, should drug abuse be prevented by increasing enforcement of drug laws or by making young people more aware of the potential dangers of drugs? Is drug abuse caused by heredity, personality characteristics, or environment? Is drug abuse a medical, legal, or social problem? Are individuals who inject drugs best served by the provision of clean needles or improved treatment? Are self-help groups the most effective treatment for drug abusers?

There are many implications to how the preceding questions are answered. If addiction to drugs is viewed as hereditary rather than as the result of flaws in one's character or personality, then a biological rather than a psychosocial approach to treatment may be pursued. If the consensus is that the prevention of drug abuse can be achieved by eliminating the availability of drugs, then more money and effort will be allocated for interdiction and law enforcement than education. If drug abuse is viewed as a legal problem, then prosecution and incarceration will be the goal. If drug abuse is identified as a medical problem, then abusers will be given treatment. However, if drug abuse is deemed a social problem, then energy will be directed at underlying social factors, such as poverty, unemployment, health care, and education. Not all of the issues have clear answers. One may favor increasing penalties for drug violations *and* improving treatment services. And it is possible to view drug abuse as a medical *and* social *and* legal problem.

The issues debated in this volume deal with both legal and illegal drugs. Although society seems most interested in illegal drugs, it is quite pertinent to address issues related to legal drugs because they cause more deaths and disabilities. No one is untouched by drugs, and everybody is affected by drug use and abuse. Billions of tax dollars are channeled into the war on drugs. Thousands of people are treated for drug abuse, often at public expense. The drug trade spawns crime and violence. Medical treatment for illnesses and injuries resulting from drug use and abuse creates additional burdens to an already extended health care system. Babies born to mothers who used drugs while pregnant are entering schools, and teachers are expected to meet the educational needs of these children. Ritalin is prescribed to tens of thousands of students to deal with their lack of attention in the classroom. Drunk drivers represent a serious threat to our health and safety while raising the cost of everyone's auto insurance. The issues debated here are not on whether or not drug abuse is a problem but what should be done to rectify this problem.

Many of these issues have an immediate impact on the reader. For example, Issue 3, *Will a Lower Blood Alcohol Level for Drunk Driving Reduce Automobile Accidents?* will affect the amount of alcohol that people consume before driving. Issue 14, *Should Nonsmokers Be Concerned About the Effects of Secondhand Smoke?* is relevant to smokers and nonsmokers alike because restrictions on smoking are discussed. Issue 10, *Should Doctors Promote Alcohol for Their Patients?* is important because millions of people have been diagnosed with alcoholism yet millions more have heart disease, the risk for which might be reduced by alcohol. And the question *Should Marijuana Be Legal for Medicinal Purposes?* (Issue 9) may become relevant for many readers or their loved ones someday.

**Plan of the book**    In this fifth edition of *Taking Sides: Clashing Views on Controversial Issues in Drugs and Society,* there are 38 selections dealing with 19 issues. Each issue is preceded by an *introduction* and followed by a *postscript.* The purpose of the introduction is to provide some background information and to set the stage for the debate as it is argued in the "yes" and "no" selections. The postscript summarizes the debate and challenges some of the ideas brought out in the two selections, which can enable the reader to see the issue in other ways. Included in the postscripts are additional suggested readings on the issue. Also, Internet site addresses (URLs) have been provided at the beginning of each part, which should prove useful as starting points for further research. The issues, introductions, and postscripts are designed to stimulate readers to think about and achieve an informed view of some of the critical issues facing society today. At the back of the book is a list of all the *contributors to this volume,* which gives information on the physicians, professors, and policymakers whose views are debated here.

*Taking Sides: Clashing Views on Controversial Issues in Drugs and Society* is a tool to encourage critical thinking. In reading an issue and forming your own opinion you should not feel confined to adopt one or the other of the positions presented. Some readers may see important points on both sides of an issue and may construct for themselves a new and creative approach. Such an approach might incorporate the best of both sides, or it might provide an entirely new vantage point for understanding.

**Changes to this edition**    This fifth edition represents a significant revision. Seven of the 19 issues are completely new: *Will a Lower Blood Alcohol Level for Drunk Driving Reduce Automobile Accidents?* (Issue 3); *Is Drug Addiction a Choice?* (Issue 6); *Are the Adverse Effects of Smoking Exaggerated?* (Issue 8); *Do the Consequences of Caffeine Outweigh the Benefits?* (Issue 11); *Should Advertisements for Prescription Drugs Be Regulated?* (Issue 13); *Should Nonsmokers Be Concerned About the Effects of Secondhand Smoke?* (Issue 14); and *Should Employees Be Required to Participate in Drug Testing?* (Issue 17). For 7 of the issues retained from the previous edition, one or both selections were replaced to reflect more current points of view: Issue 1 on the legalization of drugs; Issue 2 on whether or not more emphasis should be put on stopping the importation of drugs; Issue 5 on prosecuting pregnant drug users; Issue 7 on harm reduction as a drug control policy goal; Issue 9 on legalizing marijuana for medicinal purposes; Issue 15 on total abstinence for alcoholics; and Issue 19 on the effectiveness of antidrug media campaigns. In all, there are 22 new selections.

**A word to the instructor**  To facilitate the use of *Taking Sides,* an *Instructor's Manual With Test Questions* (multiple-choice and essay) and a general guide-book called *Using Taking Sides in the Classroom*, which discusses methods and techniques for implementing the pro-con approach into any classroom setting, can be obtained through the publisher. An online version of *Using Taking Sides in the Classroom* and a correspondence service for Taking Sides adopters can be found at http://www.dushkin.com/usingts/.

    *Taking Sides: Clashing Views on Controversial Issues in Drugs and Society* is only one title in the Taking Sides series. If you are interested in seeing the table of contents for any of the other titles, please visit the Taking Sides Web site at http://www.dushkin.com/takingsides/.

**Acknowledgments**  A number of people have been most helpful in putting together this fifth edition. I would like to thank those professors who adopted the fourth edition of this book and took the time to make suggestions for this subsequent edition:

**Lauren Barrow**
*John Jay College of Criminal Justice*

**David E. Corbin**
*University of Nebraska–Omaha*

**Donald Brodeur**
*Sacred Heart University*

**Mark Kaelin**
*Montclair State University*

**Owen Cater**
*California State University–Sacramento*

    I am also grateful to my students and colleagues, who did not hesitate to share their perceptions and to let me know what they liked and disliked about the fourth edition. Without the editorial staff at McGraw-Hill/Dushkin, this book would not exist. The insightful and professional contributions of Ted Knight, list manager for the Taking Sides program, were most valuable. His thoughtful perceptions and encouragement were most appreciated. In no small way can my family be thanked. I am grateful for their patience and support.

**Raymond Goldberg**
*State University of New York College at Cortland*

# Contents In Brief

# Contents

Ethan A. Nadelmann, director of the Lindesmith Center, maintains that the war on drugs has been futile and counterproductive. He feels that drug abstinence cannot be achieved through legal mandates and that a pragmatic approach is needed. Eric A. Voth, chairman of the International Drug Strategy Institute, contends that the war on drugs is not a failure and that legalizing drugs would worsen drug-related problems. Voth maintains that a restrictive yet compassionate approach toward drug use is the best policy to adopt.

Barry R. McCaffrey, former director of the Office of National Drug Control Policy, argues that the importation of drugs must be stopped to reduce drug use and abuse. If the supply of drugs being trafficked across American borders is reduced, then there will be fewer drug-related problems. He maintains that a coordinated international effort is needed to combat the increased production of heroin, cocaine, and marijuana. Mathea Falco, president of Drug Strategies, a nonprofit policy institute, asserts that the emphasis should not be on curtailing the availability of drugs but on factors that contribute to Americans' use of drugs. She contends that blaming other countries for drug-related problems in the United States is one way for politicians to deflect criticism from themselves. Moreover, she argues, people involved in the drug trade in other countries have little incentive to end their involvement.

Ralph W. Hingson, Timothy Heeren, and Michael R. Winter, of the Boston University School of Public Health, support lowering the legal limit for drunk driving. They note that many states have had fewer alcohol-related automobile accidents after lowering the blood alcohol level for drunk driving. In addition, they contend that drivers are impaired with a relatively small amount of alcohol in their bloodstream. The General Accounting Office (GAO) states that the evidence supporting the beneficial effects of establishing a lower blood alcohol level for drunk driving is inconclusive. The GAO maintains that the government's methods for determining the effectiveness of instituting a lower blood alcohol level are faulty. Also, rates for drunk driving declined regardless of changes in the legal limits for blood alcohol level.

## Issue 4.    Should Needle Exchange Programs Be Supported?    56

In their review of various studies, professor of epidemiology and medicine David Vlahov and Benjamin Junge, evaluation director for the Baltimore Needle Exchange Program, found that needle exchange programs successfully reduced the transmission of the virus that causes AIDS. In addition, many people who participated in needle exchange programs reduced their drug use and sought drug abuse treatment. The Office of National Drug Control Policy, an executive agency that determines policies and objectives for the U.S. drug control program, sees needle exchange programs as an admission of defeat and a retreat from the ongoing battle against drug use, and it argues that compassion and treatment are needed, not needles.

## Issue 5.    Should Pregnant Drug Users Be Prosecuted?    76

Paul A. Logli, an Illinois prosecuting attorney, argues that it is the government's duty to enforce every child's right to begin life with a healthy, drug-free mind and body. Logli maintains that pregnant women who use drugs should be prosecuted because they may harm the life of their unborn children. He feels that it is the state's responsibility to ensure that every baby is born as healthy as possible. Researcher Drew Humphries argues that the prosecution of women who use drugs while pregnant has resulted from overzealous efforts on the part of a handful of state prosecutors. Humphries asserts that the prosecution of pregnant drug users is unfair because poor women are more likely to be the targets of such prosecution and that these cases do not hold up to legal standards.

Psychotherapist Jeffrey A. Schaler maintains that drug addiction should not be considered a disease, a condition over which one has no control. Schaler states that diseases have distinct characteristics and that drug addiction does not share these characteristics. Classifying behavior as socially unacceptable does not prove that it is a disease, according to Schaler. Professor of psychology Alice M. Young points out that a small number of drugs produce pleasurable sensations in the brain, increasing the likelihood that drug-taking behavior will be repeated. In addition, tolerance and dependency may result when drugs are taken frequently. If tolerance develops, then the drug user must increase the dosage level to achieve the desired effect, increasing the possibility of dependency.

Robert J. MacCoun, an associate professor in the Graduate School of Public Policy at the University of California, Berkeley, supports efforts to minimize problems associated with drugs. He states that a harm reduction approach will not resolve all drug problems, but he feels that reducing those problems is a desirable goal. Sociology professor Grazyna Zajdow questions a policy that strives to reduce the harm of drugs. She maintains that drug use will remain a serious health problem regardless of whether or not harm reduction is the goal. Zajdow contends that using methadone to help heroin addicts overcome their addiction is merely the replacement of one addiction for another.

# PART 2   DRUGS AND SOCIAL POLICY   141

Author Stephen Goode interviews Robert Levy, of the Cato Institute, who maintains that government statistics distort and exaggerate the dangers of cigarette smoking. Levy argues that smokers are less likely to eat nutritional meals or exercise and that many are poor and uneducated. Thus, factors besides smoking may contribute to the poor health and decreased longevity of many tobacco users. The World Health Organization's report on the increase in smoking delineates the health and economic expense of tobacco use throughout the world. The report indicates that one barrier to stemming smoking is a lack of information about the risks of tobacco use. The report also states that tobacco is addictive and that tobacco manufacturers are expanding because of the tremendous profits they make.

Professor of psychiatry Lester Grinspoon argues that anecdotal evidence indicates that marijuana has medical benefits for patients suffering from chemotherapy nausea, AIDS, glaucoma, chronic pain, epilepsy, and migraine headaches. He asserts that the federal government is prohibiting its use without justification. James R. McDonough, director of the Florida Office of Drug Control, agrees that compounds in marijuana, such as THC, may have the potential to be medically valuable. However, smoked marijuana has not been proven to be of medicinal value. In addition, states McDonough, there are existing, approved drugs that are more effective for conditions that may be helped by marijuana use.

Psychologist Stanton Peele, an expert on alcoholism and addiction, asserts that physicians should recommend that their patients drink alcohol in moderate amounts. He maintains that numerous studies demonstrate the benefits of moderate alcohol use in reducing the risk of coronary heart disease, the leading cause of death in the United States. Albert B. Lowenfels, a professor at New York Medical College, contends that recommending moderate alcohol consumption is not prudent, especially since many people come from families with histories of alcohol abuse. He argues that it is inappropriate to extol the merits of moderate alcohol use to people who have abstained throughout their lives.

Writer Nell Boyce states that caffeine is more addictive than most people realize. Boyce maintains that caffeine not only causes dependency but also has a myriad of other effects. Caffeine raises blood pressure, a factor leading to heart disease, and there is also evidence that caffeine consumption during pregnancy involves some risk for the fetus. The editors of *Choice* magazine argue that many of the risks associated with moderate amounts of caffeine are exaggerated. They admit that caffeine produces some mild effects, such as dependence and high blood pressure. However, they maintain that the research showing that moderate caffeine use causes heart disease, osteoporosis, and cancer is inconclusive.

Harvard Medical School professor Richard Bromfield contends that physicians are often too eager to prescribe Ritalin for children with attention deficit/hyperactivity disorder (ADHD). Bromfield is concerned that Ritalin's long-term effects have not been adequately researched and that its overuse may be masking other childhood disorders. George Washington Medical School professor Jerry Wiener maintains that Ritalin has been proven to be safe and effective. Wiener argues that attention deficit/hyperactivity disorder is underdiagnosed in many instances and that children who could benefit from the use of Ritalin often do not receive it.

Matthew F. Hollon, a physician, maintains that doctors may compromise their judgment when patients insist on being given drugs that they see advertised in the media. He asserts that pharmaceutical manufacturers advertise directly to consumers to increase their profits, not to help patients. Alan F. Holmer, president of Pharmaceutical Research and Manufacturers of America, contends that advertisements for prescription drugs serve to educate the consumer, that such advertisements provide a benefit to the public's health, and that patients are more likely to comply with treatment if they request it.

John R. Garrison, CEO of the American Lung Association, contends that evidence of adverse effects of secondhand smoke on nonsmokers is strong. He asserts that years of research clearly show that second-hand smoke is a factor in the development of lung cancer, heart disease, asthma, and respiratory infections. Statisticians J. B. Copas and J. Q. Shi argue that research demonstrating that passive smoking is harmful is biased. They argue that many journals are more likely to publish articles if passive smoking is shown to be deleterious and that the findings of many studies exaggerate the adverse effects of passive smoking.

Professor of health Thomas Byrd maintains that Alcoholics Anonymous (AA) provides more effective treatment for alcoholics than psychiatrists, members of the clergy, or hospital treatment centers. Byrd contends that AA is the most powerful and scientific program, in contrast to all other therapies. Addiction treatment specialist Joseph Volpicelli and journalist Maia Szalavitz advocate a moderate drinking approach for individuals with drinking problems. They argue that abstinence may be counterproductive for many problem drinkers.

Researcher Michele Alicia Harmon reports that Drug Abuse Resistance Education (DARE) had a positive impact on fifth-grade students in terms of attitudes against substance abuse, assertiveness, positive peer asso-ciation, association with drug-using peers, alcohol use within the previous year, and prosocial norms. Drug researchers Richard R. Clayton et al. maintain that despite DARE's popularity, it does not produce less drug use among its participants. They argue that the money that is spent by the federal government to fund DARE could be used for more effective drug prevention programs.

# Introduction

## Drugs: Divergent Views

Raymond Goldberg

## An Overview of the Problem

No one is immune to the effects of drugs. Very few topics generate as much debate and concern as drugs. Drugs and issues related to drugs are evident in every aspect of life. There is much dismay that drug use and abuse cause many of the problems that plague society. Individuals, families, and communities are adversely affected by drug abuse, and many people wonder if morality will continue to decay because of drugs. The news media are replete with horrendous stories about people under the influence of drugs committing crimes against others, senseless drug-related deaths, men and women who compromise themselves for drugs, and women who deliver babies that are addicted to or impaired by drugs.

From conception until death, almost everyone is touched by drug use. In some cases, stimulants such as Ritalin are prescribed for children so that they can learn or behave better in school. Some students take stimulants so that they can stay up late to write a term paper or lose a few pounds. Many teenagers take drugs because they want to be accepted by their friends who use drugs or to deal with daily stress. For many people, young and old, the elixir for relaxation may be sipped, swallowed, smoked, or sniffed. Some people who live in poverty-stricken conditions anesthetize themselves with drugs as a way to escape from their environment. On the other hand, some individuals who seem to have everything immerse themselves in drugs, possibly out of boredom. To cope with the ailments that come with getting older, the elderly often rely on drugs. Many people use drugs to confront their pains, problems, frustrations, and disappointments. Others take drugs simply because they like the effects or out of curiosity.

## Background on Drugs

Despite one's feelings about drug use, drugs are an integral part of society. The popularity of various drugs rises and falls with the times. For example, according to annual surveys of 8th-, 10th-, and 12th-grade students in the United States, the use of LSD and marijuana increased throughout the 1990s despite a decline in use throughout the 1980s (Johnston, O'Malley, and Bachman, 2000).

Especially alarming is the fact that the largest increase in drug use in the 1990s occurred among 8th-grade students.

Understanding the history and role of drugs in society is critical to our ability to address drug-related problems. Drugs are believed to have been used throughout human history. Alcohol played a significant role in the early history of the United States. According to Lee (1963), for example, the Pilgrims landed at Plymouth Rock because they ran out of beer. Marijuana use dates back nearly 5,000 years, when the Chinese Emperor Shen Nung prescribed it for medical ailments like malaria, gout, rheumatism, and gas pains. Hallucinogens have existed since the beginning of humankind. About 150 of the estimated 500,000 different plant species have been used for hallucinogenic purposes (Schultes and Hofmann, 1979).

Opium, from which narcotics are derived, was alluded to often by the ancient Greeks and Romans; opium is referred to in Homer's *Odyssey* (circa 1000 B.C.). In the Arab world opium and hashish were widely used (primarily because alcohol was forbidden). The Arabs were introduced to opium through their trading in India and China. Arab physician Avicenna (A.D. 1000) wrote an extremely complete medical textbook in which he describes the benefits of opium. Ironically, Avicenna died from an overdose of opium and wine. Eventually, opium played a central role in a war between China and the British government.

Caffeine is believed to be the most commonly consumed drug throughout the world. More than 9 out of every 10 Americans consume caffeine. Coffee dates back to A.D. 900, when, to stay awake during lengthy religious vigils, Muslims in Arabia drank coffee. However, coffee was later condemned because the Koran, the holy book of Islam, described coffee as an intoxicant (Brecher, 1972). Drinking coffee became a popular activity in Europe, although it was banned for a short time. In the mid-1600s, coffeehouses were prime locations for men to converse, relax, and do business. Medical benefits were associated with coffee, although England's King Charles II and English physicians tried to prohibit its use. Caffeine is still a source of controversy today. Issue 11 discusses whether or not the consequences of caffeine outweigh its benefits.

One function of coffeehouses was as places of learning. For a one-cent cup of coffee, one could listen to well-known literary and political leaders (Meyer, 1954). Lloyd's of London, the famous insurance company, started around 1700 from Edward Lloyd's coffeehouse. However, not everyone was pleased with these "penny universities," as they were called. In 1674, in response to the countless hours men spent at the coffeehouses, a group of women published a pamphlet titled *The Women's Petition Against Coffee*, which criticized coffee use. Despite the protestations against coffee, its use proliferated. Today, more than 325 years later, coffeehouses are still flourishing as centers for relaxation and conversation.

Coca leaves, from which cocaine is derived, have been chewed since before recorded history. Drawings found on South American pottery illustrate that coca chewing was practiced before the rise of the Incan Empire. The coca plant was held in high regard: considered a present from the gods, it was used in religious rituals and burial ceremonies. When the Spaniards arrived in South America, they tried to regulate coca chewing by the natives but were unsuccessful. Cocaine was later included in the popular soft drink Coca-Cola. Another stimulant, amphetamine, was developed in the 1920s and was originally used to treat narcolepsy. It was later prescribed for treating asthma and for weight loss. Today the stimulant Ritalin is given to more than 1 million school-age children annually to address attention deficit disorders. This raises the question of whether or not Ritalin is being overprescribed (Issue 12).

Minor tranquilizers, also called "antianxiety drugs," were first marketed in the early 1950s. The sales of these drugs were astronomical. Drugs to reduce anxiety were in high demand. Another group of antianxiety drugs are benzodiazepines. Two well-known benzodiazepines are Librium and Valium; the latter ranks as the most widely prescribed drug in the history of American medicine. Xanax, which has replaced Valium as the tranquilizer of choice, is one of the five most precribed drugs in the United States today. Minor tranquilizers are noteworthy because they are legally prescribed to alter one's consciousness. Mind-altering drugs existed prior to minor tranquilizers, but they were not prescribed for that purpose. In many instances consumers request prescription drugs from their physicians after seeing those drugs advertised in the media. Whether or not there should be more regulation on prescription drug advertising is examined in Issue 13.

# Combating Drug Problems

The debates in *Taking Sides: Clashing Views on Controversial Issues in Drugs and Society* confront many important drug-related issues. For example, what is the most effective way to reduce drug abuse? Should laws preventing drug use and abuse be more strongly enforced, or should drug laws be less punitive? How can the needs of individuals be met while serving the greater good of society? Should drug abuse be seen as a public health problem or a legal problem? Are drugs an American problem or an international problem? The debate regarding whether or not the drug problem should be fought nationally or internationally is addressed in Issue 2. One could argue that America would benefit most by focusing its attention on stopping the proliferation of drugs in other countries.

One of the oldest debates concerns whether or not drug use should be legal. Issue 1 deals with this question. In recent years this debate has become more intense because well-known individuals such as political analyst William F. Buckley, Jr., and economist Milton Friedman have come out in support of legalization. For many people the issue is not whether drug use is good or bad but whether or not people should be punished for taking drugs. One question that is basic to this debate is whether drug legalization causes more or less damage than drug criminalization. A related issue, Issue 7, discusses whether or not the United States should adopt a drug policy that focuses on harm reduction. A pertinent issue concerns needle exchange programs, in which clean needles are provided to individuals who inject themselves with drugs (Issue 4). There are obvious inherent dangers to injecting drugs; yet does the provision of sterile needles help these people? Should people be given equipment that is used for an illegal act? What has been the effect of needle exchange programs in cities where they have been instituted?

In a related matter, should potentially harmful drugs be restricted even if they may be of medical benefit? Some people are concerned that drugs used for medical reasons may be illegally diverted. Yet most people agree that patients should have access to the best medicine available. In referenda in numerous states, voters have approved the medical use of marijuana. Is the federal government consistent in allowing potentially harmful drugs to be used for medical purposes? For example, narcotics are often prescribed for pain relief. Is there a chance that patients who are given narcotics will become addicted? Issue 9 debates whether or not marijuana has a legitimate medical use. Issue 6 looks at the issue of drug addiction, specifically whether addiction is based on heredity or whether it is a choice that people make.

Many of the issues discussed in this book deal with drug prevention. As with most controversial issues, there is a lack of consensus on how to prevent drug-related problems. For example, Issue 5 debates whether or not prosecuting women who use drugs during pregnancy will affect drug use by other women who become pregnant. Will pregnant women avoid prenatal care because they fear prosecution? Will newborns be better served if pregnant women who use drugs are charged with child abuse? Are these laws discriminatory, since most cases that are prosecuted involve poor women?

Some contend that drug laws discriminate not only according to social class but also according to age and ethnicity. Many drug laws in the United States were initiated because of their association with different ethnic groups: Opium smoking was made illegal after it was associated with Chinese immigrants (Musto, 1991); cocaine became illegal after it was linked with blacks; and marijuana was outlawed after it was linked with Hispanics.

Drug-related issues are not limited to illegal drugs. Tobacco and alcohol are two pervasive legal drugs that generate much debate. For example, are the adverse effects of smoking exaggerated (Issue 8)? Also, should nonsmokers be concerned about the effects of secondhand smoke (Issue 14)? With regard to alcohol, Issue 10 looks at whether or not physicians should promote moderate alcohol use. A factor in this debate is whether or not alcoholism is hereditary, which may determine whether alcoholics should totally abstain from alcohol or whether they can learn to drink moderately (Issue 15). Another issue relating to legal drugs deals with whether or not the legal blood alcohol concentration limit for driving while intoxicated should be lowered (Issue 3).

## Gateway Drugs

An inhalant is a type of drug that is popular with many young people. Like tobacco and alcohol, inhalants are considered "gateway" drugs, which are drugs that are often used as a prelude to other, usually illegal, drugs. Inhalants are composed of numerous products, ranging from paints and solvents to glues, aerosol sprays, petroleum products, cleaning supplies, and nitrous oxide (laughing gas). Inhalant abuse in the United States is a relatively new phenomenon. It seems that until the media started reporting on the dangers of inhalant abuse, its use was not particularly common (Brecher, 1972). This raises a question regarding the impact of the media on drug use. Issue 19 examines the effect of public service announcements on teen drug use.

Advertisements are an integral part of the media, and their influence can be seen in the growing popularity of cigarette smoking among adolescents. In the 1880s cigarette smoking escalated in the United States. One of the most important factors contributing to cigarettes' popularity at that time was the development of the cigarette-rolling machine (previously, cigarettes could be rolled at a rate of only four per minute). Also, cigarette smoking, which was considered an activity reserved for men, began to be seen as an option for women. As cigarettes began to be marketed toward women, cigarette smoking became more widespread. As one can see from this introduction, numerous factors affect drug use. One argument is that if young people were better educated about the hazards of drugs and were taught how to understand the role of the media, then limits on advertising would not be necessary.

## Drug Prevention and Treatment

Some people maintain that educating young people about drugs is one way to prevent drug use and abuse. Studies show that by delaying the onset of drug use, the likelihood of drug abuse is reduced. In the past, however, drug education had little impact on drug-taking behavior (Goldberg, 2000). Some programs have actually resulted in increased drug use because they stimulated curiosity. Does this suggest that drug education is detrimental or that more effective programs need to be developed? One nationwide program that deals with drug use is Drug Abuse Resistance Education (DARE). Issue 16 examines whether or not DARE effectively reduces the incidence of drug use and abuse.

Another way to reduce drug abuse that has been heavily promoted is drug abuse treatment. However, is drug abuse treatment effective? Does it prevent recurring drug abuse, reduce criminal activity and violence, and halt the spread of drug-related disease? Issue 18 examines whether or not drug abuse treatment affects these outcomes. A study by Glass (1995) showed that methadone maintenance, a treatment for heroin addiction, may have some benefits. But do those benefits outweigh the costs of the treatment? If society feels that treatment is a better alternative to incarceration, it is imperative to know if treatment works.

## Distinguishing Between Drug Use, Misuse, and Abuse

Although the terms *drug, drug misuse,* and *drug abuse* are commonly used, they have different meanings to different people. Defining these terms may seem simple at first, but many factors affect how they are defined. Should a definition for a drug be based on its behavioral effects, its effects on society, its pharmacological properties, or its chemical composition? One simple, concise definition of a drug is "any substance that produces an effect on the mind, body, or both."

One could also define a drug by how it is used. For example, if watching television or listening to music are forms of escape from daily problems, then they may be considered drugs.

Legal drugs cause far more death and disability than illegal drugs, but society appears to be most concerned with the use of illegal drugs. The potential harms of legal drugs tend to be minimized. By viewing drugs as illicit substances only, people can fail to recognize that commonly used substances such as caffeine, tobacco, alcohol, and over-the-counter preparations are drugs. If these substances are not perceived as drugs, then people might not acknowledge that they can be misused or abused.

Definitions for misuse and abuse are not affected by a drug's legal status. Drug misuse refers to the inappropriate or unintentional use of drugs. Someone who smokes marijuana to improve his or her study skills is misusing marijuana because the drug impairs short-term memory. Drug abuse alludes to physical, emotional, financial, intellectual, or social consequences arising from chronic drug use. Under this definition, can a person abuse food, aspirin, soft drinks, or chocolate? Also, should a person be free to make potentially unhealthy choices?

## The Cost of the War on Drugs

The U.S. government spends billions of dollars each year to curb the rise in drug use. A major portion of that money goes toward law enforcement. Vast sums of money are used by the military to intercept drug shipments, while foreign governments are given money to help them with their own wars on drugs. A smaller portion of the funds is used for treating and preventing drug abuse. One strategy to eliminate drug use is drug testing. Currently, men and women in the military, athletes, industry employees, and others are subject to random drug testing.

The expense of drug abuse to industries is staggering: Experts estimate that almost 20 percent of workers in the United States use dangerous drugs while at work; and the cost of drug abuse to employers is approximately $120 billion each year (Brookler, 1992). Compared to nonaddicted employees, drug-dependent employees are absent from their jobs more often, and drug users are less likely to maintain stable job histories than nonusers (Kandel, Murphy, and Kraus, 1985). In its report *America's Habit: Drug Abuse, Drug Trafficking and Organized Crime,* the President's Commission on Organized Crime supported testing all federal workers for drugs. It further recommended that federal contracts be withheld from private employers who do not implement drug-testing procedures (Brinkley, 1986).

A prerequisite to being hired by many companies is passing a drug test. Drug testing may be having a positive effect. From 1987 to 1994 the number of workers testing positive declined 57 percent (Center for Substance Abuse Prevention, 1995). Many companies have reported a decrease in accidents and injuries after the initiation of drug testing (Angarola, 1991). However, most Americans consider drug testing degrading and dehumanizing (Walsh and Trumble, 1991). An important question is, What is the purpose of drug testing? Drug testing raises three other important questions: (1) Does drug testing prevent drug use? (2) Is the point of drug testing to help employees with drug problems or to get rid of employees who use drugs? and (3) How can the civil rights of employees be balanced against the rights of companies? Issue 17 examines whether or not employees should be required to participate in drug testing.

How serious is the drug problem? Is it real, or is there simply an unreasonable hysteria regarding drugs? In the United States there has been a growing intolerance toward drug use during the last 20 years (Musto, 1991). Drugs are a problem for many people. Drugs can affect one's physical, social, intellectual, and emotional health. Ironically, some people take drugs *because* they produce these effects. Individuals who take drugs receive some kind of reward from the drug; the reward may come from being associated with others who use drugs or from the feelings derived from the drug. If these rewards were not present, people would likely cease using drugs.

The disadvantages of drugs are numerous: they interfere with career aspirations and individual maturation. They have also been associated with violent behavior; addiction; discord among siblings, children, parents, spouses, and friends; work-related problems; financial troubles; problems in school; legal predicaments; accidents; injuries; and death. Yet are drugs the cause or the symptom of the problems that people have? Perhaps drugs are one aspect of a larger scenario in which society is experiencing much change and in which drug use is merely another thread in the social fabric.

# References

R. T. Angarola, "Substance-Abuse Testing in the Workplace: Legal Issues and Corporate Responses," in R. H. Coombs and L. J. West, eds., *Drug Testing: Issues and Options* (Oxford University Press, 1991).

E. M. Brecher, *Licit and Illicit Drugs* (Little, Brown, 1972).

J. Brinkley, "Drug Use Held Mostly Stable or Better," *The New York Times* (October 10, 1986).

R. Brookler, "Industry Standards in Workplace Drug Testing," *Personnel Journal* (April 1992), pp. 128–132.

*Drug-Free for a New Century,* Center for Substance Abuse Prevention, Substance Abuse and Mental Health Services Administration (1995).

R. M. Glass, "Methadone Maintenance: New Research on a Controversial Treatment," *Journal of the American Medical Association* (vol. 269, no. 15, 1995), pp. 1995–1996.

R. Goldberg, *Drugs Across the Spectrum* (Wadsworth, 2000).

L. D. Johnston, P. O. O'Malley, and J. G. Bachman, *Monitoring the Future* (National Institute on Drug Abuse, 2000).

D. B. Kandel, D. Murphy, and D. Kraus, "Cocaine Use in Young Adulthood: Patterns of Use and Psychosocial Correlates," in N. J. Kozel and E. H. Adams, eds., *Cocaine Use in America: Epidemiologic and Clinical Perspectives* (National Institute on Drug Abuse, 1985).

H. Lee, *How Dry We Were: Prohibition Revisited* (Prentice Hall, 1963).

H. Meyer, *Old English Coffee Houses* (Rodale Press, 1954).

D. F. Musto, "Opium, Cocaine and Marijuana in American History," *Scientific American* (July 1991), pp. 40–47.

R. E. Schultes and A. Hofmann, *Plants of the Gods: Origins of Hallucinogenic Use* (McGraw-Hill, 1979).

J. M. Walsh and J. G. Trumble, "The Politics of Drug Testing," in R. H. Coombs and L. J. West, eds., *Drug Testing: Issues and Options* (Oxford University Press, 1991).

### The Drug Reform Coordination Network (DRCNet)

The Drug Reform Coordination Network is a national network of nearly 20,000 activists and concerned citizens—including parents, educators, students, lawyers, health care professionals, academics, and others—working for drug policy reform from a variety of perspectives, including harm reduction, reform of sentencing and forfeiture laws, medicalization of currently Schedule I drugs, and promotion of an open debate on drug prohibition.

http://www.drcnet.org/index.html

### .08 BAC Limit

This site of the National Highway Traffic Safety Administration (NHTSA) features a handful of links on .08 blood alcohol concentration (BAC) laws, including a progress report on President Bill Clinton's 1998 initiative to make .08 BAC the national legal limit and three studies evaluating .08 laws.

http://www.nhtsa.dot.gov/people/injury/alcohol/
limit.08/index.html

### The North American Syringe Exchange Network (NASEN)

The North American Syringe Exchange Network (NASEN) is dedicated to the creation, expansion, and continued existence of syringe exchange programs as a proven method of stopping the transmission of blood-borne pathogens in the drug-injecting community.

. http://www.nasen.org

### Association of Persons Affected by Addiction (APAA)

The Association of Persons Affected by Addiction (APPA) provides a channel through which the collective voice of the members of the recovery community may be heard in matters directly affecting them. This site includes a discussion forum and many related links to organizations and sites on a variety of addictions.

http://www.apaarc.org

### International Drug Control Policy Links and Resources

This simple site provides links to domestic organizations, foreign policy organizations, U.S. government links, and other resources related to international drug control policies.

http://www.wola.org/drugpollinks.html

# PART 1

# Drugs and Public Policy

*D*rug abuse causes a myriad of problems for society: The psychological and physical effects of drug abuse can be devastating; many drugs are addictive; drugs wreak havoc on families; disability and death result from drug overdoses; and drugs are frequently implicated in crimes, especially violent crimes. Identifying drug-related problems is not difficult. What is unclear is the best course of action to take when dealing with these problems.

Three scenarios exist for dealing with drugs: policies can be made more restrictive, they can be made less restrictive, or they can remain the same. The position one takes depends on whether drug use and abuse are seen as legal, social, or medical problems. Perhaps the issue is not whether drugs are good or bad but how to minimize the harm of drugs. The debates in this section explore these issues.

- Should Drugs Be Legalized?

- Should the United States Put More Emphasis on Stopping the Importation of Drugs?

- Will a Lower Blood Alcohol Level for Drunk Driving Reduce Automobile Accidents?

- Should Needle Exchange Programs Be Supported?

- Should Pregnant Drug Users Be Prosecuted?

- Is Drug Addiction a Choice?

- Is Harm Reduction a Desirable National Drug Control Policy Goal?

# ISSUE 1

## Should Drugs Be Legalized?

**YES: Ethan A. Nadelmann**, from "Commonsense Drug Policy," *Foreign Affairs* (January/February 1998)

**NO: Eric A. Voth**, from "America's Longest 'War,'" *The World & I* (February 2000)

### ISSUE SUMMARY

**YES:** Ethan A. Nadelmann, director of the Lindesmith Center, maintains that the war on drugs has been futile and counterproductive. He feels that drug abstinence cannot be achieved through legal mandates and that a pragmatic approach is needed.

**NO:** Eric A. Voth, chairman of the International Drug Strategy Institute, contends that the war on drugs is not a failure and that legalizing drugs would worsen drug-related problems. Voth maintains that a restrictive yet compassionate approach toward drug use is the best policy to adopt.

In 1999 the federal government allocated $19 billion to control drug use and to enforce laws that are designed to protect society from the perils created by drug use. Some people believe that the government's war on drugs could be more effective but that governmental agencies and communities are not fighting hard enough to stop drug use. They also hold that laws to halt drug use are too few and too lenient. Others contend that the war against drugs is unnecessary; that, in fact, society has already lost the war on drugs. These individuals feel that the best way to remedy drug problems is to end the fight altogether by ending the criminalization of drug use.

There are conflicting views among both liberals and conservatives on whether or not legislation has had the intended result of curtailing the problems of drug use. Many argue that legislation and the criminalization of drugs has been counterproductive in controlling drug problems. Some suggest that the criminalization of drugs has actually contributed to and worsened the social ills associated with drugs. Proponents of drug legalization maintain that the war on drugs, not drugs themselves, is damaging to American society. They do not advocate drug use; they argue only that laws against drugs exacerbate problems related to drugs.

Proponents of drug legalization argue that the strict enforcement of drug laws damages American society because it drives people to violence and crime. These people overburden the court system, thus rendering it ineffective. Moreover, proponents contend that the criminalization of drugs fuels organized crime, allows children to be pulled into the drug business, and makes illegal drugs themselves more dangerous because they are manufactured without government standards or regulations. Hence, drugs may be adulterated or of unidentified potency. Legalization advocates also argue that legalization would take the profits out of drug sales, thereby decreasing the value of and demand for drugs. In addition, the costs resulting from law enforcement are far greater to society than the benefits of criminalization.

Some legalization advocates argue that the federal government's prohibition stance on drugs is an immoral and impossible objective. To achieve a "drug-free society" is self-defeating and a misnomer because drugs have always been a part of human culture. Furthermore, prohibition efforts indicate a disregard for the private freedom of individuals because they assume that individuals are incapable of making their own choices. Drug proponents assert that their personal sovereignty should be respected over any government agenda, including the war on drugs.

People who favor legalizing drugs feel that legalization would give the government more control over the purity and potency of drugs and that the international drug trade would be regulated more effectively. Legalization, they argue, would take the emphasis off of law enforcement policies and allow more effort to be put toward education, prevention, and treatment. Decriminalization advocates assert that most of the negative implications of drug prohibition would disappear.

Opponents of this view maintain that legalization is not the solution to drug problems and that it is a very dangerous idea. Legalization, they assert, will drastically increase drug use because if drugs are more accessible, more people will turn to drugs. This upsurge in drug use will come at an incredibly high price: American society will be overrun with drug-related accidents, loss in worker productivity, and hospital emergency rooms filled with drug-related emergencies. Drug treatment efforts would be futile because users would have no legal incentive to stop taking drugs. Also, users may prefer drugs rather than rehabilitation, and education programs may be ineffective in dissuading children from using drugs. Advocates of drug legalization maintain that drug abuse is a "victimless crime" in which the only person being hurt is the drug user. Legalization opponents argue that this notion is ludicrous and dangerous because drug use has dire repercussions for all of society. Drugs can destroy the minds and bodies of many people. Also, regulations to control drug use have a legitimate social aim to protect society and its citizens from the harm of drugs.

In the following selections, Ethan A. Nadelmann explains why he feels drugs should be legalized, while Eric A. Voth describes the detrimental effects that he believes would occur as a result of drug legalization.

**Ethan A. Nadelmann**

 **YES**

# Commonsense Drug Policy

In 1988 Congress passed a resolution proclaiming its goal of "a drug-free America by 1995." U.S. drug policy has failed persistently over the decades because it has preferred such rhetoric to reality, and moralism to pragmatism. Politicians confess their youthful indiscretions, then call for tougher drug laws. Drug control officials make assertions with no basis in fact or science. Police officers, generals, politicians, and guardians of public morals qualify as drug czars—but not, to date, a single doctor or public health figure. Independent commissions are appointed to evaluate drug policies, only to see their recommendations ignored as politically risky. And drug policies are designed, implemented, and enforced with virtually no input from the millions of Americans they affect most: drug users. Drug abuse is a serious problem, both for individual citizens and society at large, but the "war on drugs" has made matters worse, not better.

Drug warriors often point to the 1980s as a time in which the drug war really worked. Illicit drug use by teenagers peaked around 1980, then fell more than 50 percent over the next 12 years. During the 1996 presidential campaign, Republican challenger Bob Dole made much of the recent rise in teenagers' use of illicit drugs, contrasting it with the sharp drop during the Reagan and Bush administrations. President [Bill] Clinton's response was tepid, in part because he accepted the notion that teen drug use is the principal measure of drug policy's success or failure; at best, he could point out that the level was still barely half what it had been in 1980.

In 1980, however, no one had ever heard of the cheap, smokable form of cocaine called crack, or drug-related HIV infection or AIDS. By the 1990s, both had reached epidemic proportions in American cities, largely driven by prohibitionist economics and morals indifferent to the human consequences of the drug war. In 1980, the federal budget for drug control was about $1 billion, and state and local budgets were perhaps two or three times that. By 1997, the federal drug control budget had ballooned to $16 billion, two-thirds of it for law enforcement agencies, and state and local funding to at least that. On any day in 1980, approximately 50,000 people were behind bars for violating a drug law. By 1997, the number had increased eightfold, to about 400,000. These are

From Ethan A. Nadelmann, "Commonsense Drug Policy," *Foreign Affairs*, vol. 77, no. 1 (January/February 1998). Copyright © 1998 by The Council on Foreign Relations, Inc. Reprinted by permission of *Foreign Affairs*.

the results of a drug policy overreliant on criminal justice "solutions," ideologically wedded to abstinence-only treatment, and insulated from cost-benefit analysis.

Imagine instead a policy that starts by acknowledging that drugs are here to stay, and that we have no choice but to learn how to live with them so that they cause the least possible harm. Imagine a policy that focuses on reducing not illicit drug use per se but the crime and misery caused by both drug abuse and prohibitionist policies. And imagine a drug policy based not on the fear, prejudice, and ignorance that drive America's current approach but rather on common sense, science, public health concerns, and human rights. Such a policy is possible in the United States, especially if Americans are willing to learn from the experiences of other countries where such policies are emerging. . . .

## Reefer Sanity

Cannabis, in the form of marijuana and hashish, is by far the most popular illicit drug in the United States. More than a quarter of Americans admit to having tried it. Marijuana's popularity peaked in 1980, dropped steadily until the early 1990s, and is now on the rise again. Although it is not entirely safe, especially when consumed by children, smoked heavily, or used when driving, it is clearly among the least dangerous psychoactive drugs in common use. In 1988 the administrative law judge for the Drug Enforcement Administration, Francis Young, reviewed the evidence and concluded that "marihuana, in its natural form, is one of the safest therapeutically active substances known to man."

As with needle exchange and methadone treatment, American politicians have ignored or spurned the findings of government commissions and scientific organizations concerning marijuana policy. In 1972 the National Commission on Marihuana and Drug Abuse—created by President Nixon and chaired by a former Republican governor, Raymond Shafer—recommended that possession of up to one ounce of marijuana be decriminalized. Nixon rejected the recommendation. In 1982 a panel appointed by the National Academy of Sciences reached the same conclusion as the Shafer Commission.

Between 1973 and 1978, with attitudes changing, 11 states approved decriminalization statutes that reclassified marijuana possession as a misdemeanor, petty offense, or civil violation punishable by no more than a $100 fine. Consumption trends in those states and in states that retained stricter sanctions were indistinguishable. A 1988 scholarly evaluation of the Moscone Act, California's 1976 decriminalization law, estimated that the state had saved half a billion dollars in arrest costs since the law's passage. Nonetheless, public opinion began to shift in 1978. No other states decriminalized marijuana, and some eventually recriminalized it.

Between 1973 and 1989, annual arrests on marijuana charges by state and local police ranged between 360,000 and 460,000. The annual total fell to 283,700 in 1991, but has since more than doubled. In 1996, 641,642 people were arrested for marijuana, 85 percent of them for possession, not sale, of the drug. Prompted by concern over rising marijuana use among adolescents and fears of being labeled soft on drugs, the Clinton administration launched its own anti-marijuana campaign in 1995. But the administration's claims to have identified new risks of marijuana consumption—including a purported link between marijuana and violent behavior—have not withstood scrutiny.[1] Neither Congress nor the White House seems likely to put the issue of marijuana policy before a truly independent advisory commission, given the consistency with which such commissions have reached politically unacceptable conclusions.

In contrast, governments in Europe and Australia, notably in the Netherlands, have reconsidered their cannabis policies. In 1976 the Baan Commission in the Netherlands recommended, and the Dutch government adopted, a policy of separating the "soft" and "hard" drug markets. Criminal penalties for and police efforts against heroin trafficking were increased, while those against cannabis were relaxed. Marijuana and hashish can now be bought in hundreds of "coffeeshops" throughout the country. Advertising, open displays, and sales to minors are prohibited. Police quickly close coffeeshops caught selling hard drugs. Almost no one is arrested or even fined for cannabis possession, and the government collects taxes on the gray market sales.

In the Netherlands today, cannabis consumption for most age groups is similar to that in the United States. Young Dutch teenagers, however, are less likely to sample marijuana than their American peers; from 1992 to 1994, only 7.2 percent of Dutch youths between the ages of 12 and 15 reported having tried marijuana, compared to 13.5 percent of Americans in that age bracket. Far fewer Dutch youths, moreover, experiment with cocaine, buttressing officials' claims of success in separating the markets for hard and soft drugs. Most Dutch parents regard the "reefer madness" anti-marijuana campaigns of the United States as silly.

Dutch coffeeshops have not been problem free. Many citizens have complained about the proliferation of coffeeshops, as well as nuisances created by foreign youth flocking to party in Dutch border cities. Organized crime involvement in the growing domestic cannabis industry is of increasing concern. The Dutch government's efforts to address the problem by more openly and systematically regulating supplies to coffeeshops, along with some of its other drug policy initiatives, have run up against pressure from abroad, notably from Paris, Stockholm, Bonn, and Washington. In late 1995 French President Jacques Chirac began publicly berating The Hague for its drug policies, even threatening to suspend implementation of the Schengen Agreement allowing the free movement of people across borders of European Union (EU) countries. Some of Chirac's political allies called the Netherlands a narco-state. Dutch officials responded with evidence of the relative success of their policies, while pointing out that most cannabis seized in France originates in Morocco (which Chirac has refrained from criticizing because of his government's close relations with King Hassan). The Hague, however, did announce reductions in the number of coffeeshops and the amount of cannabis customers can buy there. But it still sanctions the coffeeshops, and a few municipalities actually operate them.

Notwithstanding the attacks, in the 1990s the trend toward decriminalization of cannabis has accelerated in Europe. Across much of Western Europe, possession and even minor sales of the drug are effectively decriminalized.

Spain decriminalized private use of cannabis in 1983. In Germany, the Federal Constitutional Court effectively sanctioned a cautious liberalization of cannabis policy in a widely publicized 1994 decision. German states vary considerably in their attitude; some, like Bavaria, persist in a highly punitive policy, but most now favor the Dutch approach. So far the Kohl administration has refused to approve state proposals to legalize and regulate cannabis sales, but it appears aware of the rising support in the country for Dutch and Swiss approaches to local drug problems.

In June 1996 Luxembourg's parliament voted to decriminalize cannabis and push for standardization of drug laws in the Benelux countries. The Belgian government is now considering a more modest decriminalization of cannabis combined with tougher measures against organized crime and heroin traffickers. In Australia, cannabis has been decriminalized in South Australia, the Australian Capital Territory (Canberra), and the Northern Territory, and other states are considering the step. Even in France, Chirac's outburst followed recommendations of cannabis decriminalization by three distinguished national commissions. Chirac must now contend with a new prime minister, Lionel Jospin, who declared himself in favor of decriminalization before his Socialist Party won the 1997 parliamentary elections. Public opinion is clearly shifting. A recent poll found that 51 percent of Canadians favor decriminalizing marijuana.

## Will It Work?

Both at home and abroad, the U.S. government has attempted to block resolutions supporting harm reduction, suppress scientific studies that reached politically inconvenient conclusions, and silence critics of official drug policy. In May 1994 the State Department forced the last-minute cancellation of a World Bank conference on drug trafficking to which critics of U.S. drug policy had been invited. That December the U.S. delegation to an international meeting of the U.N. Drug Control Program refused to sign any statement incorporating the phrase "harm reduction." In early 1995 the State Department successfully pressured the World Health Organization to scuttle the release of a report it had commissioned from a panel that included many of the world's leading experts on cocaine because it included the scientifically incontrovertible observations that traditional use of coca leaf in the Andes causes little harm to users and that most consumers of cocaine use the drug in moderation with few detrimental effects. Hundreds of congressional hearings have addressed multitudinous aspects of the drug problem, but few have inquired into the European harm-reduction policies described above. When former Secretary of State George Shultz, then–Surgeon General M. Joycelyn Elders, and Baltimore Mayor Kurt Schmoke pointed to the failure of current policies and called for new approaches, they were mocked, fired, and ignored, respectively—and thereafter mischaracterized as advocating the outright legalization of drugs.

In Europe, in contrast, informed, public debate about drug policy is increasingly common in government, even at the EU level. In June 1995 the European Parliament issued a report acknowledging that "there will always be a demand for drugs in our societies . . . the policies followed so far have not been able to prevent the illegal drug trade from flourishing." The EU called for serious consideration of the Frankfurt Resolution, a statement of harm-reduction principles supported by a transnational coalition of 31 cities and regions. In October 1996 Emma Bonino, the European commissioner for consumer policy, advocated decriminalizing soft drugs and initiating a broad prescription program for hard drugs. Greece's minister for European affairs, George Papandreou, seconded her. Last February the monarch of Liechtenstein, Prince Hans Adam, spoke out in favor of controlled drug legalization. Even Raymond Kendall, secretary general of Interpol, was quoted in the August 20, 1994, *Guardian* as saying, "The prosecution of thousands of otherwise law-abiding citizens every year is both hypocritical and an affront to individual, civil and human rights... Drug use should no longer be a criminal offense. I am totally against legalization, but in favor of decriminalization for the user."

One can, of course, exaggerate the differences between attitudes in the United States and those in Europe and Australia. Many European leaders still echo Chirac's U.S.-style antidrug pronouncements. Most capital cities endorse the Stockholm Resolution, a statement backing punitive prohibitionist policies that was drafted in response to the Frankfurt Resolution. And the Dutch have had to struggle against French and other efforts to standardize more punitive drug laws and policies within the EU.

Conversely, support for harm-reduction approaches is growing in the United States, notably and vocally among public health professionals but also, more discreetly, among urban politicians and police officials. Some of the world's most innovative needle exchange and other harm-reduction programs can be found in America. The 1996 victories at the polls for California's Proposition 215, which legalizes the medicinal use of marijuana, and Arizona's Proposition 200, which allows doctors to prescribe any drug they deem appropriate and mandates treatment rather than jail for those arrested for possession, suggest that Americans are more receptive to drug policy reform than politicians acknowledge.

But Europe and Australia are generally ahead of the United States in their willingness to discuss openly and experiment pragmatically with alternative policies that might reduce the harm to both addicts and society. Public health officials in many European cities work closely with police, politicians, private physicians, and others to coordinate efforts. Community policing treats drug dealers and users as elements of the community that need not be expelled but can be made less troublesome. Such efforts, including crackdowns on open drug scenes in Zurich, Bern, and Frankfurt, are devised and implemented in tandem with initiatives to address health and housing problems. In the United States, in contrast, politicians presented with new approaches do not ask, "Will they work?" but only, "Are they tough enough?" Many legislators are reluctant to support drug treatment programs that are not punitive, coercive, and prison-based, and many criminal justice officials still view prison as a quick and easy solution for drug problems.

The lessons from Europe and Australia are compelling. Drug control policies should focus on reducing drug-related crime, disease, and death, not the number of casual drug users. Stopping the spread of HIV by and among drug users by making sterile syringes and methadone readily available must be the first priority. American politicians need to explore, not ignore or automatically condemn, promising policy options such as cannabis decriminalization, heroin prescription, and the integration of harm-reduction principles into community policing strategies. Central governments must back, or at least not hinder, the efforts of municipal officials and citizens to devise pragmatic approaches to local drug problems. Like citizens in Europe, the American public has supported such innovations when they are adequately explained and allowed to prove themselves. As the evidence comes in, what works is increasingly apparent. All that remains is mustering the political courage.

## Note

1. Lynn Zimmer and John P. Morgan, *Marijuana Myths, Marijuana Facts: A Review of the Scientific Evidence,* New York: Lindesmith Center, 1997.

Eric A. Voth

# America's Longest "War"

$B$ashing our drug policy is a popular activity. The advocates of legalization and decriminalization repeatedly contend that restrictive drug policy is failing, in the hope that this becomes a self-fulfilling prophecy. An objective look at the history of drug policy in the United States, especially in comparison to other countries, demonstrates that, indeed, our policies are working. What we also see is the clear presence of a well-organized and well-financed drug culture lobby that seeks to tear down restrictive drug policy and replace it with permissive policies that could seriously jeopardize our country's viability.

To understand our current situation, we must examine the last 25 years. The 1970s were a time of great social turmoil for the United States, and drug use was finding its way into the fabric of society. Policymakers were uncertain how to deal with drugs. As permissive advisers dominated the discussion, drug use climbed. The National Household Survey and the Monitoring the Future Survey both confirm that drug use peaked in the late 1970s. Twenty-five million Americans were current users of drugs in 1979, 37 percent of high school seniors had used marijuana in the prior 30 days, and 10. 7 percent of them used marijuana daily. During the same time frame, 13 states embraced the permissive social attitude and legalized or decriminalized marijuana.

In the late 1970s, policymakers, parents, and law enforcement began to realize that our drug situation was leading to Armageddon. As never before, a coordinated war on drugs was set in motion that demanded a no-use message. This was largely driven by parents who were sick of their children falling prey to drugs. The "Just Say No" movement was the centerpiece of antidrug activities during the subsequent years. A solid national antidrug message was coupled with rigorous law enforcement. The results were striking. As perception of the harmfulness of drugs increased, their use dropped drastically. By 1992, marijuana use by high school students in the prior 30 days had dropped to 11.9 percent and daily use to 1.9 percent.

## Breakdown in the 1990s

Unfortunately, several major events derailed our policy successes in the early 1990s, resulting in an approximate doubling of drug use since that time. From a national vantage point, a sense of complacency set in. Satisfied that the drug war was won, we lost national leadership. Federal funding for antidrug programs became mired in bureaucracy and difficult for small prevention organizations to obtain. A new generation of drug specialists entered the scene. Lacking experience of the ravages of the 1970s, they were willing to accept softening of policy. The Internet exploded as an open forum for the dissemination of inaccurate, deceptive, and manipulative information supporting permissive policy, even discussions of how to obtain and use drugs. The greatest audience has been young people, who are exposed to a plethora of drug-permissive information without filter or validation.

The entertainment media have provided a steady diet of alcohol and drug use for young people to witness. A recent study commissioned by the White House Office of National Drug Control Policy found that alcohol appeared in more than 93 percent of movies and illicit drugs in 22 percent, of which 51 percent depicted marijuana use. Concurrently, the news media have begun to demonstrate bias toward softening of drug policy, having the net effect of changing public opinion.

The single most dramatic influence, however, came in the transformation of the drug culture from a disorganized group of legalization advocates to a well-funded and well-organized machine. With funding from several large donors, drug-culture advocates were able to initiate large-scale attacks on the media and policymakers. The most prominent funder is the billionaire George Soros, who has spent millions toward the initiation of organizations such as the Drug Policy Foundation, Lindesmith Center, medical-marijuana-advocacy and needle-handout groups, to name a few projects.

A slick strategic shift toward compartmentalizing and dissecting restrictive drug policy has resulted in what is termed the "harm reduction" movement. After all, who would oppose the idea of reducing the harm to society caused by drug use? The philosophy of the harm reduction movement is well summarized by Ethan Nadelman of the Lindesmith Center (also funded by Soros), who is considered the godfather of the legalization movement:

> Let's start by dropping the "zero tolerance" rhetoric and policies and the illusory goal of drug-free societies. Accept that drug use is here to stay and that we have no choice but to learn to live with drugs so that they cause the least possible harm. Recognize that many, perhaps most, "drug problems" in the Americas are the results not of drug use per se but of our prohibitionist policies....

The harm reduction movement has attacked the individual components of restrictive drug policy and created strategies to weaken it. Some of these strategies include giving heroin to addicts; handing out needles to addicts; encouraging use of crack cocaine instead of intravenous drugs; reducing drug-related criminal penalties; teaching "responsible" drug use to adolescents instead of working toward prevention of use; the medical marijuana movement; and the expansion of the industrial hemp movement.

# Softening Drug Policies

The move toward soft drug policy has created some strange bedfellows. On one hand, supporters of liberal policy such as Gov. Gary Johnson of New Mexico have always taken the misguided view that individuals should have a right to use whatever they want in order to feel good. They often point to their own "survival" of drug use as justification for loosening laws and letting others experiment. Interestingly, the governor's public safety secretary quit as a result of being undermined by Johnson's destructive stand on legalization. Libertarian conservatives such as Milton Friedman and William Buckley have attacked drug policy as an infringement of civil liberties and have incorrectly considered drug use to be a victimless event. Societal problems such as homelessness, domestic abuse, numerous health problems, crimes under the influence, poor job performance, decreased productivity, and declining educational levels have strong connections to drug use and cost our society financially and spiritually.

The notion that decriminalizing or legalizing drugs will drive the criminal element out of the market is flawed and reflects a total lack of understanding of drug use and addiction. Drug use creates its own market, and often the only thing limiting the amount of drugs that an addict uses is the amount of money available. Further, if drugs were legalized, what would the legal scenario be? Would anyone be allowed to sell drugs? Would they be sold by the government? If so, what strengths would be available? If there were any limitations on strength or availability, a black market would immediately develop. Most rational people can easily recognize this slippery slope.

Consistently, drug-culture advocates assert that policy has failed and is extremely costly. This is a calculated strategy to demoralize the population and turn public sentiment against restrictive policy. The real question is, has restrictive policy failed? First we should consider the issues of cost. An effective way to determine cost-effectiveness is to compare the costs to society of legal versus illegal drugs. Estimates from 1990 suggest that the costs of illegal drugs were $70 billion, as compared to that of alcohol alone at $99 billion and tobacco at $72 billion. Estimates from 1992 put the costs of alcohol dependence at $148 billion and all illegal drugs (including the criminal justice system costs) at $98 billion.

Referring to the National Household Survey data from 1998, there were 13.6 million current users of illicit drugs compared to 113 million users of alcohol and 60 million tobacco smokers. There is one difference: legal status of the drugs. The Monitoring the Future Survey of high school seniors suggests that in 1995, some 52.5 percent of seniors had been drunk within the previous year as compared to 34.7 percent who had used marijuana. *Yet*, alcohol is illegal for teenagers. The only difference is, again, the legal status of the two substances.

## Results of Legalization

Permissive drug policy has been tried both in the United States and abroad. In 1985, during the period in which Alaska legalized marijuana, the use of marijuana and cocaine among adolescents was more than twice as high as in other parts of the country. Baltimore has long been heralded as a center-piece for harm reduction drug policy. Interestingly, the rate of heroin use found among arrestees in Baltimore was higher than in any other city in the United States. Thirty-seven percent of male and 48 percent of female arrestees were positive, compared with 6–23 percent for Washington, D.C., Philadelphia, and Manhattan.

Since liberalizing its marijuana-enforcement policies, the Netherlands has found that marijuana use among 11- to 18-year-olds has increased 142 percent from 1990 to 1995. Crime has risen steadily to the point that aggravated theft and breaking and entering occur three to four times more than in the United States. Along with the staggering increases in marijuana use, the Netherlands has become one of the major suppliers of the drug Ecstacy. Australia is flirting with substantial softening of drug policy. That is already taking a toll. Drug use there among 16- to 29-year-olds is 52 percent as compared with 9 percent in Sweden, a country with a restrictive drug policy. In Vancouver in 1988, HIV prevalence among IV drug addicts was only 1–2 percent. In 1997 it was 23 percent, after wide adoption of harm reduction policies. Vancouver has the largest needle exchange in North America.

Clearly, the last few years have witnessed some very positive changes in policy and our antidrug efforts. A steady national voice opposing drug use is again being heard. Efforts are being made to increase cooperation between the treatment and law enforcement communities to allow greater access to treatment. The primary prevention movement is strong and gaining greater footholds. The increases in drug use witnessed in the early 1990s have slowed.

On the other hand, the drug culture has been successful at some efforts to soften drug policy. Medical marijuana initiatives have successfully passed in several states. These were gross examples of abuse of the ballot initiative process. Large amounts of money purchased slick media campaigns and seduced the public into supporting medical marijuana under the guise of compassion. Industrial hemp initiatives are popping up all over the country in an attempt to hurt anti-marijuana law enforcement and soften public opinion. Needle hand-outs are being touted as successes, while the evidence is clearly demonstrating failures and increases in HIV, hepatitis B, and hepatitis C. Internationally, our Canadian neighbors are moving down a very destructive road toward drug legalization and harm reduction. The Swiss are experimenting with the lives of addicts by implementing heroin handouts and selective drug legalization. In this international atmosphere, children's attitudes about the harmfulness of drugs teeter in the balance.

Future drug policy must continue to emphasize and fund primary prevention, with the goal of no use of illegal drugs and no illegal use of legal drugs. Treatment availability must be seriously enhanced, but treatment must not be a revolving door. It must be carefully designed and outcomes based. The Rand Drug Policy Research Center concluded that the costs of cocaine use could be reduced by $33.9 billion through the layering of treatment for heavy users on top of our current enforcement efforts.

Drug screening is an extremely effective means for identifying drug use. It should be widely extended into business and industry, other social arenas, and schools. Screening must be coupled with a rehabilitative approach, however, and not simply punishment. The self-serving strategies of the drug culture must be exposed. The public needs to become aware of how drug-culture advocates are manipulating public opinion in the same fashion that the tobacco industry has for so many years.

A compassionate but restrictive drug policy that partners prevention, rehabilitation, and law enforcement will continue to show the greatest chance for success. Drug policy must focus on harm prevention through clear primary prevention messages, and it must focus upon harm elimination through treatment availability and rigorous law enforcement.

# POSTSCRIPT

## Should Drugs Be Legalized?

Nadelmann asserts that utilizing the criminal justice system to eradicate drug problems simply does not work. He argues that international control efforts, interdiction, and domestic law enforcement are ineffective and that many problems associated with drug use are the consequences of drug regulation policies. He maintains that decriminalization is a feasible and desirable means of dealing with the drug crisis.

Voth charges that the advantages of maintaining illegality far outweigh any conceivable benefits of decriminalization. He professes that if drug laws were relaxed, the result would be more drug users and, thus, more drug addicts and more criminal activity. Also, there is the possibility that more drug-related social problems would occur. Voth concludes that society cannot afford to soften its position on legalization.

Legalization proponents argue that drug laws have not worked and that the drug battle has been lost. They believe that drug-related problems would disappear if legalization were implemented. Citing the legal drugs alcohol and tobacco as examples, legalization opponents argue that decriminalizing drugs would not decrease profits from the sale of drugs (the profits from cigarettes and alcohol are incredibly high). Moreover, opponents argue, legalizing a drug does not make its problems disappear (alcohol and tobacco have extremely high addiction rates as well as a myriad of other problems associated with their use).

Many European countries have a system of legalized drugs, and most have far fewer addiction rates and lower incidences of drug-related violence and crime than the United States. However, would the outcomes of decriminalization in the United States be the same as in Europe? Legalization in the United States could still be a tremendous risk because its drug problems could escalate and recriminalizing drugs would be difficult. This was the case with Prohibition in the 1920s, which, in changing the status of alcohol from legal to illegal, produced numerous crime- and alcohol-related problems.

Many good articles debate the pros and cons of drug legalization, including "Holland's Half-Baked Drug Experiment," by Larry Collins, *Foreign Affairs* (May/June 1999); "Addicted to the Drug War," by Kenneth E. Sharpe, *The Chronicle of Higher Education* (October 6, 2000); "Fighting the Real War on Drugs," by Bill Ritter, *The World & I* (February 2000); and "Strange Bedfellows: Ideology, Politics, and Drug Legalization," by Erich Goode, *Society* (May/June 1998). Also, the February 20, 1999, issue of *The Nation* features a number of prominent individuals discussing whether or not drugs should be legalized.

# ISSUE 2

## Should the United States Put More Emphasis on Stopping the Importation of Drugs?

**YES: Barry R. McCaffrey**, from *The National Drug Control Strategy: 2001 Annual Report* (January 2001)

**NO: Mathea Falco**, from "U.S. Drug Policy: Addicted to Failure," *Foreign Policy* (Spring 1996)

### ISSUE SUMMARY

**YES:** Barry R. McCaffrey, former director of the Office of National Drug Control Policy, argues that the importation of drugs must be stopped to reduce drug use and abuse. If the supply of drugs being trafficked across American borders is reduced, then there will be fewer drug-related problems. He maintains that a coordinated international effort is needed to combat the increased production of heroin, cocaine, and marijuana.

**NO:** Mathea Falco, president of Drug Strategies, a nonprofit policy institute, asserts that the emphasis should not be on curtailing the availability of drugs but on factors that contribute to Americans' use of drugs. She contends that blaming other countries for drug-related problems in the United States is one way for politicians to deflect criticism from themselves. Moreover, she argues, people involved in the drug trade in other countries have little incentive to end their involvement.

Since the beginning of the 1990s, overall drug use in the United States has increased. Up to now, interdiction has not proven to be successful in slowing the flow of drugs into the United States. Drugs continue to cross U.S. borders at record levels. This point may signal a need for stepped-up international efforts to stop the production and trafficking of drugs. Conversely, it may illustrate the inadequacy of the current strategy. Should the position of the U.S. government be to improve and strengthen current measures or to try an entirely new approach?

Some people contend that rather than attempting to limit illegal drugs from coming into the United States, more effort should be directed at reducing the demand for drugs and improving treatment for drug abusers. Foreign countries would not produce and transport drugs like heroin and cocaine into the United States if there were no market for them. Drug policies, some people maintain, should be aimed at the social and economic conditions underlying domestic drug problems, not at interfering with foreign governments.

Many U.S. government officials believe that other countries should assist in stopping the flow of drugs across their borders. Diminishing the supply of drugs by intercepting them before they reach the user is another way to eliminate or curtail drug use. Critical elements in the lucrative drug trade are multinational crime syndicates. One premise is that if the drug production, transportation, distribution, and processing functions as well as the money-laundering operations of these criminal organizations can be interrupted and eventually crippled, then the drug problem would abate.

In South American countries such as Peru, Colombia, and Bolivia, where coca—from which cocaine is processed—is cultivated, economic aid has been made available to help the governments of these countries fight the cocaine kingpins. An alleged problem is that a number of government officials in these countries are corrupt or fearful of the cocaine cartel leaders. One proposed solution is to go directly to the farmers and offer them money to plant crops other than coca. This tactic, however, failed in the mid-1970s, when the U.S. government gave money to farmers in Turkey to stop growing opium poppy crops. After one year the program was discontinued due to the enormous expense, and opium poppy crops were once again planted.

Drug problems are not limited to the Americas. Since the breakup of the Soviet Union, for example, there has been a tremendous increase in opium production in many of the former republics. These republics are in dire need of money, and one source of income is opium production. Moreover, there is lax enforcement by police officials in these republics.

There are many reasons why people are dissatisfied with the current state of the war on drugs. For example, in the war on drugs, the *casual* user is generally the primary focus of drug use deterrence. This is viewed by many people as a form of discrimination because the vast majority of drug users and sellers who are arrested and prosecuted are poor, members of minorities, homeless, unemployed, and/or disenfranchised. Also, international drug dealers who are arrested are usually not the drug bosses but lower-level people working for them. Finally, some argue that the war on drugs should be redirected away from interdiction and enforcement because they feel that the worst drug problems in society today are caused by legal drugs, primarily alcohol and tobacco.

The following selections address the issue of whether or not the war on drugs should be fought on an international level. Barry R. McCaffrey takes the view that international cooperation is absolutely necessary if we are to stem the flow of drugs and maintain world order. Mathea Falco argues that an international approach to dealing with drugs avoids the real issues that lead to drug abuse.

**Barry R. McCaffrey**

 **YES**

# The National Drug Control Strategy, 2001

## Shielding U.S. Borders From the Drug Threat

Borders delineate the sovereign territories of nation-states. Guarding our country's 9,600 miles of land and sea borders is one of the federal government's most fundamental responsibilities—especially in light of the historically open, lengthy borders with our northern and southern neighbors. The American government maintains three hundred ports-of-entry, including airports where officials inspect inbound and outbound individuals, cargo, and conveyances. All are vulnerable to the drug threat. By curtailing the flow of drugs across our borders, we reduce drug availability throughout the United States and decrease the negative consequences of drug abuse and trafficking in our communities.

In FY 2000, more than eighty million passengers and crew members arrived in the United States aboard commercial and private aircraft. Some eleven million came by marine vessels and 397 million through land border crossings. People entered America on 211,000 ships; 971,000 aircraft; and 139 million trucks, trains, buses, and automobiles. Cargo arrived in fifty-two million containers. This enormous volume of movement makes interdiction of illegal drugs difficult.

Even harder is the task of intercepting illegal drugs in cargo shipments because of the ease with which traffickers can switch modes and routes. Containerized cargo has revolutionized routes, cargo tracking, port development, and shipping companies. As the lead federal agency for detection and monitoring, the Department of Defense [DoD] provides support to law enforcement agencies involved in counter-drug operations. A recent study by the Office of Naval Intelligence indicated that over 60 percent of the world's cargo travels by container. Moreover, vessels carrying as many as six thousand containers—which have the ability to offload cargo onto rail or trucks at various ports-of-entry and then transport it into the heart of the United States—further complicate the interdiction challenge. Drug-trafficking organizations take advantage of these dynamics by hiding illegal substances in cargo or secret compartments. False seals have been used on containers so shipments can move unimpeded through initial ports-of-entry. The United States Customs Service seized more than 1.5 million pounds of illicit drugs in FY 2000—an 11 percent increase

From Barry R. McCaffrey, Office of National Drug Control Policy, *The National Drug Control Strategy: 2001 Annual Report* (January 2001). Washington, D.C.: U.S. Government Printing Office, 2001. Notes omitted.

over the previous year. To counteract this threat, the federal government is constantly seeking new technologies which, together with capable personnel and timely intelligence, facilitate a well-coordinated interdiction plan responsive to changing drug-trafficking trends.

## Organizing Against the Drug Threat

The U.S. Customs Service has primary responsibility for ensuring that all cargo and goods moving through ports-of-entry comply with federal law. Customs is the lead agency for preventing drug trafficking through airports, seaports, and land ports-of-entry. Customs shares responsibility for stemming the flow of illegal drugs into the United States via the air and sea. It accomplishes this mission by detecting and apprehending drug-smuggling aircraft and vessels trying to enter the country. The Customs' Air and Marine Interdiction Division provides seamless twenty-four-hour radar surveillance along the entire southern tier of the United States, Puerto Rico, and the Caribbean using a wide variety of civilian and military ground-based radar, tethered aerostats, reconnaissance aircraft, and other detection sensors. In fiscal year 2000, Customs seized 1,442,778 pounds of marijuana, cocaine, and heroin—a 10.1 percent increase over seizures in FY 1999. In addition, Customs has deployed over forty non-intrusive inspection systems as part of its Five-Year Technology Plan. These systems allow for the advanced detection of narcotics and other contraband in various cargo containers, trucks, automobiles, and rail cars. Such technology has been deployed to ports of entry along the southern tier of the U.S. where it assisted in the seizure of over 180,000 pounds of drugs in the past 3 years.

The U.S. Border Patrol [USBP] specifically focuses on drug smuggling between land ports of entry. In FY 1998, the USBP seized 395,316 kilograms of marijuana, 10,285 kilograms of cocaine, and fourteen kilograms of heroin. In addition, this agency made 6,402 arrests of suspected traffickers.

The Coast Guard [USCG] as the lead federal agency for maritime drug interdiction shares responsibility for air interdiction with the U.S. Customs Service. As such, the Coast Guard plays a key role in protecting our borders. Coast Guard air and surface assets patrol over six million square miles of transit zone that stretches from the Caribbean Basin to the eastern Pacific Ocean. In FY 2000, the Coast Guard set a record for the second consecutive year by seizing 132,920 pounds of cocaine—a 19 percent increase over FY 1999. This success has been a result of the service's Campaign Steel Web counterdrug strategy, intelligence, and deployment of non-lethal technologies to counter go-fast smuggling boats. All the armed forces provide support to law-enforcement agencies involved in drug-control operations, particularly in the Southwest border region.

## Drug Trafficking Across the Southwest Border

In FY 2000, 293 million people, eighty-nine million cars, four-and-a-half million trucks, and 572,000 rail cars entered the United States from Mexico. More than half of the cocaine on our streets and large quantities of heroin, marijuana, and methamphetamine come across the Southwest border. Illegal drugs are hidden in all modes of conveyance—car, truck, train, and pedestrian. The success that the Border Patrol and Customs have had at and around ports of entry (through innovative enforcement strategies and physical security improvements) have forced smugglers to move through the vast open spaces between official border crossing points. Approximately, fifty percent of the border with Mexico is under the jurisdiction of the federal land management agencies, almost all of that in rugged, remote areas with limited law enforcement presence. Drugs cross the desert in armed pack trains as well as on the backs of human "mules." They are tossed over border fences and then whisked away on foot or by vehicle. Operators of ships find gaps in U.S./Mexican interdiction coverage and position drugs close to the border for eventual transfer to the United States. Small boats in the Gulf of Mexico and eastern Pacific seek to deliver drugs directly to the United States. Whenever possible, traffickers try to exploit incidences of corruption in U.S. border agencies. It is a tribute to the vast majority of dedicated American officials that integrity, courage, and respect for human rights overwhelmingly characterize their service. Rapidly growing commerce between the United States and Mexico complicates the attempt to keep drugs out of cross-border traffic. Since the Southwest border is currently the most porous part of the nation's periphery, we must mount a determined effort to stop the flow of drugs there. At the same time, we cannot concentrate resources along the Southwest border at the expense of other vulnerable regions because traffickers follow the path of least resistance and funnel drugs to less defended areas.

Five principal departments—Treasury, Justice [DOJ], Transportation, State, and Defense—are concerned with drug-control issues along the Southwest border. These agencies have collaborated in six drug-control areas: drug interdiction, anti-money laundering, drug and immigration enforcement, prosecutions, counter-drug support, and counter-drug cooperation with Mexico. During the past decade, the federal presence along the Southwest border expanded. Customs' budget for Southwest border programs increased 72 percent since FY 1993. The number of assigned DEA [Drug Enforcement Agency] special agents increased 37 percent since FY 1990. DoD's drug-control budget for the Southwest border increased 53 percent since FY 1990. The number of U.S. attorneys handling cases there went up by 80 percent since FY 1990. The Southwest Border Initiative enabled federal agencies to coordinate intelligence and operational assignments at Customs, DOJ's Special Operations Division, HIDTA [High Intensity Drug Trafficking Areas], and state and local law-enforcement agencies.

The United States Coast Guard plays a critical role in protecting the maritime flanks of the Southwest Border. Operations *Border Shield* and *Gulf Shield* protect the coastal borders of Southern California and along the Gulf of Mexico from maritime drug smuggling with USCG air and surface interdiction assets. The Coast Guard operations are coordinated, multi-agency efforts that focus on interdiction to disrupt drug trafficking.

# All Borders

We must stop drugs everywhere they enter our country—through the Gulf Coast, Puerto Rico, the U.S. Virgin Islands, Florida, the northeastern and northwestern United States, and the Great Lakes. The vulnerability of Alaska, Hawaii, and the U.S. territories must also be recognized. Florida's location, geography, and dynamic growth will continue to make that state particularly attractive to traffickers for the foreseeable future. Florida's six hundred miles of coastline render[ed] it a major target for shore and airdrop deliveries in the 1980s. The state is located astride the drug-trafficking routes of the Caribbean and Gulf of Mexico. The busy Miami and Orlando airports and Florida's seaports—gateways to drug-source countries in South America—are used as distribution hubs by international drug rings. To varying degrees, Florida's predicament is shared by other border areas and entry points.

The Department of Justice's Southern Frontier Initiative focuses law enforcement on drug-trafficking organizations operating along the Southwest border and the Caribbean. *Operation Trinity* resulted in 1,260 arrests, including eight hundred members of the five largest drug syndicates in Mexico and Colombia. DOJ's Caribbean Initiative substantially enhanced its counterdrug capabilities in this region, with more law-enforcement agents, greater communications, and improved interception. A major element of the Coast Guard's comprehensive multi-year strategy (Campaign Steel Web) is "Operation Frontier Shield," which focuses on disrupting maritime smuggling routes into and around Puerto Rico and the U.S. Virgin Islands.

# U.S. Seaports

Criminal activity, including the illegal importation of illicit drugs and the export of controlled commodities and drug proceeds, with a nexus to U.S. seaports is a serious problem. In response to the threat that such activities pose to the people and critical infrastructures of the United States and its seaport cities, the Interagency Commission on Crime and Security in U.S. Seaports was created by Executive Memorandum in April 1999. The Commission's report, released in August 2000, provides an overview of criminal activity and security measures at the seaports; an assessment of the nature and effectiveness of ongoing coordination among federal, state, and local governmental agencies; and gives recommendations for improvement....

# Reducing the Supply of Illegal Drugs

Since 1993, the United States has emphasized that supply reduction is an essential component of a well-balanced strategic approach to drug control. When illegal drugs are readily available, the likelihood increases that they will be abused. Supply reduction has both international and domestic components. The vast majority of illicit drugs used in the United States are produced outside of our borders. Internationally, supply reduction includes working with partner nations within the source zones to reduce the cultivation and production of illicit drugs through drug-crop substitution and eradication; alternative development and strengthening public institutions; coordinated investigations; interdiction; control of precursors; anti-money laundering initiatives; and building consensus thorough bilateral, regional and global accords. Within the United States, supply reduction entails regulation (through the Controlled Substances Act), enforcement of anti-drug laws, eradication of marijuana cultivation, control of precursor chemicals, and destruction of illegal synthetic drug laboratories within our borders.

## Breaking Cocaine Sources of Supply

Coca, the raw material for cocaine, is grown primarily in the Andean region of South America. Dramatic successes in Bolivia and Peru have been tempered by the continued expansion of coca cultivation in southern Colombia. Despite more than doubling of the coca crop in Colombia between 1995–1999, successes in the rest of the Andes have helped reduce global cultivation by 15 percent. Although crop estimates for 2000 have yet to be finalized, preliminary indications suggest increases in crop production in southern Colombia that may offset eradication efforts and reduced cultivation in Bolivia and Peru.

**Bolivia**    This South American country has achieved remarkable counternarcotics successes over the past half decade. The current Banzer administration achieved a 55 percent reduction in cultivation between 1995 and 1999. This achievement, which is the result of sustained eradication and law-enforcement efforts combined with extensive alternative crop development, reduced cocaine production in Bolivia from 255 metric tons in 1994 to seventy mts in 1999. Bolivia continues to make rapid progress towards its goal of complete elimination of all illicit coca production by the end of 2002. By the end of 2000, the Chapare region—once one of the world's major suppliers of this illegal drug—will probably cease to produce any commercial level of coca. From a high of 33,900 hectares of coca fields in the Chapare in 1994, the government eliminated all but a thousand hectares by November 2000. Bolivia plans to launch an eradication campaign, preceded by alternative-development programs, in the Yungas within calendar year 2001. As eradication efforts move from the Chapare to the Yungas, the government will leave sufficient forces to monitor the region and destroy any replanted fields. More importantly, USAID [United States Agency for International Development] Bolivia is contributing to alternative-development programs, using both regular and supplemental budgets to turn farmers away from illegal coca in favor of other crops.

In addition to eradication and alternative development, the United States is helping Bolivia pursue an aggressive drug and chemical precursor-interdiction campaign. Increased success in the interdiction of smuggled substances, particularly in the Chapare region, has raised the price of many essential chemicals, forcing Bolivian lab operators to use inferior substitutes, recycled solvents, and a streamlined production process that virtually eliminates the oxidation stage. The result has been radically diminished drug purity to a record low of 47 percent. This development dramatically affected the marketability of Bolivian cocaine in Brazil and elsewhere.

A limiting factor in Bolivia's continued success against illegal coca cultivation will be the government's ability to work with the cocalerias. In Fall 2000, government eradication efforts were beset by civil strife resulting in ten deaths and approximately a hundred injuries. Funnelling alternative-development aid to the Chapare and Yungas will likely determine whether the Banzer government is able to meet its eradication goals.

**Peru**   Like Bolivia, the government of Peru made enormous strides toward eliminating illegal coca cultivation in the past five years. Despite the rehabilitation of some previously abandoned coca fields, 24 percent of Peruvian coca was eliminated in 1999 with an overall reduction of 66 percent over the last four years. Contributing to this figure was a 1999 total of fifteen thousand fewer hectares under manual coca cultivation. Peru's counternarcotics alternative-development program, working through a hundred local governments, seven hundred communities, and fifteen thousand farmers significantly strengthened the social and economic infrastructure in these areas and helped shift the economic balance in favor of licit activities.

In 2000, the government of Peru continued its eradication campaign for coca. The country hoped to eliminate some twenty-two thousand acres (nine thousand hectares) of coca. However, a deteriorating political situation increased discontent among coca growers in the Huallaga valley, and potential spillover from southern Colombia could affect the positive direction in Peru. In November 2000, growers in the central upper Huallaga valley conducted the biggest protests in a decade, slowed eradication efforts, and endangered Peru's ability to meet its eradication objectives. However, with sustained U.S. law enforcement, alternative development, interdiction assistance, and support for eradication, Peru will continue to reduce coca cultivation.

**Colombia**   President [Andres] Pastrana and his reform-minded government took office in August of 1998. Pastrana faced multiple challenges from the outset of his administration. Ongoing, inter-related crises in Colombia threaten U.S. national interests, including: stemming the flow of cocaine and heroin into the United States, support for democratic government and the rule of law, respect for human rights, promoting efforts to reach a negotiated settlement in Colombia's long-running internal conflict, maintaining regional stability, and promoting legitimate trade and investment.

Rapidly growing cocaine production in Colombia constitutes a threat to U.S. security and the well-being of our citizens. Ninety percent of the cocaine entering the United States originates in or passes through Colombia. Over the last decade, drug production in Colombia has increased dramatically. In spite of an aggressive aerial eradication campaign, Colombian cultivation of coca, the raw material for cocaine, has more than tripled since 1992. New information about the potency of Colombian coca, the time required for crops to reach maturity, and efficiency in the cocaine conversion process has led to a revision in estimates of Colombia's 1998 potential cocaine production from 165 metric tons to 435 metric tons. The 1999 figures indicate that both the number of hectares of coca under cultivation and the amount of cocaine produced from those crops continue to skyrocket. Colombian coca cultivation rose 20 percent to 122,500 hectares in 1999; there was a corresponding 20 percent increase in potential cocaine production to 520 metric tons. Left unchecked, these massive increases in drug production and trafficking could reverse gains achieved over the last four years in Peru and Bolivia. Continued expansion of drug production in Colombia is likely to result in more drugs being shipped to the United States....

## Breaking Heroin Sources of Supply

The U.S. heroin problem is supplied entirely by foreign sources of opium. Efforts to reduce domestic heroin availability face significant problems. Unlike cocaine, where the supply is concentrated in the Andean region of South America, heroin available in the United States is produced in four distinct parts of the world: South America, Mexico, Southeast Asia, and Southwest Asia. Worldwide potential heroin production was estimated at 287 metric tons in 1999.

Latin America has emerged in recent years as the primary supplier of heroin to the United States. Colombian and Mexican heroin comprises 65 and 17 percent respectively of the heroin seized today in the United States. The heroin industry in Colombia is still young and growing. Reports of some opium poppy fields surfaced in the mid-1980s, but not until the early 1990s was any significant cultivation confirmed. By the mid-1990s, the Colombian heroin industry was producing enough high-purity white heroin to capture the U.S. East Coast market. Between 1995 and 1998, opium production in Colombia was sufficient to support more than six metric tons of heroin annually. In 1999, however, increased cultivation resulted in a larger crop, increasing potential heroin production to nearly eight metric tons.

Today, the Colombian heroin trade closely mirrors the heroin industry in Mexico rather than operations in Southeast or Southwest Asia. Heroin processing labs in Colombia operate on a small scale; heroin production is not dominated by large, well-armed trafficking organizations; there are no multi-hundred-kilogram internal movements of opiate products; and Colombian traffickers rarely attempt to smuggle large shipments of heroin into other countries. Like the Mexican industry , the heroin trade in Colombia services the U.S. market almost exclusively. Production of heroin is more fragmented, with smaller trafficking groups playing a major role. Individual couriers smuggle heroin into the United States daily in small, single-kilogram amounts. In addition, Colombia's heroin industry—like Mexico's—must cope with significant government opium-poppy eradication.

Significant diversion of the essential precursor acetic anhydride suggests that Colombian traffickers are prepared to increase heroin production. In 1999, about ninety-six metric tons of acetic anhydride—six percent of Colombia's legal imports of this chemical for pharmaceutical use—were hijacked or stolen after arriving in Colombia. The illegal diversion of acetic anhydride in 1999 alone would be enough to meet heroin production requirements for the next three to five years.

Low-level opium-poppy cultivation in Venezuela and even more limited growing in Peru currently serve only marginal heroin production but could become the foundation for an expanding opium and heroin industry beyond Colombia. Opium-poppy cultivation in Venezuela is limited to the mountains opposite Colombia's growing area and appears to be a spillover from cultivation on the Colombian side of the border. Since 1994, when a thousand hectares of opium poppy were discovered during a joint U.S.-Venezuelan aerial reconnaissance mission, Caracas has conducted periodic eradication operations that reduced the size of the annual crop to fewer than fifty hectares. The cultivation, harvesting, and processing of Venezuela's poppy crop is done primarily by Colombians who access the growing area from Colombia. Many of the farmers arrested by Venezuelan authorities for growing opium are Colombian nationals. The Venezuelan side of the border is readily accessible from trails and unimproved roads originating in Colombia.

Reports indicate that opium poppy cultivation in Peru over the last several years is nearly negligible. However, the seizure of more than fifty kilograms of opium by police in 1999 suggests that opium production in Peru may be heading for commercial levels. In Peru, Colombian backers provide farmers with poppy seed, teach processing methods, and buy Peruvian opium; most of the opium produced in Peru is reportedly shipped to Colombia. While the cultivation pattern in Peru is similar to that in Colombia, so far there has been no widespread deforestation as there was in Colombia when opium-poppy cultivation virtually exploded.

An intensification of eradication efforts in Colombia significant enough to reduce opium production might spur increased cultivation in Peru and Venezuela. Both governments, however, appear committed to preventing opium cultivation from becoming a significant problem. Successful elimination of opium-poppy cultivation in Venezuela will depend, to a large extent, on Colombia's ability to suppress cultivation on its side of the border and for both Bogota and Caracas to control the mountainous region where Colombian guerrillas operate on both sides of the border. The prospects for significant increases in opium production would be greater in Peru if cultivation were firmly established there because the growing areas are isolated and nearly inaccessible to authorities, making large-scale eradication more difficult.

With long-established trafficking and distribution networks and exclusive markets for black tar and brown powder heroin, Mexico's hold on the U.S. heroin market in the West seems secure. Mexico grows only about two percent of the world's illicit opium, but virtually the entire crop is converted into heroin for the U.S. market. Despite significant historical production in Mexico, local consumption of opium and heroin has never been more than marginal. Unlike in the far larger source countries of Southeast and Southwest Asia, opium-poppy cultivation in Mexico—as in Colombia—occurs year-round because of the favorable climate. With a hundred-day growing cycle, single opium fields in Mexico can yield up to three crops per year although the size and quality of the plants typically depends on seasonal variations. The largest crop is generally achieved in the relatively mild and wet months of December through April. Mexican officials report that many growers are planting new varieties of opium poppy in an effort to increase opium yields.

Opium cultivation and production in Mexico have been relatively stable through most of the 1990s. Between 1993 and 1998, according to the U.S. government's annual imagery-based crop survey, Mexico's opium harvest averaged fifty-four metric tons, allowing Mexican traffickers to produce five to six metric tons of heroin annually. In 1999, a drought in the best growing season reduced opium cultivation and stunned opium-poppy growth in many of the fields where plants reached maturity.

Poppy-crop eradication is the primary constraint against increased opium production. The Mexican Army's manual eradication effort, using more than twenty-thousand soldiers on any given day, is responsible for roughly 75 percent of the eradicated crop each year. The Attorney General's Office (PGR) destroys about one-quarter of the eradicated crop through helicopter aerial fumigation. However, a lack of roads and infrastructure in the remote growing areas makes manual and spray operations difficult and dangerous. Moreover, counterinsurgency operations and disaster-relief missions in recent years overburdened military personnel and may have caused the transfer of some personnel away from eradication efforts. However, this change does not seem to have had an appreciable impact on overall eradication effort. The combination of drought and eradication decreased Mexico's heroin production to slightly more than four metric tons in 1999.

Historically, most of the world's illicit opium for heroin has been grown in the Golden Triangle of Southeast Asia. Burma alone has accounted for more than half of all global production of opium and heroin for most of the last decade. In the absence of sustained alternative crop-substitution programs and consistent narcotics crop-eradication efforts (except in Thailand), only weather fluctuations have had a significant impact on opium-poppy cultivation and production. Major droughts in 1994, 1998, and 1999 caused the region's opium production to plummet.

No other country surpasses Burma in terms of hectares of opium cultivation. However, crop yields are much lower than those in Southwest Asia are. Consequently, even if normal weather conditions were to again prevail in Southeast Asia, Burma would not challenge Afghanistan as the world's leading source of heroin. Although the Burmese government showed both a willingness and capability to ban poppy cultivation in areas under its control the last two years, authorities refrain from entering prime opium-growing areas controlled by ethnic Wa insurgents.

In Thailand, aggressive eradication and crop-substitution programs have reduced opium production to less than one percent of the region's total. Thailand is now a net importer of opium to meet its addicts' demands. Without a meaningful eradication effort of its own and with little change in the status of UN-supported crop-substitution projects, Laos remains the world's third-largest producer of illicit opium. Opium production in that country was less affected by drought than was Burma. Laos accounted for about 12 percent of Southeast

Asia's opium production in 1999, as compared to less than 10 percent through most of the 1990s.

The profitability of growing opium poppy as a cash crop and the lack of resources or commitment by regional governments to implement crop substitution, alternative development, or eradication are key factors that predict a significant rebound in opium production within Southeast Asia. The remote location and rugged terrain of poppy-growing areas in Burma and Laos are major obstacles to establishing crop-substitution programs. The lack of transportation infrastructure in most opium-producing regions further complicates crop substitution because farmers have difficulty moving alternative crops to distant markets. Opium buyers, by contrast, typically come to the farmer, saving him a long trek to the nearest village or city. Although significant efforts by transit countries over the past led to the seizure of large amounts of heroin, the key to curbing heroin production and trafficking in Southeast Asia lies with the source countries—particularly Burma.

The explosive growth of opium production and development of an imposing opiate-processing infrastructure in Afghanistan during the 1990s made Southwest Asia the world's leading source of heroin. While Southwest Asian heroin is unlikely to penetrate much of the American market share anytime soon, the region's drug trade significantly affects U.S. strategic interests—including political stability and counterterrorism—in that volatile region. In 1999, Southwest Asia produced an estimated 2,898 metric tons of opium, compared to 1,236 metric tons in drought-stricken Southeast Asia. Afghanistan, whose estimated opium production increased 22 percent from 2,390 metric tons in 1998 to 2,861 metric tons, was solely responsible for Southwest Asia becoming the world's leading source of heroin. By comparison, opium production in Pakistan—the region's other source country—declined by half for the second consecutive year to thirty-seven metric tons.

In the coming decade, additional progress is achievable if governments can cordon off growing areas, increase their commitment, and implement counternarcotics programs. U.S.-backed crop-control programs reduced illicit opium cultivation in Guatemala, Mexico, Pakistan, Thailand, and Turkey. Both Colombia and Mexico have aggressive heroin-control programs. Mexico has destroyed between 60 and 70 percent of the crop each year for the past several years. In Colombia, some eight thousand hectares of poppies were fumigated from the air in 1999. However, little progress is likely if the ruling Taliban in Afghanistan doesn't commit to narcotics control. In Burma, the future is also uncertain as long as the country fails to muster the political will to make in-roads against the opium cultivation in areas ruled by the Wa Army.

The United States continues to help strengthen law-enforcement in heroin source countries by supporting training programs, information sharing, extradition of fugitives, and anti-money laundering measures. In addition, America will work through diplomatic and public channels to increase the level of international cooperation and support the ambitious UNDCP [UN International Drug Control Program] initiative to eradicate illicit opium-poppy cultivation in ten years.

Mathea Falco  **NO**

# U.S. Drug Policy: Addicted to Failure

$A$s Americans struggle to define their national security interests in the post–Cold War world, drug control enjoys strong political support from both parties. When asked to rank "very important" foreign policy goals, 85 per cent of the American public place "stopping the flow of drugs" at the top of the list, according to the 1995 Chicago Council on Foreign Relations national survey. For that reason, international drug-control programs will survive the congressional assault on the foreign affairs budget. Voter opposition to foreign aid does not yet extend to eradication and interdiction programs intended to stem the flow of drugs from abroad. Indeed, U.S.-supported antidrug programs in Latin America now represent almost 20 per cent of total American foreign assistance to the region, compared with only 3 per cent a decade ago.

The popular view that other countries are largely responsible for America's drug problems has deep historic roots. When the first drug laws were adopted early in this century, drugs were associated with immigrant groups and minorities: opium with Chinese laborers in the West; cocaine with blacks; and marijuana with Mexican immigrants in the Southwest. These drugs were seen as foreign threats to America's social fabric, undermining traditional moral values and political stability. Today the perceived link between foreigners and drugs still prompts the U.S. government to use diplomacy, coercion, money, and even military force to try to stop drugs from entering the country.

The supply-side approach is logically compelling. If there were no drugs coming in, the argument goes, then there would be no drug problem. And even if foreign drugs cannot be eliminated entirely, the laws of the marketplace dictate that reducing the supply will drive up the price, which in turn will deter potential users from trying drugs and force addicts to either go "cold turkey" or seek treatment. The critical assumption is that curtailing foreign supplies is the most effective way to cut drug abuse in the United States.

This supply-side approach to drugs has powerful political appeal. Blaming foreigners for America's recurring drug epidemics provides convenient if distant targets for public anger that might otherwise be directed toward elected officials. Getting foreign farmers to stop growing drug crops seems easier than curbing America's appetite for drugs. Moreover, intercepting incoming drugs in the air or on the high seas appears to be the kind of technological challenge

Americans are uniquely capable of meeting. If our scientists could land men on the moon, then surely we can shut off the drug traffic.

The supply-side approach to drug control has been thoroughly tested by both Republican and Democratic administrations. President Richard Nixon, faced with rising heroin and marijuana use in the late 1960s, closed a key U.S.-Mexican border crossing to convince Mexico to take action against illegal drug production. He also stepped up diplomatic pressure against Turkey, a major opium source for the notorious "French Connection" heroin traffickers, and provided narcotics-control assistance to Mexico and Turkey. Presidents Gerald Ford and Jimmy Carter continued programs of crop eradication, substitution, and overseas law-enforcement spending tens of millions of dollars during the 1970s.

At the end of the seventies, Turkey was no longer a significant source far illegal heroin, although the government allowed some farmers to grow opium for the international pharmaceutical industry. Due to intensive aerial opium eradication, Mexico's share of the U.S. heroin market declined sharply, from between 70 and 80 per cent in 1975 to 30 per cent in 1979. During the same period, heroin addiction in the United States also declined, in large part because addicts faced with rising heroin prices went into treatment, which was then widely available.

Unfortunately, the success of these supply-reduction programs was limited and brief. Production in other regions quickly expanded to fill American demand: Southeast Asia's Golden Triangle (Burma, Laos, and Thailand) and South Asia's Golden Crescent (Afghanistan, Iran, and Pakistan) became primary heroin sources. By 1983, Mexico had again become a major supplier, as opium cultivation spread to more remote areas only nominally controlled by the government.

President Ronald Reagan gave unprecedented resources to supply-control efforts. Just as he intended to shield the United States from Soviet missiles through the Strategic Defense Initiative, so, too, did Reagan try to seal the borders against the flow of drugs that threatened the nation's security. Funding for interdiction and international supply-control programs jumped from $416 million in 1981 to $1.6 billion in 1987, constituting about one-third of total federal antidrug spending.

President George Bush followed similar policies. In September 1989, in his first televised presidential address, Bush announced that, "we will for the first time make available the appropriate resources of America's armed forces. We will intensify our efforts against drug smugglers on the high seas, in international airspace, and at our borders."

The Defense Department initially resisted congressional efforts to enlist the military in the drug war. However, when faced with major budget cuts after the collapse of the Soviet Union, the Defense Department embraced a drug-fighting mission, protecting some endangered programs by reclassifying them as drug-related. For example, over-the-horizon radar systems designed to guard against Soviet missiles overflying Canada were redirected southward to watch for drug-smuggling aircraft. By 1991, the Defense Department had captured the largest share of the $2 billion drug-interdiction budget.

Although President Bill Clinton has generally endorsed his predecessors' emphasis on curtailing drug supplies, voices within the administration and the Congress express increasing skepticism about the effectiveness of America's international drug war. In September 1993, a National Security Council (NSC) interagency review concluded that interdiction had not succeeded in slowing the flow of cocaine, confirming the findings of several previous General Accounting Office (GAO) studies. Although interdiction funding had been cut substantially in the Bush administration's last budget, funding fell further under Clinton, dropping to approximately $1.3 billion by 1995.

The NSC policy review argued that stopping drugs close to their source of production might prove a more effective strategy than traditional interdiction efforts. Funding for overseas narcotics-control programs had declined from an estimated $660 million in 1992 to about $330 million in 1994. Following the NSC recommendation, the administration requested substantial increases in the fiscal 1995 budget for source-country programs, but the Democratic-controlled Congress refused to fund them. Noting that Congress had approved the $2.2 billion five-year Andean Strategy, begun in 1989 under the Bush administration to help Bolivia, Colombia, and Peru reduce illicit drug activities, the House Appropriations Committee's 1995 report on foreign operations concluded that

> there are no signs that actual levels of cocaine reaching U.S. shores has changed.... We thus find ourselves continuing to march steadily down a path towards devoting more and more resources to helicopters, vehicles, police and army bases, and weaponry, while not doing enough to fund comprehensive economic solutions.... The program has done little in its country programs to ensure sustainability, and thus the Committee has no confidence that the reforms achieved so far will stick.

The new Republican Congress has sharply criticized Clinton's shift away from interdiction, calling this a litmus test of his determination to combat drugs. In July 1995, the House of Representatives voted to eliminate the White House Office of National Drug Control Policy (ONDCP), which develops the administration's annual drug strategy and coordinates federal antidrug efforts. While the Senate subsequently restored ONDCP under threat of presidential veto, its budget was cut by one-third. Critics contended that ONDCP's budget would be better spent on interdiction. According to Senator Richard Shelby (R-Alabama), his appropriations subcommittee "voted to terminate" ONDCP in order to provide "full funding for... drug interdiction efforts with the $10 million in savings."

Congressional enthusiasm for interdiction does not extend to source-country programs, which two key House committee chairmen characterized as "tried-and-failed crop eradication and alternative development initiatives" in an open letter to Clinton in 1995. Congress cut $98 million from the Clinton administration's requested $213 million for the State Department's source-country efforts in the fiscal 1996 budget.

# Supply-Control Scorecard

Since 1981, American taxpayers have spent $23 billion on international drug control. Yet drug supplies have increased substantially both at home and abroad. Worldwide opium production has more than doubled in the past decade and now exceeds 3,400 tons per year, the equivalent of 340 tons of heroin. From 1984 to 1994, coca production almost doubled, although the United States provided more than $2 billion in narcotics-control assistance to Bolivia, Colombia, and Peru, the world's largest coca producers. Meanwhile, drug prices in the United States have fallen precipitously. Heroin now sells for less than half its 1981 street price, and heroin purity exceeds 60 per cent in many cities, compared with only 7 per cent in 1981. Cocaine prices have dropped by two-thirds. The administrator of the Drug Enforcement Administration (DEA), Thomas Constantine, testified before the House International Relations Subcommittee on the Western Hemisphere in March 1995 that "drug availability and purity of cocaine and heroin are at an all-time high."

Some congressional critics blame the apparent failure of interdiction on a lack of resources, arguing that budget cuts of one-third since 1992 have hindered federal efforts to intercept foreign drug traffic. Others blame Clinton's strategic shift away from efforts to interrupt drug traffic through the Caribbean, Central America, and Mexico in favor of trying to eliminate the *production* of drugs in Bolivia, Colombia, and Peru. In June 1995, Joseph Kelley, a top analyst for international affairs at the GAO, testified that the U.S. international antidrug effort suffers from weak management and poor coordination.

The underlying problem, however, is not operational. Increased resources and better implementation will not make foreign supply-control efforts more successful in driving up drug prices in the United States. The supply-side strategy is fatally flawed for several reasons, which follow.

**The economics of drug cultivation mitigate against sustained reductions in supply**   Drug crops can be grown very cheaply almost anywhere in the world, and poor farmers have strong economic incentives to adapt to changing conditions. If one production area is wiped out, lost crops can easily be replaced. In Peru, for example, a fungal infestation of coca crops in the early 1990s pushed cultivation into more remote, previously uncultivated areas of the Huallaga Valley. In the 1970s in Mexico, the government's opium-eradication campaign drove farmers to change their cultivation techniques, growing opium poppies in much smaller patches under large-leafed crops, such as banana trees, which made aerial detection difficult.

The number of countries producing drugs has significantly increased in the past two decades. Although coca is a traditional crop in Bolivia, Colombia, and Peru, it is now being grown in other South American countries, and worldwide poppy cultivation continues to expand. In the Central Asian republics, opium is an important source of revenue, while cocaine traffickers in Colombia are diversifying into heroin from locally grown opium poppies. (Before 1991, Colombia had never grown opium.) Marijuana is essentially a weed grown in every temperate region of the world, including many parts of the United States.

Drug crops are the mainstay of many poor countries, where farmers have few comparable alternatives. In Bolivia, for example, where the per capita gross national product (GNP) is $770 a year, an acre of coca yields about $475 annually, compared with $35–$250 for crops such as bananas and grapefruit—if there are buyers. In Kyrgyzstan, per capita GNP was only $610 in 1994, but a pound of opium brings $400 in local markets or can be bartered for canned goods, cooking oil, and other commodities.

The real but brief success of U.S. efforts to reduce Turkish and Mexican drug production in the 1970s has not been matched. Despite continuing U.S. pressure, source-country governments have been unable or unwilling to undertake sustained drug-eradication campaigns. The reductions in cultivation that do occur are symbolic, since the eradicated crops tend to be more than offset by new plantings. For example, from 1987 to 1993, the Bolivian government devoted $48 million in U.S. aid to pay farmers to eradicate 26,000 hectares of coca. During the same period, Bolivian farmers planted more than 35,000 new hectares of coca. Some observers have concluded that U.S. eradication efforts in Bolivia are little more than a coca support program at U.S. taxpayers' expense.

The only successful example of a large-scale reduction in illicit drug cultivation in recent years occurred in Thailand, where rapid economic growth has produced opportunities more lucrative than opium farming. After decades of supplying the world heroin market, Thailand now imports opium from neighboring Burma to support its own addicts. However, some Thais continue to play a significant role in international drug trafficking and money laundering.

**The United States consumes a relatively small portion of worldwide drug production**     In 1993, Americans used eight metric tons of heroin, less than 4 per cent of worldwide production, according to the DEA. The U.S. cocaine market absorbs less than one-third of total global production. Domestic marijuana consumption accounts for 817 tons per year: As much as half of that total is grown illegally in the United States.

The great bulk of foreign drug production is consumed in countries other than the United States—often in the regions where the drug crops are grown. Burma, Laos, and Thailand, for example, have almost 500,000 opium and heroin addicts, while India, Iran, and Pakistan account for several million more. According to the World Health Organization, drug abuse is regarded as an emerging "public health and social problem" in Central and East European countries. Cocaine supply appears to be on the rise; heroin addiction is also either increasing or maintaining high levels throughout Europe. In recent years, the abuse of coca paste (known as *basuco*) and cocaine has become a major problem in the South American producer and transit countries. Even if the U.S. demand for drugs declined precipitously, foreign drug suppliers have ready markets in every region of the world and would not stop production.

**America's annual drug demand can be supplied from a relatively small growing area and transported in a few airplanes**     The illegal drugs Americans consume are grown worldwide and can be cultivated on very little acreage. A poppy field roughly the area of northwest Washington, D.C.—25 square miles—can supply the American heroin market for a year. The annual demand for cocaine can be met from coca fields less than one-quarter the size of Rhode Island, or about 300 square miles.

Effectively reducing the flow of drugs into the United States is exceedingly difficult not only because America's borders are long and porous, but because relatively small amounts of heroin and cocaine are involved. Three DC-3A or five Cessna Caravan turboprop planes could carry the nation's annual heroin supply, while three Boeing 747 cargo planes or 12 trailer trucks could transport the necessary cocaine.

**The price structure of the drug market severely limits the potential impact of interdiction and source-country programs**   By far, the largest drug-trade profits are made at the level of street sales, not in foreign poppy or coca fields or on the high seas. The total cost of cultivating, refining, and smuggling cocaine to the United States accounts for less than 12 per cent of retail prices here. RAND estimates that the total cost of growing and importing heroin accounts for an even smaller fraction of the retail price. Even if the United States were able to seize half the cocaine coming from South America—or eradicate half the coca crop—the price of cocaine in U.S. cities would increase by less than 5 per cent. Thus, massive interdiction and drug-eradication efforts are far less effective in making drugs more expensive than is enforcement directed at U.S. street markets. Police patrols aimed at increasing the "hassle" factor that drug dealers and drug buyers face exert a much greater impact in discouraging domestic drug abuse and drug crime. These patrols also help deter street violence related to drug dealing.

# Concentrate on Domestic Demand

After a century of criticizing other countries for being the source of America's drug problem, it is time to recognize that any lasting solutions lie here at home. In the continuing debate over the supply-side drug strategy, we should remember that the steepest declines in drug use occurred during a period when drug availability was rapidly increasing. In 1982, the National Household Survey showed that 23.3 million Americans used illicit drugs. By 1991, when drug prices hit record lows, only 12.5 million people reported illicit drug use. This dramatic decline reflected public awareness that drugs were harmful as well as growing social disapproval of drug use. Following the death of sports star Len Bias from a cocaine overdose in 1986, cocaine use declined by half, particularly among better-educated Americans inclined to respond to health information.

Unfortunately, these downward trends have now reversed. Marijuana use among eighth graders has doubled since 1992, and illicit drug use among high school seniors is climbing for the first time in a decade. Recent surveys reveal that a majority of both teenagers and adults view drugs as less harmful than they did four years ago. This shift in public attitudes presages further increases in drug problems, particularly among young people for whom the 1980s are ancient history.

Moreover, the drugs of choice in the recent upsurge are primarily domestic, not foreign. Teenagers are using marijuana, LSD, and amphetamines—all of which are produced illegally within the United States. Younger children are turning to common household substances, such as glue, solvents, and aerosols, that are virtually impossible to control. In 1995, one in five eighth graders reported using these inhalants, which produce instant highs and can be lethal.

Experience has shown that reducing demand is the key to sustained progress against drug abuse. A 1994 RAND study, *Controlling Cocaine: Supply Versus Demand Programs,* found that treatment is far more effective than either interdiction or source-country programs in reducing cocaine consumption. Specifically, $34 million invested in treatment reduces annual cocaine use by the same amount as $366 million invested in interdiction or $783 million in source-country programs.

Most Americans do not realize that treatment works—not always, and often not the first time, but eventually. National studies that have followed tens of thousands of addicts through different kinds of programs report that one of the most important factors is the length of time in treatment. One-third of those who stay in treatment longer than three months are drug-free a year after leaving treatment. The success rate jumps to two-thirds when treatment lasts a year or longer. And some programs that provide intensive, highly structured therapy report even better results.

Yet since the early 1980s, treatment has been a low priority nationwide as drug interdiction and enforcement have dominated state and federal spending. In 1995, treatment represented only one-fifth of the more than $13 billion federal drug budget compared with one-quarter 10 years earlier, well before the cocaine epidemic created millions of new addicts. About 40 per cent of the nation's drug addicts cannot get treatment due to inadequate funding for treatment facilities.

Education is the key to protecting our children from drugs, no matter where the offending substances are produced. In the past decade, prevention programs have been developed that significantly reduce new drug use among teenagers. These programs, built on social-learning theory, teach children how to recognize pressures that influence them to smoke, drink, and use drugs and how to resist these pressures through role-playing in the classroom. The impact of these programs is much greater when prevention includes families, media, and the community in a comprehensive effort to discourage drug use. Nonetheless, Congress cut funding for in-school drug education by reducing the Safe and Drug Free Schools Program budget for 1996 from $441 million to $200 million—less than one-sixth the total federal budget for interdiction.

## Toward a New Drug Policy

Since America's international drug strategy has not reduced drug problems in this country, should the United States support *any* international efforts to control the illicit drug trade? Yes, to the extent that global cooperation can be effective against the multinational drug networks that undermine the stability of political and financial institutions throughout the world. For example, countries formerly controlled by the Soviet Union in Central Asia and Eastern Europe, as well as Russia itself, are being weakened by the activities of transnational criminal drug syndicates. Many burgeoning entrepreneurs in the newly independent republics have learned that hard drugs are a ready substitute for hard currency in international markets. Opium production in Tajikistan, Turkmenistan, and Uzbekistan has doubled since 1990. Law enforcement in the former Soviet Union is now sporadic at best and is already riven by rampant corruption. In many areas, drug traffickers operate unchallenged.

In this hemisphere, the power of the drug traffickers directly threatens two important democracies, Colombia and Mexico. Although the arrests of the Cali drug lords in August 1995 were an important victory for the Colombian government in its bloody war against the cocaine cartels, Colombia continues to be the world's primary cocaine producer. Evidence that President Ernesto Samper Pizano and some of his Cabinet ministers may have taken cartel money has severely strained Colombia's relations with the United States. Continuing allegations of corruption raise doubts about the government's viability.

The "Colombianization" of Mexico, where drug traffickers penetrated the highest levels of the former Salinas administration and may be involved in high-level assassinations, directly threatens U.S. economic and political interests. Recent revelations that Raul Salinas de Gortari banked at least $84 million in drug money in Switzerland while his brother was president have rocked public confidence in the political system that has governed Mexico for more than 60 years. Although the current president, Ernesto Zedillo, has pledged to clean up drug corruption, he may not have sufficient power to do so. Shortly after Zedillo's most recent pledge, in November 1995, a jet owned by the Cali cartel, loaded with cocaine, landed in Baja California. Witnesses report that the plane was unloaded by uniformed Mexican federal police, who subsequently attempted to conceal the fuselage. The cocaine, estimated to be worth $100 million, has "disappeared."

The failure of American efforts to curtail the flow of drugs into the United States should not cause us to abandon the effort at a time when drug traffic is growing rapidly. The passage of the North American Free Trade Agreement (NAFTA) raised concerns among many in this country that Mexican traffickers would now be able to operate unchecked across the border. Outspoken NAFTA opponents, such as California Democratic senator Dianne Feinstein, have threatened to overturn the treaty largely because of these concerns. Although border controls have very little practical impact on drug availability in America, tough inspections send an important political message that the United States will not tolerate traffickers. The U.S. decision in December 1995 to delay NAFTA's unrestricted-trucking provisions reflects the administration's concern about negative public reaction to removing existing restraints—however weak—on cross-border traffic.

The globalization of national economies broadens the reach of the traffickers, who conduct annual business estimated to be valued at $180 to $300 billion worldwide. In this rapidly evolving scenario, the United States has much to share with other countries in the areas of narcotics intelligence, law enforcement, judicial reform, education, and treatment. For example, DEA intelligence was critically important in facilitating the Colombian government's arrests of the Cali cartel leaders. The FBI, the DEA, and other U.S. enforcement agencies are currently training their Russian counterparts in crime-control techniques, including the surveillance of drug networks.

In addition, the United States can take a leading role in improving international efforts to undermine the money-laundering activities that safeguard the profits of drug traffickers. More than 100 governments have ratified the 1988 United Nations Convention Against Illicit Traffic in Narcotic Drugs and Psychotropic Substances, a worldwide framework for attacking money laundering and bank secrecy. But a dozen governments representing major financial centers have yet to ratify the convention, and enforcement by participating governments remains inconsistent. While some progress has been made in opening up traditional safe havens for drug money—such as Switzerland and the Bahamas—money laundering is increasing in the rapidly growing East Asian and Pacific financial centers. In his October 1995 speech at the United Nations's 50th anniversary, President Clinton highlighted the need for greater international cooperation against money laundering, threatening economic sanctions against countries that refuse to adopt antilaundering measures.

The computer-aided expansion of world trade and financial services complicates monitoring and enforcement for even the most capable governments. Indeed, according to the State Department, "U.S. financial systems continue to be exploited, at levels probably not approached by any other country." Major banks and investment firms in the United States have been implicated in money laundering, and, in June 1995, three former Justice Department officials were indicted for obstructing justice and assisting the Cali cartel in laundering its profits. By pursuing such major corruption cases, the United States can set an example for other countries beset by high-level involvement in drug trafficking. Still, the $375 million combined budget of the U.S. Organized Crime Drug Enforcement Task Forces—an interagency program that investigates and prosecutes high-level drug traffickers—remains less than one-fourth the level of federal spending on interdiction and international supply-control programs.

International narcotics control, if no longer subject to the elusive counts of drugs eradicated or seized, can serve America's larger interests in strengthening democratic institutions and freeing countries from the grip of criminal organizations. The arrests of the Cali cartel may not have made an appreciable difference in cocaine's availability in the United States, but they are an encouraging indication of that government's determination to fight the drug traffickers. Still, it is important to remember that lasting answers to America's drug problem lie here at home, not abroad. Providing drug-prevention programs for every school child will curb domestic drug abuse more than trying to reduce overseas drug crops. In the final analysis, offering treatment to the nation's addicts will do more to reduce drug consumption than additional drug seizures at the source of production, on the high seas, or at the border.

# POSTSCRIPT

## Should the United States Put More Emphasis on Stopping the Importation of Drugs?

The drug trade spawns violence; people die from using drugs or by dealing with people in the drug trade; families are ruined by the effects of drugs on family members; prisons are filled with tens of thousands of people who were and probably still are involved with illegal drugs; and drugs can devastate aspirations and careers. The adverse consequences of drugs can be seen everywhere in society. How should the government determine the best course of action to follow in remedying the negative effects of drugs?

Two paths that are traditionally followed involve reducing either the supply or the demand for drugs. Four major agencies involved in the fight against drugs in the United States—the Drug Enforcement Administration (DEA), the Federal Bureau of Investigation (FBI), the U.S. Customs Service, and the U.S. Coast Guard—have seized thousands of pounds of marijuana, cocaine, and heroin during the past few years. Drug interdiction appears to be reducing the availability of drugs. But what effect does drug availability have on use?

Annual surveys of 8th-, 10th-, and 12th-grade students indicate that availability is not a major factor in drug use. Throughout the 1980s drug use declined dramatically even though marijuana and cocaine could be obtained easily. According to the surveys, the perceived harm of these drugs, not their availability, is what affects students' drug use. As individuals' perceptions of drugs as being harmful increase, usage decreases; as perceptions of harm decrease, usage increases.

Efforts to prevent drug use may prove fruitless if people have a natural desire to alter their consciousness. In his 1989 book *Intoxication: Life in the Pursuit of Artificial Paradise* (E. P. Dutton), Ronald Siegel contends that the urge to alter consciousness is as universal as the craving for food and sex.

Articles that examine international efforts to deal with the issue of drugs include "A Global Empirical Review of Drug Crop Eradication and the United Nations' Crop Substitution and Alternative Development Strategies," by Graham Farrell, *Journal of Drug Issues* (vol. 2, 1998); "Global Reach: The Threat of International Drug Trafficking," by Rensselaer Lee, *Current History* (May 1995); and "Addicted to the Drug War," by Kenneth Sharpe, *The Chronicle of Higher Education* (October 6, 2000). Finally, Philippe Bordes, in "Drugs: Surveillance or Punishment?" *UNESCO Courier* (October 1998), looks at the drug problem from an international perspective.

# ISSUE 3

## Will a Lower Blood Alcohol Level for Drunk Driving Reduce Automobile Accidents?

**YES: Ralph W. Hingson, Timothy Heeren, and Michael R. Winter**, from "Preventing Impaired Driving," *Alcohol Research & Health* (Winter 1999)

**NO: General Accounting Office**, from "How Effective Are '.08' Drunk-Driving Laws?" *Consumers' Research* (August 1999)

### ISSUE SUMMARY

**YES:** Ralph W. Hingson, Timothy Heeren, and Michael R. Winter, of the Boston University School of Public Health, support lowering the legal limit for drunk driving. They note that many states have had fewer alcohol-related automobile accidents after lowering the blood alcohol level for drunk driving. In addition, they contend that drivers are impaired with a relatively small amount of alcohol in their bloodstream.

**NO:** The General Accounting Office (GAO) states that the evidence supporting the beneficial effects of establishing a lower blood alcohol level for drunk driving is inconclusive. The GAO maintains that the government's methods for determining the effectiveness of instituting a lower blood alcohol level are faulty. Also, rates for drunk driving declined regardless of changes in the legal limits for blood alcohol level.

When discussions of drinking and driving arise, many justifiably express concern. Too many people die needlessly because of others' poor judgment regarding whether or not they can safely operate a motor vehicle after consuming alcohol. However, the news is not all bad. In the last 20 years, the number of alcohol-related driving fatalities in the United States has decreased significantly. In the early 1980s approximately 26,000 people died each year because of drivers under the influence of alcohol. In 1998 the number of people killed in automobile accidents on American highways because of drunk drivers was around 17,000. This represents a 30 percent decline. Despite this significant reduction, few would argue against further improvement.

The figure of 17,000 alcohol-related automobile fatalities represents the number of people who were killed by a driver who was legally intoxicated at the time of the accident. Missing from this figure is the number of people who were killed by drivers who may have been drinking but who were not legally drunk. However, one does not need to be drunk to be impaired. A number of studies have demonstrated that driving ability is impaired with a blood alcohol concentration (BAC) level as low .04.

The BAC is the amount of alcohol that is in a person's body as measured by the weight of the alcohol in a certain volume of blood. A person's BAC can be measured by testing the blood, breath, urine, or saliva. The federal government wants states to adopt a national blood alcohol level standard of .08. States that refuse to adopt this new standard will be in jeopardy of losing federal funding for highways. The U.S. Senate debated whether or not the federal government should interfere in what many senators see as a state's option. Research indicates that lowering the BAC limit from .10 or higher to .08 reduces the number of people who get behind the wheel of a car after drinking. However, the senators are not debating whether or not a lower standard such as .08 is desirable. They are arguing what the role of the federal government should be in this matter. As of 1998, 15 states have implemented a BAC standard of .08, and 5 more are considering adopting a similar standard.

The precedent for penalizing states that refuse to adopt the .08 blood alcohol level standard was set in the early 1980s when President Ronald Reagan threatened to withdraw highway funds from states that did not raise the drinking age to 21. That situation, like the current issue, raises a fundamental question: Should the federal government have the right to dictate to individual states what is an acceptable BAC standard? Is the role of government to conduct research in order to allow states to make informed decisions? If, as Senator Jack Reed (D-Rhode Island) has indicated, a .08 BAC saves between 500 and 600 lives a year, shouldn't the federal government take a more strident stand? Yet is the research cited by these senators accurate? Should government impose laws where the supporting research is suspect?

In the following selections, Ralph W. Hingson, Timothy Heeren, and Michael R. Winter argue that the need to lower the acceptable blood alcohol level for drunk driving is clear. The federal government should enact a national blood alcohol concentration standard of .08 for driving while intoxicated in order to save lives and to prevent serious injuries. The General Accounting Office does not dispute the fact that automobile accidents have declined over the past two decades. However, it questions the validity of the studies that provide evidence that it is the lowering of blood alcohol levels that has caused the decline. The GAO asserts that the decline in automobile accidents may have occurred anyway, regardless of changes in the law.

**Ralph W. Hingson, Timothy Heeren, and Michael R. Winter**

# Preventing Impaired Driving

$A$driver does not necessarily have to be intoxicated to be impaired by alcohol. Even moderate drinking, defined as drinking no more than two drinks per day for men and no more than one drink per day for women (National Institute on Alcohol Abuse and Alcoholism [NIAAA] 1995), may impair driving performance. This level of drinking generally results in a blood alcohol concentration (BAC) of 0.03 percent for both men and women (if the drinks are consumed in 1 hour on an empty stomach). A person's risk of involvement in a fatal crash nearly doubles with each 0.02-percent increase in BAC (Zador 1991). In 1997, 18 percent of fatally injured drivers who tested positive for alcohol had BACs between 0.01 and 0.09 percent (National Highway Traffic Safety Administration [NHTSA] 1998a), a range that falls below the legal BAC limit for drivers in most States. Eight percent of these drivers had BACs between 0.01 and 0.04 percent.

This article explores the relationship between alcohol consumption and impairment and examines legislative aproaches for reducing alcohol-impaired driving, including laws lowering the legal BAC limits for drivers, sanctions imposed for impaired driving, and strategies for restricting alcohol's availability.

## Moderate Drinking and Impairment

Even at low BAC levels, alcohol impairs driving performance by reducing the driver's reaction time and slowing his or her decisionmaking process (Moskowitz et al. 1985). A driver's ability to divide his or her attention between two or more visual stimuli can be impaired at BACs of 0.02 percent or lower (Starmer 1989; Howat et al. 1991; Moskowitz et al. 1985). Starting at BACs of 0.05 percent, drivers exhibit impairment in eye movement, glare resistance, visual perception, reaction time, certain types of steering tasks, information processing, and other driving components (Starmer 1989; Howat et al. 1991; Hindmarch et al. 1992; Finnegan and Hammersley 1992). Currently, the legal BAC limit for noncommercial drivers in most States is 0.10 percent. Thus, although moderate drinking may impair driving ability, most States have legal BAC limits for drivers that exceed the BAC level reached as a result of moderate drinking. Consequently, moderate drinkers, although often impaired, can still drive legally.

From Ralph W. Hingson, Timothy Heeren, and Michael R. Winter, "Preventing Impaired Driving," *Alcohol Research & Health*, vol. 23, no. 1 (Winter 1999). Washington, D.C.: U.S. Government Printing Office, 1999. References omitted.

Alcohol absorption and metabolism vary among people, depending on such factors as drinking pace, food consumption, age, gender, and the proportion of body mass that is fatty tissue. Typically, a 170-pound man would need to consume five drinks in 1 hour on an empty stomach to reach a BAC of 0.10 percent. To reach a BAC of 0.08 percent, the legal limit in 17 States, a 170-pound man would need to consume four drinks in 1 hour on an empty stomach.

Women absorb and metabolize alcohol differently than do men. In general, compared with men, women contain a smaller amount of body water to absorb each drink. Women also exhibit lower activity levels of the alcohol-metabolizing enzyme alcohol dehydrogenase (ADH) in the stomach, causing a larger portion of ingested alcohol to reach the blood (NIAAA 1997). A 137-pound woman would need to consume three drinks in 1 hour on an empty stomach to reach a 0.08-percent BAC and four drinks in 2 hours to reach a 0.10-percent BAC. Drinking over a longer period of time and eating while drinking extend the number of drinks required to reach these BAC levels (NHTSA 1997).

Although moderate drinking may not cause a person's BAC to exceed the legal limit for driving, moderate drinking increases the risk of being involved in a fatal crash. Compared with drivers who have not consumed alcohol, drivers with BACs between 0.02 and 0.04 percent are 1.4 times as likely to be involved in a single-vehicle fatal crash. Furthermore, this risk increases to an estimated 11.1 times higher for drivers with BACs between 0.05 and 0.09 percent, 48 times higher for drivers with BACs between 0.10 and 0.14 percent, and 380 times higher for drivers with BACs at or above 0.15 percent (Zador 1991).

For drivers under age 21, fatal crash risk increases more with each 0.02-percent increase in BAC than it does for older drivers (Zador 1991). At all BAC levels including zero, the fatal crash risk for female drivers ages 16 to 20 is at least double the risk for female drivers age 25 and over, and the risk for male drivers ages 16 to 20 is triple the risk for male drivers age 25 and over (Zador 1991). Young drivers generally have less driving experience than older drivers and are more likely to take risks in traffic, such as speeding, disobeying traffic signals, and not wearing safety belts (Hingson and Howland 1993). Because alcohol consumption further increases the risk of crash involvement for young drivers, all States have adopted zero-tolerance laws for drivers under age 21, prohibiting driving after any alcohol consumption.

Recognizing the threat to the public safety associated with even moderate drinking and driving by transportation workers, the Federal government prohibits commercial truck drivers, railroad and mass transit workers, marine employees, and aircraft pilots from operating their vehicles with a BAC at or greater than 0.04 percent. To reach this relatively low BAC limit, however, most people would have to drink above the level of moderate drinking. The American Medical Association (1986) has endorsed lowering the legal BAC limit to 0.05 percent for all drivers; however, no State has yet adopted this standard.

Several other countries' legal BAC limits for drivers come closer than the United States to restricting drivers to moderate drinking. The legal limit in Canada, Austria, and the United Kingdom is 0.08 percent. Legal limits in Australia range from 0.05 to 0.08 percent. The Netherlands, Finland, France, Germany, and Japan all have 0.05-percent legal limits. Sweden has lowered the legal BAC limit for drivers to 0.02 percent (NHTSA 1997).

# Legislative Measures

Society has implemented a variety of legislative measures to reduce alcohol-impaired driving. To date, U.S. laws have not attempted to restrict adult drivers to moderate drinking. Nonetheless, research indicates that laws adopted in the United States have reduced alcohol-related traffic deaths among both moderate drinkers and those who have very high blood alcohol levels. Current U.S. laws that limit drivers' BACs to 0.10 and 0.08 percent have been found effective for reducing alcohol-related crashes, as have license revocation/suspension and other penalties for exceeding those limits as well as laws restricting access to alcohol.

## Legal BAC Limits for Drivers

Reducing the BAC level at which people can legally drive can effectively reduce alcohol-related traffic crashes (e.g., Johnson and Fell 1995; Hingson et al. 1996). Drivers under age 21 are subject to lower BAC limits than older drivers, and a few States have set lower limits for drivers previously convicted of driving while intoxicated (DWI).

## Lowering the Legal BAC Limits to 0.08 Percent for Drivers Over Age 21

Seventeen states have lowered the criminal per se legal BAC limit from 0.10 to 0.08 percent for noncommercial drivers age 21 and older (lower limits have been established for drivers younger than age 21 and are discussed later in this article). According to the criminal per se provision, prosecutors are not required to introduce evidence other than a BAC of 0.08 percent or higher to demonstrate impairment, thereby making convictions easier to obtain. These laws also have administrative license revocation (ALR) provisions, which permit police officers to immediately seize the license of any driver with a BAC of 0.08 percent or higher. The person's license is then suspended until either a hearing or trial is conducted.

Several studies have examined the effects of 0.08 laws on fatal crash trends. In California, the largest State to adopt a 0.08 law, researchers found a 12-percent decline in alcohol-related fatal crashes after the law was adopted. Because California also adopted an ALR law 6 months after the criminal per se law, the separate effects of each law are difficult to determine (NHTSA 1991). According to one study, most of the effects occurred after the ALR provisions were added (Rogers 1995).

Johnson and Fell (1995) monitored six measures of driver alcohol involvement in the first five States to adopt 0.08 laws (Utah, Oregon, Maine, California, and Vermont) and identified several statistically significant pre- to post-law decreases. Because the study did not compare States with the 0.08 law with States that did not have the law, researchers could not determine whether the changes were independent of general regional trends. The researchers concluded that the effects of the law were independent of national trends.

In a subsequent analysis, Hingson and colleagues (1996) paired the aforementioned first five States to adopt a 0.08 law with five nearby States that retained the 0.10-percent legal BAC limit (Idaho, Washington, Massachusetts, Texas, and New Hampshire). Relative to the comparison States, the States that adopted the 0.08 law experienced a significant reduction (i.e., 16 percent) in the proportion of fatal crashes involving fatally injured drivers with BACs of 0.08 percent or higher. These results resembled those reported in both the United Kingdom and France when those countries first combined 0.08 laws with automatic license revocation provisions (Ross 1973; Ross 1982).

The majority of drivers killed in traffic crashes in 1997 who tested positive for alcohol had BACs of 0.15 percent or higher. The first five States to adopt the 0.08 law also experienced a significant decline (i.e., 18 percent) relative to the comparison States in the proportion of fatal crashes involving fatally injured drivers with BACs of 0.15 percent or higher (Hingson et al. 1996). Compared with 0.10-percent States, the 0.08-percent States may have been more concerned about alcohol-impaired driving and more only 54 percent of residents in States with 0.08 laws and only 38 percent of residents in States with 0.10 laws could correctly identify their State's BAC limit. When the legal BAC limits for drivers are lowered, the need to educate the public about these changes is apparent. Research indicates that public education to promote awareness of a State's new legal BAC limit can enhance the legislation's effects (Blomberg 1992).

Public education also is needed to increase drivers' knowledge about the impairments associated with different levels of alcohol consumption. Among drivers surveyed, 75 percent thought that at least one-half of all drivers would be dangerous if they drove after consuming five drinks in 2 hours, but only 28 percent of the respondents thought all drivers would be unsafe under those conditions (NHTSA 1996).

**Zero-tolerance laws for drivers under age 21**    Although all States prohibit people under age 21 from purchasing, possessing, or consuming alcohol, drinking remains prevalent among teenagers (Johnston et al. 1998). Zero-tolerance laws are designed to reduce drinking and driving among young people by making it illegal for persons under 21 to drive after any drinking. These laws set the legal BAC limit for drivers under age 21 at 0.00 or 0.02 percent. In the fall of 1995, the U.S. Congress mandated that Federal highway funds be withheld from States that did not adopt zero-tolerance laws. At that time, only one-half of the States had such laws.

A recent study (Hingson et al. 1994) found that the first eight States to adopt zero-tolerance laws experienced a 20-percent greater decline in the proportion of nighttime single-vehicle fatal crashes among 15- to 20-year-old drivers compared with eight nearby States without zero-tolerance laws. Single-vehicle nighttime crashes are the type of fatal crash most likely to involve alcohol.

States that did not adopt zero-tolerance laws but lowered their BAC limits for drivers under age 21 to either 0.04 or 0.06 percent experienced declines of 6 to 7 percent relative to States with no BAC limit specific to drivers under age 21 (Hingson et al. 1994). Setting BAC limits for young drivers at 0.04 or 0.06 percent allows youth to speculate about how much they can drink and still drive legally. Conversely, zero-tolerance laws send a clear message to young drivers that it is illegal to drive after engaging in any drinking. By the summer of 1998, all 50 States had passed zero-tolerance laws.

Unfortunately, some States have experienced difficulty in achieving broad public awareness of zero-tolerance laws. Studies in both California and Massachusetts found that 45 to 50 percent of young drivers were unaware of the law (Martin et al. 1996). Obviously, increasing awareness of the zero-tolerance law can enhance its effects. Blomberg (1992) found a one-third greater decline in alcohol-involved crashes among young drivers in Maryland counties where public service announcements about the State's zero-tolerance law were aired compared with drivers in other counties.

As a result of all States raising the minimum legal drinking age (MLDA) to 21 and adopting zero-tolerance laws for persons under age 21, the greatest reductions in alcohol-related traffic crashes in recent years have occurred among drivers under 21. Since NHTSA first began conducting national estimates of alcohol involvement in fatal crashes, alcohol-related fatalities among 15- to 20-year-olds have declined 59 percent, from 5,380 in 1982 to 2,209 in 1997. By comparison, alcohol-related fatalities among all other age groups declined 29 percent, from 19,785 to 13,980 (NHTSA 1998a). The proportion of all fatal crashes among 15- to 20-year-olds that involved alcohol declined 44 percent compared with 30 percent for all other age groups from 1982 to 1997.

**Lower legal BAC limits for drivers convicted of driving while intoxicated**
Similar to drivers under age 21, drivers with prior DWI convictions are disproportionately at a risk for alcohol-related fatal crash involvement. One study found that drivers killed in alcohol-related crashes were eight times more likely to have had a DWI conviction in the previous 5 years than drivers randomly selected from the general population of licensed drivers (Brewer et al. 1994).

In August 1988 Maine lowered the legal BAC limit for drivers previously convicted of DWI to 0.05 percent. In 1995 the law was modified to make it illegal for these drivers to drive after engaging in any drinking. The law allows first-time DWI offenders' licenses to be reinstated after a mandatory suspension of 2 months on the condition that they not drive with a positive BAC for 1 year. Licenses of second-time offenders are reinstated on the condition that the offenders not drive with a positive BAC for 10 years. Convicted DWI offenders who are apprehended with positive BACs receive a 1-year administrative license suspension or revocation and may receive court-imposed penalties.

One method for measuring the effectiveness of laws lowering BAC limits for DWI-convicted drivers is to determine any pre- to post-law changes in the extent to which DWI offenders are involved in fatal crashes. During the first 6 years after Maine adopted its 0.05-percent BAC limit for drivers with prior DWI convictions, the proportion of fatal crashes involving drivers with prior DWI convictions declined 25 percent, compared with the 6 years before the law took effect. The proportion of fatal crashes involving drivers with prior DWI convictions and BACs of 0.05 percent or higher declined 31 percent (Hingson et al. 1998).

Opponents of lowering the legal BAC limits for drivers have argued that these measures target "social drinkers" and have no effect on drivers with high BACs or prior DWI convictions. However, during the 6 years after Maine adopted its 0.05-percent law for drivers with prior DWI convictions, the proportion of fatal crashes involving drivers with prior DWI convictions and BACs of 0.15 percent or higher declined 35 percent. During those 6 years, compared with the previous 6 years, the rest of the United States experienced minimal change in the proportion of fatal crashes involving drivers with prior DWI convictions and positive BACs. In the rest of New England, the proportion of fatal crashes involving drivers with prior DWI convictions and positive BACs increased over 40 percent (Hingson et al. 1998).

In 1995 Maine became the first State to adopt a zero-tolerance law for convicted DWI offenders. Maine was also the first State to adopt a zero-tolerance law for drivers under age 21 in 1983. Because of the benefits of that law, by the end of 1998, all States had adopted a zero-tolerance law for drivers under 21. Further research is needed to evaluate the effects of Maine's second zero-tolerance law.

## Sanctions for Drivers Convicted of DWI

Other measures to reduce recidivism among persons convicted of DWI include such sanctions as jail sentences, mandatory alcoholism treatment, and license plate or vehicle impoundment. In a meta-analysis of over 200 studies, Wells-Parker and colleagues (1995) reported that alcoholism treatment was associated with a 7- to 9-percent reduction in alcohol-related crashes compared with standard sanctions (e.g., jail or fines). Sanctions combining punishment, education, and therapy with monitoring and aftercare were more effective for both first-time and repeat offenders than any single approach.

Various studies also have found that impounding of DWI offenders' vehicles or license plates reduces recidivism (Voas et al. 1997, 1998; Rodgers 1994), as does the use of ignition interlock devices that prevent vehicle operation when a driver's breath alcohol exceeds a designated limit (Beck et al. in press).

## Restricting Access to Alcohol

Another approach to reducing drinking and driving is to lower the accessibility of alcohol. Decreased accessibility can be accomplished by raising the price of alcohol through increased taxes, restricting both alcohol outlet density (i.e., the number of alcohol outlets in an area) and hours of operation, maintaining State control of alcohol sales, and implementing laws to restrict alcohol sales to inebriated persons or persons under age 21 (Kenkel and Manning 1996; Gruenewald et al. 1996; DeJong and Hingson 1998). Research shows that alcohol-related traffic fatalities can be reduced by increasing taxes on alcohol (Cook 1981; Saffer and Grossman 1987a; 1987b; Grossman et al. 1991) and enforcing laws that hold alcohol servers responsible for actions taken by underage persons or intoxicated patrons who were sold alcohol (McKnight 1993; McKnight and Streff

1994; Wagenaar and Holder 1991b; Sloan et al. 1994). The operation of alcohol outlets by private owners rather than government agencies has been associated with increased alcohol consumption (Gruenewald et al. 1993; Gruenewald and Ponicki 1995; Wagenaar and Holder 1991a; Holder and Wagenaar 1990), and increased outlet density has been associated with increased alcohol-related traffic fatalities (Scribner et al. 1994).

**Minimum legal drinking age**    Raising the MLDA to 21 was designed to reduce impaired driving by restricting the accessibility of alcohol to everyone under age 21. This law tried to eliminate even moderate drinking by adolescent drivers. In 1984, when the Federal Government passed the National Minimum Drinking Age Act, 25 States had MLDAs of 21. By 1988 all 50 States had adopted MLDAs of 21.

Survey results show a decline in drinking among young people following the increase in the MLDA. The proportion of high school seniors who reported drinking during the year before being surveyed declined from 88 percent in 1980 to 75 percent in 1997. The proportion of high-school seniors who reported consuming five or more drinks on at least one occasion in the past 2 weeks declined from 41 to 31 percent (Johnston et al. 1998). In addition to the decrease in drinking observed among persons under age 21 following the increase in the MLDA, research also suggests that raising the MLDA resulted in reduced drinking among 21- to 25-year-olds who grew up in States with a MLDA of 21 compared with those who grew up in other States (O'Malley and Wagenaar 1991).

Numerous studies have indicated that raising the MLDA to 21 reduces alcohol-related fatal crash involvement among drivers under age 21 (United States General Accounting Office 1987). Of the 29 studies completed since the early 1980s that evaluated increases in the MLDA, 20 studies showed significant decreases in traffic crashes and crash fatalities for persons under age 21. Only three studies found no change in traffic crashes involving youth. The remaining six studies had equivocal results (Toomey et al. 1996).

States adopting MLDAs of 21 in the early 1980s experienced a 10- to 15-percent decline in alcohol-related traffic deaths among young drivers compared with States that did not adopt such laws. NHTSA (1998b) has estimated that the raising of the MLDA to 21 has prevented more than 17,300 traffic deaths among persons under age 21 since 1975, approximately 700 to 1,000 deaths annually for the past decade. Research has not examined whether MLDA laws have also reduced alcohol-related crash involvement among 21- to 25-year-olds who grew up in States with a MLDA of 21 relative to those who grew up in other States.

Despite the declines in teenage drinking and fatal crashes associated with prohibiting the purchase and possession of alcohol by persons under age 21, underage youth throughout the United States still can obtain alcohol easily from many sources. Heightened enforcement of MLDA laws can reduce youth access to alcohol, however. Preusser and colleagues (1994) reported that alcohol sales to underage youth declined dramatically following an enforcement campaign targeted at retail alcohol vendors. The campaign involved four "sting operations" over 10 months in which underage male police cadets attempted to purchase alcohol at liquor, grocery, and drug stores. Store owners received warnings if cadets were able to purchase alcohol on their first attempt. Stores that sold alcohol to the cadets during subsequent attempts were penalized accordingly. Over the 10-month period the cadets' rate of successful purchase declined from 59 to 26 percent.

## Conclusion

Although moderate drinking can impair driving performance, this level of alcohol consumption would not cause a person's BAC to reach the legal limit for most drivers in the United States. In most States, the legal BAC limit for drivers age 21 and older is 0.10 percent. Based on this standard, the public may incorrectly assume that a driver is not impaired at BACs lower than 0.10 percent. In one study, only 28 percent of the drivers surveyed reportedly believed that all drivers would be unsafe after consuming amounts of alcohol that would increase a person's BAC to 0.08 percent.

However, virtually all drivers are seriously impaired at this BAC level. Drivers must become more informed about alcohol consumption's effects on BAC levels and the various impairments a person experiences as a result of increasing BAC levels. Educational programs about alcohol consumption and impairment must be developed, implemented, and evaluated in an effort to reduce alcohol-related traffic crashes.

Research has demonstrated the effectiveness of lowering the legal BAC limit to 0.08 percent for drivers over age 21 and to 0.05 percent for drivers with prior DWI convictions, as well as implementing zero-tolerance laws for drivers under age 21. Further research is needed to determine whether Maine's zero-tolerance law for drivers with prior DWI convictions will further reduce their involvement in fatal crashes just as zero-tolerance laws did for drivers under age 21. The decline in alcohol-related fatal crashes associated with Maine's 0.05 law for convicted DWI offenders suggests that it warrants consideration and study in other States as well. Increased knowledge of what constitutes moderate drinking and the amount of alcohol a person can reasonably consume before becoming impaired would help raise people's sense of responsibility, both as drinkers and as drivers, ultimately saving thousands of lives.

 **NO**

# How Effective Are ".08" Drunk-Driving Laws?

## Inconclusive Results

*State efforts to combat drunk driving have, by all accounts, worked to good effect. Alcohol-related fatalities have declined sharply over the past 15 years. Currently, it is illegal in every state to drive while under the influence of alcohol. In addition, all but two have blood alcohol "per se" laws—laws that make it unlawful for a person to drive with a specific amount of alcohol in his blood. How low this amount should be has drawn controversy. Thirty-two states have set this limit at .10 BAC (blood alcohol content). In 16 states, however the per se limit is 20% lower, or .08 BAC and the Clinton Administration has pushed to extend this limit to other states, raising concerns that drivers who pose little threat on the highways will be unfairly penalized. As the following excerpts from a recent General Accounting Office report reveal, the effectiveness of these '.08' limits has not been sufficiently supported by the safety data, despite official assertions to the contrary.—Ed.*

Since 1970, the National Highway Traffic Safety Administration (NHTSA) has espoused a "systems approach" to reducing drunk driving, including enforcement, judicial, legislative, licensing, and public information components. In 1997, NHTSA published an action plan developed with other participants to reduce alcohol-related driving fatalities to 11,000 by the year 2005. This plan recommended that all states pass a wide range of laws, including ones establishing .08 BAC limits, license revocation laws—under which a person deemed to be driving under the influence has his or her driving privileges suspended or revoked—comprehensive screening and treatment programs for alcohol offenders, vehicle impoundment, "zero tolerance" BAC and other laws for youth, and primary enforcement laws for safety belts. The plan also called for increased public awareness campaigns, with an emphasis on target populations such as young people and repeat offenders.

The value of public education and enforcement has been demonstrated in a number of studies. A recent NHTSA evaluation of a sobriety checkpoint

From General Accounting Office, "How Effective Are '.08' Drunk-Driving Laws?" *Consumers' Research*, vol. 82, no. 8 (August 1999). Copyright © 1999 by Consumers' Research, Inc. This article was excerpted from *Highway Safety: Effectiveness of State .08 Blood Alcohol Laws*, General Accounting Office (June 23, 1999). Washington, D.C.: U.S. Government Printing Office, 1999. Reprinted by permission of *Consumers' Research*.

program in Tennessee, a state with a .10 BAC limit, concluded that the program and its attendant publicity reduced alcohol-related fatal accidents in that state by 20.4%.

⁕

One of NHTSA's principal arguments for nationwide adoption of .08 BAC laws is that the medical evidence of drivers' impairment at that level is substantial and conclusive. According to NHTSA, reaction time, tracking and steering, and emergency responses are impaired at even low levels, and substantially impaired at .08 BAC. As a result, the risk of being in a motor vehicle crash increases when alcohol is involved, and increases dramatically at .08 BAC and higher levels. In contrast to NHTSA's position, industry associations critical of .08 BAC laws contend that .08 BAC is an acceptable level of impairment for driving a motor vehicle and that these laws penalize "responsible social drinking."

These associations also believe that .08 BAC laws do not address the problem of drunk driving because many more drivers using alcohol are reported at the "high" BAC levels (above .10 BAC) than at the lower BAC levels. Because we were directed to review the impact of .08 BAC laws on the number and severity of crashes involving alcohol, we did not review the medical evidence on impairment or other arguments in favor of or in opposition to .08 BAC laws.

NHTSA also believes that lowering the BAC limit to .08 is a proven effective measure that will reduce the number of crashes and save lives. For example, in a December 1997 publication, NHTSA stated that "recent research... has been quite conclusive in showing the impaired driving reductions already attributable to .08, as well as the potential for saving additional lives if all states adopted .08 BAC laws." In May 1998, the NHTSA Administrator stated, "The traffic safety administration is aware of four published studies, ... [and] each study has shown that lowering the illegal blood alcohol limit to .08 is associated with significant reductions in alcohol-related fatal crashes." In a fact sheet distributed to state legislatures considering these laws, NHTSA stated that the agency's "analysis of five states that lowered the BAC limit to .08 showed that significant decreases in alcohol-related fatal crashes occurred in four out of the five states as a result of the legislation." NHTSA used these study results to encourage states to enact .08 BAC laws, testifying in one instance before a state legislature: "We conservatively project a 10% reduction in alcohol-related crashes, deaths, and injuries" in the state.

Seven studies have been published assessing the effect of .08 BAC laws on motor vehicle crashes and fatalities in the United States. Four studies published between 1991 and 1996 assessed the effectiveness of .08 BAC laws in the five states that enacted them between 1983 and 1991. On April 28, 1999, NHTSA released three additional studies.

**Early studies had limitations and raised methodological concerns** Although NHTSA characterized the first four studies on the effectiveness of .08 BAC laws as conclusively establishing that .08 BAC laws resulted in substantial reductions in fatalities involving alcohol, we found that three of the four studies had limitations and raised methodological concerns that called their conclusions into question. For example, while a NHTSA-endorsed Boston University study concluded that 500 to 600 fewer fatal crashes would occur each year if all states adopted .08 BAC laws, this study has been criticized for, among other reasons, its method of comparing states; and a recent NHTSA study characterized the earlier study's conclusion as "unwarranted." The fourth study reported mixed results. Therefore, these studies did not provide conclusive evidence that .08 BAC laws by themselves have resulted in reductions in drunk driving crashes and fatalities. A task force of the New Jersey State Senate examined this evidence and, in a report issued in December 1998, reached a similar conclusion.

◦◦❀◦◦

**Recent studies are more comprehensive, but results are mixed**    On April 28, 1999, NHTSA released three studies that it sponsored. These studies are more comprehensive than the earlier studies and show many positive results but fall short of conclusively establishing that .08 BAC laws by themselves have resulted in reductions in alcohol-related fatalities. For example, during the early 1990s, when the involvement of alcohol in traffic fatalities declined from around 50% to nearly 40%—a trend in states with both .08 BAC and .10 BAC laws—eight states' .08 BAC laws became effective, and the recent studies disagree on the degree to which .08 BAC laws played a role. Two of the studies reached different conclusions about the effect of one state's .08 BAC law; one concluded that the law brought about reductions in drunk driving deaths in North Carolina, while another concluded that the state's reductions occurred as the result of a long-term trend that began before the law was enacted.

In a statement releasing the three studies, NHTSA credited the nation's progress in reducing drunk driving to a combination of strict state laws and tougher enforcement, and stated that "these three studies provide additional support for the premise that .08 BAC laws help to reduce alcohol-related fatalities, particularly when they are implemented in conjunction with other impaired driving laws and programs."

**Eleven-state study**    An April 1999 NHTSA study of 11 states with .08 BAC laws assessed whether the states experienced statistically significant reductions in three measures of alcohol involvement in crashes after the law took effect: (1) the number of fatalities in crashes in which any alcohol was involved, (2) the number of fatalities in crashes where drivers had a BAC of .10 or greater ("high BAC"), and (3) the proportion of fatalities involving "high BAC" drivers to fatalities involving sober drivers. The study performed a similar analysis for license revocation laws and also modeled and controlled for any pre-existing long-term declining trends these states may have been experiencing when their .08 BAC laws went into effect. The study found that five of the 11 states had reductions in at least one measure and that two of the 11 states had reductions in all three measures.

❧

The study was careful not to draw a causal relationship between the reductions it found and the passage of .08 BAC laws by themselves. Rather, it concluded that .08 BAC laws added to the impact that enforcement, public information, and legislative activities, particularly license revocation laws, were having. In addition to the two states where .08 BAC and license revocation laws were found to be effective in combination, the study noted that the five states with .08 BAC laws that showed reductions already had license revocation laws in place. One of the authors told us that this suggested the .08 BAC laws had the effect of expanding the scope of the license revocation laws to a new portion of the driving public.

**University of North Carolina study**   A NHTSA-sponsored study by the University of North Carolina concluded, in contrast to the 11-state study, that the .08 BAC law in North Carolina had little clear effect. The study examined alcohol-related crashes and crashes involving drivers with BACs greater than .10 from 1991 through 1995; compared fatalities among drivers with BACs greater than .10 in North Carolina with such fatalities in 11 other states; and compared six measures of alcohol involvement in North Carolina and 37 states that did not have .08 BAC laws at that time. The study controlled for and commented on external factors that could confound the results, such as the state's sobriety checkpoints, enforcement, and media coverage. The study found the following:

- No statistically significant decrease in alcohol-related crashes after passage of North Carolina's .08 BAC law in three direct and two "proxy" measures.
- A continual decline in the proportion of fatally injured drivers with BACs equal to or greater than .10 but no abrupt change in fatalities that could be attributed to the .08 BAC law.
- Decreases in alcohol-related crashes in North Carolina and in the 11 other states studied. While North Carolina's decreases were greater, the study concluded that no specific effects could be attributed to the .08 BAC law.
- No statistically significant difference between North Carolina and 37 states without .08 BAC laws in four of the six measures. While reductions in police-reported and estimated instances of alcohol involvement were found to be statistically significant, these reductions happened 18 months before North Carolina lowered its BAC limit. The authors attributed these decreases, in part, to increased enforcement.

The study concluded that the .08 BAC law had little clear effect on alcohol-related fatalities in North Carolina, that a downward trend was already occurring before North Carolina enacted its .08 BAC law, and that this trend was not affected by the law. The authors offered several possible explanations, including (1) the effects of the .08 BAC laws were obscured by a broader change in drinking-driving behavior that was already occurring; (2) North Carolina had made substantial progress combating drunk driving and that the remaining drinking and driving population in North Carolina was simply not responsive to the lower BAC law; and (3) .08 BAC laws are not effective in measurably affecting the behavior of drinking drivers.

**50-state study**   The third April 1999 NHTSA study evaluated .08 BAC laws by comparing two groups—states with .08 BAC laws with states with .10 BAC laws, before and after the laws were passed. This study concluded that states that enacted .08 BAC laws experienced an 8% reduction in the involvement of drivers with both high and low BACs when compared with the involvement of sober drivers. The study estimated that 274 lives have been saved in the states that enacted .08 BAC laws and that 590 lives could be saved annually if all states enacted .08 BAC laws.

While more comprehensive than other studies, the study used a method to calculate the 8% reduction that is different from, and thus not directly comparable, to those for fatality estimates reported in other studies and publications. In particular, this method can produce a numerical effect that is larger than other methods.

⋅⦿⋅

Another reason why this study's results cannot be directly compared to other studies' is because it did not include data for drivers under 21. In 1997, drivers under 21 accounted for around 14% of the drivers in fatal crashes and about 12% of the drivers in fatal crashes involving alcohol.

Including persons under 21 years old would have changed these study results. In particular, the study would have found no statistically significant reductions associated with .08 BAC laws for drivers at low BAC levels. The findings regarding drivers at high BAC levels—a group that contains over three times as many drivers—would have remained substantially unchanged.

The study warns that "it is important to interpret estimates of lives saved due to any single law with considerable caution." In particular, as the study notes, factors such as public education, enforcement, and changes in societal norms and attitudes toward alcohol have produced long-term reductions in drunk driving deaths over many years. This study did more to control for extraneous factors than any of the other multi-state studies, but this is inherently difficult to do, and in this case the authors estimate that 50% to 60% of the reductions in alcohol-related fatalities are explained by the laws it reviewed and the other factors it considered, a moderate level for statistical analyses of this type. Because of the uncertainties, the study's estimate of lives saved is also expressed as a range—and the number of lives saved in states with .08 BAC laws could have been as few as 88 or as many as 472.

While the study reported results for the three laws it reviewed, including .08 BAC laws, the study also concluded that "the attribution of savings to any single law should be made with caution since each new law builds to some extent on existing legislation and on other ongoing trends and activities."

While indications are that .08 BAC laws in combination with other drunk-driving laws, as well as sustained public education and information efforts and strong enforcement, can be effective, the evidence does not conclusively establish that .08 BAC laws by themselves result in reductions in the number and severity of crashes involving alcohol. Until recently, limited published evidence existed on the effectiveness of .08 BAC laws, and NHTSA's position—that this evidence was conclusive—was overstated. In 1999, more comprehensive studies have been published that show many positive results, and NHTSA's characterization of the results has been more balanced. Nevertheless, these studies fall short of providing conclusive evidence that .08 BAC laws by themselves have been responsible for reductions in fatal crashes.

Because a state enacting a .08 BAC law may or may not see a decline in alcohol-related fatalities, it is difficult to predict accurately how many lives would be saved if all states passed .08 BAC laws. The effect of a .08 BAC law depends on a number of factors, including the degree to which the law is publicized; how well it is enforced; other drunk driving laws in effect; and the unique culture of each state, particularly public attitudes concerning alcohol.

As drunk driving continues to claim the lives of thousands of Americans each year, governments at all levels seek solutions. Many states are considering enacting .08 BAC laws, and the Congress is considering requiring all states to enact these laws. Although a strong causal link between .08 BAC laws by themselves and reductions in traffic fatalities is absent, other evidence, including medical evidence on impairment, should be considered when evaluating the effectiveness of .08 BAC laws. A .08 BAC law can be an important component of a state's overall highway safety program, but a .08 BAC law alone is not a "silver bullet." Highway safety research shows that the best countermeasure against drunk driving is a combination of laws, sustained public education, and vigorous enforcement.

## Five Bottles of Beer

On average, according to NHTSA, a 170-pound man reaches .08 BAC after consuming five 12-ounce beers (4.5% alcohol by volume) over a two-hour period. A 120-pound woman reaches the same level after consuming three beers over the same period. NHTSA publishes a BAC estimator that computes the level of alcohol in a person's blood on the basis of the person's weight and gender and the amount of alcohol consumed over a specified period of time.

This estimator assumes average physical attributes in the population; in reality, alcohol affects individuals differently, and this guide cannot precisely predict its effect on everyone. For example, younger people have higher concentrations of body water than older people; therefore, after consuming the same amount of alcohol, a 170-pound 20-year-old man attains a lower BAC level on average than a 170-pound 50-year-old man.

NHTSA's estimator shows that the difference between the .08 BAC and .10 BAC levels for a 170-pound man is one beer over two hours. The difference between the .08 BAC and .10 BAC levels for a 120-pound woman is one-half a beer over the same time period.

Alcohol use is a significant factor in fatal motor vehicle crashes. In 1997, the most recent year for which data are available, there were 16,189 alcohol-related fatalities, representing 38.6% of the nearly 42,000 people killed in fatal crashes that year. In the states with .08 BAC laws, alcohol was involved in 36% of all traffic fatalities, lower than the national average and the 39.5% rate of alcohol involvement in the rest of the states. Utah had the lowest level at 20.6%; the District of Columbia had the highest at 58.5%. Among the 10 states with the lowest levels of alcohol-related fatalities, three were states with .08 BAC laws and seven were states with .10 BAC laws. Among the 10 states with the highest levels of alcohol-related fatalities, two were states with .08 BAC laws, seven were states with .10 BAC laws, and one had no BAC per se law.

Although alcohol use remains a significant factor in fatal crashes, fatalities involving alcohol have declined sharply over the past 15 years. In 1982, 25,165 people died in crashes involving alcohol, 57.3% of the nearly 44,000 traffic fatalities that year. The proportion of fatal crashes that involved alcohol declined during the 1980s, falling below 50% for the first time in 1989. The involvement of alcohol in fatal crashes declined markedly in the early 1990s, from about 50% of the fatal crashes in 1990 to nearly 40% in 1994. During this time, the number of people killed in crashes involving alcohol declined by around 25%. The proportion of fatalities involving alcohol rose slightly in the next two years before falling, in 1997, to its lowest level since 1982.

# POSTSCRIPT

## Will a Lower Blood Alcohol Level for Drunk Driving Reduce Automobile Accidents?

An important follow-up question to the discussion of whether or not a national BAC standard of .08 for driving while intoxicated would reduce the number of alcohol-related accidents is, Is the federal government unreasonably imposing laws concerning blood alcohol levels due to the fact that the evidence for those laws can be seen as questionable? Is the federal government being presumptuous in trying to implement a policy that it feels is best for its citizens? On the other hand, if it has been shown that a .08 BAC limit lowers the rate of alcohol-related accidents, doesn't the federal government have a moral and ethical obligation to prevent these accidents?

Alcohol abuse is a serious problem. Although restricting a person from drinking and driving may not reduce the incidence of alcohol abuse, it may reduce other problems. Driving a motor vehicle after drinking alcohol is clearly dangerous. Not only are the drinker and the drinker's passengers endangered, but anyone else who may be driving a car in the vicinity of the intoxicated driver is at risk. Thousands of people, including pedestrians, are killed or maimed each year by drunk drivers. Lowering the blood alcohol limit to .08 may not reduce alcohol abuse, but will it reduce the risks faced by others?

Balancing the rights of individual states to establish their own laws against the need of the federal government to implement a policy that it believes is right is a recurring issue. There is a lack of consistency in the matter of federal and state laws. During the oil crisis of the 1970s, for example, the federal government required states to have speed limits no higher than 55 miles per hour. Yet each state has its own laws regarding the sale of alcohol. There is little debate that reducing the number of alcohol-related accidents is a high priority. However, how far should the federal government go to ensure that this occurs?

The National Safety Council and the National Highway Traffic Safety Administration's publication *Setting Limits, Saving Lives* (2000) addresses the effects of a .08 blood alcohol level on automobile accidents. Other publications include "Drinking and Driving: Factors Influencing Accident Risk," by the National Institute on Alcohol Abuse and Alcoholism, *Alcohol Alert No. 31* (January 1996); the National Highway Traffic Safety Administration report *Zero-Tolerance Laws to Reduce Alcohol-Impaired Driving by Youth* (January 1998); and *Drunk Driving: Should Each State Be Required to Enact a 0.08 Blood Alcohol Concentration (BAC) Law?* by Paul F. Rothberg (January 12, 1998), published by the Library of Congress's Congressional Research Service.

# ISSUE 4

## Should Needle Exchange Programs Be Supported?

**YES: David Vlahov and Benjamin Junge**, from "The Role of Needle Exchange Programs in HIV Prevention," *Public Health Reports* (June 1998)

**NO: Office of National Drug Control Policy**, from "Needle Exchange Programs: Are They Effective?" *ONDCP Bulletin No. 7* (July 1992)

### ISSUE SUMMARY

**YES:** In their review of various studies, professor of epidemiology and medicine David Vlahov and Benjamin Junge, evaluation director for the Baltimore Needle Exchange Program, found that needle exchange programs successfully reduced the transmission of the virus that causes AIDS. In addition, many people who participated in needle exchange programs reduced their drug use and sought drug abuse treatment.

**NO:** The Office of National Drug Control Policy, an executive agency that determines policies and objectives for the U.S. drug control program, sees needle exchange programs as an admission of defeat and a retreat from the ongoing battle against drug use, and it argues that compassion and treatment are needed, not needles.

$\mathbf{B}$oth selections presented here refer to intravenous drug use as a factor in the escalating incidence of AIDS (acquired immunodeficiency syndrome). One point needs to be clarified: Any type of drug injection, whether it is intravenous (mainlining), intramuscular, or just below the surface of the skin (skin popping), can result in the transmission of AIDS. Technically, what is transmitted is not AIDS but the human immunodeficiency virus (HIV), which ultimately leads to the development of AIDS.

Until a cure for AIDS is found or a vaccine against HIV has proven to be effective, the relationship between AIDS and injecting drugs will remain a cause of great concern. According to the Centers for Disease Control, approximately one-third of AIDS cases in the United States are directly or indirectly associated with drug injection, and half of all new HIV infections occur among users of injected drugs.

No one disagrees that the spread of AIDS is a problem and that the number of people who inject drugs is a problem. The issue that needs to be addressed is, What is the best course of action to take to reduce drug injection and the transmission of AIDS? Is it better to set up more drug treatment facilities, as the Office of National Drug Control Policy (ONDCP) suggests, or to allow people who inject drugs access to clean needles?

One concern of needle exchange opponents is that endorsement of these programs conveys the wrong message concerning drug use. Instead of discouraging drug use, they feel that such programs merely teach people how to use drugs or encourage drug use. Needle exchange advocates point to studies showing that these programs have not resulted in an increase of intravenous drug users. Other studies indicate that many drug users involved in needle exchange programs drop out and that drug users who remain in the programs are not as likely to share needles in the first place.

Proponents of needle exchange programs argue that HIV is easily transmitted when needles are shared and that something needs to be done to stem the practice. Opponents argue that whether or not needle exchange programs are available, needles will be shared. Three reasons cited by drug users for sharing needles are (1) they do not have access to clean needles, (2) they do not own their own needles, and (3) they cannot afford to buy needles. If clean needles were readily available, would drug addicts necessarily use them? Some studies show that people who inject drugs are concerned about contracting AIDS and will alter their drug-taking behavior if presented with a viable alternative.

Although needle exchange programs may result in the use of clean needles and encourage people to obtain treatment, they do not get at the root cause of drug addiction. Drug abuse and many of its concomitant problems stem from inadequate or nonexistent employment opportunities, unsafe neighborhoods, underfunded schools, and insufficient health care. Some argue that until these underlying causes of drug abuse are addressed, stopgap measures like needle exchange programs should be implemented. Needle exchange programs, however, may forestall the implementation of other programs that could prove to be more helpful.

Needle exchange programs generate a number of legal and social questions. Since heroin and cocaine are illegal, giving needles to people for the purpose of injecting these drugs contributes to illegal behavior. Should people who are addicted to drugs be seen as criminals or as victims who need compassion? Should drug users, especially drug addicts, be incarcerated or treated? The majority of drug users involved with needle exchange programs are members of minority groups. Could needle exchange programs promote the continuation of drug use and, hence, the enslavement of minorities?

In the following selections, David Vlahov and Benjamin Junge address the benefits of needle exchange programs and respond to criticisms of these programs. The ONDCP points out the inadequacies of previous research regarding needle exchange programs and argues that these programs exacerbate drug abuse problems by facilitating drug use.

**David Vlahov and Benjamin Junge**

 **YES**

# The Role of Needle Exchange Programs in HIV Prevention

## Synopsis

Injecting drug users (IDUs) are at high risk for infection by human immuno-deficiency virus (HIV) and other blood-borne pathogens. In the United States, IDUs account for nearly one-third of the cases of acquired immunodeficiency syndrome (AIDS), either directly or indirectly (heterosexual and perinatal cases of AIDS where the source of infection was an IDU). IDUs also account for a substantial proportion of cases of hepatitis B (HBV) and hepatitis C (HCV) virus infections. The primary mode of transmission for HIV among IDUs is par-enteral, through direct needle sharing or multiperson use of syringes. Despite high levels of knowledge about risk, multiperson use of needles and syringes is due primarily to fear of arrest and incarceration for violation of drug para-phernalia laws and ordinances that prohibit manufacture, sale, distribution, or possession of equipment and materials intended to be used with narcotics. It is estimated that in 1997 there were approximately 110 needle exchange programs (NEPs) in North America. In part, because of the ban on the use of Federal funds for the operation of needle exchange, it has been difficult to evaluate the effi-cacy of these programs. This [selection] presents data from the studies that have evaluated the role of NEPs in HIV prevention.

Evidence for the efficacy of NEPs comes from three sources: (1) stud-ies originally focused on the effectiveness of NEPs in non-HIV blood-borne infections, (2) mathematical modeling of data on needle exchange on HIV seroincidence, and (3) studies that examine the positive and negative impact of NEPs on HIV and AIDS. Case-control studies have provided powerful data on the positive effect of NEPs on reduction of two blood-borne viral infections (HBV and HCV). For example, a case-control study in Tacoma, Washington, showed that a six-fold increase in HBV and a seven-fold increase in HCV infections in IDUs were associated with nonuse of the NEP.

The first federally funded study of needle exchange was an evaluation of the New Haven NEP, which is legally operated by the New Haven Health Depart-ment. Rather than relying on self-report of reduced risky injection drug use, this

From David Vlahov and Benjamin Junge, "The Role of Needle Exchange Programs in HIV Preven-tion," *Public Health Reports* (June 1998). Washington, D.C.: U.S. Government Printing Office, 1998. References omitted.

study utilized mathematical and statistical modeling, using data from a syringe tracking and testing system. Incidence of HIV infection among needle exchange participants was estimated to have decreased by 33% as a result of the NEP.

A series of Government-commissioned reports have reviewed the data on positive and negative outcomes of NEPs. The major reports are from the National Commission on AIDS; the U.S. General Accounting Office; the Centers for Disease Control/University of California; and the National Academy of Sciences. The latter two reports are used in this [selection].

The aggregated results support the positive benefit of NEPs and do not support negative outcomes from NEPs. When legal restrictions on both purchase and possession of syringes are removed, IDUs will change their syringe-sharing behaviors in ways that can reduce HIV transmission. NEPs do not result in increased drug use among participants or the recruitment of first-time drug users.

⋅◈⋅

Injecting drug users (IDUs) are at risk for human immunodeficiency virus (HIV) and other blood-borne infections. The principal mode of transmission is parenteral through multiperson use of needles and syringes. The mechanism of contamination is through a behavior called registering, whereby drug users draw back on the plunger of a syringe after venous insertion to ensure venous placement before injecting drug solutions. Strategies to prevent or reduce parenteral transmission of HIV infection need to focus on reducing, if not eliminating altogether, the multiperson use of syringes that have been contaminated. The principle underlying these strategies has been stated clearly in the recommendations of the 1995 National Academy of Sciences Report on preventing HIV infection as follows: "For injection drugs the once only use of sterile needles and syringes remains the safest, most effective approach for limiting HIV transmission." This principle was echoed in the 1996 American Medical Association's booklet *A Physician's Guide to HIV Prevention* and in 1995 in the booklet of the U.S. Preventive Services Task Force *Guide to Clinical Preventive Services.* More recently, this principle has been codified in a multiagency *HIV Prevention Bulletin.*

The first line of prevention is to encourage IDUs to stop using drugs altogether. However, for drug users who cannot or will not stop drug use, owing to their addiction, other approaches are needed. Two major approaches have been developed to provide sufficient sterile needles and syringes to drug users to reduce transmission of HIV and other blood-borne infections. The first is needle exchange programs (NEPs), and the second is modification of syringe prescription and paraphernalia possession laws or ordinances. Hereafter, we will refer to the latter as deregulation of prescription and paraphernalia laws.

**NEPs**    There are now more than 110 NEPs in the United States. By comparison, there are 2000 or more outlets in Australia and hundreds in Great Britain. The exchange programs are varied in terms of organizational characteristics. Some operate out of fixed sites; others are mobile. Some are legally authorized; others are not. Funding, staffing patterns, policies, and hours of operation vary considerably among the different programs.

Despite different organizational characteristics, the basic description and goals of NEPs are the same. They provide sterile needles in exchange for contaminated or used needles to increase access to sterile needles and to remove contaminated syringes from circulation in the community. Equally important, needle exchanges are there to establish contact with otherwise hard-to-reach populations to deliver health services, such as HIV testing and counseling, as well as referrals to treatment for drug abuse.

Over time, numerous questions have arisen about NEPs, such as whether these programs encourage drug use and whether they result in lower HIV incidence. These questions have been summarized and examined in a series of published reviews and Government-sponsored reports. The Government-sponsored reports include those from the National Commission on AIDS in 1991, the U.S. General Accounting Office in 1993, the University of California and Centers for Disease Control (CDC) Report in 1993, and the National Academy of Sciences in 1995.

As to whether NEPs increase drug use among participants, the 1993 California report examined published reports that involved comparison groups (Table 1). Because the sampling and data collection methods varied considerably among studies, the summary has been reduced here to show whether needle exchange was associated with a beneficial, neutral, or adverse effect. Of the eight reports that examined the issue of injection frequency, three showed a reduction in injection frequency, four showed a mixed or neutral effect (no change), and one initially recorded an increase in injection frequency.

*Table 1*

### Summary of Studies of Behavioral Change Within NEPs

| Outcome measures | Beneficial NEP effect | Mixed or neutral NEP effect | Adverse NEP effect |
|---|---|---|---|
| Drug risk: | | | |
|    Sharing frequency | 10 | 4 | – |
|    Give away syringes | 3 | 1 | 1 |
|    Needle cleaning | 3 | 1 | – |
|    Injection frequency | 3 | 4 | 1 |
| Sex risk: | | | |
|    Number of partners | 2 | 1 | – |
|    Partner choice | 1 | 1 | – |
|    Condom use | 1 | 1 | 1 |

In terms of attracting youth or new individuals into NEPs in the United States, programs that have no minimum age restriction have reported that recruitment of participants who are younger than 18 years old was consistently less than 1%; this low rate of use was noted in studies that were conducted in San Francisco and New Haven and in our recent studies in Baltimore. However, recent studies also have shown that new injectors who are adolescent or young adults also are at extremely high risk for HIV infection. In response to this problem, Los Angeles has recently developed an NEP specifically directed at new initiates into injection drug use (P. Kerndt, personal communication, February 10, 1996).

Another question is whether the presence of NEPs in a community conveys a message to youth that condones and encourages drug use. This issue is particularly difficult to study. In 1993, the authors of the University of California-CDC report examined longitudinal national drug use indicator data (data from the DAWN Project), which monitors emergency-room mentions of drug-abuse-related admissions. Comparisons of data before and after the opening of needle exchanges and between cities with and without NEPs showed no significant trends.

The only systematic study to date of trends in drug use within a community following the opening of a needle exchange comes from Amsterdam. Using data on admissions to treatment for drug abuse, Buning and colleagues noted that the proportion of drug users younger than 22 declined from 14% in 1981 to 5% in 1986; the NEP opened in 1984. The opening of the needle exchange increased neither the proportion of drug users overall nor the proportion of those younger than 22 years. Thus, the currently available data argue against the belief that needle exchange encourages drug use.

Another issue is whether needle exchanges will result in more contaminated syringes found on the street. If a needle exchange is designed as a one-for-one exchange, the answer is no. In Baltimore, a carefully designed systematic street survey showed no increase in discarded needles following the opening of an NEP. An update following two years of surveys has shown a similar trend of no increase.

Findings of behavioral change associated with needle exchange are varied. A number of published studies have compared levels of risky behavior among IDUs participating and those not participating in needle exchange. As the University of California-CDC report noted, methods varied considerably among these published reports, so that the summary here (Table 1) sorts the studies into whether and how the needle exchange has shown an effect—risk reduction, no effect, or adverse effect.

In terms of drug risks, Table 1 shows that there were 14 studies that looked at the frequency of needle sharing, the most dangerous behavior in terms of drug-related risk of HIV transmission. In those studies, 10 showed a reduction in needle sharing frequency, four had no effect, and none showed any increase in needle sharing.

Similar trends were noted for the practice of giving away syringes: three showed a reduction in this practice, one no effect, and one an increase. Three out of four studies reporting on this needle cleaning showed a positive effect.

Finally, in terms of sexual risk behavior, few studies overall have examined the impact of needle exchange on sexual risks. Sexual transmission among IDUs is an important area that merits further investigation.

The next question about NEPs is whether such programs actually reduce the incidence of HIV infection in IDUs. While the idea of using only sterile needles makes the question of efficacy seem obvious, the real question centers on how effective the programs are in practice and how subject such programs are to the ubiquitous "law of unintended consequences."

Studies of the impact of needle exchange on the incidence of HIV infection in the United States are few, primarily because funding for such evaluations is relatively recent and sample size requirements are large. The first study (shown in Table 2) was conducted by Hagan and colleagues in Tacoma, Washington. In that city, the prevalence and, therefore, the incidence of HIV were extremely low. A needle exchange was initiated with the goal of maintaining HIV incidence at a low level. Two case-controlled analyses used hepatitis B and hepatitis C virus infection as outcome variables because the epidemiology of these two viruses is similar to HIV, although transmission of hepatitis is more efficient than HIV. In these studies, needle exchange participation was associated with more than an 80% reduction in the incidence of hepatitis infection. Over time, HIV prevalence has not risen.

*Table 2*

**Impact of NEPs on Incidence of Blood-Borne Infections in the United States**

| Author | City | Design | Outcome | Percent reduction |
| --- | --- | --- | --- | --- |
| Hagan et al. | Tacoma | Case-control | HBV | 83 |
|  |  |  | HCV | 86 |
| Kaplan et al. | New Haven | Mathematical modeling based on testing of syringes returned to NEP | HIV | 33 |
| Des Jarlais et al. | New York | Prospective study of seroconversion; NEP is external cohort and IDUs in neighboring regions | HIV | 70 |

In terms of HIV studies, Kaplan and Heimer at Yale utilized information about HIV test results of washes from syringes returned to the New Haven Needle Exchange Program by constructing an elegant statistical model to estimate that needle exchange reduced HIV incidence by 33%. This model has been reviewed by three independent statistical reviewers who have judged the model sound in estimates as reasonable or even conservative.

More recently, Des Jarlais and colleagues from New York City published a prospective study of seroconversion between attendees and nonattendees of needle exchange. In this study, they estimated a 70% reduction in HIV incidence. Several other studies are ongoing in San Francisco, Chicago, and Baltimore, but their findings are too preliminary to present at this time.

In terms of HIV seroconversion studies from needle exchanges with comparison groups from outside the United States, data are available from Amsterdam and Montreal. In Amsterdam, data from a case-control study nested within an ongoing cohort study identified a slightly increased risk of HIV seroconversion with needle exchange use. However, when the analyses were examined by calendar time, the needle exchange was initially protective, but the association reversed over time. The authors attributed their results to the needle exchange losing lower risk users to pharmacy access over time, leaving a core of highest risk users within the exchange.

More recently a study was published using a case-control analysis nested within a cohort study in Montreal. Of 974 HIV-seronegative subjects followed an average of 22 months, 89 subjects seroconverted. Consistent use of needle exchange compared with nonuse was associated with an odds ratio for HIV seroconversion of 10.5, which remained elevated even during multivariate adjustment. The authors concluded that NEPs were associated with higher HIV rates and speculated that the exchange may have facilitated formation of new social networks that might have permitted broader HIV transmission. In an accompanying commentary, Lurie criticized the Montreal study saying that the more likely explanation for the findings was that powerful selection forces attracted the most risky IDUs as evidenced by substantial differences in the baseline data for the exchangers *vs.* nonexchangers: exchangers had higher injection frequencies, were less likely to have a history of drug abuse treatment, were more likely to share needles and use shooting galleries, and had a high HIV prevalence. Lurie attributed the differences to the hours and locations of the exchange (late night in the red-light district) attracting only a select subset of users.

In Vancouver, Strathdee reported on HIV incidence in a cohort of IDUs of whom 92% were enrolled in needle exchange. The incidence of 18.6 (100 person-years) was associated with low education, unstable housing, commercial sex, borrowing needles, injecting with others, and frequent use of needle exchange. The related study by Archibald and colleagues demonstrates a selection of higher risk individuals into needle exchange in Vancouver.

The point to consider is what accounts for the discrepancy between the U.S. and non-U.S. studies. From a methodological perspective, selection factors could be operating. For example, in Vancouver, a study compared characteristics of exchangers with those of nonexchangers, or high frequency *vs.* low frequency exchangers; this study showed that the high frequency exchangers were more likely to engage in high risk activities. While the Vancouver study showed that self-selection into needle exchange results in leaving a comparison group that is not similar in other respects, the data do suggest that needle exchange has been successful in recruiting high risk users.

At another level, the U.S. studies involve evaluation of a needle exchange in comparison with people who do not have access to an NEP or to sterile needles through other sources. In contrast, the Canadian and Dutch studies have involved comparisons that do have an alternative source for sterile needles, principally through pharmacies; their studies may have selected into the needle exchange the people who cannot get needles from pharmacies. The effectiveness of NEPs depends on understanding who constitutes the comparison group.

More recently, an ecological analysis was published with serial HIV seroprevalence data for 29 cities with NEPs and 52 cities without such programs. The results, although subject to a possible ecological fallacy, indicated a 5.8% decline in HIV prevalence per year in cities with NEPs and a 5.9% increase in cities without exchange.

**Deregulating syringe prescription and paraphernalia laws**   In 1992, Connecticut changed the state laws to permit sale and possession of up to 10 syringes at a time. The CDC, in conjunction with the state of Connecticut, conducted initial studies that examined whether IDUs utilized pharmacies and discovered that they did. The CDC and the state of Connecticut then examined how pharmacy utilization affected needle-sharing behaviors in the two samples of IDUs that were interviewed: 52% reported sharing needles before the law changed, and 31% did so after the law changed. While these data are encouraging, data on needle disposal and HIV incidence are not yet available.

## Summary

Access to sterile needles and syringes is an important, even vital, component of a comprehensive HIV prevention program for IDUs. The data on needle exchange in the United States are consistent with the conclusion that these programs do not encourage during use and that needle exchanges can be effective in reducing HIV incidence. Other data show that NEPs help people stop drug use through referral to drug treatment programs. The studies outside of the United States are important for reminding us that unintended consequences can occur. While changes in needle prescription and possession laws and regulations have shown promise, the identification of organizational components that improve or hinder effectiveness of needle exchange and pharmacy-based access are needed.

**NO** ⬅

**Office of National Drug
Control Policy**

# Needle Exchange Programs: Are They Effective?

**W**hen President Bush took office, most Americans regarded the use of illegal drugs as the most serious problem confronting the Nation. Since that time, the Nation has made substantial progress in reducing drug use. But now, in response to the AIDS epidemic, there are those who are ready to sound a retreat in the war against drugs by distributing clean needles to intravenous drug users in the hope that this will slow the spread of AIDS. I believe this would be a serious mistake. We must not lose sight of the fact that illegal drugs still pose a serious threat to our Nation. Nor can we allow our concern for AIDS to undermine our determination to win the war on drugs.

In 1988, 14.5 million Americans and nearly two million young people, aged 12–17, were using drugs. In response to the devastation caused by drug use, the President boldly announced the first National Drug Control Strategy in a televised address to the Nation in 1989. That Strategy was a landmark document. Not only did it establish a coherent, coordinated policy for the national effort against drugs, but it committed unprecedented new resources for fighting drug use.

The Strategy is working; the use of illegal drugs by Americans is declining. Between 1988 and 1991, almost two million fewer Americans were using drugs, a drop of almost 13 percent. And by 1991, about half a million fewer young people were current users of drugs, a drop of 27 percent. Since 1985, the number of Americans using drugs has fallen by over 10 million.

Key to the success of the Strategy has been increasing Americans' intolerance of illicit drugs. But, for those already caught in the deadly web of addiction, we must act with compassion. The Administration therefore vigorously supports efforts to provide effective drug treatment to those who want it and can benefit from it, and has increased funding for drug treatment from $1.1 billion in 1989 to a proposed $2.1 billion for 1993.

Our gains against drug use have been hard-won, and this is no time to jeopardize them by instituting needle exchange programs. Despite all the arguments made by proponents of needle exchange, there is no getting around the fact that distributing needles facilitates drug use and undercuts the credibility

From Office of National Drug Control Policy, Executive Office of the President, "Needle Exchange Programs: Are They Effective?" *ONDCP Bulletin No. 7* (July 1992). Washington, D.C.: U.S. Government Printing Office, 1992. Some notes omitted.

of society's message that using drugs is illegal and morally wrong. And just as important, there is no conclusive evidence that exchange programs reduce the spread of AIDS.

The Administration's concerns about needle exchange are widely shared. Recently, for example, the Congress extended a prohibition on the use of most Federal drug treatment funds to support needle exchange programs. And in June 1992, the National Association of State Alcohol and Drug Abuse Directors informed every member of Congress of its support for continuing this prohibition. Also, in February 1992, the National District Attorneys Association passed an official policy position condemning needle exchange.

The Administration will continue to work with the Congress, and with State and local officials to support alternatives to needle exchange, including expanded and improved drug treatment and aggressive outreach programs. These efforts will provide addicts with something that needle exchange programs cannot: hope and a chance for real recovery from drug addiction.

# Needle Exchange Programs in the United States

**Intravenous drug use and HIV/AIDS**[1]    Intravenous drug users in the United States are one of the groups most at risk for contracting AIDS. AIDS prevention and education programs, which have had a measurable effect on the behavior of other high-risk groups, have not been so successful with intravenous drug users. In fact, the Centers for Disease Control estimates that about 32 percent of the diagnosed AIDS cases in this country, involving nearly 70,000 individuals, resulted from intravenous drug use or sexual contact with intravenous drug users. In addition, intravenous drug use is responsible for half of the AIDS cases among women.

AIDS is spread among intravenous drug users primarily through the sharing of hypodermic syringes, or "needles," and other drug-using paraphernalia (e.g., cotton and water) that have been contaminated with the AIDS virus, and secondarily by high-risk sexual behavior. Thus, intravenous drug users pose a threat not only to themselves, but to their sexual partners and offspring as well. In fact, 58 percent of all reported pediatric AIDS cases are associated with intravenous drug use.

Faced with the growing link between intravenous drug use and AIDS, some cities and communities have instituted or are contemplating programs to provide clean needles to addicts in the hope that this will help reduce the sharing of needles, and hence, the spread of the HIV virus.

**Needle exchange programs**    Needle exchange programs provide free, clean needles to intravenous drug users in an attempt to reduce the likelihood that they will share needles with other users. Some programs operate from fixed locations such as city government offices or pharmacies. Others are mobile, using outreach workers in vans, on foot, and at temporary sites. Some programs provide a new needle only in exchange for an old one, while others provide at least one "starter" needle. Most programs limit the number of needles that can be exchanged at any one time. Some programs provide needles to persons only if they have a verifiable history of drug injection, and most have age limits. Most programs are privately funded; others are supported with State or municipal government funds.[2]

Needle exchange programs also differ in scope. Some only exchange needles, while others are more comprehensive and provide counseling, referral to testing and drug treatment, bleach to clean needles, and safer sex information.

**Needle exchange and the law**   In 39 States and the District of Columbia, sterile needles can be purchased inexpensively without a prescription in many pharmacies.[3] In most of the remaining 11 States, a prescription is required. However, four of the 11 are considering legislation that would broaden access to needles. Only one State, Alabama, is considering legislation that would restrict accessibility by making it a criminal offense for those other than licensed pharmacists or practitioners to sell needles.

Forty-nine States, the District of Columbia, and numerous local jurisdictions have laws to prohibit the sale and distribution of drug paraphernalia. The majority of these laws conform with the Model Drug Paraphernalia Act, which was released by the Drug Enforcement Administration in August 1979. The Model Drug Paraphernalia Act would make it a crime to possess, deliver, or manufacture needles with the intent to violate anti-drug laws. Therefore, operating needle exchange programs may be a violation of the law in many States and local jurisdictions. Furthermore, operating such programs may subject municipalities to civil liability in some jurisdictions.

**What the research shows**   Several studies on the efficacy of needle exchange programs have been conducted in the United States and abroad. Some of these studies have been cited by proponents of needle exchange as evidence that such programs work. However, all of the needle exchange programs studied have yielded either ambiguous or discouraging results. Moreover, the methodology used to conduct these studies has been flawed. For example:

- Many studies make long-term projections of addict behavior based on short-term results;
- Many use a small or insufficient sample size and then project results to larger populations;
- Despite claims that needle sharing was reduced, none of the studies conducted objective tests (e.g., analysis of blood types on returned needles) to determine whether needles were shared;
- Most do not use valid comparison or control groups; and
- Most have program staff, rather than independent evaluators, conduct client interviews on which the findings of the studies are based.

There are four other significant problems with the research. First, needle exchange programs are plagued by high levels of attrition. Programs may have initial contact with intravenous drug users who are at the highest risk of sharing needles and contracting AIDS, but only as few as 20 percent may return for a second or third visit.

Second, needle exchange programs tend to attract and retain a self-selecting group of older, long-term intravenous drug users who are less likely to share needles than less experienced, more promiscuous users. Therefore, positive reports on the effectiveness of exchange programs may be due *more* to the behavior of this less risky subset of the intravenous drug using population and *less* to the availability of clean needles.

Third, programs offering needle exchange often provide bleach for cleaning needles, referrals to testing and treatment, and other services. However, the research conducted to date has not isolated the specific impact that exchanging needles has had on reducing the transmission of AIDS compared with these other factors. Most researchers have simply attributed positive results to needle exchange.

The fourth weakness with the research relates to the dynamics of addiction. No matter what addicts promise when they are not on drugs, they may still share needles when they shoot up heroin or cocaine. In many cases it is simply part of the ritual of taking drugs. More often, a drug-induced state overwhelms rational thinking. Many addicts know that they can get AIDS from dirty needles. Yet hazards to their health—even deadly ones—do not weigh heavily on their minds. Rather, they are primarily concerned with the instant gratification of drugs.

To expect an individual locked in the grip of drug addiction to act responsibly by not sharing needles is unrealistic. Such a change in behavior requires self-discipline and a willingness to postpone gratification and plan for the future—all of which are contrary to the drug-using lifestyle. The fact that addicts can purchase clean needles cheaply, without prescription, in many pharmacies in most States, but often fail to do so, is evidence of their irresponsible behavior.[4] In fact, the only proven way to change an addict's behavior is through structured interventions, such as drug treatment.

**The New Haven study**    A 1991 interim study of a needle exchange program in New Haven, Connecticut, is cited by many needle exchange advocates as evidence of the benefits of needle exchange.[5] The study asserts numerous positive findings, most of which are not supported by the data.

The study states that retention rates stabilized after a high attrition rate early in the program. But, of the 720 addicts who initially contacted the New Haven program over an eight-month period, only 288 (40 percent) returned at least once to exchange a used needle (Figure 1). The New Haven study defines the 288 returning intravenous drug users as "program participants," but does not distinguish between those who exchanged needles once and those who exchanged needles more frequently.[6] The loose definition of "program participation" exaggerates the program's reported retention rate and calls into question the claim that participation in the program stabilized. In addition, the study does not provide information on the 288 individuals who remained in the program and whether they shared needles before the program started. In fact,

*Figure 1*

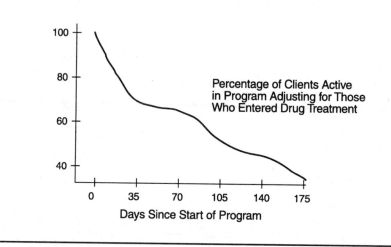

Percentage of Clients Active
in Program Adjusting for Those
Who Entered Drug Treatment

Days Since Start of Program

*Source:* The New Haven Study, July 1991.

the study reports that of the 720 addicts who contacted the program, 436 (61 percent) reported never sharing needles before the program began (Table 1).

The study also states that about half of the 10,180 needles distributed by the program between November 1990 and June 1991 were returned, and that an additional 4,236 "street" or nonprogram needles were brought in for exchange. However, the study fails to account for the 4,917 needles—50 percent of those given out—that were not returned. Based on this information, the study claims that the circulation time for needles was reduced and that fewer contaminated needles were appearing in public places. However, no data are presented to directly support such conclusions.

The authors also report that 107 intravenous drug users (about 15 percent of those who contacted the program) entered treatment over an eight-month period through contact with the New Haven program, but there are no data on how many of these individuals were "program participants" (e.g., had exchanged needles more than once). Therefore, the study does not present any basis for correlating the *exchange* of needles to entry into drug treatment. Also, no data on treatment retention or completion are presented.

The study also claims that intravenous drug use in the community did not increase. Although this may be true, it is not supported by convincing data. The study indicates that 92 percent of those who initially contacted the program were experienced users who had been injecting drugs for one year or more. The study uses this statistic to demonstrate that the availability of free needles did not entice individuals to begin using intravenous drugs. However, there is no evidence to verify that experienced users did not use needles distributed by the program to initiate new users. The study also cites an unchanged rate in drug

*Table 1*

### Extent of Needle Sharing Reported at Initial Contact With Program

| How Often Shared Works | | |
| --- | --- | --- |
| Always (100%) | 16 | (2%) |
| Almost Always (67–99%) | 16 | (2%) |
| Half the Time (34–66%) | 43 | (6%) |
| Sometimes (1–33%) | 196 | (27%) |
| Never (0%) | 436 | (61%) |
| (Missing) | 13 | (2%) |

*Source:* The New Haven Study, July 1991.

arrests as evidence that no increase in intravenous drug use occurred due to the program. However, the New Haven program had only been in operation for two months and had been contacted by fewer than 200 addicts at the time statistics on drug arrests were recorded. Therefore, it is unlikely that the program could have had any impact on the rate of drug arrests.

The most striking finding of the New Haven study—that the incidence of new HIV infections was reduced by one-third among those participating in the program—is based on tenuous data. The study indicates that 789 needles—581 from the program, 160 from the street, and 48 from a local "shooting gallery"[7] —were tested for the presence of HIV.[8] The tests found that program needles were much less likely to be HIV positive than street or gallery needles. The tests also indicated that "dedicated" program needles (e.g., those returned by the original recipient) were much less likely to be HIV positive than other program needles. Based on this information, the study concludes that "dedicated" needles were not shared, *although no tests were conducted to determine if different blood types appeared on the needles or the blood type on the needle matched that of the program participant.* Without conducting such tests, accurate conclusions as to whether needles were shared cannot be drawn, and a reduction in the spread of HIV cannot be attributed to needle exchange.

Finally, the study projects that expanding the availability of clean needles to New Haven's entire intravenous drug using population would also reduce the incidence of new HIV infections by one-third. The projection is based on a highly complex mathematical model involving eight different factors that are supported by numerous assumptions, estimates, probabilities, and rates. While the model may be valid, its projections are based on the tenuous assumption that the 288 intravenous drug users "participating" in the New Haven program are representative of the general intravenous drug using population. However, the high attrition rate of the New Haven program demonstrates that such an assumption cannot be made.

# Foreign Needle Exchange Programs

In recent years, other countries—most notably the Netherlands and the United Kingdom—have established needle exchange programs. Studies of these programs have also produced mixed results. Most reflect the problems noted in existing research on needle exchange. Many report anecdotal or other unquantified information. Furthermore, some base "success" on the number of needles distributed.

In Amsterdam, a program started in 1984 reported that the number of participants grew more than tenfold in four years. The program also reported that during the first four years participants shared fewer needles, the HIV prevalence rate among intravenous drug users stabilized, and instances of Hepatitis B decreased.

In England, about 120 exchange programs distribute approximately four million needles annually. These programs reportedly reach users who have not been in contact with drug treatment services, decrease needle sharing, and increase contact with other social services by participants.

Sweden's three needle exchange sites reported after three years that no project participant had become infected with HIV, that needle sharing had declined, and that many users not previously in contact with drug treatment had been attracted to the program.

Although generally positive, the reports on these programs are scientifically weak and present very few objective indicators of success. All claim that needle exchange reduced the number of needles shared, but none of the programs conducted the tests (e.g., blood-type tests) necessary to make that determination.

In addition, the attrition rates in foreign programs are extremely high. A 1989 study of 15 needle exchange programs in England and Scotland reported that only 33 percent of intravenous drug users who initially contacted the programs returned up to five times. As in the United States, needle exchange programs in other countries are more likely to attract and retain intravenous drug users who are already predisposed not to share needles, and who therefore are at lower risk of contracting AIDS than other, less cautious, users.

# Alternatives to Needle Exchange

The challenges to society presented by drug use and HIV/AIDS require the steady development of scientific understanding and the promotion of effective interventions. Requested Federal funding for AIDS prevention, treatment, research, and income maintenance in 1993 is $4.9 billion—a 69 percent increase since 1990 (Figure 2). The President's National Drug Control Strategy supports using a portion of these funds for research, experiments, and demonstrations to seek out high-risk drug users; to encourage and support their entry into drug treatment; and to provide them with information on the destructiveness of their behavior and ways to change it. The Strategy also supports efforts to expand the capacity and effectiveness of drug treatment for intravenous drug users.

*Figure 2*

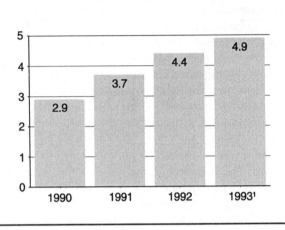

Federal Funding for HIV/AIDS, 1990–1993

[1] Requested

*Source:* Office of Management and Budget, 1992

**Outreach programs**  The most effective method of reducing the spread of AIDS among intravenous drug users is to treat successfully their drug addiction. However, Federal studies estimate that more than 40 percent of intravenous drug users have never been in treatment, even though many have used drugs intravenously for more than 10 years. Therefore, it is essential to continue efforts to aggressively recruit intravenous drug users into treatment.

Since 1987, the Department of Health and Human Service's National Institute on Drug Abuse has funded projects in more than 40 cities to help identify intravenous drug users and persuade them to enter treatment. In these cities, squads of outreach workers contact addicts and encourage them to avoid sharing needles and other risky behaviors and to enter treatment. Outreach workers also provide addicts with information on the threat of AIDS and dispense materials (e.g., bleach and condoms) to reduce the risk of HIV infection.

Between 1987 and 1992, outreach workers contacted approximately 150,000 intravenous drug users. Of these, 45,000 addicts (54 percent of whom reported regularly sharing needles) and 9,500 sexual partners were provided with information on treatment, counseling and methods for reducing the risk of infection. Program participants were assigned to standard and enhanced interventions. Follow-up surveys were conducted six months after the assignments were made, and the results of those surveys indicated that:

- 31 percent of the intravenous drug users had enrolled in formal drug treatment programs;
- 38 percent were sharing needles less frequently;

- 44 percent had begun to always clean their needles, always use a new needle, or had stopped injecting completely; and
- 47 percent had stopped injecting or reduced their frequency of injection.

The success of this effort demonstrates that outreach programs are highly effective in persuading intravenous drug users to avoid sharing needles and to seek treatment. By comparison, only 15 percent of those who contacted the New Haven program entered treatment. The Federal government will continue to support outreach programs by awarding approximately 60 grants in 1992 and 1993.

The Centers for Disease Control also administers an extensive outreach program for preventing the spread of the HIV virus among intravenous drug users. This program, which is operated through State departments of health and community-based organizations, offers intravenous drug users counseling, testing, and referral to treatment. An evaluation of the program will be completed in about two years.

**Expanding treatment capacity**    The Federal government continues to support expanded treatment capacity for intravenous drug users, primarily through the Alcohol, Drug Abuse and Mental Health Services Block Grant program, which requires States to use at least 50 percent of their drug allotment for outreach and treatment of these drug users. Also, the Capacity Expansion Program, which was created by the Bush Administration in Fiscal Year 1992, will increase the number of drug treatment slots for areas and populations in the greatest need of treatment, including intravenous drug users. If Congress fully funds this program in Fiscal Year 1993 (the Administration has requested $86 million), an additional 38,000 addicts—many of whom will be intravenous drug users—will be provided with drug treatment.

**Medications development**    The Federal government is continuing its efforts to develop medications to treat heroin addiction. New pharmacological therapies, such as LAAM (a longer-acting alternative to methadone), depot naltrexone, and buprenorphine, are showing considerable promise in treating heroin addiction and should be available within the next few years.[9] In addition, performance standards and clinical protocols are being developed for methadone treatment programs to enhance their safety and effectiveness in treating heroin addiction.[10]

# Conclusion

The rapid spread of AIDS has prompted officials of some of America's cities to institute programs that distribute clean needles to intravenous drug users. Such programs are questionable public policy, however, because they facilitate addicts' continued use of drugs and undercut the credibility of society's message that drug use is illegal and morally wrong. Further, there is no compelling research that needle exchange programs are effective in preventing intravenous drug users from sharing needles, reducing the spread of AIDS, or encouraging addicts to seek drug treatment.

Research does show, however, that aggressive outreach efforts are an effective way to get intravenous drug users to end their high-risk behavior and seek treatment. Therefore, the National Drug Control Strategy will continue to support such outreach programs. It also will continue to support expanded treatment capacity for high-risk populations, including intravenous drug users; the development of medications for treating heroin addiction; and the exploration of other options that may offer intravenous drug users a real chance for recovery.

## Notes

1. Human Immunodeficiency Virus/Acquired Immunodeficiency Syndrome.
2. Federal law prohibits the use of Alcohol, Drug Abuse, and Mental Health Services Block Grant funds—the major source of Federal support for drug treatment—to pay for needle exchange programs.
3. In some States, such as California, needles may be sold without prescription for the administration of insulin or adrenaline if the pharmacist can identify the purchaser and records the purchase.
4. Syringes cost about $.30 each. For example, in a recent study of pharmacies in St. Louis, Compton et al. found the cost of a package of 10, 28-gauge, 100-unit insulin syringes to range from $1.92 to $4.28.

    See Compton, W., et al. "Legal Needle Buying in St. Louis," *American Journal of Public Health*, April 1992, Vol. 82, No. 4.
5. In Fiscal Year 1992, the National Institute on Drug Abuse awarded a grant to Yale University to conduct a rigorous evaluation of the New Haven program over a three-year period. Results of the evaluation will be available in 1995.
6. Researchers estimate that intravenous heroin users on average inject two or more times a day, heavy users four to six times a day. Intravenous cocaine users invariably inject more frequently. There is very little data yet available on the number of injections an average user gets from a needle before it is discarded, although a 1989 California survey of 257 users found a mean of 22.5 uses (with 27 reporting one use and 15 reporting over 100).
7. A "shooting gallery" is a communal injection site notorious for inadequate sterilization of injection equipment.
8. The study does not specify the method used to select program and street needles or whether they are considered random or representative samples.
9. LAAM is a longer-acting alternative to methadone, depot naltrexone is a long-acting heroin blocker, and buprenorphine is being investigated for treating individuals addicted to both heroin and cocaine.
10. Methadone is a synthetic medication used to treat heroin addicts by relieving withdrawal symptoms and craving for heroin for 24 hours. Methadone is only administered as part of a supervised treatment program.

# POSTSCRIPT

## Should Needle Exchange Programs Be Supported?

The implementation of needle exchange programs arouses several ethical and practical concerns. Opponents challenge the wisdom of giving drug addicts needles to inject themselves with illegal drugs. They ask, What might impressionable adolescents think if the government funds programs in which drug addicts are given needles? Some people reason that those who inject drugs into their bodies know the risks and should live with the consequences of their actions. Others wonder whether the distribution of needles will lead to an increase or a decrease in drug use.

One potential advantage of needle exchange programs is that needles may be safely discarded after they have been used. Unsafely discarded needles may accidentally prick someone (including nonusers) and lead to HIV transmission. A second potential benefit is that when people come to needle exchange sites, they can be encouraged to enter drug treatment programs.

Despite the difficulties of studying people who inject drugs, long-term studies are needed to determine the impact of needle exchange programs on (1) the incidence of AIDS, (2) the continuation or reduction of drug use, (3) whether or not these programs attract new users to the drug culture, (4) the likelihood of program participants entering drug treatment programs, and (5) the impact on other high-risk behaviors. Preliminary studies into the effectiveness of needle exchange programs are contradictory. One such program was introduced in Tacoma, Washington, and needle sharing declined 30 percent. Programs in New York City and New Haven, Connecticut, resulted in fewer reports of HIV infection without an increase in drug use. Conversely, in a program in Louisville, Kentucky, nearly two-thirds of people who inject drugs continued to share needles. In Louisville, however, needles are obtained through a prescription, which may have a different effect in the long run than receiving needles through an exchange program.

Several articles that address the benefits of needle exchange programs are "Prevention of HIV/AIDS and Other Blood-Borne Diseases Among Injection Drug Users: A National Survey on the Regulation of Syringes and Needles," by Lawrence Gostin et al., *JAMA* (January 1, 1997); "Needed: A Zero-Tolerance Policy on AIDS," by Peter Lurie, *Drug Policy Letter* (Summer 1995); and "On Pins and Needles," by Will Van Sant, *National Journal* (May 15, 1999). Articles that oppose needle exchange programs include "Killing Them Softly," by Joe Loconte, *Policy Review* (July–August 1998) and "Clean Needles May Be Bad Medicine," by David Murray, *The Wall Street Journal* (April 22, 1998).

# ISSUE 5

## Should Pregnant Drug Users Be Prosecuted?

**YES: Paul A. Logli**, from "Drugs in the Womb: The Newest Battlefield in the War on Drugs," *Criminal Justice Ethics* (Winter/Spring 1990)

**NO: Drew Humphries**, from *Crack Mothers: Pregnancy, Drugs, and the Media* (Ohio State University Press, 1999)

### ISSUE SUMMARY

**YES:** Paul A. Logli, an Illinois prosecuting attorney, argues that it is the government's duty to enforce every child's right to begin life with a healthy, drug-free mind and body. Logli maintains that pregnant women who use drugs should be prosecuted because they may harm the life of their unborn children. He feels that it is the state's responsibility to ensure that every baby is born as healthy as possible.

**NO:** Researcher Drew Humphries argues that the prosecution of women who use drugs while pregnant has resulted from overzealous efforts on the part of a handful of state prosecutors. Humphries asserts that the prosecution of pregnant drug users is unfair because poor women are more likely to be the targets of such prosecution and that these cases do not hold up to legal standards.

The effects that drugs have on a fetus can be mild and temporary or severe and permanent, depending on the extent of drug use by the mother, the type of substance used, and the stage of fetal development at the time the drug crosses the placental barrier and enters the bloodstream of the fetus. Both illegal and legal drugs, such as cocaine, crack, marijuana, alcohol, and nicotine, are increasingly found to be responsible for incidents of premature births, congenital abnormalities, fetal alcohol syndrome, mental retardation, and other serious birth defects. The exposure of the fetus to these substances and the long-term involuntary physical, intellectual, and emotional effects are disturbing. In addition, the medical, social, and economic costs to treat and care for babies who are exposed to or become addicted to drugs while in utero (in the uterus) warrant serious concern.

An important consideration regarding the prosecution of pregnant drug users is whether this is a legal problem or a medical problem. In recent years, attempts have been made to establish laws that would allow the incarceration of drug-using pregnant women on the basis of "fetal abuse." Some cases have been successfully prosecuted: mothers have been denied custody of their infants until they enter appropriate treatment programs, and criminal charges have been brought against mothers whose children were born with drug-related complications. The underlying presumption is that the unborn fetus should be afforded protection against the harmful actions of another person, specifically the use of harmful drugs by the mother.

Those who profess that prosecuting pregnant women who use drugs is necessary insist that the health and welfare of the unborn child is the highest priority. They contend that the possibility that these women will avoid obtaining health care for themselves or their babies because they fear punishment does not absolve the state from the responsibility of protecting the babies. They also argue that criminalizing these acts is imperative to protect fetuses and newborns who cannot protect themselves. It is the duty of the legal system to deter pregnant women from engaging in future criminal drug use and to protect the best interests of infants.

Others maintain that drug use and dependency by pregnant women is a medical problem, not a criminal one. Many pregnant women seek treatment, but they often find that rehabilitation programs are limited or unavailable. Shortages of openings in chemical dependency programs may keep a prospective client waiting for months, during which time she will most likely continue to use the drugs to which she is addicted and prolong her fetus's drug exposure. Many low-income women do not receive drug treatment and adequate prenatal care due to financial constraints. And women who fear criminal prosecution because of their drug use may simply avoid prenatal care altogether.

Some suggest that medical intervention, drug prevention, and education —not prosecution—are needed for pregnant drug users. Prosecution, they contend, drives women who need medical attention away from the very help they and their babies need. Others respond that prosecuting pregnant women who use drugs will help identify those who need attention, at which point adequate medical and social welfare services can be provided to treat and protect the mother and child.

In the following selections, Paul A. Logli, arguing for the prosecution of pregnant drug users, contends that it is the state's responsibility to protect the unborn and the newborn because they are least able to protect themselves. He charges that it is the prosecutor's responsibility to deter future criminal drug use by mothers who he feels violate the rights of their potential newborns to have an opportunity for a healthy and normal life. Drew Humphries contends that many of the pregnant women who are prosecuted are minorities and that there is therefore a racist element to such prosecution. She asserts that prosecuting pregnant drug users may be counterproductive to improving the quality of infant and maternal health. The threat of arrest and incarceration may decrease the likelihood that pregnant drug users will seek out adequate prenatal care.

Paul A. Logli

 **YES**

# Drugs in the Womb: The Newest Battlefield in the War on Drugs

## Introduction

The reported incidence of drug-related births has risen dramatically over the last several years. The legal system and, in particular, local prosecutors have attempted to properly respond to the suffering, death, and economic costs which result from a pregnant woman's use of drugs. The ensuing debate has raised serious constitutional and practical issues which are far from resolution.

Prosecutors have achieved mixed results in using current criminal and juvenile statutes as a basis for legal action intended to prosecute mothers and protect children. As a result, state and federal legislators have begun the difficult task of drafting appropriate laws to deal with the problem, while at the same time acknowledging the concerns of medical authorities, child protection groups, and advocates for individual rights.

## The Problem

The plight of "cocaine babies," children addicted at birth to narcotic substances or otherwise affected by maternal drug use during pregnancy, has prompted prosecutors in some jurisdictions to bring criminal charges against drug-abusing mothers. Not only have these prosecutions generated heated debates both inside and outside of the nation's courtrooms, but they have also expanded the war on drugs to a controversial new battlefield—the mother's womb.

A 1988 survey of hospitals conducted by Dr. Ira Chasnoff, Associate Professor of Northwestern University Medical School and President of the National Association for Perinatal Addiction Research and Education (NAPARE) indicated that as many as 375,000 infants may be affected by maternal cocaine use during pregnancy each year. Chasnoff's survey included 36 hospitals across the country and showed incidence rates ranging from 1 percent to 27 percent. It also indicated that the problem was not restricted to urban populations or particular racial or socio-economic groups. More recently a study at Hutzel Hospital in

From Paul A. Logli, "Drugs in the Womb: The Newest Battlefield in the War on Drugs," *Criminal Justice Ethics*, vol. 9, no. 1 (Winter/Spring 1990), pp. 23–29. Copyright © 1990 by *Criminal Justice Ethics*. Reprinted by permission of The Institute for Criminal Justice Ethics, 555 West 57th Street, Suite 601, New York, NY 10019-1029. Notes omitted.

Detroit's inner city found that 42.7 percent of its newborn babies were exposed to drugs while in their mothers' wombs.

The effects of maternal use of cocaine and other drugs during pregnancy on the mother and her newborn child have by now been well-documented and will not be repeated here. The effects are severe and can cause numerous threats to the short-term health of the child. In a few cases it can even result in death.

Medical authorities have just begun to evaluate the long-term effects of cocaine exposure on children as they grow older. Early findings show that many of these infants show serious difficulties in relating and reacting to adults and environments, as well as in organizing creative play, and they appear similar to mildly autistic or personality-disordered children.

The human costs related to the pain, suffering, and deaths resulting from maternal cocaine use during pregnancy are simply incalculable. In economic terms, the typical intensive-care costs for treating babies exposed to drugs range from $7,500 to $31,000. In some cases medical bills go as high as $150,000.

The costs grow enormously as more and more hospitals encounter the problem of "boarder babies"—those children literally abandoned at the hospital by an addicted mother, and left to be cared for by the nursing staff. Future costs to society for simply educating a generation of drug-affected children can only be the object of speculation. It is clear, however, that besides pain, suffering, and death the economic costs to society of drug use by pregnant women is presently enormous and is certainly growing larger.

## The Prosecutor's Response

It is against this backdrop and fueled by the evergrowing emphasis on an aggressively waged war on drugs that prosecutors have begun a number of actions against women who have given birth to drug-affected children. A review of at least two cases will illustrate the potential success or failure of attempts to use existing statutes.

*People v. Melanie Green*    On February 4, 1989, at a Rockford, Illinois hospital, two-day-old Bianca Green lost her brief struggle for life. At the time of Bianca's birth both she and her mother, twenty-four-year-old Melanie Green, tested positive for the presence of cocaine in their systems.

Pathologists in Rockford and Madison, Wisconsin, indicated that the death of the baby was the result of a prenatal injury related to cocaine used by the mother during the pregnancy. They asserted that maternal cocaine use had caused the placenta to prematurely rupture, which deprived the fetus of oxygen before and during delivery. As a result of oxygen deprivation, the child's brain began to swell and she eventually died.

After an investigation by the Rockford Police Department and the State of Illinois Department of Children and Family Services, prosecutors allowed a criminal complaint to be filed on May 9, 1989, charging Melanie Green with the offenses of Involuntary Manslaughter and Delivery of a Controlled Substance.

On May 25, 1989, testimony was presented to the Winnebago County Grand Jury by prosecutors seeking a formal indictment. The Grand Jury, however, declined to indict Green on either charge. Since Grand Jury proceedings in the State of Illinois are secret, as are the jurors' deliberations and votes, the reason for the decision of the Grand Jury in this case is determined more by conjecture than any direct knowledge. Prosecutors involved in the presentation observed that the jurors exhibited a certain amount of sympathy for the young woman who had been brought before the Grand Jury at the jurors' request. It is also likely that the jurors were uncomfortable with the use of statutes that were not intended to be used in these circumstances.

It would also be difficult to disregard the fact that, after the criminal complaints were announced on May 9th and prior to the Grand Jury deliberations of May 25th, a national debate had ensued revolving around the charges brought in Rockford, Illinois, and their implications for the ever-increasing problem of women who use drugs during pregnancy.

*People v. Jennifer Clarise Johnson*    On July 13, 1989, a Seminole County, Florida judge found Jennifer Johnson guilty of delivery of a controlled substance to a child. The judge found that delivery, for purposes of the statute, occurred through the umbilical cord after the birth of the child and before the cord was severed. Jeff Deen, the Assistant State's Attorney who prosecuted the case, has since pointed out that Johnson, age 23, had previously given birth to three other cocaine-affected babies, and in this case was arrested at a crack house. "We needed to make sure this woman does not give birth to another cocaine baby."

Johnson was sentenced to fifteen years of probation including strict supervision, drug treatment, random drug testing, educational and vocational training, and an intensive prenatal care program if she ever became pregnant again.

## Support for the Prosecution of Maternal Drug Abuse

Both cases reported above relied on a single important fact as a basis for the prosecution of the drug-abusing mother: that the child was born alive and exhibited the consequences of prenatal injury.

In the Melanie Green case, Illinois prosecutors relied on the "born alive" rule set out earlier in *People v. Bolar.* In *Bolar* the defendant was convicted of the offense of reckless homicide. The case involved an accident between a car driven by the defendant, who was found to be drunk, and another automobile containing a pregnant woman. As a result, the woman delivered her baby by emergency caesarean section within hours of the collision. Although the newborn child exhibited only a few heart beats and lived for approximately two minutes, the court found that the child was born alive and was therefore a person for purposes of the criminal statutes of the State of Illinois.

The Florida prosecution relied on a live birth in an entirely different fashion. The prosecutor argued in that case that the delivery of the controlled substance occurred after the live birth via the umbilical cord and prior to the cutting of the cord. Thus, it was argued, that the delivery of the controlled substance occurred not to a fetus but to a person who enjoyed the protection of the criminal code of the State of Florida.

Further support for the State's role in protecting the health of newborns even against prenatal injury is found in the statutes which provide protection for the fetus. These statutes proscribe actions by a person, usually other than the mother, which either intentionally or recklessly harm or kill a fetus. In other words, even in the absence of a live birth, most states afford protection to the unborn fetus against the harmful actions of another person. Arguably, the same protection should be afforded the infant against intentional harmful actions by a drug-abusing mother.

The state also receives support for a position in favor of the protection of the health of a newborn from a number of non-criminal cases. A line of civil cases in several states would appear to stand for the principle that a child has a right to begin life with a sound mind and body, and a person who interferes with that right may be subject to civil liability. In two cases decided within months of each other, the Supreme Court of Michigan upheld two actions for recovery of damages that were caused by the infliction of prenatal injury. In *Womack v. Buckhorn* the court upheld an action on behalf of an eight-year-old surviving child for prenatal brain injuries apparently suffered during the fourth month of the pregnancy in an automobile accident. The court adopted with approval the reasoning of a New Jersey Supreme Court decision and "recognized that a child has a legal right to begin life with a sound mind and body." Similarly, in *O'Neill v. Morse* the court found that a cause of action was allowed for prenatal injuries that caused the death of an eight-month-old viable fetus.

Illinois courts have allowed civil recovery on behalf of an infant for a negligently administered blood transfusion given to the mother prior to conception which resulted in damage to the child at birth. However, the same Illinois court would not extend a similar cause of action for prebirth injuries as between a child and its own mother. The court, however, went on to say that a right to such a cause of action could be statutorily enacted by the Legislature.

Additional support for the state's role in protecting the health of newborns is found in the principles annunciated in recent decisions of the United States Supreme Court. The often cited case of *Roe v. Wade* set out that although a woman's right of privacy is broad enough to cover the abortion decision, the right is not absolute and is subject to limitations, "and that at some point the state's interest as to protection of health, medical standards and prenatal life, becomes dominant."

More recently, in the case of *Webster v. Reproductive Health Services*, the court expanded the state's interest in protecting potential human life by setting aside viability as a rigid line that had previously allowed state regulation only after viability had been shown but prohibited it before viability. The court goes on to say that the "fundamental right" to abortion as described in *Roe* is now accorded the lesser status of a "liberty interest." Such language surely supports a prosecutor's argument that the state's compelling interest in potential human life would allow the criminalization of acts which if committed by a pregnant woman can damage not just a viable fetus but eventually a born-alive infant. It follows that, once a pregnant woman has abandoned her right to abort and has decided to carry the fetus to term, society can well impose a duty on the mother to insure that the fetus is born as healthy as possible.

A further argument in support of the state's interest in prosecuting women who engage in conduct which is damaging to the health of a newborn child is especially compelling in regard to maternal drug use during pregnancy. Simply put, there is no fundamental right or even a liberty interest in the use of psychoactive drugs. A perceived right of privacy has never formed an absolute barrier against state prosecutions of those who use or possess narcotics. Certainly no exception can be made simply because the person using drugs happens to be pregnant.

Critics of the prosecutor's role argue that any statute that would punish mothers who create a substantial risk of harm to their fetus will run afoul of constitutional requirements, including prohibitions on vagueness, guarantees of liberty and privacy, and rights of due process and equal protection. . . .

In spite of such criticism, the state's role in protecting those citizens who are least able to protect themselves, namely the newborn, mandates an aggressive posture. Much of the criticism of prosecutorial efforts is based on speculation as to the consequences of prosecution and ignores the basic tenet of criminal law that prosecutions deter the prosecuted and others from committing additional crimes. To assume that it will only drive persons further underground is to somehow argue that certain prosecutions of crime will only force perpetrators to make even more aggressive efforts to escape apprehension, thus making arrest and prosecution unadvisable. Neither could this be accepted as an argument justifying even the weakening of criminal sanctions. . . .

The concern that pregnant addicts will avoid obtaining health care for themselves or their infants because of the fear of prosecution cannot justify the absence of state action to protect the newborn. If the state were to accept such reasoning, then existing child abuse laws would have to be reconsidered since they might deter parents from obtaining medical care for physically or sexually abused children. That argument has not been accepted as a valid reason for abolishing child abuse laws or for not prosecuting child abusers. . . .

The far better policy is for the state to acknowledge its responsibility not only to provide a deterrant to criminal and destructive behavior by pregnant addicts but also to provide adequate opportunities for those who might seek help to discontinue their addiction. Prosecution has a role in its ability to deter future criminal behavior and to protect the best interests of the child. The medical and social welfare establishment must assume an even greater responsibility to encourage legislators to provide adequate funding and facilities so that no pregnant woman who is addicted to drugs will be denied the opportunity to seek appropriate prenatal care and treatment for her addiction.

## One State's Response

The Legislature of the State of Illinois at the urging of local prosecutors moved quickly to amend its juvenile court act in order to provide protection to those children born drug-affected. Previously, Illinois law provided that a court could assume jurisdiction over addicted minors or a minor who is generally declared neglected or abused.

Effective January 1, 1990, the juvenile court act was amended to expand the definition of a neglected or abused minor....

> those who are neglected include... any newborn infant whose blood or urine contains any amount of a controlled substance....

The purpose of the new statute is to make it easier for the court to assert jurisdiction over a newborn infant born drug-affected. The state is not required to show either the addiction of the child or harmful effects on the child in order to remove the child from a drug-abusing mother. Used in this context, prosecutors can work with the mother in a rather coercive atmosphere to encourage her to enter into drug rehabilitation and, upon the successful completion of the program, be reunited with her child.

Additional legislation before the Illinois Legislature is House Bill 2835 sponsored by Representatives John Hallock (R-Rockford) and Edolo "Zeke" Giorgi (D-Rockford). This bill represents the first attempt to specifically address the prosecution of drug-abusing pregnant women....

The statute provides for a class 4 felony disposition upon conviction. A class 4 felony is a probationable felony which can also result in a term of imprisonment from one to three years.

Subsequent paragraphs set out certain defenses available to the accused.

> It shall not be a violation of this section if a woman knowingly or intentionally uses a narcotic or dangerous drug in the first twelve weeks of pregnancy and: 1. She has no knowledge that she is pregnant; or 2. Subsequently, within the first twelve weeks of pregnancy, undergoes medical treatment for substance abuse or treatment or rehabilitation in a program or facility approved by the Illinois Department of Alcoholism and Substance Abuse, and thereafter discontinues any further use of drugs or narcotics as previously set forth.

... A woman, under this statute, could not be prosecuted for self-reporting her addiction in the early stages of the pregnancy. Nor could she be prosecuted under this statute if, even during the subsequent stages of the pregnancy, she discontinued her drug use to the extent that no drugs were present in her system or the baby's system at the time of birth. The statute, as drafted, is clearly intended to allow prosecutors to invoke the criminal statutes in the most serious of cases.

## Conclusion

Local prosecutors have a legitimate role in responding to the increasing problem of drug-abusing pregnant women and their drug-affected children. Eliminating the pain, suffering and death resulting from drug exposure in newborns must be a prosecutor's priority. However, the use of existing statutes to address the problem may meet with limited success since they are burdened with

numerous constitutional problems dealing with original intent, notice, vagueness, and due process.

The juvenile courts may offer perhaps the best initial response in working
to protect the interests of a surviving child. However, in order to address more
serious cases, legislative efforts may be required to provide new statutes that
will specifically address the problem and hopefully deter future criminal conduct which deprives children of their important right to a healthy and normal
birth.

The long-term solution does not rest with the prosecutor alone. Society,
including the medical and social welfare establishment, must be more responsive in providing readily accessible prenatal care and treatment alternatives for
pregnant addicts. In the short term however, prosecutors must be prepared to
play a vital role in protecting children and deterring women from engaging
in conduct which will harm the newborn child. If prosecutors fail to respond,
then they are simply closing the doors of the criminal justice system to those
persons, the newborn, who are least able to open the doors for themselves.

# NO ←

Drew Humphries

# The Point of Moral Panic

In any moral panic the decisive moment arrives when moral entrepreneurs —experts, spokespeople, officials—determine that disapproved conduct exceeds the boundaries of permissible behavior. In this case, too many cocaine mothers had harmed their babies, or a few cocaine mothers had inflicted too great a harm on their babies. However overstated such claims might be, the point is that moral entrepreneurs came to believe that existing systems of social control no longer sufficed. Pregnant drug users were perceived as ignoring medical warnings, physician advice, and referrals to drug treatment or prenatal care. Termination of parental rights, a sanction available through social services, was not seen as a severe enough penalty to force drug users to halt maternal cocaine use. Firmer action was required.

Reacting to these perceptions, a handful of county prosecutors took the step that triggered the panic: treating cocaine mothers as criminals. Across the nation prosecutors brought over 160 criminal cases against women who used crack or cocaine during pregnancy. Although most cases were dismissed or overturned on appeal, the county prosecutors profiled in this [selection] pursued the high-publicity cases that defined the issues and turned the crack mothers episode into a classic case of moral panic.

Consider what the prosecutions were not. They did not arise in America's big cities, nor did they necessarily reflect local epidemics of crack babies. The communities that generated them were like many other small- and medium-sized towns and cities. They ran the gamut from wealthy suburb to worn-out industrial center. They were overwhelmingly white; minority populations did not exceed the national average. So, many of the explanations developing from the symbolic implications of the prosecutions are ill suited to actual circumstances. The prosecutions did not arise in communities where affluent white groups felt threatened by unemployment, poverty, or minorities.

The prosecutions were localized responses to national priorities. Crack was the drug targeted by federal authorities. Any politically astute, ambitious, or ideologically inclined prosecutor understood that crack was also the target drug at the local level. At this level crack was a powerful symbol. It epitomized all the ills associated with America's urban centers. County prosecutors—white professionals occupying positions of power and privilege in small cities and

From Drew Humphries, *Crack Mothers: Pregnancy, Drugs, and the Media* (Ohio State University Press, 1999). Copyright © 1999 by Drew Humphries. Reprinted by permission of Ohio State University Press. Notes omitted.

85

medium-sized towns—labored to keep crack and big cities' problems out. As the suburbs turned against the big cities, prosecutors turned against cocaine mothers. The highly publicized cases that resulted galvanized hostility, directing it against some of the most vulnerable women in America.

It can be said that county prosecutors brought the cases in part because they could. Prosecutors have far-reaching latitude in how they conduct the business of prosecution (Jacoby, 1979): County prosecutors decide whether to prosecute a case. They make decisions that affect who is prosecuted, the charges that are to be filed, and the kinds of plea bargains that are struck. They decide which cases are to be pursued more aggressively than others. In this [selection], we will see how reports of crack mothers reached prosecutors, and we will examine some of the factors that influenced the decision to prosecute in the first place, to charge at the high end of the penalty spectrum, and to prosecute aggressively. The kind of power held over defendants, even before a judge gets involved, reflects the unparalleled role prosecutors play in the criminal justice system.

Across the country most prosecutors declined to prosecute women who had used drugs during pregnancy. States like Florida and California limited or declined to authorize criminal prosecution in cases of cocaine-exposed infants under the child abuse and neglect laws (Spitzer, 1987; Gomez, 1997). Alternatives existed. The statutes on possession and distribution of drugs applied to women, pregnant or not. Child protective services investigated cocaine-exposed newborns and, where warranted, brought abusive or negligent parents into family or juvenile court to terminate parental rights. And the federal Ad Hoc Drug Policy Group had by 1991 recommended prevention and treatment for the mothers as well as shifts in the mission of child welfare services to cope with maternal drug use and drug-exposed children. The group's recommendations reflected a broader, but less visible, consensus about the efficacy of services over prosecution (U.S. Department of Health and Human Services, 1992).

Legal precedents made it unlikely that any attempt to criminally prosecute cocaine mothers would be successful. A fetus is not, legally speaking, a person. The state may act to protect fetal life, and often it imposes criminal sanctions for intentionally harming a fetus—but typically only someone else's fetus. In *Roe v. Wade* (1973) and later in *Webster v. Reproductive Health Services* (1989), the Supreme Court left no doubt that the state's interest in protecting fetal life is outweighed by a woman's interest in controlling her own reproductive life. Thus, a woman's fetus may be protected from other people, but not really from herself.

The fetal-rights advocates have never accepted this, asking, if a third party can be punished for harming a fetus, why can't the mother be punished, too? For years they have pushed at the limits of *Roe v. Wade* (1973), trying to read much into the "important and legitimate interest" the Supreme Court Justices said the state may have in a first- or second-trimester fetus. Knowing a declaration that legal life begins at conception is beyond them, right-to-life jurists have tried to work around the edges, using related issues like maternal drug use to advance their cause.

In no state was there a criminal statute in place applying to the specific circumstances of cocaine-exposed newborns. This meant that prosecutors drew from the statutes available, stretching the meaning of their provisions beyond the legislature's original intentions (Maschke, 1995). A 1986 case in San Diego shows the lengths to which prosecutors went in finding applicable statutes (Moss, 1988). Pamela Rae Stewart was charged with child abuse for failing to provide "medical attendance" for her unborn child. Stewart had disregarded doctor's instructions to avoid cocaine and other illicit drugs and to avoid sexual intercourse. And she delayed getting help when she started to hemorrhage. When she reached the hospital, the infant she delivered tested positive for cocaine, and it died of brain damage. The statute used to charge Stewart had been designed to force fathers to provide for the women they had impregnated. It had been amended, however, to require mothers to support their children as well. The prosecutors seized on this later provision to charge Stewart, but because the legislature had not intended it to penalize conduct during pregnancy, the case was dismissed.

A few years later, riding a wave of anti-drug hysteria, county prosecutors in a handful of other states acted. Karen Maschke suggests that these prosecutors had a "conviction psychology" (1995). Some had prosecuted child abuse cases; others were strong advocates of victims' rights. They all believed that babies had a right to be born free of defect—a variant of the defeated fetal-rights argument. They all believed that the mothers should be held responsible.

But the county prosecutors who tried the cocaine mother cases shared other things as well. As elected officials, they identified voters as their primary constituency (Jacoby, 1979), and their need to remain visible led them to make politically popular decisions. The early Stewart case had set off a national controversy without settling the issues; other statutes remained to be tested. Publicity earned by prosecuting a high-profile case had carryover value in winning higher office or attracting the attention of national decision makers. Indeed, their need to remain visible led prosecutors to legally questionable decisions. Paul Logli, the state's attorney from Rockford, Illinois, said the plight of cocaine-exposed babies was so severe in Winnebago County that one could do no less than to exploit all avenues of the law. Other prosecutors were every bit as adamant and inventive. Using manslaughter, drug-trafficking, and child-abuse statutes, they applied existing laws to a situation never envisaged by the legislature: a mother and her cocaine-exposed newborn.

Irrespective of how individual prosecutors justified their action, the decision to prosecute reflects the isolation of public prosecutors as a group of privileged white professionals. Dwight Greene, who wrote about Tony Tague, the Michigan county prosecutor discussed below, calls this isolation "pluralistic ignorance" (Greene, 1991). Tague made his decisions about the case, said Greene, on the basis of "false knowledge"—misconceptions about women, race, and poverty that he shared with other attorneys. It's hard to know whether any of the prosecutors reviewed in this chapter saw the women they prosecuted as real people; they apparently saw them as symbolic targets in a battle to save children. What they did not see or would not admit were the increasing depth of urban poverty, the desperation of the people burdened by it, and the impact of crack on the lives of people, especially of young women. Prosecutors instead saw women who had refused to help themselves, who had used up all their chances, and who required the full impact of the criminal sanction to get them to carry out their duties as mothers.

Here, then, are the highly publicized cases that signaled the moral panic. The defendants were for the most part poor, single mothers who had succumbed to crack because it defined the social worlds in which they lived. Two defendants were white. The case against Lynn Bremer, a white attorney, helped county prosecutor Tony Tague fend off accusations of racism for having charged Kimberly Hardy, a black single mother whose baby tested positive for cocaine. Josephine Pelligrini, the other white defendant, came from a middle-class family in Brockton, Massachusetts, but the father of her infant was black. The remaining defendants were poor, black, single mothers: Melanie Green in Illinois, Jennifer Johnson in Florida, and Kimberly Hardy in Michigan. Several additional cases grew out of a program in Charleston, South Carolina; defendants in these cases were almost all black, too. Charges filed against these women included involuntary manslaughter, delivery of a controlled substance to a minor, and child abuse or neglect. The cases were filed in Illinois, Florida, Michigan, Massachusetts, and South Carolina. Paul Logli, state's attorney for Winnebago County; Jeffrey Deen, assistant state attorney in Seminole County; Anthony Tague, county attorney for Muskegon County; William O'Malley, district attorney in Plymouth County; and Charles M. Condon, ninth circuit solicitor in Charleston prosecuted the cases.

## Melanie Green and Involuntary Manslaughter

Melanie Green, 24, was the first cocaine mother in the country to be charged with manslaughter in the death of her baby. She was as unlikely as any other poor, single mother to find herself at the center of a national debate about women's rights and drug abuse. Raised in a large working-class black family in Rockford, Illinois, she had dropped out of high school before drifting into drug use. When she was 17, she pleaded guilty to shoplifting charges; later she attributed her problems to having got involved with the wrong people. She gave birth to her son, Damen, in 1983.

Green was pregnant with her second child in September of 1988. Back in Illinois from an extended stay in Iowa, she was on welfare and had sought help for a drug problem, but the waiting list was too long, so she tried on her own to cut back. Six months later, Green gave birth to a daughter, Bianca, and both tested positive for cocaine. Bianca was underweight, had suffered brain damage, and she died within days of her birth. Later Melanie described the loss of her daughter as the most difficult days of her life. When another close family member died in April, Melanie Green was emotionally less prepared than ever for what was to come. Three months after the death of her daughter, she was arrested at her home as she waited for her son Damen to return from school.

The state's attorney for Winnebago County, Paul Logli, had in the meantime been pondering the legal situation presented by the death of Bianca Green. "It was a living, breathing baby that died, for no other reason, we believe, than that cocaine was ingested by the mother," Logli said. "To ignore that is unconscionable. It borders on barbarism" (Stein, 1989). His frustrations were with the law. If a living infant was prenatally exposed to cocaine, an Illinois prosecutor can bring the mother before the juvenile court for a hearing to determine custody. If, on the other hand, the cocaine-exposed infant dies, the Illinois law provides no remedy. "The statutes of this state," Logli said in a published interview, "specifically exempt mothers from the aggravated battery or manslaughter of a fetus." He went on to explain, "That's so prosecutors like me can't use that to get around the [U.S. Supreme Court abortion] decision [in *Roe v. Wade*]" (Reardon, 1989, May 14).

Logli disputed suggestions that his Roman Catholic background—he attended Catholic high school and a Catholic-affiliated college—had any bearing on his decision in the Green case (Stein, 1989). As the legal test that he proposed and later wrote about, Logli reported finding precedent for filing criminal charges against Melanie Green in a 1982 Illinois reckless homicide case (Logli, 1992). The facts were straightforward: a car driven by the drunken defendant collided with another car in which a pregnant woman rode as a passenger. Within hours of the collision, the woman delivered a baby who died a few minutes later. The injury to the baby was prenatal. But because the baby was born alive—like Bianca Green—Logli hoped this could be the precedent for holding Melanie Green responsible for her own child's death. Thus, the Rockford office of the state's attorney presented to the grand jury one charge of involuntary manslaughter in the death of Green's daughter and one count of delivering drugs to a minor.

The obstacles to the involuntary manslaughter charge were serious (Reardon, 1989, May 28). The American Civil Liberties Union (ACLU) had entered the case, pointing out that the injury was prenatal. In attempting to hold a mother criminally responsible for prenatal injury to her own child, the ACLU argued, Logli ran afoul of the U.S. Supreme Court ruling in *Roe v. Wade*: the fetus is not a person with protectable rights (Kreiter, 1989, May 10). Prosecuting a woman for acts to her own body is an unconstitutional intrusion into the right to privacy (Kreiter, 1989, May 27). Harvey Grossman, legal director of the ACLU in Chicago, defended Melanie Green and said of the case, "It's a question of how society related to women, period. She is not simply a vessel for carrying a fetus. She doesn't lose her rights to personal autonomy because of pregnancy" (Parson, 1993).

The eight women and four men on the grand jury agreed and chose not to indict Green on either the manslaughter or the drug delivery charge. Bowing to defeat, Logli admitted that manslaughter may not have been the best mechanism for charging women who used drugs during pregnancy (Lamb, 1989). Questions asked by the grand jurors, he conceded, showed that they had concerns about Green's right to privacy, that is, her right to make decisions about her body free from government interference. There were also some risks, Logli admitted, in criminalizing the behavior in question (Reardon, 1989, May 28).

From where did this high-profile prosecution come? Logli cited the local epidemic of crack babies, although Winnebago County, Illinois, was not the most likely place for a prosecutorial campaign (Logli, 1990). While 27 babies born to women allegedly using cocaine had been identified in the hospitals between the summer of 1988 and May of 1989, this figure is small in contrast with the much larger estimates from urban centers like New York City or Los Angeles (Stein, 1989).

Logli may have been more concerned with keeping big-city problems, including crack babies, from taking hold in the smaller community of Rockford. And Logli was frustrated with the war on drugs (Logli, 1990). "We undertook this prosecution in an effort to find one more way to fight a cocaine war that all society is presently losing," Logli wrote in a 1990 law journal article (Logli, 1990). "Concerned citizens and child welfare authorities" who wanted to remedy the problem of substance-abused infants had asked him to step in, he said (Logli, 1992). Criminal sanctions, Logli maintained, remained an effective remedy. They "raised the consequences of maternal drug use to a tough enough position that these persons... might be encouraged to seek the treatment, the help they need" (Primetime Live, 1989).

The Green case gave Paul Logli national exposure. On the day he filed charges against Green, he flew to New York City to appear on two national television shows (Reardon, 1989, May 11), and television talk show hosts continued to provide a forum for him to express his prosecutorial views. Reports circulating in the late 1980s had it that Paul Logli was considering a run for Congress, but he remained state's attorney for Winnebago County well into the 1990s (Stein, 1989). He became president of the Illinois State's Attorney Association in 1996.

Melanie Green, on the other hand, tried to escape the publicity that surrounded her case. Even though she was unavailable for interviews, the troubles she experienced in 1989 were played out on national television. As she mourned the death of her daughter and an aunt, she faced very serious criminal charges: the drug distribution charge carried a sentence of 15 years in prison, the manslaughter charge, of 5. And had Logli tacked on the drug possession charge he threatened to file after the grand jury dismissed the others, Green would have faced 3 years in prison. After the grand jury dismissed charges against her, Green left Rockford to enter a three-week day-treatment program. To avoid the permanent stigma of being Rockford's most infamous crack mother, she announced plans to relocate....

## Crack Mothers in Charleston, South Carolina

Charles Malony Condon, South Carolina's ninth circuit solicitor from 1980 to 1991, served both Charleston and Berkeley Counties. One of the things that attracted Condon to the job of solicitor was its promise of autonomy and discretion. In an article profiling his career, he told interviewers that the job allowed him to pick his cases, discarding bad ones to concentrate on good ones: "I think the prosecutor should always wear the white hat. And if you don't wear the white hat, you're not doing your job" (MacDougall, 1991).

In the late 1990s, now state attorney general for South Carolina, Charles Condon looks back on a career that includes developing the program he says reduced the number of cocaine-addicted babies in Charleston (MacDougall,

1991). Hospital officials from the Medical University of South Carolina (MUSC) had originally called in the Circuit Solicitor's Office when nurses and doctors began seeing five or six pregnant women a week who had used cocaine or crack, some with hemorrhaging or other complications related to pregnancy (Lewin, 1990). Physicians linked the symptoms to cocaine, and because they felt they were witnessing a crime, went to the circuit solicitor (Siegel, 1994).

Condon had already enlisted in the war on drugs, and with a politician's eye to a winning issue, agreed that the hospital had an obligation to report such cases (Siegel, 1994). In a *Los Angeles Times* article, Condon is reported to have admonished hospital officials, "It's nice you came in... But the fact is, you have to come in. There's no patient-doctor privilege on this. If you don't report it, it's a crime" (Siegel, 1994). In response, Dr. Edgar Horger and nurse Shirley Brown, both from MUSC, joined Condon in developing a program for drug-using pregnant women that sent a deterrent message: Seek drug treatment or face arrest and jail time (Condon, 1995).

The program developed in three stages. From October 1988 to September 1989, during clinic visits urine drug tests were administered to pregnant women suspected of using cocaine or other illicit drugs. The testing program identified 119 cases of cocaine use among pregnant women. For most, the drug test coincided with the delivery of their babies. Referrals for drug rehabilitation were made for 15 women tested for drugs early in their pregnancies, but their babies tested positive for cocaine when they returned to the hospital for delivery.

In the program's shock stage, arrests were made. In October, November, and December 1989, patients were arrested if they or their newborns tested positive for cocaine. Ten women were arrested, their babies turned over to foster care. In a final stage, beginning in January 1990, the program modified its procedures so that patients could avoid arrest by successfully completing drug counseling. The threat of arrest, made real by the program's shock period, was thereafter used to "leverage" women into treatment. Over the program's five-year life, 42 women were arrested, some of whom avoided charges by agreeing to drug treatment (Associated Press, 1994).

Following an investigation in January 1990, the ACLU and the Center for Reproductive Law and Policy pointed to serious deficiencies in the MUSC program (Goetz, Fox, and Bates, 1990). Screening procedures were discriminatory. Doctors began by screening patients on a discretionary basis, but implementation of a nine-point protocol intended to reduce bias still permitted selective drug screening. Combined with the fact that MUSC served poor patients, this meant that poor women, the majority of whom were black, were singled out as drug-abusing mothers.

The MUSC program was also punitive. Once the hospital identified drug-using women, the circuit solicitor recommended against releasing them on their own recognizance, insisting instead on bail. The judge set bail, which had the effect of keeping cash-strapped, postpartum women in jail and away from adequate medical attention or drug treatment. The MUSC program purported to give mothers a choice between treatment and jail, but treatment was either nonexistent or inappropriate. Initially, the hospital had not developed treatment options for women, but when it did, the program did not work well for most. This population needed day treatment, child care, and transportation, or residential facilities with accommodations for children—none of which existed in Charleston.

Still, Condon defended the program as effective in reducing the number of cocaine babies (MacDougall, 1991). The program's evaluation reportedly showed that MUSC had reduced the number of drug-using women coming to the hospital for delivery, but a flawed methodology made it a poor demonstration of effectiveness (Horger, Brown, and Condon, 1990). Nonetheless, in a 1990 interview on *Nightline*, Condon summed up the MUSC experience: "We have been able to demonstrate quite clearly that with an effective prosecution program available as a last resort and the women knowing that something will in fact happen to them eventually, they [the women] have simply stopped using cocaine" (1990). And because there had been growing criticism that prosecutions like those in South Carolina frightened women away from needed prenatal care, he added, "And there's absolutely no evidence here locally that the women are not seeking prenatal care.... They go to the same hospitals as before."

His experience in South Carolina, Condon said, showed that without the threat of prosecution, women who used cocaine during pregnancy would do nothing to help themselves or their future children: "When the women have been coming into the hospital and have been told simply and educated simply that cocaine use is bad, it can hurt you or your fetus and can cause great damage, many women continue to use cocaine" (Nightline, 1990). In a different context, Condon predicted, "Until they [cocaine mothers] suffer sanctions, ... you're going to see the problem increase" (Sataline, 1991). Moreover, he argued, if it is against the law in South Carolina to use cocaine, then it is against the law for pregnant women to use it, too. If the law applies to pregnant women, then no woman has the right to bear a drug-affected baby (Sataline, 1991)

In the midst of what was shaping up as a major debate on public health policy, the ACLU and the Center for Reproductive Law and Policy publicized details about the women who had been jailed because of the MUSC program (Siegel, 1994). They were black, poor, and as single mothers in their late twenties and thirties, they had used crack or cocaine, and they had several children. On the basis of a positive drug screen, they were arrested on charges of possession and delivery of drugs to a minor.

One example, Theresa Joseph, 35, was the mother of several children, only one of whom lived with her. Although she avoided the hospital throughout her pregnancy for fear of prosecution—she had seen Condon's public service announcement threatening jail for pregnant substance abusers—an infection brought her to MUSC. There the staff told her to get drug treatment, but fearing prosecution, she fled. She returned for further medical care but did not keep the appointment for drug treatment. Back at the hospital for the birth of her baby, she was arrested and taken to jail after the baby tested positive for cocaine.

In addition to fear, the lack of appropriate options in the MUSC program kept women away from treatment. Crystal Ferguson, 31 years old and the mother of three children, was referred late in her pregnancy to MUSC, where she tested positive for cocaine. She was given the option of getting treatment or going to jail, but she felt she could not leave her children, and treatment facilities had no room for children. Ferguson returned to her children, rejecting the offer of treatment, and tried to stop on her own. When she went to the hospital to give birth to her daughter, she tested positive for drugs, and Ferguson was arrested and jailed.

Defense attorneys easily got the charges (drug possession and drug delivery to a minor) against Ferguson and Joseph dismissed (Siegel, 1994). In 1992 an appellate court overturned the child-neglect conviction of a pregnant substance abuser, holding that the law had been misapplied. So when Lynn Paltrow of the Center for Reproductive Law and Policy and the ACLU and Charleston public defender Ted Phillips moved to quash the distribution charges against Joseph and Ferguson, the new ninth circuit solicitor, David Schwacke, who replaced Condon when Condon became state attorney general, did not put up a fight. Schwacke dismissed the charges and rescinded the bench warrants on five other women also charged with possession and delivery of drugs to a minor, hoping to avoid a ruling that the drug delivery charge was misapplied as well.

The Center for Reproductive Law and Policy assembled an impressive array of experts and public health organizations (Siegel, 1994). All had gone on record opposing the MUSC program on public health grounds: prosecution was the least effective way to deal with maternal drug use. Dr. Barry Zuckerman, chairman of the department of pediatrics at the Boston University School of Medicine and Boston City Hospital, and Dr. Jay Katz, professor emeritus of law, medicine, and psychiatry at the Yale University, raised objections to the MUSC program. The American Medical Association, American Academy of Pediatrics, American Public Health Association, American Nurses Association, March of Dimes, and other groups opposed the threat of arrest to force pregnant women into drug treatment programs. Women's groups, including the National Organization for Women, opposed prosecution for public health reasons and because it threatened women's right to make reproductive decisions free of government interference. They were also concerned because prosecution might give anti-abortion advocates grounds for expanding fetal rights.

The Center for Reproductive Law and Policy devised a two-pronged strategy in South Carolina (Siegel, 1994). It first complained to the National Institutes of Health that the evaluation of the MUSC program had not met federal guidelines requiring the consent of human subjects in research. Subjects had not consented to participate in the evaluation research that was later published in a medical journal. MUSC and the study's authors (Dr Edgar Horger, nurse Shirley Brown, and circuit solicitor Charles Condon) stood accused of conducting unethical experiments on African American women. The U.S. Department of Health and Human Services reviewed the charges and threatened to cut off federal funding unless MUSC corrected its procedures. To avoid losing federal funding, MUSC shut down the program in 1994.

Second, the Center for Reproductive Law and Policy filed a $3-million class-action suit against MUSC, the city of Charleston, and local law enforcement officials and agencies (Siegel, 1994). The suit asked for compensatory and punitive damages for 10 women whose civil rights had been violated by MUSC's arrest-and-jail policy. In January 1997 a federal jury decided, however, that the choice between drug treatment or jail was not racially motivated, nor did the conduct of the hospital in turning over the results of drug tests to prosecutors amount to an illegal search. The U.S. district judge, Westin Houck, had six months to determine whether the search itself was unconstitutional, whether MUSC violated confidentiality of medical information, women's right to procreate, and the Federal Civil Rights Act (Baxley, 1997). Although Lynn Paltrow did not believe that the case was over, the judge failed to act within the time limit, and the issues remain unresolved.

The federal suit in Charleston stirred up local prejudices against the outsiders who defended cocaine mothers (Siegel, 1994). The ACLU, feminists, and "California-type liberals" were rebuked by officials for moralizing and interfering with the way things were done in Charleston. "The left-wing ACLU doesn't represent the American people," said Condon at a press conference during a break in the federal class-action suit. "MUSC deserves an award. If the plaintiff [the women jailed by MUSC] prevails, in effect we'd be legalizing the use of crack cocaine during pregnancy" (Siegel, 1994). As Condon turned back to his private conversation, *Los Angeles Times* correspondent Barry Siegel recorded his comments: "Tell Lynn [Paltrow] thanks for suing me. Running in South Carolina for attorney general, the best thing you can have happen is to be sued by the ACLU" (1994).

⌖

With the 1996 federal court decision in South Carolina, the moral panic ground to a halt. One by one, the cases built by prosecutors had unraveled. While the media and the public understood the prosecutions as legitimate attempts to deal with the problem, the judiciary cast a more critical eye. The Rockford grand jury doubted the wisdom of Logli's manslaughter strategy, and in an unusual move for any grand jury, refused to indict Melanie Green. The grand jury in Brockton, less suspicious of O'Malley's drug-delivery strategy, indicted Josephine Pelligrini, and O'Malley managed to get the case to court, but the judge quickly dismissed it and effectively ended such prosecutions in Massachusetts. Tague took advantage of sympathetic lower-court judges to get both his cases bound over for trial, but the Michigan Court of Appeals threw out the charges. The prosecutor in Florida managed to convict Jennifer Johnson, but the Supreme Court of Florida refused to uphold it and ended the cocaine baby cases there.

The five prosecutors had surprisingly little support within their own professional circles. In the National District Attorneys Association (NDAA), one subcommittee, Substance Abused Infants and Children, strongly endorsed their efforts. But most other NDAA sections were less enthusiastic, including the American Prosecutors Research Institute (APRI), the research arm of the association ("Substance Abused Infants," 1990). Charles Condon, Anthony Tague, and Jeffrey Deen figured prominently in an APRI conference, "Substance Abused Infants: A Prosecutor's Dilemma," held in Chicago in July 1990. But the conference failed to endorse the high-profile prosecutions. Jill Hiatt and Janet Dinsmore, spokespeople for the National Center for Prosecution of Child Abuse, distanced APRI and NDAA from the "very few but highly publicized cases, involving novel use of laws to prosecute women who have given birth to drug-affected babies" ("Pregnant Addicts," 1990).

Prosecutors made it easier both morally and politically to cut social service spending, to push fetal rights, and to attack racial preferences. Their crusade appealed to the prejudices of white audiences who watched the panic unfold on the nightly news, but their limited racial experience blinded them to the racial implications of the prosecutions (Greene, 1991). Misconceptions fit into a long line of stereotypes about black sexuality and incompetent mothering (Roberts, 1991). As another dehumanizing wave of restrictions on reproduction, the prosecutions showed that state officials were all too willing to punish black women for having babies. Under slavery, an owner's profit dictated the reproductive choices of black women. Later, involuntary sterilization eliminated the choices arising from fertility. Pronatalist attitudes combined with restrictions on Medicaid abortions made termination unlikely. The crusade against crack mothers, consequently, served as punishment for women who carried their pregnancies to term and delivered babies (Roberts, 1991).

# POSTSCRIPT

## Should Pregnant Drug Users Be Prosecuted?

**B**abies born with health problems as a result of their mothers' drug use is a tragedy that needs to be rectified. The issue is not whether or not this problem needs to be addressed but what course of action is best. The need for medical intervention and specialized treatment programs serving pregnant women with drug problems has been recognized. The groundwork has been set for funding and developing such programs. The Office of Substance Abuse Prevention is funding chemical dependency programs specifically for pregnant women in several states.

It has been argued that drug use by pregnant women is a medical problem that requires medical, not criminal, attention. One can contend that pregnant drug users and their drug-exposed infants are victims of drug abuse. Humphries feels that there is an element of discrimination in the practice of prosecuting women who use drugs during pregnancy because these women are primarily low-income, single, members of minorities, and recipients of public assistance. Possible factors leading to their drug use—poverty, unemployment, poor education, and lack of vocational training—are not addressed when the solution to drug use during pregnancy is incarceration. Moreover, many pregnant women are denied access to treatment programs.

Prosecution proponents contend that medical intervention is not adequate in preventing pregnant women from using drugs and that criminal prosecution is necessary. Logli argues that "eliminating the pain, suffering and death resulting from drug exposure in newborns must be a prosecutor's priority." He maintains that the criminal justice system should protect newborns and, if legal cause does exist for prosecution, then statutes should provide protection for the fetus. However, will prosecution result in more protection or less protection for the fetus? If a mother stops using drugs for fear of prosecution, then the fetus benefits. If the mother avoids prenatal care because of potential legal punishment, then the fetus suffers.

If women can be prosecuted for using illegal drugs such as cocaine and narcotics during pregnancy because they harm the fetus, then should women who smoke cigarettes and drink alcohol during pregnancy also be prosecuted? The evidence is clear that tobacco and alcohol place the fetus at great risk; however, most discussions of prosecuting pregnant drug users overlook women who use these drugs. Also, the adverse health effects from secondhand smoke are well documented. Should people be prosecuted if they smoke around pregnant women?

Two articles that address the effects of prenatal exposure to drugs are "Drinking Moderately and Pregnancy," by Joseph Jacobson and Sandra Jacobson, *Alcohol Research and Health* (Winter 1999) and "The Impact of Maternal Cocaine Use on Neonates in Socioeconomic Disadvantaged Population," by Wei Yue Sun and William Chen, *Journal of Drug Education* (vol. 27, no. 4, 1997). In "The Wrong Race, Committing Crime, Doing Drugs, and Maladjusted for Motherhood: The Nation's Fury Over Crack Babies," *Social Justice* (Spring 1999), Enid Logan addresses the effects of race and class in cases in which pregnant, drug-using women are prosecuted. Rachel Roth writes about the civil rights of pregnant drug users in "Policing Pregnancy," *The Nation* (October 16, 2000). And in her book *Crack Cocaine, Crime, and Women: Legal Social, and Treatment Issues* (Sage, 1996), Sue Mahan maintains that women and their babies would be better served by prenatal care and treatment rather than incarceration.

# ISSUE 6

## Is Drug Addiction a Choice?

**YES: Jeffrey A. Schaler**, from *Addiction Is a Choice* (Open Court, 2000)

**NO: Alice M. Young**, from "Addictive Drugs and the Brain," *National Forum* (Fall 1999)

### ISSUE SUMMARY

**YES:** Psychotherapist Jeffrey A. Schaler maintains that drug addiction should not be considered a disease, a condition over which one has no control. Schaler states that diseases have distinct characteristics and that drug addiction does not share these characteristics. Classifying behavior as socially unacceptable does not prove that it is a disease, according to Schaler.

**NO:** Professor of psychology Alice M. Young points out that a small number of drugs produce pleasurable sensations in the brain, increasing the likelihood that drug-taking behavior will be repeated. In addition, tolerance and dependency may result when drugs are taken frequently. If tolerance develops, then the drug user must increase the dosage level to achieve the desired effect, increasing the possibility of dependency.

I s drug addiction caused by an illness or disease or is it caused by inappropriate behavioral patterns? This distinction is important because it has both legal and medical implications. Should people be held accountable for behaviors that stem from an illness of which they have no control? For example, if a person cannot help being an alcoholic and hurts or kills someone as a result of being drunk, should that person be treated for addiction or incarcerated? Likewise, if an individual's addiction is due to lack of self-control rather than due to a disease, should taxpayer money be used to pay for that person's treatment?

It can be argued that the disease concept of drug addiction legitimizes or excuses behaviors. If addiction is an illness, then blame for poor behavior can be shifted to the disease and away from the individual. Moreover, if drug addiction is incurable, addicts should not be held responsible for their behavior.

Jeffrey A. Schaler contends that addicts should be held responsible for their behavior and that loss of control is not inevitable. He asserts that the ability of alcoholics to stop excessive consumption is not determined by a physiological reaction to alcohol. Moreover, it has been shown that many cocaine and heroin users do not lose control while using these drugs. In their study of U.S. service personnel in Vietnam, epidemiologist Lee N. Robins and colleagues showed that most of the soldiers who used narcotics regularly during the war did not continue using them once they returned home. Many service personnel in Vietnam reportedly used drugs because they were in a situation that they did not want to be in. Additionally, without the support of loved ones and the constraints of society, they were freer to gravitate to behaviors that would not be tolerated by their families and friends.

Alice M. Young states that certain neurotransmitters in the brain contribute to the reward response and that humans repeatedly engage in behaviors that produce pleasurable feelings. Psychological factors are important but biological factors are important as well. Young contends that psychology tells the body to repeat behaviors, but biology "contributes the concept of chemical communication systems in the brain, systems critical to learning and memory." Drugs produce changes in the brain that provide a pleasurable response.

According to the disease perspective, an important step for addicts to take in order to benefit from treatment is to admit that they are powerless against their addiction. They need to acknowledge that their drug addiction controls them and that drug addiction is a lifelong problem. The implication of this view is that addicts are never cured. Addicts must therefore abstain from drugs for their entire lives.

Is addiction caused by psychological or biological factors? Can drugs produce changes in the brain that result in drug addiction? How much control do drug addicts have over their use of drugs? In the following selections, Schaler argues that drug use is a matter of free will, while Young contends that drugs produce changes in the brain that result in repeating behaviors leading to drug addiction.

 **YES**

# Is Addiction Really a Disease?

Being addicted to a melancholy as she is.

— William Shakespeare, *Twelfth Night*

If you watch TV, read the newspaper, or listen to almost any social worker or religious minister, you soon pick up the idea that addiction is a condition in which addicts just physically cannot control themselves, and that this condition is a medical disease.

The federal government views alcohol addiction as a disease characterized by *loss of control*, with a physiological 'etiology' (cause) independent of volition. According to a typical statement of the government's view by Otis R. Bowen, former secretary of health and human services,

> millions of children have a genetic predisposition to alcoholism... alcohol use by young people has been found to be a 'gateway' drug preceding other drug use... about 1 out of every 15 kids will eventually become an alcoholic.... alcoholism is a disease, and this disease is highly treatable. (Bowen 1988, pp. 559, 563)

You may easily conclude that all the experts agree with this kind of thinking. Most people with no special interest in the subject probably never get to hear another point of view.

The true situation is a bit more complicated. Public opinion overwhelmingly accepts the claim that addiction is a disease, but the general public's views are seriously inconsistent. A 1987 study of public views on alcoholism showed that over 85 percent of people believe that alcoholism is a disease, but most of them also believe things that contradict the disease theory. Many people seem to support and reject the disease theory at the same time. For instance, they often say they believe that alcoholism is a disease and also that it is a sign of moral weakness (Caetano 1987, p. 158).

The addiction treatment providers, the many thousands of people who make their living in the addiction treatment industry, mostly accept the disease theory. They are, in fact, for the most part, 'recovered addicts' themselves, redeemed sinners who spend their lives being paid to preach the gospel that social deviants are sick.

Among those psychologists and others who think, write, discuss, and conduct research in this area, however, opinion is much more divided. In this small world, there is an ongoing battle between the 'disease model' and the 'free-will model'.

Biomedical and psychosocial scientists range across both sides of the controversy (Fillmore and Sigvardsson 1988). Some biomedical researchers accept the disease model and assert that genetic and physiological differences account for alcoholism (for example, D.W. Goodwin 1988; F.K. Goodwin 1988; Blum et al. 1990; Tabakoff and Hoffman 1988). Other biomedical researchers have investigated their claims and pronounced them invalid (Lester 1989; Bolos et al. 1990; Billings 1990). Many social scientists reject the idea that alcoholics or other addicts constitute a homogeneous group. They hold that individual differences, personal values, expectations, and environmental factors are key correlates to heavy drinking and drug-taking. Others reject strictly psychological theories (Maltzman 1991; Madsen 1989; Vaillant 1983; Milam and Ketcham 1983; Prince, Glatt, and Pullar-Strecker 1966). Some sociologists regard the disease model of alcoholism as a human construction based on desire for social control (Room 1983; Fillmore 1988). Some embrace the disease model even while agreeing that addiction may not be a real disease—they hold that utility warrants labeling it as such (Kissin 1983; Vaillant 1990). Their opponents believe the disease model does more harm than good (Szasz 1972; Fingarette 1988; Alexander 1990a; 1990b; Crawford et al. 1989; Fillmore and Kelso 1987; Heather, Winton, and Rollnick 1982; Schaler 1996b).

My impression is that the disease model is steadily losing ground. It may not be too much to hope that the notion of addiction as a disease will be completely discredited and abandoned in years to come, perhaps as early as the next 20 years.

If this seems like a fanciful speculation, remember that other recognized 'diseases' have been quite swiftly discredited. The most recent example is homosexuality. Being sexually attracted to members of one's own sex was, overwhelmingly, considered a disease by the psychiatric profession, and therefore by the medical profession as a whole, until the 1960s. Psychiatry and medicine completely reversed themselves on this issue within a few years. Homosexuality was declassified as an illness by the American Psychiatric Association in 1973. It is now officially considered a non-disease, unless the homosexual wishes he were not a homosexual. This doesn't go far enough, but imagine the same principle extended to drug addiction: the addict is not at all sick unless he says he is unhappy being addicted!

Before homosexuality, there were the recognized diseases of masturbation, negritude (having a black skin), Judaism (described as a disease by the German government in the 1930s), and being critical of the Soviet government, which 'treated' political dissidents in mental hospitals (see Rush 1799; Szasz 1970; Robitscher 1980; Lifton 1986; Conrad and Schneider 1992; and Breggin 1993). A similar fate may be in store for the 'disease' of drug addiction.

Many people accept the disease model of addiction on the basis of respect for the messenger. Addiction is a disease because doctors say it's a disease (social psychologists call this peripheral-route processing) rather than critical evaluation of the message itself (central-route processing). Peripheral-route processing has more in common with faith than reason, and research shows that in general its appeal is greatest among the less educated. Reason and faith are not always compatible. Reason requires evidence, faith does not.

Clinical and public policy should not be based on faith, whether the source is drunken anecdote, the proclamations of self-assigned experts, or the measured statements of addiction doctors. Rather, empirical evidence and sound reasoning are required. Both are lacking in the assertion that addiction is a disease.

If it were ever to be shown that there existed a genetic disease causing a powerful craving for a drug, this would not demonstrate that the afflicted person had no choice as to whether to take the drug. Nor would it show that the action of taking the drug was itself a disease.

There are various skin rashes, for example, which often arouse a powerful urge to scratch the inflamed area. It's usually enough to explain the harmful consequences of scratching, and the patient will choose not to scratch. Though scratching may cause diseases (by promoting infection of the area) and is a response to physiological sensations, the activity of scratching is not itself considered a disease.

## What Is a Disease?

Is addiction really a disease? Let's clarify a few matters. The classification of behavior as socially unacceptable does not prove its label as a disease. Adherents of the disease model sometimes respond to the claim that addiction is not a disease by emphasizing the terrible problems people create as a result of their addictions, but that is entirely beside the point. The fact that some behavior has horrible consequences does not show that it's a disease.

The 'success' of 'treatment programs' run by people who view addiction as a disease would not demonstrate that addiction was a disease—any more than the success of other religious groups in converting people from vicious practices would prove the theological tenets of these religious groups. However, this possibility need not concern us, since all known treatment programs are, in fact, ineffective.

I will not go into the claims of a genetic basis for 'alcoholism' or other addictions. A genetic predisposition toward some kind of behavior, say, speaking in tongues, would not show that those with the predisposition had a disease. Variations in skin and eye color, for example, are genetically determined, but are not diseases. Fair-skinned people sunburn easily. The fairness of their skin is genetically determined, yet their susceptibility to sunburn is not considered a disease. Neither would a genetic predisposition toward some kind of behavior necessarily show that the predisposed persons could not consciously change their behavior.

With so much commonsense evidence to refute it, why is the view of drug addiction as a disease so prevalent? Incredible as it may seem, because doctors say so. A leading alcoholism researcher once asserted that alcoholism is a disease simply because people go to doctors for it. Undoubtedly, drug 'addicts' seek help from doctors for two reasons. Many addicts have a significant psychological investment in maintaining this view, having been told, and come to believe, that their eventual recovery depends on believing they have a disease. They may even have come to accept that they will die if they question the disease model of addiction. And treatment professionals have a significant economic investment at stake. The more behaviors are diagnosed as diseases, the more they will be paid by health insurance companies for 'treating' these diseases.

When we consider whether drug addiction is a disease we are concerned with what causes the drug to get *into* the body. It's quite irrelevant what the drug does *after* it's in the body. I certainly don't for a moment doubt that the taking of many drugs *causes* disease. Prolonged heavy drinking of alcoholic beverages can cause cirrhosis of the liver. Prolonged smoking of cigarettes somewhat raises the risk of various diseases such as lung cancer. But this uncontroversial fact is quite distinct from any claim that the activity is itself a disease (Szasz 1989b).

Some doctors make a specialty of occupation-linked disorders. For example, there is a pattern of lung and other diseases associated with working down a coal mine. But this does not show that mining coal is itself a disease. Other enterprising physicians specialize in treating diseases arising from sports: there is a pattern of diseases resulting from swimming, another from football, yet another from long-distance running. This does not demonstrate that these sports, or the inclination to pursue these sports, are themselves diseases. So, for instance, the fact that a doctor may be exceptionally knowledgeable about the effects of alcohol on the body, and may therefore be accepted as an expert on 'alcoholism', does nothing to show that alcoholism itself is a legitimate medical concept.

## Addiction, a Physical Disease?

If addiction is a disease, then presumably it's either a bodily or a mental disease. What criteria might justify defining addiction as a physical illness? Pathologists use nosology—the classification of diseases—to select, from among the phenomena they study, those that qualify as true diseases. Diseases are listed in standard pathology textbooks because they meet the nosological criteria for disease classification. A simple test of a true physical disease is whether it can be shown to exist in a corpse. There are no bodily signs of addiction itself (as opposed to its effects) that can be identified in a dead body. Addiction is therefore not listed in standard pathology textbooks.

Pathology, as revolutionized by Rudolf Virchow (1821–1902), requires an identifiable alteration in bodily tissue, a change in the cells of the body, for disease classification. No such identifiable pathology has been found in the bodies of heavy drinkers and drug users. This alone justifies the view that addiction is not a physical disease (Szasz 1991; 1994).

A symptom is subjective evidence from the patient: the patient reports certain pains and other sensations. A sign is something that can be identified in the patient's body, irrespective of the patient's reported experiences. In standard medical practice, the diagnosis of disease can be based on signs alone or on a combination of signs and symptoms, but only rarely on symptoms alone. A sign is objective physical evidence such as a lesion or chemical imbalance. Signs may be found through medical tests.

Sometimes a routine physical examination reveals signs of disease when no symptoms are reported. In such cases the disease is said to be 'asymptomatic' —without symptoms. For example, sugar in the urine combined with other signs may lead to a diagnosis of asymptomatic diabetes. Such a diagnosis is made solely on the basis of signs. It is inconceivable that addiction could ever be diagnosed on the basis of bodily signs alone. (The *effects* of heavy alcohol consumption can of course be inferred from bodily signs, but that, remember, is a different matter.) To speak of 'asymptomatic addiction' would be absurd.

True, conditions such as migraine and epilepsy are diagnosed primarily on the basis of symptoms. But, in general, it is not standard medical practice to diagnose disease on the basis of symptoms alone. The putative disease called addiction is diagnosed solely by symptoms in the form of conduct, never by signs, that is, by physical evidence in the patient's body. (A doctor might conclude that someone with cirrhosis of the liver and other bodily signs had partaken of alcoholic beverages heavily over a long period, and might infer that the patient was an 'alcoholic', but actually the doctor would be unable to distinguish this from the hypothetical case of someone who had been kept a prisoner and dosed with alcohol against her will. So, again, strictly speaking, *there cannot possibly be a bodily sign of an addiction.*)

If you visited your physician because of a dull pain in your epigastric region, would you want her to make a diagnosis without confirming it through objective tests? Wouldn't you doubt the validity of a diagnosis of heart disease without at least the results of an EKG? You would want to see reliable evidence of signs. But in the diagnosis of the disease called addiction, there are no signs, only symptoms (Szasz 1987).

We continually hear that 'addiction is a disease just like diabetes'. Yet there is no such thing as asymptomatic addiction, and *logically there could not be.* Moreover, the analogy cannot be turned around. It would be awkward to tell a person with diabetes that his condition was 'just like addiction' and inaccurate too: When a person with diabetes is deprived of insulin he will suffer and in severe cases may even die. When a heavy drinker or other drug user is deprived of alcohol or other drugs his physical health most often improves.

## A Mental or Metaphorical Disease?

Mental illnesses are diagnosed on the basis of symptoms, not signs. Perhaps, then, addiction is a mental illness, a psychiatric disease. Where does it fit into the scheme of psychiatric disorders?

Psychiatric disorders can be categorized in three groups: organic disorders, functional disorders, and antisocial behavior (Szasz 1988). Organic disorders include various forms of dementia such as those caused by HIV-1 infection, acute alcohol intoxication, brain tumor or injury, dementia of the Alzheimer's type, general paresis, and multi-infarct dementia. These are physical diseases with identifiable bodily signs. Addiction has no such identifiable signs.

Functional disorders include fears (anxiety disorders), discouragements (mood disorders), and stupidities (cognitive disorders). These are mental in the sense that they involve mental activities. As Szasz has pointed out, they are diseases "only in a metaphorical sense."

Forms of antisocial behavior categorized as psychiatric illness include crime, suicide, personality disorders, and maladaptive and maladjusted behavior. Some people consider these 'disorders' because they vary from the norm and involve danger to self or others. According to Szasz, however, they are "neither 'mental' nor 'diseases'" (Szasz 1988, pp. 249–251). If addiction qualifies as an antisocial behavior, this does not necessarily imply that it is mental or a disease.

Addiction is not listed in the American Psychiatric Association's Diagnostic and Statistical Manual of Mental Disorders IV (DSM-IV). What was once listed as alcoholism is now referred to as alcohol dependence and abuse. These are listed under the category of substance-related disorders. They would not fit the category of organic disorders because they are described in terms of behavior only. They would conceivably fit the functional disorder category but probably would be subordinated to one of the established disorders such as discouragement or anxiety.

Thus, it's difficult to classify addiction as either a physical or a mental disease. Many human problems may be described *metaphorically* as diseases. We hear media pundits speak of a 'sick economy' or 'sick culture'. Declining empires, such as the Ottoman empire at the end of the nineteenth century and the Soviet empire in the 1980s, are said to be 'sick'. There is little harm in resorting to this metaphor, and therefore describing negative addictions as diseases—except that there is the danger that some people will take the metaphor literally.

Today any socially-unacceptable behavior is likely to be diagnosed as an 'addiction'. So we have shopping addiction, videogame addiction, sex addiction, Dungeons and Dragons addiction, running addiction, chocolate addiction, Internet addiction, addiction to abusive relationships, and so forth. This would be fine if it merely represented a return to the traditional, non-medical usage, in which addiction means being given over to some pursuit. However, all of these new 'addictions' are now claimed to be medical illnesses, characterized by self-destructiveness, compulsion, loss of control, and some mysterious, as-yet-unidentified physiological component. This is entirely fanciful.

People become classified as 'addicts' or 'alcoholics' because of their behavior. 'Behavior' in humans refers to intentional conduct. As was pointed out long ago by Wilhelm Dilthey, Max Weber, and Ludwig von Mises, among others, the motions of the human body are either involuntary reflexes or meaningful human action. Human action is governed by the meaning it has for the acting person. The behavior of heavy drinking is not a form of neurological reflex but is the expression of values through action. As Herbert Fingarette puts it:

> A pattern of conduct must be distinguished from a mere sequence of reflex-like reactions. A reflex knee jerk is not conduct. If we regard something as a pattern of conduct... we assume that it is mediated by the mind, that it reflects consideration of reasons and preferences, the election of a preferred

means to the end, and the election of the end itself from among alternatives. The complex, purposeful, and often ingenious projects with which many an addict may be occupied in his daily hustlings to maintain his drug supply are examples of conduct, not automatic reflex reactions to a singly biological cause. (1975, p. 435)

Thomas Szasz agrees that

by behavior we mean the person's 'mode of conducting himself' or his 'deportment'... the name we attach to a living being's conduct in the daily pursuit of life.... bodily movements that are the products of neurophysiological discharges or reflexes are not behavior.... behavior implies action, and action implies conduct pursued by an agent seeking to attain a goal. (1987, p. 343)

The term 'alcoholism' has become so loaded with prescriptive intent that it no longer describes any drinking behavior accurately and should be abandoned. 'Heavy drinking' is a more descriptive term (Fingarette 1988). It is imprecise, but so is 'alcoholism'.

If we continue to use the term 'alcoholism', however, we should bear in mind that there is no precisely defined condition, activity, or entity called alcoholism in the way there is a precise condition known as lymphosarcoma of the mesenteric glands, for example. The actual usage of the term 'alcoholism', like 'addiction', has become primarily normative and prescriptive: a derogatory, stigmatizing word applied to people who drink 'too much'. The definition of 'too much' depends on the values of the speaker, which may be different from those of the person doing the drinking.

Calling addiction a 'disease' tells us more about the labeler than the labelee. Diseases are medical conditions. They can be discovered on the basis of bodily signs. They are something people have. They are involuntary. For example, the disease of syphilis was discovered. It is identified by specific signs. It is not a form of activity and is not based in human values. While certain behaviors increase the likelihood of acquiring syphilis, and while the acquisition of syphilis has consequences for subsequent social interaction, the behavior and the disease are separate phenomena. Syphilis meets the nosological criteria for disease classification in a pathology textbook. Unlike addiction, syphilis is a disease that can be diagnosed in a corpse.

Once we recognize that addiction cannot be classified as a literal disease, its nature as an ethical choice becomes clearer. A person starts, moderates, or abstains from drinking because that person wants to. People do the same thing with heroin, cocaine, and tobacco. Such choices reflect the person's values. The person, a moral agent, chooses to use drugs or refrains from using drugs because he or she finds meaning in doing so.

# NO ⟵

Alice M. Young

# Addictive Drugs and the Brain

Thomas De Quincey's 1821 essay, *Confessions of an English Opium-Eater,* vividly captures the psychological power of addictive drugs: "...thou hast the keys of Paradise, oh, just, subtle, and mighty opium!" How does opium or its modern relative, heroin, produce the compulsive drug use that we call addiction? Does addictive use of other drugs follow a similar course? Emerging answers to such questions suggest that all addictive drugs may co-opt normal brain processes of learning and emotion.

When De Quincey smoked opium, the smoke delivered morphine and codeine (and numerous other agents contained in opium) into his lungs. These agents moved directly from his lungs into his bloodstream and out through his body. They reached his brain in seconds. Similarly, when a modern user injects, smokes, or snorts heroin, blood carries the drug throughout the body and into the brain. As heroin reaches the brain, it is rapidly metabolized to morphine, which disperses over the surfaces of the brain's nerve cells, or neurons. In some areas of the brain, the morphine encounters small specialized proteins lodged in the outer membranes of certain neurons. These proteins are called opioid receptors ('receptor' for their ability to receive information from the neuron's surroundings, and 'opioid' because they detect opium-like substances). Morphine rapidly attaches and detaches from these opioid receptors. As it does so, it initiates a cascade of actions in the neurons housing the opioid receptors and in the neurons with which they communicate. These actions produce the profound psychological and physiological effects of morphine and other opioids. Some of these actions may underlie addiction.

Current ideas about the brain's role in addiction arise from both psychology and biology. Psychology contributes the concepts of reward and conditioning. These concepts link drug addiction to two important human attributes—our ability to learn and remember through experience and our tendency to repeat actions that had reinforcing consequences in the past. Biology contributes the concept of chemical communication systems in the brain, systems critical to learning and memory.

# Learning Processes Linked to Drug Seeking and Drug Taking

Experimental psychology has shown that, for humans as for other organisms, voluntary behaviors are influenced by their consequences. A voluntary behavior that has a positive consequence today is likely to be repeated in the future. Put another way, we repeatedly engage in behaviors that produce pleasurable feelings and positive reinforcers or rewards. We also repeat behaviors that avoid or escape noxious feelings or negative reinforcers. This fundamental learning process, often called instrumental or operant conditioning, is a primary way that we learn skillful and complex voluntary behaviors.

Our biological, cultural, and social histories have given us normal tendencies to repeat voluntary behaviors that produce a range of natural rewards. These rewards include food, water, sex, social contact, and avoidance of aggressive or painful encounters. Our responsiveness to these natural rewards helps ensure that we engage in behaviors that are critical for our survival as individuals and as a species—behaviors of eating, drinking, procreating, nurturing, and escaping from danger. Neuroscientists are beginning to identify pathways and circuits in the brain that organize our responsiveness to these naturally rewarding activities. Among the chief candidates are circuits involved in behavioral integration, learning, and cognition. These circuits are linked to other circuits that serve perceptual and motor behaviors, and they may be particularly important in forging strong motivations and drives.

We also respond to such artificial rewards as money, consumer goods, and drugs. Artificial rewards engage the same brain circuits as do natural rewards. Addictive drugs may be particularly effective rewards, producing a strong tendency for the user to engage repeatedly in drug seeking and drug use. Indeed, drug rewards can control long sequences of complex and highly directed behaviors that rival activities usually directed at more profitable goals such as strong family ties or professional rewards. Moreover, the effectiveness of addictive drugs as rewards may allow them to compete too effectively with other, more beneficial, rewards, leading to severe disruptions in many areas of a drug abuser's life.

Our natural response to rewards has another element that plays a crucial role in addiction. Over repeated encounters with effective rewards, we begin to associate the reward and the feelings it engenders with the surroundings in which we encounter it. Features or stimuli in those surroundings become associated with rewarding or other effects of drugs by a second fundamental learning process, that of Pavlovian conditioning. With repeated drug use, such conditioning can establish strong memories of drug use or drug effects. These memories can compel strong urges to seek or take the drug itself. Later in an individual's life, these memories can be triggered by encounters with small amounts of the drug or even by the stimuli alone. Such triggered memories probably underlie the cravings and relapses that characterize addictive drug use.

Addictive drugs use multiple strategies to commandeer natural processes and compel strong memories of drug use. Among the most important are their abilities to mimic or modulate brain neurotransmitters and trigger adaptive changes in brain circuits involved in basic learning and emotional processes.

## Addictive Drugs and Brain Neurotransmitters

Drugs that have the potential to be addictive for their users actually represent a small minority of the types of drugs we use to affect biological function. The great majority of drugs do not have the ability to establish and reinforce strong behavioral repertoires or compel conditioned memories. The key features of addictive drugs are their special effects on brain chemistry.

The addictive drugs comprise a diverse set of chemicals that differ in their structure and affinity for biological tissues, in their ability to be carried by the body's natural absorption and distribution routes, and in their susceptibility to the body's natural metabolic and excretion systems. It is important to note that the different addictive drugs produce different effects on body systems and markedly different immediate or long-term health consequences. In addition to these differences, however, addictive drugs share a common ability to influence brain chemistry involved in basic processes of reinforcement, learning, and memory.

As a user drinks alcohol, snorts cocaine, or smokes a cigarette, the body's natural systems deliver the chemicals in the drug source throughout the body. The specific drug used and its amount and route of administration will determine its speed of entry into the brain, but most addictive drugs enter the brain very rapidly. Once in the brain, they initiate their actions via the brain's own neurotransmitters. Neurotransmitters are the natural chemicals that neurons use to communicate among themselves and with the rest of the body. Addictive drugs initiate their actions, including those actions that lead to addiction, by mimicking or blocking the brain's neurotransmitters, or by modulating their activity. For example, nicotine (a key addictive component of tobacco products) mimics the natural neurotransmitter acetylcholine. Caffeine, the active drug in coffee, blocks the neurotransmitter adenosine. Cocaine, derived from the coca plant, alters levels of three natural neurotransmitters: dopamine, serotonin, and norepinephrine.

Other addictive drugs influence neurotransmitter systems that were unknown until neuroscientists looked for their targets in the brain. The brain's own opioid neurotransmitters—the endorphins, enkephalins, and dynorphins —were found by researchers investigating how heroin and morphine produce their addictive actions. Avram Goldstein, who spearheaded the discovery of dynorphin, provides a highly readable account of the search for neurotransmitters linked to addictive drugs in his book *Addiction* (W.H. Freeman, 1994). He notes that, "If not for the brain receptors, with their amazing specificity, all the addictive drugs would have the same biologic actions (or more likely, none at all)" (p. 311). The last point is important, because it highlights the fact that the ability of addictive drugs to interact with the brain's normal receptors makes these chemicals 'drugs' rather than poisons or inert agents.

Addictive drugs seem to have a preferential ability to mimic, block, or modulate the neurotransmitters that our brains use to learn and remember highly reinforcing activities. To state the case baldly, addictive drugs may hijack our brains' natural responses to rewards. Drugs such as alcohol, nicotine, heroin, and cocaine may short-circuit the natural reward pathways that have evolved to ensure that we engage in activities critical to our survival.

One working hypothesis in this area suggests that addictive drugs may share a common ability to alter the levels of dopamine in brain areas critical for learning. Although this hypothesis is surely too simplistic, it has guided productive studies that have illuminated how addictive drugs can interact with brain chemistry.

Studies in animals suggest that many addictive drugs change the levels of dopamine in brain pathways linked to the reward circuits described above. One suggested circuit involves areas called the ventral tegmental area (VTA), the nucleus accumbens, and the frontal cortex. The VTA communicates with the nucleus accumbens by releasing the neurotransmitter dopamine, and such release is correlated with activities that animals find highly rewarding. Cocaine and amphetamine powerfully increase the levels of dopamine at the juncture of the VTA and the nucleus accumbens. They do so by blocking the uptake processes that neurons normally use to stop dopamine's actions and, in the case of amphetamine, by causing neurons to release dopamine. The resulting increase in dopamine levels may be critical to the addictive properties of cocaine and amphetamine. Several lines of evidence support this idea. Included in the evidence is the finding that drugs which block the actions of dopamine at its targets can dampen the addictive power of cocaine or amphetamine. Moreover, recent studies suggest that changes in genes that code for receptors for dopamine can produce marked, and unexpected, changes in the avidity with which genetically altered animals seek addictive drugs.

Other addictive drugs also influence the circuit linking the VTA, nucleus accumbens, and frontal cortex. This circuit is rich in neurochemicals, regulating its normal activities via numerous neurotransmitters and their receptors. Its normal neurotransmitters include those targeted by major classes of addictive drugs, including opioids (heroin, morphine, and their relatives), sedatives (alcohol, barbiturates, and benzodiazepines), and nicotine. The working hypothesis described above has been expanded to suggest that these drugs exert addictive actions by regulating the release of dopamine in the circuit, often by complex interlocking mechanisms.

These interactions of drugs with brain reward systems—including the compulsive quality of the behaviors they engender—may be similar to those evoked by other highly reinforcing human activities. Recent imaging studies suggest that the brain areas involved in our reactions to stimuli associated with addictive drugs may be similar to those involved in other compulsive activities such as gambling. More work is required to understand the implications of such similarities.

## Changes in Brain Actions With Repeated Drug Use

The interactions among drugs and their brain targets may change when drugs are used repeatedly. At least three different types of change are important for addictive drug use. First, repeated use of a drug can produce tolerance, so that a higher dose must be used to achieve a given level of response. In the case of some drugs, such tolerance occurs because the body begins to break the drug down more efficiently. In the case of many other drugs, tolerance appears to occur at the neurons themselves. For example, when morphine binds to opioid receptors in some brain areas, it initiates a cascade of actions in the neuron. One of these actions slows the activity of an enzyme (adenylate cyclase) that orchestrates the chemical reactions needed for proper neuronal firing. After repeated activation of the opioid receptor by morphine, the enzyme adapts so that the morphine no longer stimulates changes in neuronal firing. Thus, the effect of a given dose of morphine is diminished.

Second, repeated use of some drugs can produce a state of dependence (often called physical dependence), in which nerves in the brain and elsewhere adapt to repeated drug exposure and function normally only in the presence of the drug. If the drug is withdrawn, severe physiological reactions occur. These are often called a 'withdrawal syndrome.' The withdrawal syndrome can be relatively mild (as when I miss my morning cup of coffee), pronounced (as when a high-dose heroin user misses a fix), or life-threatening (as when a severely dependent alcoholic stops drinking suddenly). The brain areas involved in withdrawal reactions may differ from those involved in the rewarding or conditioned effects of drugs, but the psychological reactions to withdrawal can alter these effects.

A third way in which experience alters brain chemistry is in the operation of the reward pathways themselves. With repeated use of cocaine or amphetamine, for example, the neurons in the VTA may decrease their production of dopamine, probably by invoking feedback mechanisms normally used to counter excess production of dopamine. Thus, the cocaine-using individual may begin to have a deficient production of dopamine. If this deficient production is not corrected when cocaine use ceases, the individual may have an altered brain reward system. Such long-term changes in brain chemistry may support conditioning processes that trigger cravings and relapses.

## Caveats

Our understanding of the brain's role in addiction is complicated by another feature of addictive drugs. Specifically, patients who use these drugs as clinical medicines usually do not become addicted.

In the case of opioids, the basis for continued medical use was stated succinctly by Sydenham in 1680: "Among the remedies which it has pleased Almighty God to give to man to relieve his sufferings, none is so universal and so efficacious as opium" (Goodman & Gilman. *The Pharmacological Basis of Therapeutics*. MacMillan, 1941, p. 186). Modern opioids, including highly addictive agents, remain a critical therapy for acute and chronic pain. The patient who receives morphine or other opioids for management of severe pain encounters all of the brain actions of opioids discussed above. Indeed, patients receiving opioids for pain may use higher doses, and develop more severe physical dependence, than do opioid addicts. And yet, most of these patients face little risk of addiction. This contrasts with the repetitive drug seeking and drug taking that characterize opioid abusers. What underlies such profound differences in vulnerability to addictive drug use?

It is likely that this question has multiple answers, only some of which can be glimpsed now. First, individuals may differ in their biological or genetic vulnerability to the rewarding or conditioned actions of addictive drugs. Studies in animals suggest that this is true for vulnerability to the rewarding actions of alcohol and opioids, and similar differences may occur in people. Second, the setting and expectancies associated with drug use influence the development of addiction. Third, individuals may differ in learned vulnerability. Individuals who have learned abusive use of one drug may more easily relearn abusive use of the same or a second drug than will an individual who has never abused a drug. Alternatively, other early experiences may increase susceptibility to the rewarding effects of drugs. For example, animal studies suggest that highly stressful experiences may alter susceptibility to drug reward. Finally, voluntary self-administration of a drug may activate chemical systems in the brain different from those activated when the same drug is administered by an outside party. Again, studies in animals suggest that animals which voluntarily seek out and self-administer cocaine or opioids show different changes in neurotransmitter activities than do animals which receive identical doses involuntarily. These differences highlight the importance of individual experience in shaping the neurochemical impact of addictive drugs.

In summary, addictive drugs may be said to capture their users by hijacking brain systems that support reward processes required for survival. On the other hand, the user's individual experience and genetic heritage shape the neurochemical impact of addictive drugs. Thus, addiction is not an inevitable outcome of drug exposure. Addiction requires active interactions among the potential user's brain chemistry, genetic vulnerability, and individual experience. [T]his view of addiction has important implications for our design of prevention and treatment efforts.

# POSTSCRIPT

## Is Drug Addiction a Choice?

There is little debate that drug addiction is a major problem. Drug addiction wreaks havoc for society and ruins the lives of numerous individuals. The causes of drug addiction are divergent. Because drug abuse can be viewed as a matter of free will and as a brain disorder, there are also different views on how society should deal with drug abusers. Should drug addicts be incarcerated or treated?

One could argue that free will and the concept of a brain disorder both apply to drug addiction. People do not choose to become addicted when they choose to use drugs, and what may start out as an occasional behavior may become abusive. For example, a person may use alcohol for social purposes, but eventually his or her use could develop into a chronic pattern that cannot be stopped. Initially, one can stop using alcohol without too much discomfort. As time passes, however, and drinking becomes heavier, stopping for some becomes difficult. By its very definition, social drinkers can stop drinking at will. Alcoholics drink out of necessity.

In addition, many people who use addictive drugs do not become dependent on them. Perhaps there are factors beyond free will and changes in the brain that account for those who become dependent. Is it possible that social factors also come into play? Can friends and colleagues and their attitudes about drugs influence whether or not a drug user becomes a drug abuser? In the final analysis, drug addiction may result from the interaction of numerous factors and not simply be a dichotomy between psychology and biology.

Alan Leshner, director of the National Institute on Drug Abuse, states that there are 72 risk factors for drug abuse and addiction. Of course, one may have many of these risk factors yet not become drug dependent. Not all risk factors are equally important, according to Leshner. Like Young, Leshner states that drug addiction is caused by changes in the brain. More of Leshner's views are discussed in Jerry Stilkind, "Addiction Is a Brain Disease: An Interview With Dr. Alan Leshner," *USIA Electronic Journal* (June 1997). Sally Satel, in "The Fallacies of No-Fault Addiction," *Public Interest* (Winter 1999), describes the views of numerous drug addiction experts. An article that supports the idea that drug addiction is primarily genetic is Ronald Kotaluk, "Nearly Everyone Inherits Genetic Vulnerability to Drug Abuse," *Chicago Tribune* (March 14, 1999).

# ISSUE 7

# Is Harm Reduction a Desirable National Drug Control Policy Goal?

**YES: Robert J. MacCoun**, from "Toward a Psychology of Harm Reduction," *American Psychologist* (November 1998)

**NO: Grazyna Zajdow**, from "Harm Reduction for Whom?" *Arena Magazine* (April 1999)

### ISSUE SUMMARY

**YES:** Robert J. MacCoun, an associate professor in the Graduate School of Public Policy at the University of California, Berkeley, supports efforts to minimize problems associated with drugs. He states that a harm reduction approach will not resolve all drug problems, but he feels that reducing those problems is a desirable goal.

**NO:** Sociology professor Grazyna Zajdow questions a policy that strives to reduce the harm of drugs. She maintains that drug use will remain a serious health problem regardless of whether or not harm reduction is the goal. Zajdow contends that using methadone to help heroin addicts overcome their addiction is merely the replacement of one addiction for another.

There is little debate as to whether or not drug use has the potential to cause adverse physical and psychological effects upon the user. Moreover, the families and communities of drug users are affected as well. It would be desirable if people always did that which was good for themselves, their families, and their communities. However, people do not always act in health-promoting ways. Tens of millions of people engage in unhealthy behaviors such as ingesting cocaine, smoking marijuana, drinking large quantities of alcohol, inhaling solvents, smoking cigarettes, and injecting heroin. The question is not whether drug use is harmful to the individual or whether drug use is the cause of many of the problems in our society. Rather, one needs to ask, What strategy is most likely to limit or reduce problems resulting from drug use?

There are various approaches that can be taken to address drug use. One approach focuses on harm reduction. Another approach focuses on supply reduction. The harm reduction approach attempts to minimize the dangers of drug use. The premise behind this approach is that since millions of people take drugs and that many will continue to take drugs regardless of whether or not they are legal, it is logical to teach people how to lessen the problems associated with using drugs. A harm reduction approach attempts to curtail drug-related problems while also trying to diminish drug use. Reducing the demand for drugs is an important component of this approach.

Even if individuals do cause harm to themselves, are there policies that can be enacted to limit the risks that drugs pose to other members of society? Harm reduction opponents argue that all members of society would be better served by improving and expanding enforcement of existing drug laws. Harm reduction advocates maintain that current restrictive policies that strive for supply reduction by emphasizing drug enforcement, prosecution, and interdiction have been ineffective and that alternatives need to be explored.

Some of the goals of harm reduction include reducing violence related to the drug trade, lowering death rates directly attributable to drugs, reducing infectious diseases caused by drug use, and preventing the ravages of drugs from affecting family members. Another benefit may be economical in that less money would go for enforcement and prosecution, although more funds would be needed for drug prevention, education, and treatment. On the other hand, harm reduction may result in greater drug use and more people seeking drug treatment. Harm reduction opponents maintain that stiff drug laws act as important deterrents. Moreover, many people who are arrested for drug-related offenses receive treatment for their drug abuse while incarcerated.

Opponents of harm reduction feel that its advocates are hypocritical and point out that its advocates demand more stringent policies regarding tobacco advertising, smoking restrictions, and driving while under the influence of alcohol, while calling for a reduction in the penalties for illegal drug use. It is true that tobacco and alcohol cause more deaths and disabilities than illegal drugs do. However, it is not known whether or not a policy of harm reduction would increase the number of deaths and disabilities from illegal drugs.

Drug prohibition proponents state that, following the decriminalization of marijuana in the Netherlands, there was an increase in shootings, robberies, and car thefts, as well as a rise in the rate of drug addiction. Even if the evidence demonstrated that decriminalization of marijuana in the Netherlands had beneficial effects, would it mean that marijuana decriminalization in the United States would have the same effects?

The following selections debate whether or not a policy of harm reduction would lessen the adverse health and social effects that come from using illegal drugs. Robert J. MacCoun contends that a harm reduction approach should be expanded because it has been shown to be effective. Grazyna Zajdow questions the contention that a policy of harm reduction would eliminate the negative consequences of drugs and argues that restrictive policies are necessary because they deter drug use.

**Robert J. MacCoun**

 **YES**

# Toward a Psychology of Harm Reduction

This article discusses 3 different strategies for dealing with the harmful consequences of drug use and other risky behaviors: We can discourage people from engaging in the behavior (prevalence reduction), we can encourage people to reduce the frequency or extent of the behavior (quantity reduction), or we can try to reduce the harmful consequences of the behavior when it occurs (harm reduction). These strategies are not mutually exclusive; this article offers a framework for integrating them. The framework is useful for examining frequent claims that harm reduction "sends the wrong message." Opposition to harm reduction is based in part on a recognition of potential trade-offs among the strategies, but it is also fueled by several more symbolic psychological factors. Strategies for successfully integrating prevalence reduction, quantity reduction, and harm reduction are explored.

During the 1980s, a grassroots movement called *harm reduction* (or harm minimization) emerged in Amsterdam, Rotterdam, and Liverpool as a response to pervasive drug-related public health problems (Heather, Wodak, Nadelmann, & O'Hare, 1993). The movement gradually spread to many other European cities, eventually influencing the policies of several nations (MacCoun, Saiger, Kahan, & Reuter, 1993). Harm reduction is not yet a well-developed approach. Rather, it is a set of programs that share certain public health goals and assumptions. Central among them is the belief that it is possible to modify the behavior of drug users, and the conditions in which they use, in order to reduce many of the most serious risks that drugs pose to public health and safety. Examples of specific harm reduction interventions for drug use include needle and syringe exchange, low-threshold methadone maintenance, "safe-use" educational campaigns, and the use of treatment as an alternative to incarceration for convicted drug offenders.

## The Ends of Drug Control

Table 1 lists and briefly defines six overlapping drug control strategies. The first two have dominated the American drug policy debate, centered on the appropriate balance between *supply reduction* (interdiction, source country control,

From Robert J. MacCoun, "Toward a Psychology of Harm Reduction," *American Psychologist*, vol. 53, no. 11 (November 1998). Copyright © 1998 by The American Psychological Association. Adapted with permission. References omitted.

domestic drug law enforcement) and *demand reduction* (treatment, prevention) in the federal budget. But despite their disagreements, demand-side and supply-side advocates share a common allegiance to what might be called the use reduction paradigm—the view that the highest, if not the exclusive, goal of drug policy should be to reduce (and hopefully eliminate) psychoactive drug use. In both practice and rhetoric, use reduction usually means *prevalence reduction.* That is, the goal has been to reduce the total number of users by discouraging initiation on the part of nonusers, and by promoting abstinence for current users. Table 1 introduces three newer terms—*quantity reduction, micro harm reduction,* and *macro harm reduction*—that are described in more detail below. These terms add more jargon to an already jargon-laden domain, but I hope to show that they make it possible to think more strategically about options for effective drug control.

*Table 1*

### Overlapping Drug Control Strategies

| Strategy | Goal |
| --- | --- |
| Supply reduction | Reduce total supply of drugs |
| Demand reduction | Reduce total demand for drugs |
| Prevalence reduction | Reduce total number of drug users |
| Quantity reduction | Reduce total quantity consumed |
| Micro harm reduction | Reduced average harm per use of drugs |
| Macro harm reduction | Reduce total drug-related harm |

The harm reduction critique of the enforcement-oriented U.S. drug strategy is twofold. First, prevalence-reduction policies have failed to eliminate drug use, leaving its harms largely intact. Second, these harsh enforcement policies are themselves a *source* of many drug-related harms, either directly or by exacerbating the harmful consequences of drug use (Nadelmann, 1989). Although many drug-related harms result from the psychopharmacologic effects of drug consumption, many others are mostly attributable to drug prohibition and its enforcement (MacCoun, Reuter, & Schelling, 1996). These harms would be greatly reduced, if not eliminated, under a regime of legal availability. The acknowledgment that prohibition is a source of harm does not imply that legalizing drugs would necessarily lead to a net reduction in harm; as we shall see, much depends on the effects of legal change on levels of drug use (MacCoun, 1993; MacCoun & Reuter, 1997). But by almost exclusively relying on use reduction—especially drug law enforcement—as an indirect means of reducing harm, we are foregoing opportunities to reduce harm directly. We are even increasing some harms in the process.

## American Resistance to Harm Reduction

With remarkable consistency, the U.S. government has aggressively resisted harm reduction (Kirp & Bayer, 1993; Reuter & MacCoun, 1995). For example, there are probably more than 1 million injecting drug users in this country, and injection drug use accounts for about one third of all AIDS cases. Though the evidence is not unanimous, a considerable body of evidence demonstrates that needle exchange programs can bring about significant reductions in HIV transmission (Des Jarlais, Friedman, & Ward, 1993; General Accounting Office, 1993; Hurley, Jolley, & Kaldor, 1997; Lurie & Reingold, 1991).[1] Lurie and Drucker (1997) recently estimated that between 4,394 and 9,666 HIV infections could have been prevented in the United States between 1987 and 1995 if a national needle exchange program had been in place. Yet there are fewer than 100 needle exchange programs operating in the United States. Why? Because prescription laws, paraphernalia laws, and local "drug-free zone" ordinances ban needle exchange programs in most of the country. Indeed, almost half of the existing programs are operating under an illicit or quasi-legal status. Despite the fact that these programs have been endorsed by the Centers for Disease Control, the National Academy of Sciences, and various leading medical journals and health organizations, drug policy officials in the federal government and most state governments have actively opposed needle exchange. In 1998, Department of Health and Human Services (DHHS) Secretary Donna Shalala publicly endorsed needle exchange on scientific grounds, but subsequently announced that the administration had decided that federal funding of needle exchanges would be unwise. A *Washington Post* story claimed that DHHS officials had arranged her press conference in the mistaken belief that the President would support needle exchange funding; Secretary Shalala's memo of talking points announcing his support was reported to say "the evidence is airtight" and "from the beginning of this effort, it has been about science, science, science" (J. F. Harris & Goldstein, 1998).

Our almost exclusive emphasis on use reduction rather than harm reduction probably has many causes (Reuter & MacCoun, 1995). One is the fear that harm reduction is a Trojan horse for the drug legalization movement (e.g., McCaffrey, 1998). Another factor might be that whereas harm reduction focuses on harms to users, drug-related violence and other harms to *nonusers* are more salient in the United States than in Europe. In addition, prevalence is more readily measurable than harms, and few harm-reduction programs, with the notable exception of needle exchange, have been rigorously evaluated—though political opposition to harm reduction is itself a major cause of the lack of relevant data. But other objections involve beliefs about behavior. For example, it may seem only logical that reducing use is the best way to reduce harm.

But this logic holds only if the elimination of drug use is nearly complete, and if efforts to reduce use do not themselves cause harm. Unfortunately, many prevalence-reduction policies often fail on one or both counts. Although it is true that abstinence from drugs (or teenage sex, or drinking among alcoholics) is "100% effective" at reducing harm, the key policy question is whether we are 100% effective at convincing people to *become* abstinent. Finally, the most frequent objection to harm reduction is the claim that harm reduction programs will "send the wrong message." The logic by which harm reduction "sends the wrong message" is rarely articulated in any detail, suggesting that for its proponents, the proposition is self-evident. It seems likely that harm-reduction advocates will continue to face opposition in the United States until they successfully address this concern.

# Harm Reduction in Other Policy Domains

The tension between preventing a behavior and reducing the harmfulness of that behavior is not unique to the debate about illicit drugs. Table 2 lists some intriguing parallels in other contemporary American policy debates. Despite many superficial differences, each domain involves a behavior that poses risks to both the actor and others. And each raises the question about the relative efficacy of policies that aim to reduce the harmful consequences of a risky behavior (harm reduction) versus policies designed to discourage the behavior itself (prevalence or quantity reduction).

The first row of Table 2—safety standards for consumer products—is notable for its relative lack of controversy outside of the halls of Congress. Even though these safety regulations clearly have a harm-reduction rationale—albeit one generally not recognized as such—recent Congressional efforts to scale them back have received a remarkably lukewarm public response. But in the other domains listed in Table 2, a debate centers on the fear that an intervention to reduce harm—harm reduction in spirit if not in name—will in some way "send the wrong message," encouraging the risky behavior. The parallels to drugs are particularly striking for the topic of condom distribution in schools (and to a lesser degree, sex education). Advocates argue that condom distribution is needed to reduce the risks of unplanned pregnancies and sexually transmitted diseases, whereas opponents vociferously argue that distribution programs and other safe sex interventions actually promote sexual activity (Mauldon & Luker, 1996). On the other hand, recent U.S. debates about welfare and immigration benefits may seem to have little to do with concepts like risk regulation or harm reduction. But at an abstract level, the issues are similar. Assertions are made that policies designed to mitigate the harmful consequences of being unemployed, or of immigrating to the United States, actually encourage people to become (or remain) unemployed, or to immigrate to the United States. Aside from brief excursions into the lessons of motor vehicle safety standards and tobacco and alcohol policy, this article focuses almost exclusively on harm reduction for illicit drugs. But it seems possible that the analysis might provide insights for other domains of risk reduction—in part because my arguments

*Table 2*

### Policies Aimed at Reducing Harms Associated With Risky Behaviors

| Policy | Risky behavior | Harms that policy tries to reduce |
|---|---|---|
| Mandated safety standards for motor vehicles, toys, sports equipment, food, pharmaceuticals, and so on | Driving, participation in sports, consumption of products, and so on | Physical injury, illness, death |
| Needle exchange | Intravenous drug use | HIV transmission |
| Teaching of controlled drinking skills | Drinking by diagnosed alcoholics | Social, psychological, and physical harms of alcohol abuse |
| School condom programs | Unprotected sexual contact among teens | Sexually transmitted diseases, unwanted pregnancies |
| Welfare | Becoming or remaining unemployed | Poor quality of life (housing, health, education), especially for children |
| Provision of benefits for illegal immigrants | Illegal immigration to the United States | Poor quality of life (housing, health, education), especially for children |

were often informed by those literatures but also because it seems unlikely that the underlying behavioral questions are unique to the drug domain.

## Overview

The remainder of this [selection] explores critics' concerns about harm reduction. This [selection] does not attempt a comprehensive review of the evaluation literature on harm reduction or on the specifics of interventions at the clinical level (see Des Jarlais, Friedman, & Ward, 1993; Heather et al., 1993). Instead, the [selection] has four goals: (a) to demonstrate the value of distinguishing microlevel harm from macrolevel harm, and prevalence of a behavior from the quantity or frequency of that behavior; (b) to identify potential trade-offs between prevalence reduction, quantity reduction, and micro harm reduction; (c) to explore some nonconsequentialist psychological bases for opposition to harm reduction; and (d) to offer some tentative suggestions for successfully integrating harm reduction into our national drug control strategy. The next section examines two different senses in which harm reduction might "send the wrong message," either directly through its rhetorical effects or indirectly by making drug use less risky. I offer a theoretical framework for integrating prevalence-reduction and harm-reduction policies. I believe it offers a way of thinking about harm reduction that might reduce some of the barriers to a more flexible public health orientation to U.S. drug policy. But not necessarily. The tone of the harm-reduction debate suggests that attitudes toward drug policies—on both sides—are influenced by deeply rooted and strongly felt symbolic factors that are largely independent of concerns about policy effectiveness per se. These factors are explored in a later section.

# Use Reduction and Harm Reduction: An Integrative Framework

## Micro Versus Macro Harm Reduction

The efficacy of harm reduction depends on behavioral responses to policy interventions. In explaining this point, it is important to make a distinction between levels of analysis that is sometimes obscured in the harm-reduction literature. Let me begin with a truism that is largely overlooked in the harm-reduction debate: *Total Harm = Average Harm per Use × Total Use*, where total use is a function of the number of users and the quantity each user consumes, and average harm per use is a function of two vectors of specific drug-related harms, one involving harms to users (e.g., overdoses, addiction, AIDS), and the other involving harms to nonusers (e.g., HIV transmission, criminal victimization; MacCoun & Caulkins, 1996; Reuter & MacCoun, 1995).

Figure 1 depicts this relationship graphically using a causal path diagram. Links *a* and *b* depict the intended effects of harm-reduction and use-reduction policies, respectively. Links *c, d,* and *e* depict the ancillary harmful effects —unintended and often unanticipated—these policies might have. Link *c* denotes the unintended harms caused by prohibiting a risky behavior (e.g., the lack of clean needles, lack of drug quality control, violence associated with illicit markets, inflated prices that encourage income-generating crime, and so on; Nadelmann, 1989). This category of unintended harms is of central concern to any assessment of alternative legal regimes for drug control (MacCoun, Reuter, & Schelling, 1996). But here I focus on a second set of unintended consequences, those resulting from harm-reduction policies, to see whether objections to harm reduction have merit. If a harm-reduction strategy reduces harm per incident but leads to increases in drug use (links *d* and *e*), the policy might still achieve *net* harm reduction; on the other hand, a sufficiently large increase in use could actually result in an *increase* in total harm. There are two potential mechanisms for such an unintended consequence, one direct and one indirect. For reasons to be explained, link *d* can be conceptualized as the direct *rhetorical* effect (if any) of harm reduction on total use; link *e* is an indirect *compensatory behavior* effect. Either might be interpreted as "sending the wrong message."

## Direct Version: Does Harm Reduction Literally Send the Wrong Message?

The rhetorical hypothesis is that irrespective of their effectiveness in reducing harms, harm-reduction programs literally communicate messages that encourage drug use. As noted earlier, those who espouse this rhetorical hypothesis rarely explain how it is supposed to work. The most plausible interpretation is that without intending to do so, harm reduction sends tacit messages that are construed as approval—or at least the absence of strong disapproval—of drug consumption.

*Figure 1*

### Use Reduction and Harm Reduction: An Integrative Framework

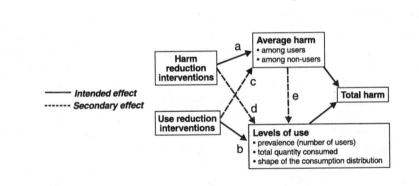

If harm reduction service providers *intend* to send a message, it is something like this: "We view drugs as harmful. We discourage you from using them, and we are eager to help you to quit if you've started. But if you will not quit using drugs, we can help you to use them less harmfully." Is that the only message? Psycholinguistic theory and research do suggest that people readily draw additional inferences that are *pragmatically implied* by an actor's conduct, regardless of whether those inferences were intended, or even endorsed, by the actor (R. J. Harris & Monaco, 1978; Wyer & Gruenfeld, 1995). Thus if we provide heroin users with clean needles, they might infer that we don't expect them to quit using heroin—if we did, why give them needles? Arguably, this perception could undermine their motivation to quit.

But would users infer that we believe heroin use is *good*, or at least "not bad"? It is not obvious how harm reduction might actually imply *endorsement* of drug use. Ultimately, whether any such rhetorical effects occur is an empirical question. It would be useful to assess the kinds of unintended inferences that users and nonusers draw from harm-reduction messages, and from the mere existence of harm-reduction programs. But in the absence of such evidence, the rhetorical hypothesis that harm-reduction conveys approval of drug use is purely speculative.

Moreover, it is difficult to reconcile this notion with the secondary prevention and treatment efforts that frequently accompany actual harm-reduction interventions. Through such efforts, users are informed that their behavior is dangerous to themselves and others and that assistance and support are available to help them if they wish to quit drug use. Braithwaite's (1989) research on *reintegrative shaming* indicates that it is possible simultaneously to send a social message that certain acts are socially unacceptable while still helping the actors to repair their lives. Braithwaite suggests that this approach is integral to Japanese culture, but it is also reflected in the Christian tradition of "hating the sin but loving the sinner."

## Indirect Version: Does a Reduction in Harm Make Drugs More Attractive?

Even if no one took harm reduction to imply government endorsement of drugs, harm reduction might still influence levels of drug use *indirectly* through its intended effect, that is, by reducing the riskiness of drug use. This is a second interpretation of "sending the wrong message." Though there are ample grounds for being skeptical of a pure "rational-choice" analysis of drug use (MacCoun, 1993), the notion that reductions in risk might influence drug use is certainly plausible and would be consistent with a growing body of evidence of compensatory behavioral responses to safety interventions. Thus we should be mindful of potential trade-offs between harm reduction and use reduction.

Risk assessors have known for some time that engineers tend to overestimate the benefits of technological improvements in the safety of traffic signals, automobiles, cigarettes, and other products. The reason is that engineers often fail to anticipate that technological improvements lead to changes in behavior. When technological innovations successfully reduce the probability of harm given unsafe conduct, they make that conduct less risky. And if the perceived risks were motivating actors to behave somewhat self-protectively, a reduction in risk should lead them to take fewer precautions than before, raising the probability of their unsafe conduct to a higher level. This notion has been variously labeled *compensatory behavior, risk compensation, offsetting behavior,* or in its most extreme form, *risk homeostasis*—a term that implies efforts to maintain a constant level of risk (Wilde, 1982). Although some find this general idea counterintuitive, one economist has noted that, on reflection, it is hardly surprising that "soldiers walk more gingerly when crossing minefields than when crossing wheat fields," and "circus performers take fewer chances when practicing without nets" (Hemenway, 1988).

Compensatory behavioral responses to risk reduction have been identified in a variety of settings. For example, everything else being equal, drivers have responded to seat belts and other improvements in the safety of automobiles by driving faster and more recklessly than they would in a less safe vehicle (Chirinko & Harper, 1993). Similarly, filters and low-tar tobacco each reduce the harmfulness per unit of tobacco, yet numerous studies have demonstrated that smokers compensate by smoking more cigarettes, inhaling more deeply, or blocking the filter vents (Hughes, 1995). In both domains, some of the safety gains brought about by a reduction in the probability of harm given unsafe conduct have been offset by increases in the probability of that conduct. Though early correlational studies were criticized on methodological grounds, the compensatory behavioral hypothesis has received important support from recent controlled laboratory experiments (Stetzer & Hofman, 1996).

The compensatory behavioral mechanism suggests that if reductions in average drug-related harm were to motivate sufficiently large increases in drug use, micro harm reduction would actually increase macro harm. Blower and McLean (1994) offer a similar argument based on epidemiological simulations that suggest that an HIV vaccine, unless perfectly prophylactic, could actually exacerbate the San Francisco AIDS epidemic, provided that individuals behaved less cautiously in response to their increased sense of safety. But to date, research on compensatory responses to risk reduction provides little evidence that behavioral responses produce net increases in harm, or even the constant level of harm predicted by the "homeostatic" version of the theory. Instead, most studies find that when programs reduce the probability of harm given unsafe conduct, any increases in the probability of that conduct are slight, reducing but not eliminating the gains in safety (Chirinko & Harper, 1993; Hughes, 1995; Stetzer & Hofman, 1996). As a result, in our terms, micro harm reduction produces macro harm reduction.

## Do Drug Interventions Achieve Macro Harm Reduction?

It is impossible to calculate total drug harm in any literal fashion, or to rigorously compare total harm across alternative policy regimes (MacCoun, Reuter, & Schelling, 1996). Many of the harms are difficult to quantify, and observers will differ in their weighting of the various types of harm. Thus at the strategic level of national policy formation, macro harm reduction is not a rigid analytical test but rather a heuristic principle: Are we reducing drug harms, and reducing drug use in ways that do not increase drug harm? But at the level of specific interventions, macro reduction of *specific* harms is a realistic evaluation criterion, as illustrated by the compensatory behavioral research just cited. Unfortunately, few drug policy programs are evaluated with respect to both use reduction and harm reduction. Prevention and treatment programs are generally evaluated with respect to changes in abstinence or relapse rates, whereas harm reduction evaluators tend to assess changes in crime, morbidity, and mortality rates. As a result, researchers are unable to determine whether many programs achieve macro harm reduction.

The empirical literature on needle exchange is a notable and exemplary exception. There is now a fairly sizable body of evidence that needle exchange programs produce little or no measurable increase in injecting drug use (Lurie & Reingold, 1993; Watters, Estilo, Clark, & Lorvick, 1994). Because it significantly reduces average harm, needle exchange provides both micro and macro harm reduction. But the empirical success record for needle exchange does not constitute blanket support for the harm reduction movement. Each intervention must be assessed empirically on its own terms.

Let me offer a few cautionary tales. One harm reduction intervention that has been tried and rejected is the "zone of tolerance" approach tried by Zurich officials in the Platzspitz—or, as the American press labeled it, "Needle Park." By allowing injecting drug users to congregate openly in this public park, and to shoot up without police interference, city officials were able to make clean needles and other health interventions readily available at the time and place of drug use. Even sympathetic observers agree that these benefits were ultimately offset by increases in local crime rates and in the prevalence of hard drug use in the city (Grob, 1992). Another example involves bongs and water pipes. Though these devices have been touted as a means of reducing the health risks of marijuana smoking, a recent test found that they actually increase the quantity of tars ingested. The apparent reason harkens back to the compensatory behavioral mechanism. Water pipes filter out more THC than tar, so users smoke more to achieve the same high, thereby increasing their risk (Gieringer, 1996). The Zurich case and the bong study suggest that harm-reduction strategies can fail, but it is important to note that neither failure resulted from increasing rates of *initiation* to drug use. In the Zurich case, the prevalence of drug use rose because the park attracted users from other Swiss cities and neighboring countries. Arguably, the program might have been successful had other European cities adopted the idea simultaneously. In the bong case, the filtering benefits were offset by increases in consumption levels among users, but I am unaware of any evidence that bongs and water pipes have ever encouraged nonusers to start smoking marijuana.

One can imagine hypothetical examples of how a harm-reduction strategy might plausibly attract new users. For example, from a public health perspective, we are better off if current heroin injectors switch to smoking their drug. Imagine a public information campaign designed to highlight the relative health benefits of smoking. If some fraction of nonusers have resisted heroin because of an aversion to needles (for anecdotal evidence, see Bennetto, 1998), our campaign might indeed end up encouraging some of them to take up heroin smoking, despite our best intentions. Of course, no one has seriously proposed such a campaign. But the example demonstrates that concerns about increased use are plausible in principle.

## Quantity Reduction as a Middle Ground?

As noted earlier, American drug policy rhetoric is dominated by concerns about the number of users, drawing a bright line between "users" and "nonusers." This is illustrated by our national drug indicator data. Most available measures of drug use are *prevalence* oriented: rates of lifetime use, use in the past year, or use in the past month. But drug-related harms may well be more sensitive to changes in the *total quantity consumed* than to changes in the total number of users. One million occasional drug users may pose fewer crime and health problems than 100,000 frequent users. Our nation's recent cocaine problems provide an illustration. After significant reductions in casual use in the 1980s, total consumption has become increasingly concentrated among a smaller number of heavy users. At an individual level, these heavy users are at much greater risk than casual users with respect to acute and chronic illness, accidents, job- and family-related problems, and participation in criminal activities. Thus although cocaine prevalence has declined, total cocaine consumption and its related harms have remained relatively stable (Everingham & Rydell, 1994).

This suggests that *quantity reduction* (reducing consumption levels) holds particular promise as a macro harm reduction strategy. Quantity reduction occupies a point halfway between prevalence reduction and micro harm reduction. Like prevalence reduction, quantity reduction targets use levels rather than harm levels. But like harm reduction, quantity reduction is based on the premise that when use cannot be prevented, we might at least be able to mitigate its harms.

What is less clear is the optimal targeting strategy for quantity reduction. Consider the distribution of users across consumption levels, which for most psychoactive drugs (licit and illicit) is positively skewed, with a long right tail indicating a small fraction of very heavy users. One strategy is to target those heaviest users—to "pull in" the right tail of the distribution. The marginal gains in risk reduction should be greatest at the right tail, and only a small fraction of users need be targeted.

This approach has received considerable attention—and notoriety—in the alcohol field under the rubric "controlled drinking." Few public health experts dispute the notion that problem drinkers are better off drinking lightly than drinking heavily. But there has been an extraordinary furor surrounding the notion of controlled drinking as a treatment goal. The evidence suggests that (a) although abstinence-based treatment programs experience high relapse rates, many of the relapsing clients successfully reduce their drinking to relatively problem-free levels; (b) it is possible to *teach* controlled drinking skills to many, but not all, problem drinkers; (c) we cannot yet predict which problem drinkers will be able to control their drinking at moderate levels; and (d) most treated problem drinkers fail to achieve either abstinence or controlled levels of drinking (Marlatt, Larimer, Baer, & Quigley, 1993). But opponents assert that, irrespective of any benefits to be derived from controlled drinking, the very notion undermines the goal of abstinence and discourages drinkers from achieving it. The small-scale studies conducted to date do not support that claim, but the evidence is not yet decisive.

In addition to the abstinence–moderation debate, a second quantity-reduction debate has emerged among alcohol experts. Are problem drinkers even the appropriate intervention target? An alternative quantity-reduction strategy targets the middle of the alcohol consumption distribution. For some years, many experts have argued that the total social costs of alcohol might be better reduced by lowering average consumption levels rather than concentrating on the most problematic drinkers at the right tail (Rose, 1992; Skog, 1993). If so—and this is a matter of ongoing debate in the pages of *Addiction* and other journals—broad-based efforts to reduce total drug use might indeed be the best way to achieve total harm reduction, at least for alcohol consumption. The controversy here has been more purely technical and less emotional than the controlled drinking debate, in part because few people still champion the notion of abstinence for casual drinkers. Many Americans seem quite willing to accept the notion of "nonproblem" alcohol consumption yet reject the notion of "nonproblem" marijuana or cocaine consumption.

In fact, the viability of "lower-risk" drug consumption, and the relative efficacy of the "pull in the tail" and the "lower the average" strategies, will depend on a variety of factors. One factor is the degree of skew of the consumption distribution: The greater the probability mass in the right tail, the greater the efficacy of targeting heavy users. A second is the dose-response curve for risks, which is usually S-shaped for those drug-risk combinations that have been studied. (We know a great deal more about dose-response functions for health and public safety risks involving licit drugs than for comparable risks involving illicit drugs.) When this function is very steep, even moderate consumption levels are very risky, making the "shift-the-distribution" strategy more efficacious. A third factor involves the possibility that individuals with a higher propensity for danger self-select higher consumption levels. The latter effect will spuriously inflate the quantity–risk relationship. To the extent that this effect predominates, convincing right-tail users to cut back may yield fewer benefits than anticipated.

## The Public Acceptability of Harm Reduction

Whereas American citizens and policymakers have embraced drug strategies that promote prevalence reduction, harm reduction and some forms of quantity reduction are often greeted with considerable hostility—when they are not ignored altogether. In this section, I offer a number of hypotheses about this negative reaction. The opposition to harm reduction surely has multiple causes, so these explanations are not mutually exclusive. They vary along a continuum ranging from *consequentialist* to *symbolic* grounds for opposition. Many people probably hold both kinds of views. Harm reduction opponents might be placed along this continuum based on their responses to the following hypothetical questions:

1. If new evidence suggested that needle exchange (or some other harm-reduction strategy) reduced total harm, would you still be opposed?
2. If the answer is "yes": If new evidence suggested a reduction in harm, *with no increase in use,* would you still be opposed?
3. If the answer is "yes": Would you be opposed to drug use even if it were made *completely* harmless?

Those who would say "no" to the first question are pragmatic or consequentialist in their opposition to harm reduction. Those who say "yes" to the third question are at the other extreme; for them, drug use is intrinsically immoral, irrespective of its consequences—what philosophers call a *deontological* stance. Those who would support harm reduction only if there were no increase in drug use fall somewhere in between. Their views might reflect a complex mix of instrumental and symbolic concerns.

## Consequentialist Grounds

The consequentialist grounds for opposing harm reduction are the easiest to describe. They are characterized primarily by the belief that harm reduction will be counterproductive, either by failing to reduce average harm or by increasing drug use enough to increase total harm. Those who oppose harm reduction on truly consequentialist grounds should change their mind and support it if the best available facts suggest that an intervention reduces harm without producing offsetting increases in use. In recent years, the favorable evidence for needle exchange has received increasing publicity in the mass media. This media coverage may explain why a 1996 poll found that 66% of Americans endorsed needle exchange as a means of preventing AIDS—a dramatic increase over earlier surveys (The Henry J. Kaiser Family Foundation, 1996). Of course, this may be an over-optimistic reading of the impact of empirical research (MacCoun, 1998). Program evaluations rarely yield unequivocal verdicts; even when effects are statistically reliable, they are usually open to multiple interpretations. Expert consensus on the effects of high-profile policy interventions is rare, even when the accumulated body of research is large. And the vehemence of the opposition to harm reduction suggests that attitudes toward these interventions are based on something more than purely instrumental beliefs about the effectiveness of alternative drug policies.

Attitudes toward the death penalty are instructive in this regard. Attitude research indicates that many citizens overtly endorse a *deterrence* rationale for the death penalty, believing that "it will prevent crimes." Yet most do not change their views when asked how they would feel if there were unequivocal evidence that execution provided no marginal deterrence above and beyond life imprisonment. The evidence suggests that ostensibly instrumental views are actually masking deeper retributive motives (Ellsworth & Gross, 1994). As a result, support for capital punishment is relatively impervious to research findings (Lord, Ross, & Lepper, 1979).

The nonconsequentialist grounds for opposing harm reduction are more complex than the consequentialist grounds. There are a number of distinct psychological processes that might play a role in shaping these views.[2]

## The Need for Predictability and Control

Harmonious social relations require a minimal level of predictability because we must routinely relinquish control to other people—automobile drivers, surgeons, airline pilots, our children's teachers, and so on. The notion that others are using drugs can be threatening because it suggests that they've lost some self-control. Although harm reduction can minimize the consequences of diminished control, it may be more reassuring to believe that others are completely abstinent. When we are unable to control aversive stimuli, any signal that helps us to anticipate danger will significantly reduce our anxiety (Miller,

1980). Perhaps the belief that others are abstinent from drugs works like a "safety signal" to free us from worrying about their conduct.

Our fears about others are augmented by a robust bias in risk perceptions. Most people—adults as well as adolescents—perceive themselves to be less vulnerable than the average person to risks of injury or harm (e.g., Weinstein & Klein, 1995). An apparent corollary is that most of us believe we are surrounded by people less cautious or skillful than ourselves. We may think we can control our own use of intoxicants (most of us feel that way about alcohol), but we find it harder to believe that others will do the same. Indeed, this might explain why a sizable minority of regular cannabis users opposes the complete legalization of that drug (Erickson, 1989).

## Aversion to Making Value Trade-Offs

Our attitudes toward public policy involve more than simple judgments about effectiveness and outcomes. They are symbolic expressions of our core values. Unfortunately, most difficult social problems bring core values into conflict. Drug problems are no exception; they bring personal liberty into conflict with public safety, compassion into conflict with moral accountability. Contemplating harm reduction brings these conflicts into strong relief. According to [Philip E.] Tetlock's *value pluralism model,* acknowledging such conflicts is psychologically aversive, and so many people avoid explicit trade-off reasoning, preferring simpler mental strategies (Tetlock, Peterson, & Lerner, 1996). The easiest is to deny that there is a conflict, by ignoring one value or the other. If that doesn't work, we may adopt a simple "lexicographic" ranking. Many of us engage in complex multidimensional trade-off reasoning only when we can't avoid it, as when the conflicting values are each too salient to dismiss or ignore.

In a recent content analysis of op-ed essays debating the reform of drug laws, my colleagues and I found that legalizers and decriminalizers (all of whom were harm-reduction advocates, though the converse is not necessarily true) used significantly more complex arguments than prohibitionists (MacCoun, Kahan, Gillespie, & Rhee, 1993). The reform advocates were less likely to view the drug problem in terms of a simple good–bad dichotomy; they identified multiple dimensions to the problem and were more likely to acknowledge trade-offs and counterarguments to their own position. It may be hard to persuade others to acknowledge the full complexity of harm-reduction logic unless the values that support it become more salient in drug policy discourse.

## The Propriety of Helping Drug Users

Of course, there is little basis for value conflict if one feels that drug users *should* suffer harm when they use drugs. There are a number of reasons why some people might hold this view. One is authoritarianism, a complex trait defined as a chronic tendency to cope with anxiety by expressing hostility toward outgroup members; intolerance of unconventional behavior; and submissive, unquestioning support of authority figures. Authoritarianism is strongly correlated with support for punitive drug policies (Peterson, Doty, & Winter, 1993). Indeed, several items from the Right Wing Authoritarianism Scale—a leading research instrument for measuring this trait—seem to equate authoritarianism with opposition to harm-reduction interventions almost by definition (Christie, 1991). According to Item 7, "The facts on crime, sexual immorality, and the recent public disorders all show we have to crack down harder on deviant groups and troublemakers if we are going to save our moral standards and preserve law and order." Item 12 states, "Being kind to loafers or criminals will only encourage them to take advantage of your weakness, so it's best to use a firm, tough hand when dealing with them." And authoritarians are more likely to disagree with Item 19: "The courts are right in being easy on drug offenders. Punishment would not do any good in cases like these."

But scoring high in authoritarianism is probably not a prerequisite for hostility toward drug users. There is a general antagonism to hard drug users among U.S. citizens, partly stemming from the strong association between drugs and street violence in American cities. It is much easier to see harshness as the appropriate response in the United States than in Europe, where drug use is more likely to be perceived as a health problem. Race and social distance may play a role here as well; arguably, Americans were more tolerant of drug users in the 1970s, when the mass media's prototypical drug user was an Anglo-American student in a college dorm instead of a young African American man on a city street corner (Kirp & Bayer, 1993). As a result, Americans have supported (or at least tolerated) sentencing policies that tend to disproportionately burden minority and poor offenders relative to those who are Anglo-American or middle class (Tonry, 1995).

But irrespective of race and class, the mere fact that someone uses drugs will often be sufficient to categorize them as "the other," particularly if we don't already know them. Citizens with a friend or family member who is an addict may embrace micro harm reduction, whatever its aggregate consequences, but those who don't know any addicts may prefer a strategy of isolation and containment.

Even in the absence of malice, many people may feel that addicts should suffer the consequences of their actions. Addiction is widely viewed as a voluntary state, regardless of many experts' views to the contrary (Weiner, Perry, & Magnusson, 1988). Many Americans, especially conservatives, are unwilling to extend help to actors who are responsible for their own suffering; such actors are seen as undeserving (Skitka & Tetlock, 1993). The retributive view that bad acts require punishment is deeply rooted in the Judeo-Christian tradition, particularly in Protestant fundamentalist traditions. In light of the possibility that opposition to harm reduction traces back to our nation's strong Puritan and Calvinist roots, it is quite ironic that the Dutch and the Swiss have championed such an approach in Europe.

## Disgust and Impurity

A final ground for opposing harm reduction might be the vague, spontaneous, and nonrational sense that drug use defiles the purity of the body and hence that anything that comes in contact with drug users becomes disgusting through a process of contagion. Stated so bluntly, this may sound utterly implausible; such concepts are quite alien to Western moral discourse. Nevertheless, this kind of thinking is quite explicit in other cultures, and anthropologists argue that it often lurks below the surface of our own moral judgments (Douglas, 1966; Haidt, Koller, & Dias, 1993). I know of no direct evidence that such reactions influence attitudes toward drug policy, but the hypothesis is testable in principle and worthy of further investigation.

# Conclusion

In this [selection], I have tried to take a frank look at the arguments against harm reduction, and I have suggested that, like most policy interventions, the approach has potential pitfalls. Not every harm-reduction intervention will be successful, and some might even increase aggregate harm. We are still woefully ignorant about the complex interplay between formal drug policies and informal social and self-control factors (MacCoun, 1993). Still, the evidence to date on harm reduction is encouraging (as the success of needle exchange programs makes clear), and I believe that we have much to gain by integrating harm-reduction interventions and goals into our national drug control strategy. I conclude by offering five hypotheses about how harm reduction might be more successful—successful both in reducing aggregate harm and in attracting and retaining a viable level of political support.

1. Harm-reduction interventions should have the greatest political viability when they can demonstrate a reduction in average harm—especially harms that affect nonusers—without increasing drug use levels. Interventions that lead to increases in drug use are likely to encounter stiff opposition, even if they yield demonstrable net reductions in aggregate harm. Thus, harm-reduction interventions need to be rigorously evaluated with respect to four types of outcome: effects on targeted harms, "side effects" on untargeted harms (especially harms to nonusers), effects on participants' subsequent use levels, and effects on local nonparticipants' use levels.

2. Because the compensatory behavioral mechanism is triggered by perceived changes in risk, harm-reduction efforts seem least likely to increase drug use when those harms being reduced were already significantly underestimated, discounted, or ignored by users and potential users (see Wilde, 1982). At one extreme, if perceptions of risk are serious enough, few people will use the drug in the first place. (Witness the almost complete disappearance of absinthe after its dangers became apparent in the late 19th century.) At the other extreme, those who are either ignorant of, or indifferent to, a drug's risks, seem unlikely to escalate their use when an intervention lowers those risks.

3. Similarly, interventions involving safe-use information or risk-reducing paraphernalia should be less likely to increase total use, and hence be more politically viable, when they are highly salient for heavy users but largely invisible to potential initiates to drug use. Maintenance interventions, which provide drugs or drug substitutes for addicts, should

be less likely to encourage use if the program has few barriers to entry for heavy users but high barriers to entry for casual users. (The risk of these targeting strategies is that new initiates may fail to obtain the benefits of the interventions.)

4. Reducing users' consumption levels should generally provide harm reduction, an important strategy for achieving use reduction when heavy users refuse to become abstinent.

5. Whenever feasible, harm-reduction interventions should be coupled with credible primary and secondary prevention efforts, as well as low-threshold access to treatment.

This last point is a truism among many harm-reduction providers. Still, a few in the harm-reduction movement are uncomfortable with the notion that harm-reduction programs should urge users to stop their drug use. Some take that position on libertarian grounds, but others associate traditional use-reduction efforts with dishonesty ("reefer madness"), hypocrisy ("what about alcohol and tobacco?"), or an apparent willingness to jeopardize user health (e.g., the U.S. decision to spray Mexican marijuana crops with paraquat in the 1970s). But harm-reduction advocates who categorically reject the opposition risk undermining their own cause. Americans who oppose harm reduction are unlikely to change their views until they feel their fears have been taken seriously.

## Notes

1. This finding is not universal; participation in needle exchanges was associated with elevated HIV risk in recent studies in Vancouver (Strathdee et al., 1997) and Montreal (Bruneau et al., 1997), though the authors caution that this association might reflect features that distinguish these evaluations from others in the literature; for example, they were conducted at the peak of the HIV epidemic, their clients were heavily involved in cocaine injection, and the number of needles dispersed fell well short of the amount needed to prevent needle sharing (Bruneau & Schechter, 1998). A broader comparison of 81 U.S. cities estimated a 5.9% increase in HIV seroprevalence in 52 cities without needle exchange, and a 5.8% decrease in 29 cities with needle exchange during the period 1988 to 1993 (Hurley, Jolley, & Kaldor, 1997).

2. Note that these psychological accounts by themselves do not constitute evidence for or against the wisdom of opposition to harm reduction, nor are they meant to imply that such views are somehow pathological.

# NO ↵

Grazyna Zajdow

# Harm Reduction for Whom?

## Some Guilty Thoughts on New Drug Policies

Heroin addiction is a staple story of our media today. It is generally presented with two faces. These faces belong to the grieving parents who give personal histories of trauma and destruction, or they are the faces of the drug and alcohol specialists. Often we have them together. The news cuts from the tearful parent whose child has died from an overdose to the cool professional who has a recipe of sorts to deal with this great scourge. Both stories are compelling and well-wrought, and pity the poor idiot who dares question the sentiment of the former and the knowledge of the latter.

I do not wish to become the cynical observer. The two faces are genuine and authentic, but I do want to put forward another perspective. This is one of scepticism towards the state ideology of harm reduction which governs policy in Australia. Harm reduction or harm minimisation has been presented as the only alternative to the failed 'war on drugs' which, quite rightly, has had such a bad press.

It is all or nothing according to the harm minimisation/abstinence dichotomy that is presented in the media. I want to deconstruct the false choices this sets up by looking at the results of current policies through the experience of people who have been subject to them, and suggest that the policies may not be the panaceas their proponents claim them to be. Further, I would like to ask why it is that many of us who consider ourselves politically left, and have no compunction criticising economic rationalist policies in other areas do not recognise the economic rationalist elements in harm reduction policies.

Add the cry of 'drugs are not a legal issue, but a health issue', and my blood begins to boil. Substance abuse is a social, legal, health, economic and ethical issue. We cannot keep morality out of it, although this is what scientists often want to do. We must not allow health professionals to dominate the argument now in the same way that police and lawyers have done for so long. Economic rationalism depends on technical specialists and abhors democratic debate, as John Ralston Saul points out, and drug policies in Australia are going in this very direction. The voices of the people caught in the debate are rarely heard except within a paradigm limited by professional discourses.

I am not a prohibitionist. Legalise all drugs, I say, but don't pretend that people will not disrupt their lives, disturb their families, disappoint their friends, lose their jobs and even die as a result of their addictions, legal or illegal. You only have to look at what happens to alcoholics to know that legalisation does not stop violence, mendacity, dissembling, financial chaos and physical illness. To the mothers who write about how their children have died as a result of the illegality of heroin, I would say that perhaps they might not have died there and then if legal heroin were available, but shooting galleries, legally prescribed heroin and methadone, needle exchanges and the paraphernalia of harm reduction will do little to stop the pain and heartache of seeing their loved ones suffer through addiction. Although all these strategies are necessary, they are not sufficient to deliver us from the pain. Pain is the nature of this particular beast.

The industry which has arisen around the moral panic which is heroin, namely the public health officials, doctors, nurses, pharmacists, counsellors, directors of research, psychologists, media-friendly police persons, outraged lord mayors and the rest work from particular assumptions about the nature of drug use and abuse which should be contestable. But they aren't. For the moment, harm reduction ideologues are acting as if there is no debate; as if it has been won. This reminds me of the professor of economics who, in a letter to the Melbourne Age, had the temerity to argue that there was no debate about the merits of economic rationalism in the academy: economic theory was economic rationalism and economic rationalism was economic theory. Game, set and match. Now, a few years later, some voices from the wilderness are being heard. Even the rapacious George Soros is getting into it. If we can do this with economics, why do we not do it with harm reduction?

Partly the answer lies in the fear Australians have of being called 'wowsers' if they question the nature of our 'fun-loving' culture. Call me a wowser if you like but the person with a belly full of alcohol is a pain to be around (and even dangerous) and a heroin addict after a hit is just a huge bore. A wine buff who knows his Hunter Valley red from his Yarra Valley white is just as capable of wreaking havoc on his family as the Four Roses sherry man at the Vic Market, but the political economy of alcohol limits our ability to criticise since it is so powerful. Our hand-wringing over the scourge of heroin is just an extension of the ambivalence we have always exhibited towards our alcohol culture. The pragmatism of harm reduction helps us to deny the importance of having a real debate about the nature of addictions. If we are unwilling to personally interrogate our use of substances like alcohol, we will find it impossible to continue a public debate about heroin which is serious and informed, and not wholly dependent on the 'specialists'.

What is harm reduction? Harm reduction or minimisation is a policy which aims to reduce the social and physical harm produced by the use of drugs. It accepts that drug use and abuse are inevitable and that state policy should be directed towards minimising their negative consequences. As a motherhood statement, I think this is great. The devil, as they say, is in the detail.

In the harm reduction literature researchers debate whether use reduction is strictly speaking part of harm reduction since the primary goal is the minimisation of drug-related harm, not the reduction of drug use. Abstinence is only a tangential goal of harm reduction. Pragmatic strategies such as needle-exchanges are put in place and education programs like Rave-Safe are introduced. Substitution programs such as methadone maintenance and other legal drugs are deemed part of this policy. Political economy comes into this as well since pharmaceutical companies need to produce markets for their new drugs. Indeed, a detailed analysis is needed in relation to the uses and abuses of physeptone (the generic name for methadone), naltrexone and other legal heroin-substitution drugs.

An important point to note here is that the proof of harm reduction lies in direct measurement, such as the large statistical studies used by public health scientists. Number crunching, in other words. I was reading a journal article the other day which looked at the relationship between alcohol outlets and violence in a particular US state and it argued pretty convincingly that the more alcohol outlets of any sort there were, the more violence that happened in the area. But it also found that the variables influencing the findings changed depending on whether the area under consideration was a large state-wide census tract or a local block tract. In other words, what happens on a mass scale does not easily translate to small group or individual experience. When I read, then, that it has been proven that methadone-maintenance programs reduce overdose deaths by 25 per cent, I know that each individual's risk is not lowered by 25 per cent. People still go out and die when they are on programs. And most people still use heroin while they are on programs. This is clearly illustrated in Victorian Institute of Forensic Medicine figures in the Pennington Report which show that almost all of the heroin-related deaths in the last few years also involved other illegal, legal and prescription drugs, such as alcohol and benzodiazepines (Valium and the like). More worrying for the authors were the '20 deaths caused by the diversion of "take-away" (methadone) doses in the last 3 years'. They continue: 'a further 37 persons have died (since 1989) within a week of starting a methadone maintenance program. Significant mortality is associated with the availability of methadone'. I would have thought this sort of evidence would give us pause to reflect, but no such luck. This evidence has not stopped the expansion of the methadone maintenance program in Victoria, nor have medical practitioners stopped supplying benzos and other drugs to heroin addicts, increasing their risk of harm.

Legitimate evidence is a political project as well. Apart from mortality and morbidity statistics, few other acceptable forms of evidence exist. People's negative experiences with methadone cannot be quantified in the way that scientists take seriously, but in a study I recently undertook, a number of women reported that they found methadone so dreadful they would rather have gone to jail than be forced onto a program. For whom, exactly, is the harm to be reduced? Perhaps the reduction of harm for one group might increase the harm for another, as the deaths mentioned above in the example from the Pennington Report suggest.

Harm reduction began as state ideology in the mid 1980s when the AIDS pandemic was at its height in Australia and elsewhere in the developed world. However, a reading of the literature makes it clear that the harm that needed to be reduced was that of the general population. If harm reduction also helped drug users, fine, but otherwise they were expendable. We needed to stop the needle users becoming the vectors for the virus into the 'innocent' population. Needle-exchanges were a logical outcome of this fear, and generally an effective one. However, needle-exchanges were introduced long before there was any proof of their effectiveness. They were the result of a very intelligent hunch.

Methadone was originally developed in Nazi Germany as a way of keeping conscripts fighting. It was addictive and therefore it was necessary to have a constant supply, but it did not produce the useless euphoria that characterises morphine, so the boys could keep fighting. Remember also that morphine was produced as a way of weaning opium addicts off their deadly love. Heroin was invented as a nonaddictive alternative to morphine. As a substitute for heroin, methadone was introduced in the United States in the early 1960s, long before harm reduction became a state ideology and in conjunction with the abstinence-based culture of the United States. Addicts were to be weaned off heroin by methadone and then weaned off the methadone. But of course, it was never that easy. A number of women I spoke to used heroin to wean themselves off methadone and then went into rehab to free themselves of all drugs.

Now in Victoria, there are trials of four other heroin-substitutes taking place because some people (30 per cent said one commentator, I would say much higher) cannot 'tolerate' methadone. Unlike heroin, methadone is toxic to many bodily organs and people who have been on methadone-maintenance programs for years have complained about their teeth falling out, constant constipation, aches, pains and illnesses. One woman said to me, 'I always felt like my bones were aching. I felt cold all the time, I sweated a lot and my sleep patterns were hideous'. And she was considered a success on the program! She finally became totally drug free, free of methadone and other legal drugs as well. Interestingly, I have not seen any studies which compare the lives of methadone patients with drug-free ex-addicts, only methadone patients with heroin-using non-patients. This would be a difficult but very worthwhile project.

The women I spoke to who had been through methadone programs and who were finally free of all drugs said it is the worst drug they had ever came across. In high doses it meant they could not operate at all since they would be drowsy for hours. They felt sick and the withdrawals were the worst they ever experienced. They also felt controlled by the drug itself, the doctors who wrote the scripts, the chemists who administered the doses and the welfare authorities who threatened to take away their children if they decided to come off the drug.

And this is the crux of my problem with harm reduction as a state policy; the insidious surveillance and control of the people within its purview. Following Foucault, we could say that we have moved into the surveillance stage of control when each of us, 'deviant' or not, understands that the surveillance inherent in prisons and hospitals is part of our everyday reality and we finally internalise and normalise the discourse of surveillance power. Drug-substitution programs are part of this shift, where police become less necessary because the counsellors, doctors and chemists do their work for them in conjunction with the legally addictive drug. These can be considered drug handcuffs in the same way that new electronic handcuffs monitor prisoners living outside prison. The surveillance is augmented when parents and family members are given training to detect drug problems and become part of the rehabilitative process. This is the risk-management process. We are told we are dealing with a health issue, rather than a legal issue, but the use of power is just as enveloping.

Together with the widening of surveillance comes the shrinking of the state. At the same time as concerned and well-meaning people have been arguing that we need to change our drug policies to accept the inevitability of drug use, economists have been gaining control of health and welfare budgets. Just as deinstitutionalisation of the mentally ill was hit upon as humane policy and then turned into a razor-gang exercise, so the same has happened to drug addiction policies.

Going back to the Foucauldian idea that we can see harm reduction as part of modern risk management, Stephen Mugford argued some time ago that state fiscal control would finally hit upon harm reduction as a policy. Mugford characterises the debate between harm reductionists and their opponents as one of moral concern versus pragmatic reality. You can see this in the huge debates in New York where the mayor is battling to close methadone programs and his opponents are accusing him of hypocritical moral self-righteousness. But Mugford also points out that harm reduction logic consists of an accountant's cost-benefit analysis which presents the argument as the greatest good for the greatest number at the cheapest possible cost. The costs of drug addiction are presented as costs in law enforcement, crime, infection in the larger community, and so on. The rights of individual addicts to be free of drug addiction completely are presented against the supposedly cheaper alternative of keeping them under control with legal drugs and surveillance. There is less likelihood of a drug-free existence when you realise that there is little room for workers to suggest to their clients that there is a possibility of a drug-free life. People free of all drugs cannot be monitored by the structures of harm reduction. But they need long- and medium-term housing, and this costs money. They also tend to go to non-professional self-help groups and this cuts out the power of specialists and professionals.

It seems to me that the answer to the 'problem' of drug addiction is to move away from the dichotomy inherent in the debate between harm minimisation and prohibition. Giving people the alternative of abstinence does not mean becoming a prohibitionist. It may mean, however, wresting the debate from the hands of the specialists and allowing it to reflect the voices of everyone involved. It may also mean that many of us who grew up in the '60s and '70s will have to let go of many of the libertarian notions we have about drugs and understand that limitations and boundaries are part of the social world. The women I spoke to were horrified with the notions implicit in the methadone programs they were offered. Notions such as being forever controlled by a drug and the people who dispense it They were happy being drug free and in the self-help community they became part of in the process. If they had not been able to get into long-term drug-free housing, they would never have been given this chance. Many of these programs are now being closed down. If there is only harm reduction, then these places and the people who have found them useful and congenial have no place. These are not the stories we generally view on television or read in the daily papers.

# POSTSCRIPT

## Is Harm Reduction a Desirable National Drug Control Policy Goal?

One could argue against the concept of harm reduction on the grounds that it is immoral. The question is, Is it moral to encourage people to use illegal drugs in such a way that their dangers are minimized? If a drug is illegal, then any use could be construed as harmful. By virtue of the illegality of drugs, the only way to minimize both personal and social risk is simple: do not use drugs. Another concern regarding the harm reduction approach is that some people, especially children and young adults, may get the wrong impression or receive a mixed message regarding drug use. If the federal government promotes the concept of harm reduction, young people may feel that, in the end, drug use is not that harmful.

In his selection, MacCoun does not argue in favor of drug use. He contends, however, that many of the personal and social problems emanating from drug use can be curtailed by developing a policy of harm reduction. Another point is that focusing on a program in which the primary goal is to eliminate access to drugs is inadequate because it overlooks differences among drugs, the extent of drug use, and the different types and groups of people who are using drugs. One could argue, for example, that persuading a person to switch from injecting drugs to a less dangerous form of drug use is more important than persuading an occasional marijuana user to cease use.

Zajdow doubts that a policy of harm reduction achieves its goal. She contends that lessening or abolishing criminal penalties for drug offenses, promoting needle exchange programs, and eliminating workplace drug testing has not been proven to diminish drug-related problems. Harm reduction, says Zajdow, continues to enslave drug abusers. In addition, policies should strive to help all people, not just drug abusers.

For an overview of the U.S. federal government's drug policy, read the *National Drug Control Strategy*, published annually by the Office of National Drug Control Policy. This publication outlines efforts that have been enacted toward reducing drug use and lists the government's future goals. Several chapters in the book *Drug Policy and Human Nature* edited by Warren K. Bickel and Richard J. DeGrandpre (Plenum Press, 1996) examine the debate over the harm reduction model. Jalie A. Tucker, in "From Zero Tolerance to Harm Reduction," *National Forum: Phi Kappa Phi Journal* (vol. 79, no. 4, 1999), discusses the merits of the harm reduction model. An article that is critical of the harm reduction approach is "Drug Legalization, Harm Reduction, and Drug Policy," by Robert L. DuPont and Eric A. Voth, *Annals of Internal Medicine* (vol. 123, 1995), pp. 461–465.

# On the Internet . . .

## Smoking From All Sides

This site contains links about all perspectives of smoking. Links include smoking cessation, smoking glamour, tobacco history, prosmoking documents, and statistics.

http://smokingsides.com

## The Medical Marijuana Arguments Page (Pro and Con)

This site provides dozens of links to sites on both sides of the medical marijuana debate.

http://www.cheeo.com/medical_marijuana.htm

## How Caffeine Works

This HowStuffWorks page was written by Marshall Brain, the founder, chairman, and CEO of HowStuffWorks. In it, Brain discusses what caffeine is, how caffeine affects the body, caffeine in the diet, and more. This site includes links to related articles and books.

http://www.howstuffworks.com/caffeine.htm

## Ritalin Links

This site contains a wealth of links on Ritalin and the Ritalin controversy, including laws against school system Ritalin abuse, attention deficit disorder (ADD) information, and alternative remedies to Ritalin.

http://www.scn.org/~bk269/rball_links.html

## EthicAd

EthicAd is an independent, nonprofit organization dedicated to helping the consumer, the health care professional, and the pharmaceutical and advertising industry in the area of direct-to-consumer (DTC) advertising for prescription drugs.

http://www.ethicad.org

# PART 2

# Drugs and Social Policy

*E*xcept *for the debate over legalizing marijuana for medical use, each debate in this section focuses on drugs that are already legal. Despite concerns over the effects of illegal drugs, the most frequently used drugs in society are legal drugs. Because of their prevalence and legal status, the social, psychological, and physical impact of drugs like tobacco, caffeine, alcohol, and prescription drugs are often minimized or discounted. However, tobacco and alcohol cause far more death and disability than all illegal drugs combined.*

*The recent trend toward medical self-help raises questions of how much control one should have over one's own health. The current tendency to identify nicotine as an addictive drug and to promote the moderate use of alcohol to reduce heart disease has generated much controversy. In the last several years the increase in consumers requesting prescription drugs for themselves and Ritalin for their children has also created much concern. Lastly, should marijuana be prescribed for people with certain illnesses for which some have suggested the drug could be beneficial?*

- Are the Adverse Effects of Smoking Exaggerated?

- Should Marijuana Be Legal for Medicinal Purposes?

- Should Doctors Promote Alcohol for Their Patients?

- Do the Consequences of Caffeine Outweigh the Benefits?

- Are Too Many Children Receiving Ritalin?

- Should Advertisements for Prescription Drugs Be Regulated?

# ISSUE 8

## Are the Adverse Effects of Smoking Exaggerated?

**YES: Stephen Goode**, from "Cato's Levy Challenges Federal Tobacco Myths," *Insight on the News* (January 31, 2000)

**NO: World Health Organization**, from *The World Health Report 1999: Making a Difference* (1999)

### ISSUE SUMMARY

**YES:** Author Stephen Goode interviews Robert Levy, of the Cato Institute, who maintains that government statistics distort and exaggerate the dangers of cigarette smoking. Levy argues that smokers are less likely to eat nutritional meals or exercise and that many are poor and uneducated. Thus, factors besides smoking may contribute to the poor health and decreased longevity of many tobacco users.

**NO:** The World Health Organization's report on the increase in smoking delineates the health and economic expense of tobacco use throughout the world. The report indicates that one barrier to stemming smoking is a lack of information about the risks of tobacco use. The report also states that tobacco is addictive and that tobacco manufacturers are expanding because of the tremendous profits they make.

Most people, including those who smoke, recognize that cigarette smoking is harmful. Because of tobacco's reputation as an addictive substance that jeopardizes people's health, many activists are requesting that more stringent restrictions be placed on it. Currently, cigarette packages are required to carry warnings describing the dangers of tobacco products. In many countries tobacco products cannot be advertised on television or on billboards. Laws that prevent minors from purchasing tobacco products are being enforced more vigorously than ever. However, the World Health Organization maintains that global leadership in curtailing the proliferation of cigarette smoking is lacking.

Defenders of the tobacco industry point to benefits associated with nicotine, the mild stimulant that is the chief active chemical in tobacco. In previous centuries, for example, tobacco was used to help people with a variety of ailments, including skin diseases; internal and external disorders; and diseases of the eyes, ears, mouth, and nose. Tobacco and its smoke were often employed by Native Americans for sacramental purposes. For users, nicotine provides a sense of euphoria, and smoking is a source of gratification that does not impair thinking or performance. One can drive a car, socialize, study for a test, and engage in a variety of activities while smoking. Nicotine can relieve anxiety and stress. It can also reduce weight by lessening one's appetite and by increasing metabolic activity. Many smokers assert that abstaining from smoking impairs their concentration.

Critics paint a very different picture of tobacco products, citing some of the following statistics: Tobacco is responsible for approximately 30 percent of deaths among people between the ages of 35 and 69, making it the single most prominent cause of premature death in the developed world. The relationship between cigarette smoking and cardiovascular disease, including heart attack, stroke, sudden death, peripheral vascular disease, and aortic aneurysm, is well documented. Even as few as one to four cigarettes daily can increase the risk of fatal coronary heart disease. Cigarettes have also been shown to reduce blood flow and the level of high-density lipoprotein cholesterol, which is the beneficial type of cholesterol.

Cigarette smoking is strongly associated with cancer, accounting for over 85 percent of lung cancer cases and 30 percent of all deaths due to cancer. Cancer of the pharynx, larynx, mouth, esophagus, stomach, pancreas, uterus, cervix, kidney, and bladder have been related to smoking. Studies have shown that smokers have twice the rate of cancer than nonsmokers.

According to smokers' rights advocates, the majority of smokers are already aware of the potential harm of tobacco products; in fact, most smokers tend to overestimate the dangers of smoking. Therefore, adults should be allowed to smoke if that is their wish. Many promote the idea that the Food and Drug Administration (FDA) and a number of politicians are attempting to deny smokers the right to engage in a behavior that they freely choose. On the other hand, tobacco critics maintain that due to the addictiveness of nicotine—the level of which some assert is manipulated by tobacco companies—smokers do not have the ability to stop their behavior. That is, after a certain point, smoking cannot be considered freely chosen behavior.

There is an economic element associated with this issue, as well. Should taxpayers financially assist smokers who need medical help as a result of their use of tobacco products? Much money is collected on taxes paid by smokers, but several billion dollars are needed each year to cover Medicaid costs for smoking-related illnesses. Should such illnesses be covered by government-funded medical programs?

In the following selections, Stephen Goode interviews Robert Levy, who argues that the scientific evidence demonstrating the harmful effects of tobacco use is disputable. Levy also asserts that smoking has been demonized unfairly. The World Health Organization compares cigarette smoking to an epidemic that wreaks havoc on health and the economy. Until cigarette manufacturers are reined in, it argues, problems related to smoking will continue to grow.

Stephen Goode

**YES**

# Cato's Levy Challenges Federal Tobacco Myths

For a quarter-century Robert Levy was an enormously successful businessman as founder and chief executive officer of CDA Investment Technologies Inc. In 1991, Levy left business and went to law school, graduating in 1994. Since 1997 the 58-year-old attorney has been at the Cato Institute in Washington, where he has written on issues such as the tobacco wars, Microsoft and the war against the gun industry.

Levy is no stranger to statistical analysis. His doctoral dissertation, completed for his degree in business at American University, took up quantitative modeling of the stock market. In the fall 1998 issue of *Regulation, The Cato Review of Business and Government,* Levy published "Lies, Damned Lies & 400,000 Smoking-Related Deaths," an article he co-wrote with mathematician and scientist Rosalind Marimont, examining the government's method of coming up with the claim that 400,000 die annually from tobacco-related disease.

The *Regulation* article was attacked as "unscientific and inflammatory" by the American Council on Science and Health, with which Levy has been having a running debate since the piece appeared. A nonsmoker, Levy has no doubt that smoking is dangerous and can cause diseases, including lung cancer. What he argues, though, is that the threat of tobacco has been vastly exaggerated and that we need to acquire a more balanced notion of just what that threat is.

*Insight:* In "Lies, Damned Lies, & 400,000 Smoking-Related Deaths" you concluded that the government's estimate of 400,000 annual deaths due to cigarette smoking is unreliable. What's wrong with that figure?

*Robert A. Levy:* According to the Centers for Disease Control and Prevention, tobacco-related diseases are those in which the rate of risk among smokers is higher than among nonsmokers. But epidemiologists will tell you without exception, I think, that "simply higher" is not enough. In most studies, the requirement to show a correlation is that the risk be three or four times as high.

From Stephen Goode, "Cato's Levy Challenges Federal Tobacco Myths," *Insight on the News* (January 31, 2000). Copyright © 2000 by News World Communications, Inc. Reprinted by permission of *Insight on the News.*

The reason for requiring a relative risk rate among smokers of three or four times what it is among nonsmokers before categorizing a disease as smoking-related is that epidemiological studies are subject to all sorts of statistical problems.

There's the problem of sampling error. There is the problem of bias. The third problem is what epidemiologists call "compounding variables": that is the failure to take into account variables that are correlated both with the disease and with smoking. The obvious one in this case is socioeconomic status, as smokers tend to be less affluent than nonsmokers. So because of the problems of sampling, bias and of compounding variables, epidemiologists insist that to categorize a disease as tobacco-related the disease has to have a relative risk among smokers that is three or four times that among nonsmokers.

The relative risk of smoking for many types of heart disease is less than 2-to-1, and if you eliminate even those that are just below 2-to-1 you reduce the estimated number of tobacco-related deaths by about 55 to 60 percent.

We know that smokers are poorer than nonsmokers, have worse nutritional intake, typically have less exercise and less education. Those factors contribute to the contraction of various diseases described as smoking-related. To suggest that the entire incidence among smokers is because these people smoke is to ignore that they share exposure to many other characteristics that also impact health.

*Insight:*    What's the reason for the distortion?

*RAL:*    Underlying such manipulation of statistics one often finds a political agenda, a public-policy agenda, which seeks to convince the public that something is a terrible scourge—and to do so even if the polemic violates the standards and principles of statistics and epidemiology.

This is not to say that tobacco is not a problem. Tobacco is clearly a problem. The evidence is overwhelming that use of tobacco can cause lung cancer, emphysema, bronchitis. But with respect to other diseases its role is less certain. This causes us to ask whether the government is lying to us in presenting these kinds of statistics, because, if it is, that has implications.

*Insight:*    What implications?

*RAL:*    We've seen what happened with antitobacco lawsuits. They've morphed now into antigun litigation. Shortly, it will be the HMOs [health-maintenance organizations] under attack. Who knows what will be next? Fatty foods and alcohol are other obvious candidates for such government-sponsored litigation. The corruption of science for political ends is destructive to a free society and dangerous to citizens who want their government to refrain from activities that intrude upon the rights of people to make their own choices.

Data are being massaged so as to produce outcomes that the litigants find congenial; whether those outcomes are supported by the data is disregarded. I think that's exactly what happened in the tobacco wars.

Tobacco is a problem about which 45 million people decided that it's too dangerous and they quit smoking. For more than 35 years now we've had warnings on every single pack of cigarettes that has been sold legally in the United

States. It's a product about which the risks are well-known. Those risks, in fact, have been exaggerated and this has meant that public policy has focused on the unreal, exaggerated risks to the exclusion of some other sources of risk that might better have been targeted.

Damage done from alcohol, damage done from drugs, from suicide and particularly from homicide all are vastly more important than the damage done from tobacco, I think. Tobacco is not an intoxicant. It doesn't cause crime except for those people involved in avoiding taxes or regulation of a product whose price has been pushed through the roof by legislation, taxation and regulation. Tobacco doesn't, as do drugs and alcohol, result in spousal abuse and child abuse. It doesn't break up families. It doesn't result in unemployment.

Nor does tobacco result in the deaths of young people. Drugs and alcohol, suicide and homicide are killing young people in the prime of life, with decades of life left. The average age of what are called tobacco-related deaths is 72. Those years lost after 72 are important, but they're not so significant, not of the same magnitude, as years lost to the young.

*Insight:*   We've had the tobacco wars. What are the gun wars going to be like?

*RAL:*   Well, we're about to find out because there now are about 28 cities that are suing the gun industry. My forecast is that the gun industry will cave. You had the tobacco industry cave and the tobacco industry [is far wealthier] than the gun industry, so the gun folks are likely to come to the negotiating table with the government bearing down very heavily on their necks. Of course, that's the strategy: To coordinate these lawsuits, forget about whether they have any underlying legal merit, and by sheer force and number of the suits coerce a settlement.

*Insight:*   How can the enormous power of government in these cases be brought under control?

*RAL:*   A solution is a "lose-you-pay" system. When the state is a plaintiff in a civil case—and I use the word "state" broadly to encompass government at all levels—we ought to require that it pay if it loses. The government has coercive taxing power behind it [which, for one thing, supplies an almost unlimited supply of funds], so when the government is the plaintiff in a civil case, we need this extra protection against the abuse of the government's power.

*Insight:*   Is there any means to bring under control the huge fees plaintiff lawyers have been getting in these cases?

*RAL:*   Yes. We could prohibit contingency fees for cases when the state is plaintiff. I don't have any objection to contingency fees arranged by private litigants. But when you combine the state as plaintiff and a contingency-fee contract, that is abusive. You can imagine the abuse you would have if you hired an attorney general and paid him for each indictment he got a grand jury to hand down or if you paid state troopers based on how many speeding tickets they handed out. But that's exactly what's happened with private attorneys hired by the state in these civil cases. We've seen legal fees in Texas of $92,000 an hour!

*Insight:*    Meanwhile, we've been eliminating personal responsibility by saying a person's not responsible for his or her own choice to smoke.

*RAL:*    We actually eliminated assumption of risk. In Florida, Maryland and Vermont they did it by statute. They actually said in their statutes that the tobacco industry may not use assumption of risk as a defense. Secondly, they eliminated the rule of causation. The tobacco industry, they said, could not require the states in court to show a link between any smoker's conduct and the disease. The only evidence the states had to produce were these macrostatistics we've talked about showing the higher incidence of various diseases among smokers than nonsmokers. So it was all washed away in one stroke of the pen, all the rules of causation and the assumption of risk.

That is more destructive than the impact of cigarettes themselves! Basically, we're now telling kids two things: First, you can change the rules of the game after the game has begun because all these rules were retroactive. Second, you can go out and engage in risky behavior and if it doesn't turn out like you wanted, you can force the cost onto some third party.

# Combating the Tobacco Epidemic

With current smoking patterns, about 500 million people alive today will eventually be killed by tobacco *(1)*. Tobacco deaths will occur in men already smoking, children who will become smokers, and an increasing number of women smokers. For most of these deaths to be avoided, a substantial proportion of adult smokers will have to quit and children will need to avoid taking up the habit. If half of the adult smokers stopped over the next 20 years, about one third of the tobacco deaths in 2020 would be avoided and tobacco deaths in the second quarter of the century would be halved. Such changes would avoid about 20 or 30 million tobacco deaths in the first quarter of the century and about 140 million in the second quarter.

How can the epidemic be fought? Effective tobacco control strategies already exist, and they have been proved to make a difference, benefiting both adults and children. Governments that have adopted them have succeeded in reducing, or at least slowing the increase in, tobacco use.

To build on those successes, four principles of tobacco control provide a road-map for national and global action. They include public health information combined with advertising bans, taxes and regulations, encouraging smoking cessation, and building tobacco control coalitions....

## The Health and Economic Costs of Tobacco Use

Worldwide mortality from tobacco is likely to rise from about four million deaths a year in 1998 to about 10 million a year in 2030. To put it slightly differently, tobacco will cause about 150 million deaths in the first quarter of the century and 300 million in the second quarter. Half of these deaths will occur in the 35-69 years age group, including many in productive middle age, with an average loss of 20-25 years of life.

Tobacco use results in both health and economic costs that are large and growing. This section summarizes the evidence.

### Health Consequences of Tobacco

Since about 1950, more than 70,000 scientific articles have left no scientific doubt that prolonged smoking is an important cause of premature mortality

From World Health Organization, *The World Health Report 1999: Making a Difference* (1999).

and disability worldwide. Estimates suggest that in developed countries, smoking will have caused about 62 million deaths between 1950 and 2000. WHO now estimates that smoking causes about four million deaths annually worldwide and predicts that, with current smoking patterns, this number is likely to increase dramatically.

There is, of course, some uncertainty in such estimates, both because they involve extrapolation of present hazards to future hazards, and because they involve extrapolation from studies in Western Europe, North America and China to many other populations. At present many large countries lack direct evidence on their tobacco mortality; in addition, the long delay between smoking and its mortality effects has confused governments and individuals. For example, while studies in the 1960s suggested that one in four long-term smokers died from their habit, studies in the 1990s suggest that the real ratio is now about one in two. In addition, those smokers dying between ages 35 and 69 lose about 20–25 years of life versus non-smoker life expectancy, and those dying over age 70 lose about 8 years of life.

The nature of the smoking epidemic also varies from country to country. In developed countries, cardiovascular disease, in particular ischaemic heart disease, is the most common smoking-related cause of death. In populations where cigarette smoking has been common for several decades, about 90% of lung cancer, 15–20% of other cancers, 75% of chronic bronchitis and emphysema, and 25% of deaths from cardiovascular disease at ages 35–69 years are attributable to tobacco. Tobacco-related cancer constitutes 16% of the total annual incidence of cancer cases—and 30% of cancer deaths—in developed countries, while the corresponding figure in developing countries is 10% (2). By contrast, in China, which has the world's highest number of tobacco deaths, smoking now causes far more deaths from chronic respiratory diseases than it does from cardiovascular disease. In addition, smoking causes about 12% of all tuberculosis deaths. Men in urban China smoking more than 20 cigarettes a day have double the death rate from TB of non-smokers. This could be because a lung damaged by tobacco may offer a propitious environment for the infectious tuberculosis bacillus.

Exposure to other people's smoking is associated with a somewhat higher risk of lung cancer, and with several other important health ailments in children such as sudden infant death syndrome, low birth weight, intrauterine growth retardation and children's respiratory disease. In addition, smoking is the leading cause of domestic fires in the United States, Canada and other high income countries, entailing billions of dollars of property loss annually.

Current deaths from tobacco relate to past consumption, mainly among males in developed countries and in China. In the near future, the epidemic will expand to include more developing countries and a larger number of women. Lung cancer is now the most common cause of death from cancer in women in the United States and its incidence in women is rising briskly in countries where female smoking is long established (3).

The scale of the approaching epidemic can be gauged from the estimate that there are about 1.15 billion smokers in the world today, consuming an average of 14 cigarettes each per day *(4)*. Of these smokers, 82% live in low and middle income countries—a result, in part, of inadequate tobacco controls.

Tobacco consumption fell between 1981 and 1991 in most high income countries. In the United States, the prevalence of smoking increased steadily from the 1930s and reached a peak in 1964 when more than 40% of all adult Americans, including 60% of men, smoked. Since then smoking prevalence has decreased, falling to 23% by 1997. By contrast, consumption is increasing in developing countries by about 3.4% per annum, having risen dramatically in some countries in recent years. Overall, smoking prevalence among men in developing countries is about 48%.

Thus, on current smoking patterns, by the third decade of the next century, smoking is expected to kill 10 million people annually worldwide—more than the total of deaths from malaria, maternal and major childhood conditions, and tuberculosis combined *(5)*. Over 70% of these deaths will be in the developing world. By 2020, smoking will cause about one in three of all adult deaths, up from one in six adult deaths in 1990 *(6)*.

## The Economic Costs

Tobacco obviously provides economic benefits to producers. Similarly, the fact that users are willing to pay for tobacco products means that they clearly derive measurable benefits from them. However, economic analyses conclude that even with highly conservative assumptions, the economic costs of tobacco exceed its estimated benefits.

One analysis by Barnum *(7)* tried to estimate the additional costs—in mortality, morbidity and health care—and the benefits—to consumers and producers—per year if global tobacco production were to increase by 1000 metric tons. The analysis concluded that there would be net economic losses of 13.6 million dollars per year, and said: "Tobacco is a poor investment if the objective is to enhance the future welfare of the globe." In fact there has been a 26% increase in production between 1994 and 1997—equal to almost 2.1 million metric tons, giving a total of just over 8 million metric tons....

# Obstacles to Tobacco Control

Evidence about the addictive nature of nicotine, and other ill-effects of smoking, needs to be disseminated more widely. The tobacco industry is reluctantly surrendering its secrets.

## Lack of Information on Risks

Like consumers of other goods, tobacco consumers need information about what they are buying. Tobacco, however, differs from most consumer goods in that it has harmful health consequences and is addictive. Therefore its consumers have to weigh up and additional type of information in making their decision to buy. The extent to which smokers know about the health consequences and addictive nature of their purchase is critical in determining what they believe they are buying.

Consumers can learn about the health effects of tobacco in several ways. One is through published scientific and epidemiological research which may be summarized in the media. They may also learn through warning labels directly attached to cigarette packs. A third way is through public information campaigns, or counter-advertising; a fourth is through educational initiatives, such as school and community programmes. All of these have been shown to be effective to varying degrees; further research is required on educational initiatives in high income countries in reducing demand for tobacco. A Surgeon General's report in the United States and a Royal College of Physicians report in the United Kingdom, both published in the 1960s, have been responsible for halting much of the increases in consumption in those countries. The implication is that a greater increase in the availability of health information in developing countries would be expected to lead to a significant decrease in global tobacco consumption.

All countries need to increase and improve local studies on tobacco-attributable mortality. Established vital registration systems, some of them over 100 years old, can be used in some rich countries to assess disease patterns and trends. Decades of epidemiological research have identified some of the particular causes of such trends, particularly tobacco use. This is not yet so in poorer countries.

Unfortunately, country-specific information on tobacco-related disease is weakest precisely in the countries where the epidemic looms largest. Recently, WHO collaborating centres and Chinese scientists have helped to develop an innovative model where simply asking about smoking on death certificates provides a low-cost and reliable method of monitoring the tobacco epidemic. Similar methods could be used to monitor the hazards of tobacco in many other populations. For example, in South Africa smoking status is routinely reported on the new type of death certificate, perhaps obviating the need to interview family members.

## Tobacco Use Is an Addiction

As many millions of smokers have belatedly discovered—and lack of information is partly to blame—nicotine is addictive. Some addiction experts have rated tobacco as worse than heroin or cocaine in producing dependency. The 1988 report of the United States Surgeon General, subtitled *Nicotine addiction,* concluded that: "The pharmacological and behavioural processes that determine tobacco addiction are similar to those that determine addiction to drugs such as heroin and cocaine" *(8).*

Tobacco satisfies the criteria for "dependence" in the tenth revision of the International Classification of Diseases *(9).* Classification F17 is entitled *Mental and behavioural disorders due to use of tobacco.* Sub-classification F17.2, *Dependence syndrome,* offers a description that will be familiar to most smokers: a cluster of behavioural, cognitive and physiological phenomena that develop after repeated substance use and that typically include a strong desire to take the drug, difficulties in controlling its use, persisting in use despite harmful consequences, a higher priority given to drug use than to other activities and obligations, increased tolerance, and sometimes a physical withdrawal state.

Research suggests that the process by which people decide about tobacco usage involves a "tobacco addiction cycle". This consists of the stages a person goes through when he or she changes from being a "non-smoker" into a "new smoker", then becomes a "committed smoker", then typically a "smoker trying to stop" and, for a fortunate minority, a "reformed smoker" who, alas, is liable to start the cycle all over again (6).

Many people consume tobacco primarily to obtain nicotine, which is found in all tobacco products. Cigarettes are highly refined vehicles designed to give rapid peak nicotine levels. In the words of the tobacco industry, "Think of the cigarette as a dispenser for a dose unit of nicotine" (10). The nicotine is quickly absorbed via the lungs of smokers and reaches the brain within seconds. It is the primary active ingredient in tobacco that reinforces the biomedical and behavioural process of individual smoking habits. Social and psychological influences are also important in the initiation of smoking, but the addictive nature of nicotine is the main reason why many smokers maintain their tobacco use (8), leading to tobacco-related ill-health, disability and premature death.

Nicotine addiction is not simply a matter of choice or taste. It is not irreversibly addictive, as many people can quit smoking. This explains much of the decline in smoking among adults in OECD (Organisation for Economic Co-Operation and Development) countries. But some people find quitting virtually impossible. Even smokers who quit often have to make several attempts before dropping the habit; and former smokers remain vulnerable to resuming smoking at times of stress.

Nicotine addiction takes hold almost exclusively in children and youth. About half to three-quarters of teenagers in OECD countries try smoking, and about half of those quit quickly. The rest become life-long smokers, among whom one in two will die from smoking. The joint probability of trying smoking, becoming addicted and dying prematurely is higher than for any other addiction (such as alcohol, for which the likelihood of addiction is much lower). Also, children taking up smoking are more likely to experiment with other drugs than those who do not.

Nicotine addiction creates an incentive for the tobacco industry to subsidize or give away free cigarettes to potential smokers, especially young people, in order to induce them to smoke, and otherwise to keep prices high to maximize profits. The same incentive applies to creating addiction among adults in developing countries by manipulating price.

## Tobacco Dealers Make Enormous Profits

Tobacco is big business. This year [1999], twice as many cigarettes will be smoked as were lit 30 years ago. The tobacco industry is expanding, with the world retail market in cigarettes now worth some US$ 300 billion. Tobacco companies continue to make huge profits, estimated at more than $20 billion a year.

The tobacco industry exerts its influence in countries in several ways: politically as a result of large profits, through denial of tobacco's health impacts, and by advertising and promoting cigarettes. The cigarette market is rapidly expanding among developing countries. Globally, about 6000 billion cigarettes are consumed each year, up from 3000 billion in 1970, despite the fall in countries such as Australia, Canada, Japan, New Zealand, the UK, the USA, and most northern European countries *(11)*. For example, total cigarette consumption in the United Kingdom has fallen from 138 billion to 80 billion per year over the last two decades.

Developing countries are an ideal target for market expansion. In the past few decades, transnational tobacco conglomerates have made tremendous inroads into the markets of poor and middle income nations in Africa, Asia, Eastern Europe and Latin America. Manufacturers have benefited from the globalization of trade, creating big increases in domestic tobacco consumption and imports of tobacco products in many low and middle income nations. In many countries, tobacco companies support social services, in an attempt to portray themselves as purveying "just another product".

Like other industries, the tobacco industry has no financial incentive to provide health information that would reduce consumption of its products. On the contrary, the industry has consistently hidden product information on the ill effects of smoking, used the power of its advertising dollars to dissuade lay journals from reporting on smoking's health effects, and resorted to other methods to decrease information available to smokers. Internal industry documents uncovered in recent American lawsuits confirm such practices *(12)*. Futhermore, the industry has played an active role in funding and disseminating research that casts doubt on the links between tobacco and death. The impact of such information on overall consumer knowledge is difficult to assess. But it is likely to have impeded individual assessments of the true risks of smoking, and it has slowed the spread of government-initiated anti-smoking information campaigns.

Advertising is a crucial component of the industry's expansion. It is the primary method of competition within a highly concentrated industry which has a small number of relatively large firms. These firms tend not to compete by price, but try to increase sales with advertising. The largest international tobacco companies are Philip Morris and BAT [British American Tobacco]. *Advertising age* reports that in 1996, for advertising outside of the USA, Philip Morris was the ninth largest advertiser in the world and BAT was the 44th largest. In addition, an *Advertising age* survey of Asia, Europe and the Middle East finds that tobacco companies are listed in the top ten advertisers in 21 out of 50 countries.

Huge increases in cigarette advertising and a 10% increase in total tobacco use occurred in four Asian countries when US cigarette companies entered those markets *(13)*. Increases in consumption come both from new consumers and from increased tobacco use by existing consumers. In the case of cigarettes, new consumers are often uniformed adolescents.

# References

1. Peto R et al. *Mortality from smoking in developed countries 1950–2000.* New York, Oxford University Press, 1994.

2. Parkin DM et al. At least one in seven cases of cancer is caused by smoking. Global estimates for 1985. *International journal of cancer,* 1994, **59**(4): 494–504.

3. *The world health report 1997—Conquering suffering, enriching humanity.* Geneva, World Health Organization, 1997.

4. *Curbing the epidemic: Governments and the economics of tobacco control.* Washington, The World Bank, 1999.

5. *World development report 1993—Investing in health.* New York, Oxford University Press for The World Bank, 1999.

6. Murray CJL, Lopez AD. *The global burden of disease.* Cambridge MA, Harvard University Press, 1996.

7. Barnum H. *Initial analysis of the economic costs and benefits of investing in tobacco.* Washington, The World Bank, 1993 (unpublished manuscript, Human Development Department).

8. US Department of Health and Human Services. *The health consequences of smoking: Nicotine addiction. A report of the Surgeon General.* Rockville MD, Centers for Disease Control, 1988 (DHHS Publication No. CDC 88-8406).

9. *The ICD-10 classification of mental and behavioural disorders. Clinical descriptions and diagnostic guidelines.* Geneva, World Health Organization, 1992.

10. Dunn WL Jnr. *Motives and incentives in cigarette smoking.* Philip Morris 1972. Minnesota Tobacco Trial-Exhibit 18089.

11. Jha P, Chaloupka FJ (eds). *Tobacco control policies in developing countries.* New York, Oxford University Press, 1999.

12. Hurt RD, Robertson CR. Prying open the door to the tobacco industry's secrets about nicotine: The Minnesota tobacco trial. *Journal of the American Medical Association,* 1998, 280: 1178–1181.

13. Chaloupka FJ, Laixuthai A. *US trade policy and cigarette smoking in Asia.* Cambridge MA, National Bureau of Economic Research, 1996 (NBER Working Paper 5543).

# POSTSCRIPT

## Are the Adverse Effects of Smoking Exaggerated?

$M$uch data indicates that smoking cigarettes is injurious to human health. For example, more than 400,000 people die from tobacco-related illnesses each year in the United States, costing the U.S. health care system more than $80 billion annually. Levy, however, questions the accuracy of the data. How the data are presented and interpreted may affect how one feels about the issue of placing more restrictions on tobacco products. There is currently a great deal of antismoking sentiment in society. Levy does not recommend that people use tobacco products; however, he states only that the consequences linked to it are exaggerated.

Despite the reported hazards of tobacco smoking, many proponents of smokers' rights assert that smoking is a matter of choice. However, the World Health Organization contends that smoking is not a matter of choice because smokers become addicted to nicotine. One could argue that the decision to start smoking is a matter of choice, but once dependency occurs, most smokers are in effect deprived of the choice to stop smoking. Also contributing to the tobacco dilemma is the expansion of tobacco manufacturers into many developing countries and the proliferation of advertising.

Nevertheless, tobacco proponents maintain that people make all types of choices, and if the choices that people make are ultimately harmful, then that is their responsibility.

Several times a year the SmokeFree Educational Services publishes Smoke-Free Air, a newsletter describing actions that have been taken to limit smoking in public locations. Mike Mitka's article "Surgeon General's Newest Report on Tobacco," *Journal of the American Medical Association* (September 20, 2000) describes current smoking-related statistics and efforts to stem cigarette smoking. In "Prying Open the Door to the Tobacco Industry's Secrets About Nicotine," *Journal of the American Medical Association* (October 7, 1998), Richard D. Hurt and Channing R. Robertson describe actions taken by states to get the tobacco industry to admit that it covered up industry documents that revealed that nicotine is an addictive drug and that industry strategies utilized this knowledge to increase cigarette sales. In a similar article, "The Defeat of Philip Morris' California Uniform Tobacco Control Act," *American Journal of Public Health* (December 1997), Heather MacDonald, Stella Aguinga, and Stanton A. Glantz discuss the techniques used by Philip Morris and other tobacco companies to prevent tobacco control by local municipalities.

# ISSUE 9

## Should Marijuana Be Legal for Medicinal Purposes?

**YES: Lester Grinspoon**, from "Whither Medical Marijuana?" *Contemporary Drug Problems* (Spring 2000)

**NO: James R. McDonough**, from "Marijuana on the Ballot," *Policy Review* (April/May 2000)

### ISSUE SUMMARY

**YES:** Professor of psychiatry Lester Grinspoon argues that anecdotal evidence indicates that marijuana has medical benefits for patients suffering from chemotherapy nausea, AIDS, glaucoma, chronic pain, epilepsy, and migraine headaches. He asserts that the federal government is prohibiting its use without justification.

**NO:** James R. McDonough, director of the Florida Office of Drug Control, agrees that compounds in marijuana, such as THC, may have the potential to be medically valuable. However, smoked marijuana has not been proven to be of medicinal value. In addition, states McDonough, there are existing, approved drugs that are more effective for conditions that may be helped by marijuana use.

Since the mid-1990s voters in California, Arizona, Oregon, Colorado, and other states have passed referenda to legalize marijuana for medical purposes. Despite the position of these voters, however, the federal government does not support the medical use of marijuana, and federal laws take precedence over state laws. A major concern of opponents of these referenda is that legalization of marijuana for medicinal purposes will lead to its use for recreational purposes.

Marijuana's medicinal qualities have been recognized for centuries. Marijuana was utilized medically as far back as 2737 B.C., when Chinese emperor Shen Nung recommended marijuana, or cannabis, for medical use. By the 1890s some medical reports had stated that cannabis was useful as a pain reliever. However, despite its historical significance, the use of marijuana for medical treatment is still a widely debated and controversial topic.

156

Marijuana has been tested in the treatment of glaucoma, asthma, convulsions, epilepsy, and migraine headaches, and in the reduction of nausea, vomiting, and loss of appetite associated with chemotherapy treatments. Many medical professionals and patients believe that marijuana shows promise in the treatment of these disorders and others, including spasticity in amputees and multiple sclerosis. Yet others argue that there are alternative drugs and treatments available that are more specific and effective in treating these disorders than marijuana and that marijuana cannot be considered a medical replacement.

Because of the conflicting viewpoints and what many people argue is an absence of reliable, scientific research supporting the medicinal value of marijuana, the drug and its plant materials remain in Schedule I of the Controlled Substances Act of 1970. This act established five categories, or schedules, under which drugs are classified according to their potential for abuse and their medical usefulness, which in turn determines their availability. Drugs classified under Schedule I are those that have a high potential for abuse and no scientifically proven medical use. Many marijuana proponents have called for the Drug Enforcement Administration (DEA) to move marijuana from Schedule I to Schedule II, which classifies drugs as having a high potential for abuse but also having an established medical use. A switch to Schedule II would legally allow physicians to utilize marijuana and its components in certain treatment programs. To date, however, the DEA has refused.

Currently, marijuana is used medically but not legally. Most of the controversy surrounds whether or not marijuana and its plant properties are indeed of medical value and whether or not the risks associated with its use outweigh its proposed medical benefits. Research reports and scientific studies have been inconclusive. Some physicians and many cancer patients say that marijuana greatly reduces the side effects of chemotherapy. Many glaucoma patients believe that marijuana use has greatly improved their conditions. In view of these reports by patients and the recommendations by some physicians to allow inclusion of marijuana in treatment, expectations have been raised with regard to marijuana's worth as a medical treatment.

Marijuana opponents argue that the evidence in support of marijuana as medically useful suffers from far too many deficiencies. The DEA, for example, believes that studies supporting the medical value of marijuana are scientifically limited, based on biased testimonies of ill individuals who have used marijuana and their families and friends, and grounded in the unscientific opinions of certain physicians, nurses, and other hospital personnel. Furthermore, marijuana opponents state that the safety of marijuana has not been established by reliable scientific data weighing marijuana's possible therapeutic benefits against its known negative effects.

In the following selections, Lester Grinspoon asserts that the federal government has set up needless political roadblocks to prevent needy individuals from receiving the medicinal benefits of marijuana. James R. McDonough argues that the current research on marijuana's medicinal benefits is inconclusive and that other drugs are available that preclude the need to use marijuana.

**Lester Grinspoon**

 **YES**

# Whither Medical Marijuana?

Cannabis was first admitted to Western pharmacopoeias one and a half centuries ago. In 1839 W. B. O'Shaughnessy at the Medical College of Calcutta observed its use in the indigenous treatment of various disorders and found that tincture of hemp was an effective analgesic, anticonvulsant, and muscle relaxant.[1] Publication of O'Shaughnessy's paper created a stir within a medical establishment which at that time had access to only a few effective medicines. In the next several decades, many papers on cannabis appeared in the Western medical literature. It was widely used until the first decades of the 20th century, especially as an analgesic and hypnotic. Symptoms and conditions for which it was found helpful included tetanus, neuralgia, labor pain, dysmenorrhea, convulsions, asthma, and rheumatism.[2]

Administering a medicine through smoking was unheard of until the late 19th century, when pharmaceutical house, prepared coca leaf cigars and cheroots were occasionally used in lieu of cocaine.[3] If physicians had realized that titration of the dose was easier and relief came faster when marijuana was inhaled, they might have preferred to administer it by smoking. However, in the 19th century it was prepared chiefly as a tincture (alcoholic solution), generally referred to as tincture of hemp, tincture of cannabis, or Cannabis indica. The potency and bioavailability of oral cannabis varied widely, and there were no reliable bioassay techniques. Nevertheless, physicians prescribed cannabis without much concern about overdoses or side effects, because they knew how safe it was. But understandably, they considered it less reliable as an analgesic than opium and opium derivatives. Furthermore, unlike opiates, it could not be used parenterally because it was not water-soluble. Then, at the turn of the century, the first synthetic analgesics and hypnotics (aspirin and barbiturates) became available. Physicians were immediately attracted to these drugs because their potencies were fixed and they were easily dispensed as pills.

Beginning in the 1920s, interest in cannabis as a recreational drug grew, along with a disinformation campaign calculated to discourage that use. In 1937 the first draconian federal legislation against marijuana, the Marijuana Tax Act, was passed. At that time the medical use of cannabis had already declined considerably; the Act made prescription of marijuana so cumbersome that physicians abandoned it. Now physicians themselves became victims of the "Reefer Madness" madness. Beginning with an editorial published in the *Journal of the American Medical Association* in 1945, the medical establishment became one of the most effective agents of cannabis prohibition.[4]

The modern renaissance of medicinal cannabis began in the early 1970s, when several young patients who were being treated with the recently developed cancer chemotherapies discovered that marijuana was much more effective than conventional medicines for the relief of the intense and prolonged nausea and vomiting induced by some of these agents.[5] Word spread rapidly over the cancer treatment grapevine. By mid-decade, the capacity of marijuana to lower intraocular pressure had been observed, and patients suffering from glaucoma began to experiment with it.[6] As the AIDS epidemic gathered momentum, many patients who suffered HIV-associated weight loss learned that marijuana was the most effective and least toxic treatment for this life-threatening symptom. These three new medical uses of cannabis have led to wider folk experimentation. The use of marijuana in the symptomatic treatment of convulsive disorders, migraine, insomnia, and dysmenorrhea has been rediscovered.

We have now identified more than 30 symptoms and syndromes for which patients have found cannabis useful,[7] and others will undoubtedly be discovered. Many patients regard it as more effective than conventional medicines, with fewer or less disturbing side effects. Consider the pain of osteoarthritis, which was often treated in the 19th century with tincture of cannabis. Aspirin, the first of the non-steroidal antiinflammatory drugs (NSAIDs), rapidly displaced cannabis as the treatment of choice for this and many other kinds of mild to moderate pain. But NSAIDs now take more than 7,000 lives annually in the United States alone; cannabis, by contrast, has never killed anyone using it for the relief of pain or any other purpose.[8] It is not surprising that many patients now treat their osteoarthritis with cannabis, asserting that it provides a better quality of pain relief than NSAIDs and also elevates their spirits.

The number of Americans who understand the medical uses of cannabis has grown greatly in the last few years. The passage of initiatives or legislation allowing some restricted legal use of cannabis as a medicine in eight states is the most striking political manifestation of this growing interest. The state laws have led to a battle with federal authorities who, until recently, proclaimed medical marijuana to be a hoax. Under public pressure to acknowledge the medical potential of marijuana, the director of the Office of National Drug Policy, Barry McCaffrey, authorized a review by the Institute of Medicine [IOM] of the National Academy of Science which was published in March of 1999.[9]

The report acknowledged the medical value of marijuana, but grudgingly. One of its most important shortcomings was a failure to put into perspective the vast anecdotal evidence of marijuana's striking medicinal versatility and limited toxicity. The report states that smoking is too dangerous a form of delivery, but this conclusion is based on an exaggerated evaluation of the toxicity of the smoke. The report's Recommendation Six would allow patients with what it calls "debilitating symptoms (such as intractable pain or vomiting)" to use smoked marijuana for only six months, and then only after all other approved medicines have failed. The treatment would have to be monitored with "an oversight strategy comparable to an institutional review board process."[10] This would make legal use of medical cannabis impossible in practice. The IOM would have patients who find cannabis helpful when taken by inhalation wait for years until a means of delivering smoke-free cannabinoids is developed. But there are already prototype devices which take advantage of the fact that cannabinoids vaporize at temperatures below the ignition point of dried cannabis plant material.

The authors of the IOM report discuss marijuana as if it were a drug like thalidomide, with well-established serious toxicity (phocomelia) and limited clinical usefulness (leprosy). This is inappropriate for a drug with a long history, limited toxicity, unusual versatility, and easy availability. But at least the report confirms that even government officials no longer doubt that cannabis has medical uses. Inevitably, cannabinoids will eventually be allowed to compete with other medicines in the treatment of a variety of symptoms and conditions; the only uncertainty involves the form in which they will be delivered.

When I first considered this issue in the early 1970s, I assumed that cannabis as medicine would be identical to the marijuana that is used for other purposes (the dried flowering tops of female Cannabis indica plants); its toxicity is minimal, its dosage is easily titrated and, once freed of the prohibition tariff, it will be inexpensive. I thought the main problem was its classification in Schedule I of the Comprehensive Drug Abuse and Control Act of 1970, which describes it as having a high potential for abuse, no accepted medical use in the United States, and lack of accepted safety for use under medical supervision. At that time I naively believed that a change to Schedule II would overcome a major obstacle to its legal availability as a medicine. I had already come to believe that the greatest harm in recreational use of marijuana came not from the drug itself but from the effects of prohibition. But I saw that as a separate issue; I believed that, like opiates and cocaine, cannabis could be used medically while remaining outlawed for other purposes. I thought that once it was transferred to Schedule II, clinical research on marijuana would be pursued eagerly. A quarter of a century later, I have begun to doubt this. It would be highly desirable if marijuana could be approved as a legitimate medicine within the present federal regulatory system, but it now seems to me unlikely.

Today, transferring marijuana to Schedule II (high potential for abuse, limited medical use) would not be enough to make it available as a prescription drug. Such drugs must undergo rigorous, expensive, and time-consuming tests before they are approved by the FDA [Food and Drug Administration]. This system is designed to regulate the commercial distribution of drug company products and protect the public against false or misleading claims about their efficacy and safety. The drug is generally a single synthetic chemical that a pharmaceutical company has developed and patented. The company submits an application to the FDA and tests it first for safety in animals and then for clinical safety and efficacy. The company must present evidence from double-blind controlled studies showing that the drug is more effective than a placebo and as effective as available drugs. Case reports, expert opinion, and clinical experience are not considered sufficient. The cost of this evaluation exceeds 200 million dollars per drug.

It is unlikely that whole smoked marijuana should or will ever be developed as an officially recognized medicine via this route. Thousands of years of use have demonstrated its medical value; the extensive government-supported effort of the last three decades to establish a sufficient level of toxicity to support the harsh prohibition has instead provided a record of safety that is more compelling than that of most approved medicines. The modern FDA protocol is not necessary to establish a risk-benefit estimate for a drug with such a history. To impose this protocol on cannabis would be like making the same demand of aspirin, which was accepted as a medicine more than 60 years before the advent of the double-blind controlled study. Many years of experience have shown us that aspirin has many uses and limited toxicity, yet today it could not be marshalled through the FDA approval process. The patent has long since expired, and with it the incentive to underwrite the enormous cost of this modern seal of approval. Cannabis too is unpatentable, so the only source of funding for a "start-from-scratch" approval would be the government, which is, to put it mildly, unlikely to be helpful. Other reasons for doubting that marijuana would ever be officially approved are today's anti-smoking climate and, most important, the widespread use of cannabis for purposes disapproved by the government.

To see the importance of this obstacle, consider the effects of granting marijuana legitimacy as a medicine while prohibiting it for any other use. How would the appropriate "labeled" uses be determined and how would "off-label" uses be proscribed? Then there is the question of who will provide the cannabis. The federal government now provides marijuana from its farm in Mississippi to eight patients under a now-discontinued Compassionate IND [investigational new drug] program. But surely the government could not or would not produce marijuana for many thousands of patients receiving prescriptions, any more than it does for other prescription drugs. If production is contracted out, will the farmers have to enclose their fields with security fences and protect them with security guards? How would the marijuana be distributed? If through pharmacies, how would they provide secure facilities capable of keeping fresh supplies? Would the price of pharmaceutical marijuana have to be controlled: not too high, lest patients be tempted to buy it on the street or grow their own; not too low, lest people with marginal or fictitious "medical" conditions besiege their doctors for prescriptions? What about the parallel problems with potency? When urine tests are demanded for workers, how would those who use marijuana legally as a medicine be distinguished from those who use it for other purposes?

To realize the full potential of cannabis as a medicine in the setting of the present prohibition system, we would have to address all these problems and more. A delivery system that successfully navigated this minefield would be cumbersome, inefficient, and bureaucratically top-heavy. Government and medical licensing boards would insist on tight restrictions, challenging physicians as though cannabis were a dangerous drug every time it was used for any new patient or purpose. There would be constant conflict with one of two outcomes: patients would not get all the benefits they should, or they would get the benefits by abandoning the legal system for the black market or their own gardens and closets.

A solution now being proposed, notably in the IOM Report, is what might be called the "pharmaceuticalization" of cannabis: prescription of isolated individual cannabinoids, synthetic cannabinoids, and cannabinoid analogs. The IOM Report states that "if there is any future for marijuana as a medicine, it lies in its isolated components, the cannabinoids, and their synthetic derivatives." It goes on: "Therefore, the purpose of clinical trials of smoked marijuana would not be to develop marijuana as a licensed drug, but such trials could be a first step towards the development of rapid-onset, non-smoked cannabinoid delivery systems."[11] Some cannabinoids and analogs may have advantages over whole smoked or ingested marijuana in limited circumstances. For example, cannabidiol may be more effective as an anti-anxiety medicine and an anticonvulsant when it is not taken along with THC [the chief intoxicant in marijuana], which sometimes generates anxiety. Other cannabinoids and analogs may occasionally prove more useful than marijuana because they can be administered intravenously. For example, 15 to 20 percent of patients lose consciousness after suffering a thrombotic or embolic stroke, and some people who suffer brain syndrome after a severe blow to the head become unconscious. The new analog dexanabinol (HU-211) has been shown to protect brain cells from damage by glutamate excitotoxicity in these circumstances, and it will be possible to give it intravenously to an unconscious person.[12] Presumably other analogs may offer related advantages. Some of these commercial products may also lack the psychoactive effects which make marijuana useful to some for non-medical purposes. Therefore they will not be defined as "abusable" drugs subject to the constraints of the Comprehensive Drug Abuse and Control Act. Nasal sprays, nebulizers, skin patches, pills, and suppositories can be used to avoid exposure of the lungs to the particulate matter in marijuana smoke.

The question is whether these developments will make marijuana itself medically obsolete. Surely many of these new products would be useful and safe enough for commercial development. It is uncertain, however, whether pharmaceutical companies will find them worth the enormous development costs. Some may be (for example, a cannabinoid inverse agonist that reduces appetite might be highly lucrative), but for most specific symptoms, analogs or combinations of analogs are unlikely to be more useful than natural cannabis. Nor are they likely to have a significantly wider spectrum of therapeutic uses, since the natural product contains the compounds (and synergistic combinations of compounds) from which they are derived. THC and cannabidiol, as well as dexanabinol, protect brain cells after a stroke or traumatic injury. Synthetic tetrahydrocannabinol (dronabinol or Marinol) has been available for years, but patients generally find whole smoked marijuana to be more effective.

The cannabinoids in whole marijuana can be separated from the burnt plant products by vaporization devices that will be inexpensive when manufactured in large numbers. Inhalation is a highly effective means of delivery, and faster means will not be available for analogs (except in a few situations such as parenteral injection in a patient who is unconscious or suffering from pulmonary impairment). Furthermore, any new analog will have to have an acceptable therapeutic ratio. The therapeutic ratio of marijuana is not known because it has never caused an overdose death, but it is estimated on the basis of extrapolation from animal data to be 20,000 to 40,000. The therapeutic ratio of a new analog is unlikely to be higher than that; in fact, new analogs may be less safe than smoked marijuana because it will be physically possible to ingest more of them. And there is the problem of classification under the Comprehensive Drug Abuse and Control Act for analogs with psychoactive effects. The more restrictive the classification of a drug, the less likely drug companies are to develop it and physicians to prescribe it. Recognizing this economic fact of life, Unimed, the manufacturer of Marinol, has recently succeeding in getting it reclassified from Schedule II to Schedule III. Nevertheless, many physicians will continue to avoid prescribing it for fear of the drug enforcement authorities.

A somewhat different approach to the pharmaceuticalization of cannabis is being taken by a British company, G. W. Pharmaceuticals. Recognizing the great usefulness of naturally occurring cannabinoids, this firm is developing a seed bank of cannabis strains with particular value in the treatment of various symptoms and disorders. They are also attempting to develop products and delivery systems which will skirt the two primary concerns about the use of marijuana as a medicine: the smoke and the psychoactive effects (the "high").

To avoid the need for smoking, G. W. Pharmaceuticals is exploring the possibility of delivering cannabis extracts sublingually or via nebulizers. The company expects its products to be effective therapeutically at doses too low to produce the psychoactive effects sought by recreational and other users. My clinical experience leads me to question whether this is possible in most or even many cases. Furthermore, the issue is complicated by tolerance. Recreational users soon discover that the more often they use marijuana, the less "high" they feel. A patient who smokes cannabis frequently for the relief of, say, chronic pain or elevated intraocular pressure will not experience a "high" at all. Furthermore, as a clinician who has considerable experience with medical cannabis use, I have to question whether the psychoactive effect is necessarily undesirable. Many patients suffering from serious chronic illnesses say that cannabis generally improves their spirits. If they note psychoactive effects at all, they speak of a slight mood elevation—certainly nothing unwanted or incapacitating.

In principle, administration of cannabis extracts via a nebulizer has the same advantages as smoked marijuana—rapid onset and easy titratability of the effect. But the design of the G. W. Pharmaceutical nebulizer negates this advantage. The device has electronic controls that monitor the dose and halt delivery if the patient tries to take more than the physician or pharmacist has set it to deliver. The proposal to use this cumbersome and expensive device apparently reflects a fear that patients cannot accurately titrate the amount or a concern that they might take more than they need and experience some degree of "high" (always assuming, doubtfully, that the two can easily be separated, especially when cannabis is used infrequently). Because these products will be considerably more expensive than natural marijuana, they will succeed only if patients and physicians take the health risks of smoking very seriously and feel that it is necessary to avoid any hint of a psychoactive effect.

In the end, the commercial success of any cannabinoid product will depend on how vigorously the prohibition against marijuana is enforced. It is safe to predict that new analogs and extracts will cost much more than whole smoked or ingested marijuana even at the inflated prices imposed by the prohibition tariff. I doubt that pharmaceutical companies would be interested in developing cannabinoid products if they had to compete with natural marijuana on a level playing field. The most common reason for using Marinol is the illegality of marijuana, and many patients choose to ignore the law for reasons of efficacy and price. The number of arrests on marijuana charges has been steadily increasing and has now reached nearly 700,000 annually, yet patients continue to use smoked cannabis as a medicine. I wonder whether any level of enforcement would compel enough compliance with the law to embolden drug companies to commit the many millions of dollars it would take to develop new cannabinoid products. Unimed is able to profit from the exorbitantly priced dronabinol only because the United States government underwrote much of the cost of development. Pharmaceutical companies will undoubtedly develop useful cannabinoid products, some of which may not be subject to the constraints of the Comprehensive Drug Abuse and Control Act. But this pharmaceuticalization will never displace natural marijuana for most medical purposes.

Thus two powerful forces are now colliding: the growing acceptance of medical cannabis and the proscription against any use of marijuana, medical or non-medical. There are no signs that we are moving away from absolute prohibition to a regulatory system that would allow responsible use of marijuana. As a result, we are going to have two distribution systems for medical cannabis: the conventional model of pharmacy-filled prescriptions for FDA-approved medicines, and a model closer to the distribution of alternative and herbal medicines. The only difference, an enormous one, will be the continued illegality of whole smoked or ingested cannabis. In any case, increasing medical use by either distribution pathway will inevitably make growing numbers of people familiar with cannabis and its derivatives. As they learn that its harmfulness has been greatly exaggerated and its usefulness underestimated, the pressure will increase for drastic change in the way we as a society deal with this drug.

# References

1. W. B. O'Shaughnessy. On the Preparations of the Indian Hemp, or Gunjah (*Cannabis indica*): The Effects on the Animal System in Health, and Their Utility in the Treatment of Tetanus and Other Convulsive Diseases. *Transactions of the Medical and Physical Society of Bengal* (1838–1840), p. 460.
2. L. Grinspoon. *Marihuana Reconsidered*. Cambridge, Mass.: Harvard University Press, 1971, pp. 218–230.
3. L. Grinspoon and J. B. Bakalar. *Cocaine: A Drug and Its Social Evolution*, Revised Edition. New York: Basic Books, 1985, p. 279.
4. Marihuana Problems. Editorial, *Journal of the American Medical Association*, Vol. 127 (1945), p. 1129.
5. L. Grinspoon and J. B. Bakalar. *Marihuana, the Forbidden Medicine*, Revised and Expanded Edition. New Haven: Yale University Press, 1997, pp. 25–27.

6. R. S. Hepler and I. M. Frank. Marihuana Smoking and Intraocular Pressure. *Journal of the American Medical Association*, Vol. 217 (1971), p. 1392.
7. L. Grinspoon and J. B. Bakalar. *Marihuana, the Forbidden Medicine*, Revised and Expanded Edition. New Haven: Yale University Press, 1997.
8. S. Girkipal, D. R. Ramey, D. Morfeld, G. Singh, H. T. Hatoum, and J. F. Fries. Gastrointestinal Tract Complications of Nonsteroidal Anti-inflammatory Drug Treatment in Rheumatoid Arthritis. *Archives of Internal Medicine*, Vol. 156 (July 22, 1996), pp. 1530-1536.
9. *Marijuana and Medicine: Assessing the Science Base.* J. E. Joy, S. J. Watson, Jr., and J. A. Benson, Jr., Editors. Institute of Medicine, Washington, D.C.: National Academy Press (1999).
10. Ibid, pp. 7–8.
11. Ibid, p. 11.
12. R. R. Leker, E. Shohami, O. Abramsky, and H. Ovadia. Dexanabinol; A Novel Neuroprotective Drug in Experimental Focal Cerebral Ischemia. *Journal of Neurological Science*, Vol. 162, No. 2 (January 15, 1999), pp. 114–119; E. Shohami, M. Novikov, and R. Bass. Long-term Effect of HU-211, a Novel Non-competitive NMDA Antagonist, on Motor and Memory Functions after Closed Head Injury in the Rat. *Brain Research*, Vol. 674, No. 1 (March 13, 1995), pp. 55–62.

James R. McDonough

 **NO**

# Marijuana on the Ballot

**W**hile it has long been clear that chemical compounds found in the marijuana plant offer potential for medical use, smoking the raw plant is a method of delivery supported neither by law nor recent scientific evidence. The Food and Drug Administration's approval process, which seeks to ensure the purity of chemical compounds in legitimate drugs, sets the standard for medical validation of prescription drugs as safe and effective. Diametrically opposed to this long-standing safeguard of medical science is the recent spate of state election ballots that have advocated the use of a smoked plant—the marijuana leaf—for "treating" an unspecified number of ailments. It is a tribute to the power of political activism that popular vote has displaced objective science in advancing what would be the only smoked drug in America under the guise of good medicine.

Two recent studies of the potential medical utility of marijuana advocate development of a non-smoked, rapid onset delivery system of the cannabis compounds. But state ballot initiatives that seek legalization of smoking marijuana as medicine threaten to circumvent credible research. Advocates for smoking marijuana appear to want to move ahead at all costs, irrespective of dangers to the user. They make a well-financed, emotional appeal to the voting public claiming that what they demand is humane, useful, and safe. Although they rely largely on anecdote to document their claims, they seize upon partial statements that purport to validate their assertions. At the same time, these partisans —described by Chris Wren, the highly respected journalist for the *New York Times,* as a small coalition of libertarians, liberals, humanitarians, and hedonists—reject the main conclusions of medical science: that there is little future in smoked marijuana as a medically approved medication.

## A Dearth of Scientific Support

Compounds found in marijuana may have medical potential, but science does not support smoking the plant in its crude form as an appropriate delivery system. An exploration of two comprehensive inquiries into the medical potential of marijuana indicates the following:

- Science has identified only the *potential* medical benefit of chemical compounds, such as THC, found in marijuana. Ambitious research is necessary to understand fully how these substances affect the human body.
- Experts who have dealt with all available data *do not* recommend that the goal of research should be smoked marijuana for medical conditions. Rather, they support development of a smoke-free, rapid-onset delivery system for compounds found in the plant.

In 1997, the National Institutes of Health (NIH) met "to review the scientific data concerning the potential therapeutic uses of marijuana and the need for and feasibility of additional research." The collection of experts had experience in relevant studies and clinical research, but held no preconceived opinions about the medical use of marijuana. They were asked the following questions: What is the current state of scientific knowledge; what significant questions remain unanswered; what is the medical potential; what possible uses deserve further research; and what issues should be considered if clinical trials are conducted?

Shortly thereafter, the White House Office of National Drug Control Policy (ONDCP) asked the Institute of Medicine (IOM) to execute a similar task: to form a panel that would "conduct a review of the scientific evidence to assess the potential health benefits and risks of marijuana and its constituent cannabinoids." Selected reviewers were among the most accomplished in the disciplines of neuroscience, pharmacology, immunology, drug abuse, drug laws, oncology, infectious diseases, and ophthalmology. Their analysis focused on the effects of isolated cannabinoids, risks associated with medical use of marijuana, and the use of smoked marijuana. Their findings in the IOM study stated:

> "Compared to most drugs, the accumulation of medical knowledge about marijuana has proceeded in reverse. Typically, during the course of drug development, a compound is first found to have some medical benefit. Following this, extensive tests are undertaken to determine the safety and proper dose of the drug for medical use. Marijuana, in contrast, has been widely used in the United States for decades.... The data on the adverse effects of marijuana are more extensive than the data on effectiveness. Clinical studies of marijuana are difficult to conduct."

Nevertheless, the IOM report concluded that cannabinoid drugs do have *potential* for therapeutic use. It specifically named pain, nausea and vomiting, and lack of appetite as symptoms for which cannabinoids may be of benefit, stating that cannabinoids are "moderately well suited" for AIDS wasting and nausea resulting from chemotherapy. The report found that cannabinoids "probably have a natural role in pain modulation, control of movement, and memory," but that this role "is likely to be multi-faceted and remains unclear."

In addressing the possible effects of smoked marijuana on pain, the NIH report explained that no clinical trials involving patients with "naturally occurring pain" have ever been conducted but that two credible studies of cancer pain indicated analgesic benefit. Addressing another possible benefit—the reduction of nausea related to chemotherapy—the NIH report described a study comparing oral administration of THC (via a drug called Dronabinol) and smoked marijuana. Of 20 patients, nine expressed no preference between the two, seven preferred the oral THC, and only four preferred smoked marijuana. In summary, the report states, "No scientific questions have been definitively answered about the efficacy of smoked marijuana in chemotherapy-related nausea and vomiting."

In the area of glaucoma, the effect of marijuana on intraocular pressure (the cause of optic nerve damage that typifies glaucoma) was explored, and smoked marijuana was found to reduce this pressure. However, the NIH report failed to find evidence that marijuana can "safely and effectively lower intraocular pressure enough to prevent optic nerve damage." The report concluded that the "mechanism of action" of smoked marijuana or THC in pill form on intraocular pressure is not known and calls for more research.

In addressing appetite stimulation and wasting related to AIDS, the NIH report recognized the potential benefit of marijuana. However, the report also noted the lack of pertinent data. The researchers pointed out that the evidence known to date, although plentiful, is anecdotal, and "no objective data relative to body composition alterations, HIV replication, or immunologic function in HIV patients are available."

Smoking marijuana as medicine was recommended by neither report. The IOM report called smoked marijuana a "crude THC delivery system" that is not recommended because it delivers harmful substances, pointing out that botanical products are susceptible to problems with consistency, contaminations, uncertain potencies, and instabilities. The NIH report reached the same conclusion and explained that eliminating the smoked aspect of marijuana would "remove an important obstacle" from research into the potential medical benefits of the plant.

These studies present a consistent theme: Cannabinoids in marijuana do show potential for symptom management of several conditions, but research is inadequate to explain definitively *how* cannabinoids operate to deliver these potential benefits. Nor did the studies attribute any curative effects to marijuana; at best, only the symptoms of particular medical conditions are affected. The finding most important to the debate is that the studies did not advocate smoked marijuana as medicine. To the contrary, the NIH report called for a non-smoked alternative as a focus of further research. The IOM report recommended smoking marijuana as medicine only in the most extreme circumstances *when all other medication has failed* and then only when administration of marijuana is under strict medical supervision.

These conclusions from two studies, based not on rhetorical conjecture but on credible scientific research, do not support the legalization of smoked marijuana as medicine.

# The Scientific Community's Views

The conclusions of the NIH and IOM reports are supported by commentary published in the nation's medical journals. Much of this literature focuses on the problematic aspect of smoke as a delivery system when using cannabinoids for medical purposes. One physician-authored article describes smoking "crude plant material" as "troublesome" to many doctors and "unpleasant" to many patients. Dr. Eric Voth, chairman of the International Drug Strategy Institute, stated in a 1997 article published in the *Journal of the American Medical Association* (JAMA): "To support research on smoked pot does not make sense. We're currently in a huge anti-tobacco thrust in this country, which is appropriate. So why should we waste money on drug delivery that is based on smoking?" Voth recommends non-smoked analogs to THC.

In September, 1998, the editor in chief of the *New England Journal of Medicine*, Dr. Jerome P. Kassirer, in a coauthored piece with Dr. Marcia Angell, wrote:

> "Until the 20th century, most remedies were botanical, a few of which were found through trial and error to be helpful. All of that began to change in the 20th century as a result of rapid advances in medical science. In particular, the evolution of the randomized, controlled clinical trial enabled researchers to study with precision the safety, efficacy, and dose effects of proposed treatments and the indications for them. No longer do we have to rely on trial and error and anecdotes. We have learned to ask and expect statistically reliable evidence before accepting conclusions about remedies."

Dr. Robert DuPont of the Georgetown University Department of Psychiatry points out that those who aggressively advocate smoking marijuana as medicine "undermine" the potentially beneficial roles of the NIH and IOM studies. As does Dr. Voth, DuPont discusses the possibility of nonsmoked delivery methods. He asserts that if the scientific community were to accept smoked marijuana as medicine, the public would likely perceive the decision as influenced by politics rather than science. Dupont concludes that if research is primarily concerned with the needs of the sick, it is unlikely that science will approve of smoked marijuana as medicine.

Even those who advocate smoking marijuana for medicine are occasionally driven to caution. Dr. Lester Grinspoon, a Harvard University professor and advocate of smoking marijuana, warned in a 1994 JAMA article: "The one area we have to be concerned about is pulmonary function. The lungs were not made to inhale anything but fresh air." Other experts have only disdain for the loose medical claims for smoked marijuana. Dr. Janet Lapey, executive director of Concerned Citizens for Drug Prevention, likened research on smoked marijuana to using opium pipes to test morphine. She advocates research on isolated active compounds rather than smoked marijuana.

The findings of the NIH and IOM reports, and other commentary by members of the scientific and medical communities, contradict the idea that plant smoking is an appropriate vehicle for delivering whatever compounds research may find to be of benefit.

# Enter the FDA

The mission of the Food and Drug Administration's (FDA) Center for Drug Evaluation and Research is "to assure that safe and effective drugs are available to the American people." Circumvention of the FDA approval process would remove this essential safety mechanism intended to safeguard public health. The FDA approval process is not designed to keep drugs out of the hands of the sick but to offer a system to ensure that drugs prevent, cure, or treat a medical condition. FDA approval can involve testing of hundreds of compounds, which allows scientists to alter them for improved performance. The IOM report addresses this situation explicitly: "Medicines today are expected to be of known composition and quantity. Even in cases where marijuana can provide relief from symptoms, the crude plant mixture does not meet this modern expectation."

For a proposed drug to gain approval by the FDA, a potential manufacturer must produce a new drug application. The application must provide enough information for FDA reviewers to determine (among other criteria) "whether the drug is safe and effective for its proposed use(s), whether the benefits of the drug outweigh its risks [and] whether the methods used in manufacturing the drug and the controls used to maintain the drug's quality are adequate to preserve the drug's integrity, strength, quality, and purity."

On the "benefits" side, the Institute of Medicine found that the therapeutic effects of cannabinoids are "generally modest" and that for the majority of symptoms there are approved drugs that are more effective. For example, superior glaucoma and antinausea medications have already been developed. In addition, the new drug Zofran may provide more relief than THC for chemotherapy patients. Dronabinol, the synthetic THC, offers immunocompromised HIV patients a safe alternative to inhaling marijuana smoke, which contains carcinogens.

On the "risks" side, there is strong evidence that smoking marijuana has detrimental health effects. Unrefined marijuana contains approximately 400 chemicals that become combustible when smoked, producing in turn over 2,000 impure chemicals. These substances, many of which remain unidentified, include carcinogens. The IOM report states that, when used chronically, "marijuana smoking is associated with abnormalities of cells lining the human respiratory tract. Marijuana smoke, like tobacco smoke, is associated with increased risk of cancer, lung damage, and poor pregnancy outcomes." A subsequent study by Dr. Zuo-Feng Zhary of the Jonsson Cancer Center at UCLA determined that the carcinogens in marijuana are much stronger than those in tobacco.

Chronic bronchitis and increased incidence of pulmonary disease are associated with frequent use of smoked marijuana, as are reduced sperm motility and testosterone levels in males. Decreased immune system response, which is likely to increase vulnerability to infection and tumors, is also associated with frequent use. Even a slight decrease in immune response can have major public health ramifications. Because marijuana by-products remain in body fat for several weeks, interference with normal body functioning may continue beyond the time of use. Among the known effects of smoking marijuana is impaired lung function similar to the type caused by cigarette smoking.

In addressing the efficacy of cannabinoid drugs, the IOM report—after recognizing "potential therapeutic value"—added that smoked marijuana is "a crude THC delivery system that also delivers harmful substances." Purified cannabinoid compounds are preferable to plants in crude form, which contain inconsistent chemical composition. The "therapeutic window" between the desirable and adverse effects of marijuana and THC is narrow at best and may not exist at all, in many cases.

The scientific evidence that marijuana's potential therapeutic benefits are modest, that other approved drugs are generally more effective, and that smoking marijuana is unhealthy, indicates that smoked marijuana is not a viable candidate for FDA approval. Without such approval, smoked marijuana cannot achieve legitimate status as an approved drug that patients can readily use. This reality renders the advocacy of smoking marijuana as medicine both misguided and impractical.

## Medicine by Ballot Initiave?

While ballot initiatives are an indispensable part of our democracy, they are imprudent in the context of advancing smoked marijuana as medicine because they confound our system of laws, create conflict between state and federal law, and fail to offer a proper substitute for science.

Ballot initiatives to legalize smoking marijuana as medicine have had a tumultuous history. In 1998 alone, initiatives were passed in five states, but any substantive benefits in the aftermath were lacking. For example, a Colorado proposal was ruled invalid before the election. An Ohio bill was passed but subsequently repealed. In the District of Colombia, Congress disallowed the counting of ballot results. Six other states permit patients to smoke marijuana as medicine but only by prescription, and doctors, dubious about the validity of a smoked medicine, wary of liability suits, and concerned about legal and professional risks are reluctant to prescribe it for their patients. Although voters passed Arizona's initiative, the state legislature originally blocked the measure. The version that eventually became Arizona law is problematic because it conflicts with federal statute.

Indeed, legalization at the state level creates a direct conflict between state and federal law in every case, placing patients, doctors, police, prosecutors, and public officials in a difficult position. The fundamental legal problem with prescription of marijuana is that federal law prohibits such use, rendering state law functionally ineffective.

To appreciate fully the legal ramifications of ballot initiatives, consider one specific example. California's is perhaps the most publicized, and illustrates the chaos that can result from such initiatives. Enacted in 1996, the California Compassionate Use Act (also known as Proposition 215) was a ballot initiative intended to afford legal protection to seriously ill patients who use marijuana therapeutically. The act explicitly states that marijuana used by patients must first be recommended by a physician, and refers to such use as a "right" of the people of California. According to the act, physicians and patients are not subject to prosecution if they are compliant with the terms of the legislation. The act names cancer, anorexia, AIDS, chronic pain, spasticity, glaucoma, arthritis, and migraine as conditions that may be appropriately treated by marijuana, but it also includes the proviso: "or any other illness for which marijuana provides relief."

Writing in December 1999, a California doctor, Ryan Thompson, summed up the medical problems with Proposition 215:

"As it stands, it creates vague, ill-defined guidelines that are obviously subject to abuse. The most glaring areas are as follows:

- A patient does not necessarily need to be seen, evaluated or diagnosed as having any specific medical condition to qualify for the use of marijuana.
- There is no requirement for a written prescription or even a written recommendation for its medical use.
- Once 'recommended,' the patient never needs to be seen again to assess the effectiveness of the treatment and potentially could use that 'recommendation' for the rest of his or her life.
- There is no limitation to the conditions for which it can be used, it can be recommended for virtually any condition, even if it is not believed to be effective."

The doctor concludes by stating: "Certainly as a physician I have witnessed the detrimental effects of marijuana use on patients and their families. It is not a harmless substance."

Passage of Proposition 215 resulted in conflict between California and the federal government. In February 1997, the Executive Office of the President issued its response to the California Compassionate Use Act (as well as Arizona's Proposition 200). The notice stated:

"[The] Department of Justice's (D.O.J.) position is that a practitioner's practice of recommending or prescribing Schedule I controlled substances is not consistent with the public interest (as that phrase is used in the federal Controlled Substances Act) and will lead to administrative action by the Drug Enforcement Administration (DEA) to revoke the practitioner's registration."

The notice indicated that U.S. attorneys in California and Arizona would consider cases for prosecution using certain criteria. These included lack of a bona fide doctor-patient relationship, a "high volume" of prescriptions (or recommendations) for Schedule I drugs, "significant" profits derived from such prescriptions, prescriptions to minors, and "special circumstances" like impaired driving accidents involving serious injury.

The federal government's reasons for taking such a stance are solid. Dr. Donald Vereen of the Office of National Drug Control Policy explains that "research-based evidence" must be the focus when evaluating the risks and benefits of any drug, the only approach that provides a *rational* basis for making such a determination. He also explains that since testing by the Food and Drug

Administration and other government agencies is designed to protect public health, circumvention of the process is unwise.

While the federal government supports FDA approved cannabinoid-based drugs, it maintains that ballot initiatives should not be allowed to remove marijuana evaluation from the realm of science and the drug approval process—a position based on a concern for public health. The Department of Health and Human Services has revised its regulations by making research-grade marijuana more available and intends to facilitate more research of cannabinoids. The department does not, however, intend to lower its standards of scientific proof.

Problems resulting from the California initiative are not isolated to conflict between the state and federal government. California courts themselves limited the distribution of medical marijuana. A 1997 California appellate decision held that the state's Compassionate Use Act only allowed purchase of medical marijuana from a patient's "primary caregiver," not from "drug dealers on street corners" or "sales centers such as the Cannabis Buyers' Club." This decision allowed courts to enjoin marijuana clubs.

The course of California's initiative and those of other states illustrate that such ballot-driven movements are not a legally effective or reliable way to supply the sick with whatever medical benefit the marijuana plant might hold. If the focus were shifted away from smoking the plant and toward a non-smoked alternative based on scientific research, much of this conflict could be avoided.

## Filling "Prescriptions"

It is one thing to pass a ballot initiative defining a burning plant as medicine. It is yet another to make available such "medicine" if the plant itself remains—as it should—illegal. Recreational use, after all, cannot be equated with medicinal use, and none of the ballots passed were constructed to do so.

Nonetheless, cannabis buyers' clubs were quick to present the fiction that, for medical benefit, they were now in business to provided relief for the sick. In California, 13 such clubs rapidly went into operation, selling marijuana openly under the guise that doing so had been legitimized at the polls. The problem was that these organizations were selling to people under the flimsiest of facades. One club went so far as to proclaim: "All use of marijuana is medical. It makes you smarter. It touches the right brain and allows you to slow down, to smell the flowers."

Depending on the wording of the specific ballots, legal interpretation of what was allowed became problematic. The buyers' clubs became notorious for liberal interpretations of "prescription," "doctor's recommendation," and "medical." In California, Lucy Mae Tuck obtained a prescription for marijuana to treat hot flashes. Another citizen arrested for possession claimed he was medically entitled to his stash to treat a condition exacerbated by an ingrown toenail. Undercover police in several buyers clubs reported blatant sales to minors and adults with little attention to claims of medical need or a doctor's direction. Eventually, 10 of the 13 clubs in California were closed.

Further exacerbating the confusion over smoked marijuana as medicine are doctors' concerns over medical liability. Without the Food and Drug Administration's approval, marijuana cannot become a pharmaceutical drug to be purchased at local drug stores. Nor can there be any degree of confidence that proper doses can be measured out and chemical impurities eliminated in the marijuana that is obtained. After all, we are talking about a leaf, and a burning one at that. In the meantime, the harmful effects of marijuana have been documented in greater scientific detail than any findings about the medical benefits of smoking the plant.

Given the serious illnesses (for example, cancer and AIDS) of some of those who are purported to be in need of smoked marijuana for medical relief and their vulnerability to impurities and other toxic substances present in the plant, doctors are loath to risk their patients' health and their own financial well-being by prescribing it. As Dr. Peter Byeff, an oncologist at a Connecticut cancer center, points out: "If there's no mechanism for dispensing it, that doesn't help many of my patients. They're not going to go out and grow it in their backyards." Recognizing the availability of effective prescription medications to control nausea and vomiting, Byeff adds: "There's no reason to prescribe or dispense marijuana."

Medical professionals recognize what marijuana-as-medicine advocates seek to obscure. The chemical makeup of any two marijuana plants can differ significantly due to minor variations in cultivation. For example, should one plant receive relative to another as little as four more hours of collective sunlight before cultivation, the two could turn out to be significantly different in chemical composition. Potency also varies according to climate and geographical origin; it can also be affected by the way in which the plant is harvested and stored. Differences can be so profound that under current medical standards, two marijuana plants could be considered completely different drugs. Prescribing unproven, unmeasured, impure burnt leaves to relieve symptoms of a wide range of ailments does not seem to be the high point of American medical practice.

## Illegal Because Harmful

Cannabinoids found in the marijuana plant offer the potential for medical use. However, lighting the leaves of the plant on fire and smoking them amount to an impractical delivery system that involves health risks and deleterious legal consequences. There is a profound difference between an approval process that seeks to purify isolated compounds for safe and effective delivery, and legalization of smoking the raw plant material as medicine. To advocate the latter is to bypass the safety and efficacy built into America's medical system. Ballot initiatives for smoked marijuana comprise a dangerous, impractical shortcut that circumvents the drug-approval process. The resulting decriminalization of a dangerous and harmful drug turns out to be counterproductive—legally, politically, and scientifically.

Advocacy for smoked marijuana has been cast in terms of relief from suffering. The Hippocratic oath that doctors take specifies that they must "first, do no harm." Clearly some people supporting medical marijuana are genuinely concerned about the sick. But violating established medical procedure *does* do harm, and it confounds the political, medical, and legal processes that best serve American society. In the single-minded pursuit of an extreme position that harkens back to an era of home medicine and herbal remedies, advocates for smoked marijuana as medicinal therapy not only retard legitimate scientific progress but become easy prey for less noble-minded zealots who seek to promote the acceptance and use of marijuana, an essentially harmful—and, therefore, illegal—drug.

# POSTSCRIPT

## Should Marijuana Be Legal for Medicinal Purposes?

Grinspoon strongly advocates the legalization of marijuana for medical treatment. He believes that the delay in the medicalization of marijuana stems from arduous and restrictive procedures of the federal government and that the government blocks people in need from receiving medication that is both therapeutic and benign.

From McDonough's perspective, promoting marijuana as a medicinal agent would be a mistake because it has not been proven medically useful or safe. Moreover, he feels that the availability of marijuana should not be predicated on personal accounts of its benefits or on whether or not the public supports its use. Also, McDonough asserts that studies showing that marijuana has medical value suffer from unscientific methodology and other deficiencies. The results of previous research, McDonough contends, do not lend strong credence to marijuana's medicinal value.

Some people have expressed concern about what will happen if marijuana is approved for medicinal use. Would it then become more acceptable for nonmedical, recreational use? There is also a possibility that some people would misinterpret the government's message and think that marijuana *cures* cancer when, in fact, it would only be used to treat the side effects of the chemotherapy.

A central question is, If physicians feel that marijuana use is justified to properly care for seriously ill patients, should they promote this form of medical treatment even though it falls outside the law? Does the relief of pain and suffering for patients warrant going beyond what federal legislation says is acceptable? Also, should physicians be prosecuted if they recommend marijuana to their patients? What about the unknown risks of using an illegal drug? Is it worthwhile to ignore the possibility that marijuana may produce harmful side effects in order to alleviate pain or to treat other ailments?

Many marijuana proponents contend that the effort to prevent the legalization of marijuana for medical use is purely a political battle. Detractors maintain that the issue is purely scientific—that the data supporting marijuana's medical usefulness are inconclusive and scientifically unsubstantiated. And although the chief administrative law judge of the Drug Enforcement Administration (DEA) made a recommendation to change the status of marijuana from Schedule I to Schedule II, the DEA and other federal agencies are not compelled to do so, and they have resisted any change in the law.

Lester Grinspoon and James B. Bakalar's book *Marihuana, the Forbidden Medicine*, rev. and exp. ed. (Yale University Press, 1997) provides a thorough history and overview of marijuana's medical benefits. Articles that discuss whether or not marijuana should be legalized as a medication include "Marijuana and Medicine: Assessing the Science," by Stanley Watson, John Benson, and Janet Joy, *Archives of General Psychiatry* (June 2000) and "The Adverse Effects of Cannabis," by Wayne Hall and Nadia Solowij, *The Lancet* (November 14, 1998). In an often cited study by Richard Doblin and Mark Kleiman, "Marijuana as Medicine: A Survey of Oncologists," in Arnold Trebach and Kevin Zeese, eds., *New Frontiers in Drug Policy* (Drug Policy Foundation, 1991), almost half of the oncologists surveyed recommended marijuana to their patients to help them deal with the side effects of chemotherapy.

# ISSUE 10

## Should Doctors Promote Alcohol for Their Patients?

**YES: Stanton Peele**, from "Should Physicians Recommend Alcohol to Their Patients? Yes," *Priorities* (vol. 8, no. 1, 1996)

**NO: Albert B. Lowenfels**, from "Should Physicians Recommend Alcohol to Their Patients? No," *Priorities* (vol. 8, no. 1, 1996)

### ISSUE SUMMARY

**YES:** Psychologist Stanton Peele, an expert on alcoholism and addiction, asserts that physicians should recommend that their patients drink alcohol in moderate amounts. He maintains that numerous studies demonstrate the benefits of moderate alcohol use in reducing the risk of coronary heart disease, the leading cause of death in the United States.

**NO:** Albert B. Lowenfels, a professor at New York Medical College, contends that recommending moderate alcohol consumption is not prudent, especially since many people come from families with histories of alcohol abuse. He argues that it is inappropriate to extol the merits of moderate alcohol use to people who have abstained throughout their lives.

H eart disease is the leading cause of death in the United States, so it is reasonable to assume that people are interested in reducing the risks that lead to heart disease. Magazines are replete with articles describing ways to control factors that are linked with heart disease, such as minimizing the amount of saturated fats we consume, managing stress in our lives, controlling our blood pressure, and exercising to counter the effects of a sedentary lifestyle. It has been suggested that it is possible to diminish the likelihood of heart disease through the moderate consumption of alcohol. The relationship between alcohol and heart disease and whether or not physicians should recommend moderate alcohol consumption are the focus of this issue.

Discussions regarding the effects of alcohol usually center on the consequences associated with excessive alcohol use. Alcoholism is a devastating problem; an estimated 10–20 million people are affected by it. Individuals and families are sometimes ruined by the unhealthy use of alcohol. Despite a decline since the early 1980s in the number of fatalities linked to driving while intoxicated, about 16,000 people were killed in 2000 by drivers under the influence of alcohol. Alcoholism is often described as a national epidemic that poses a threat to every member of society. Is it therefore unwise for physicians to promote the moderate use of alcohol, even though such behavior may reduce the risk of heart disease?

An important aspect of this debate is what constitutes moderate alcohol use. The concept of moderation varies from one individual to another: To a social drinker, moderation may involve one, two, or three drinks per week. To an alcoholic, moderation is probably much more. To a college student, binge drinking may be viewed as moderate if it is limited to weekends and special occasions. Also, how much alcohol does one need to drink to reduce heart disease? How much is too much? Numerous studies show that two drinks per day are beneficial. However, due to individual and cultural differences, many experts feel that no one definition of moderation is adequate.

Health researcher Stanton Peele concurs that excessive alcohol use entails potential harm, but he contends that it is reasonable to advocate moderate alcohol consumption. Peele feels that educators and public health officials are preoccupied with discussing the negative effects of alcohol; thus, moderate alcohol use is not learned by young people. He also believes that researchers downplay the positive effects of alcohol because they fear that people would drink more than a moderate amount if alcohol's benefits were promoted.

Professor of surgery Albert B. Lowenfels questions the value of promoting moderate alcohol consumption for individuals who have maintained a lifetime of sobriety. He concurs that research shows that moderate use is beneficial to people who drink, but he argues that there is no research supporting the benefits of moderate alcohol use for abstainers. Some experts maintain that the evidence demonstrating the benefits of moderate alcohol use over abstinence is misleading because these studies are based on self-reports, which are frequently inaccurate and nonrepresentative.

One major concern with regard to promoting moderate alcohol consumption to lessen the likelihood of heart disease is that some people may misconstrue the information. Heavy drinkers, for example, may rationalize their behavior, maintaining that their drinking is for health purposes. Also, if moderate alcohol use acts as a protective behavior against heart disease, some people may disregard warnings against behaviors that are clearly harmful, such as smoking, not getting enough exercise, and practicing poor nutrition. Furthermore, moderate alcohol consumption is clearly harmful in some situations, such as before driving, while on medication, and during pregnancy.

In the following selections, Peele argues that there is strong evidence that two alcoholic drinks daily act to mitigate the risk of heart disease and that there may be other benefits from publicly advancing such a message. Lowenfels contends that the benefits of moderate alcohol use over abstinence are questionable. He also indicates that promoting a moderate-use message may lead to other problems, especially for individuals with a family history of heavy drinking.

**Stanton Peele**

 **YES**

# Should Physicians Recommend Alcohol to Their Patients? Yes

**W**henever I have visited a physician over the last decade, the following scenario has been replayed: We discuss my cholesterol levels (total, LDL and HDL). We review dietary guidelines and other medical recommendations. Then I say, "Don't forget to remind me to drink a glass or two of wine daily." Invariably, the doctor demurs: "That hasn't been proven to protect you against atherosclerosis."

My doctors, all of whom I have respected and liked, are wrong. Evidence has established beyond question that alcohol reduces coronary artery disease, America's major killer. This result has been found in the Harvard Physician and Nurse studies and in studies by Kaiser Permanente and the American Cancer Society (ACS). Indeed, the evidence that alcohol reduces coronary artery disease and mortality is better than the evidence for the statin drugs, the most potent cholesterol-reducing medications.

Drinking to excess does increase mortality from several sources, such as cancer, cirrhosis and accidents. But a series of studies in the 1990s—including those conducted in conjunction with Kaiser, ACS and Harvard—in the U.S., Britain and Denmark, have found that moderate drinking reduces overall mortality.

Nonetheless, many people object to the idea that doctors should inform their patients that moderate drinking may prolong life. They fear that such advice will justify the excessive drinking some patients already engage in, or they worry that encouragement from doctors will push people who cannot handle alcohol to drink.

The view that people are so stupid or malleable that they will become alcohol abusers because doctors tell them moderate drinking is good for them is demeaning and self-defeating. If people can't regulate their own diets, drinking and exercise, then doctors should avoid giving patients any information about their health behavior, no matter how potentially helpful.

Not only can people handle such information on lifestyle, it offers the primary and best way to attack heart disease. Of course, doctors may also prescribe medications. These medications rarely solve underlying problems, however, and they often cause adverse side effects that counterbalance their positive effects.

From Stanton Peele, "Should Physicians Recommend Alcohol to Their Patients? Yes," *Priorities,* vol. 8, no. 1 (1996), pp. 24, 26, 28. Copyright © 1996 by The American Council on Science and Health. Reprinted by permission of *Priorities,* a publication of The American Council on Science and Health, 1995 Broadway, 2d Floor, New York, NY 10023-5860. www.acsh.org.

Because they are not a cure, courses of medication, once begun, are rarely discontinued.

People are the best regulators of their own behaviors. Even those who drink excessively often benefit when doctors provide straightforward, accurate information. Clinical trials conducted by the World Health Organization around the world showed that so-called brief interventions, in which medical personnel advised heavy drinkers to reduce their drinking, are the most successful therapy for problem drinking.

But far more Americans drink less, not more, than would be most healthful for them. To fail to inform these patients about the benefits of moderate drinking is both counterproductive and dishonest. Physicians may ask, "How much alcohol do you drink," "Is there any reason that you don't drink (or that you drink so little)," and (to those without religious objections, previous drinking problems, etc.), "Do you know that one or two glasses of wine or beer a day can be good for your health if you can safely consume them?"

Here are the data about alcohol and mortality:

1. In 1995 Charles Fuchs and his colleagues at Harvard found that women who drank up to two drinks a day lived longer than abstainers. Subjects were 85,700 nurses.
2. In 1995, Morten Gronbaek and colleagues found that wine drinkers survived longer than abstainers, with those drinking three to five glasses daily having the lowest death rate. Subjects were 20,000 Danes.
3. In 1994, Richard Doll and his colleagues found that men who drank up to two drinks daily lived significantly longer than abstainers. Subjects were 12,300 British doctors.
4. In 1992 Il Suh and colleagues found a 40 percent reduction in coronary mortality among men drinking three and more drinks daily. The 11,700 male subjects were in the upper 10 to 15 percent of risk for coronary heart disease based on their cholesterol, blood pressure and smoking status. Alcohol's enhancement of high density lipoproteins was identified as the protective factor.
5. In 1990, Paolo Boffetta and Lawrence Garfinkel found that men who drank occasionally—up to two drinks daily—outlived abstainers. Subjects were over a quarter of a million volunteers enrolled by the American Cancer Society.
6. In 1990, Arthur Klatsky and his colleagues found that those who drank one or two drinks daily had the lowest overall mortality rate. Subjects were 85,000 Kaiser Permanente patients of both genders and all races.

These data—from large prospective studies of people of both sexes, different occupations, several nations and varying risk profiles—all point to alcohol's life-sustaining effects. This phenomenon is now so well accepted that the U.S. dietary guidelines released in January 1996 recognize that moderate drinking can be beneficial.

The levels of drinking at which alcohol lowers death rates are still open to dispute. The new U.S. guidelines indicate that men should not drink more than

*Table 1*

---

### Temperance, Alcohol Consumption and Cardiac Mortality

| Alcohol Consumption (1990) | Temperance Nations[a] | Non-Temperance Nations[b] |
|---|---|---|
| total consumption[c] | 6.6 | 10.8 |
| percent wine | 18 | 44 |
| percent beer | 53 | 40 |
| percent spirits | 29 | 16 |
| AA groups/million population | 170 | 25 |
| coronary mortality[d] (males 50-64) | 421 | 272 |

---

[a] Norway, Sweden, U.S., U.K., Ireland, Australia, New Zealand, Canada, Finland, Iceland
[b] Italy, France, Spain, Portugal, Switzerland, Germany, Denmark, Austria, Belgium, Luxembourg, Netherlands
[c] Liters consumed per capita per year
[d] Deaths per 100,000 population

*Source:* Peele S. *Culture, alcohol, and health: the consequences of alcohol consumption among Western nations.* December 1, 1995. Morristown, NJ.

two drinks per day and women should not exceed one per day. But the British government has set its limits for "sensible drinking" at three to four drinks for men and two to three drinks for women. That abstemiousness increases the risk of death, however, can no longer be doubted. Moreover, alcohol operates at least as effectively as pharmaceuticals to reduce the risk of death for those at high risk for coronary disease.

At one point, researchers questioned whether people who had quit drinking due to previous health problems inflated the mortality rate among abstainers. But this position can no longer be maintained. The studies described above separated drinkers who had quit drinking and who had preexisting health problems from other non-drinkers. The benefits of drinking persisted with these individuals omitted.

At some point, ranging from three to six drinks daily, the negative effects of drinking for cancer, cirrhosis and accidents catch up to and surpass alcohol's beneficial cardiac impact. Moreover, women under 50—who have relatively low rates of heart disease and relatively high rates of breast cancer mortality—may not benefit from drinking.

That is, unless they have one or more cardiac risk factors. Even younger women with such risk factors benefit from light to moderate drinking. And, we must remember, most American women and men have such risk factors. (Fuchs et al. found about three quarters of the nurses in the Harvard study had at least one.) Remember, over all ages, American women are ten times as likely to die of heart disease (40 percent) as of breast cancer (4 percent).

Why, then, do Americans—physicians, public health workers, educators and political leaders—refuse to recognize alcohol's benefits? We might also ask why the United States banned the manufacture, sale and transportation of alcoholic beverages from 1920 to 1933. It is probably too obvious to mention that alcohol has never been banned—or prohibition even seriously discussed—in France, Italy, Spain and a number of other European nations.

What is it about America and some other nations that prevents them from considering that alcohol may be good for people? These so-called "temperance" nations see alcohol in a highly negative light. This is true even though nations with higher alcohol consumption have lower death rates from coronary heart disease (see Table 1). Oddly, temperance nations—despite concentrating on alcohol problem prevention and treatment—actually have more drinking problems than those in which alcohol is socially accepted and integrated.

This occurs even though temperance nations drink less alcohol. But they drink a higher percentage of their alcohol in the form of spirits. This drinking is more likely to take place in concentrated bursts among men at sporting events or in drinking establishments. This style of drinking contrasts with that in wine-drinking nations, which encourage socialized drinking among family members of both genders and all ages at meals and other social gatherings. These cultures do not teach people that alcohol is an addictive drug. Rather, moderate drinking is modeled for children and taught to them in the home. Furthermore, these cultures accept that drinking may be good for you. We should, too.

# Should Physicians Recommend Alcohol to Their Patients? No

If physicians were to encourage their patients to drink alcohol, what patients would be the target group? Certainly not heavy drinkers, whose health, job and family may already suffer from alcohol abuse or addiction; the advice for these unfortunate individuals should be to reduce alcohol consumption or, preferably, to abstain entirely from alcohol.

Light and moderate drinkers need no encouragement to drink alcohol; instead, they need advice about safe levels for drinking, the dangers of drinking while driving or operating motorized equipment and, for females, the necessity for abstinence from alcohol prior to conception and during pregnancy.

The only target group, therefore, would be those patients who are non-consumers of alcohol. Physicians would never advocate alcohol consumption for children, so our advice would be limited to nondrinking adults. The size of this group can be estimated as follows: There are currently about 200 million adults in the United States. Although the exact number of nondrinkers in that population is unknown, a good estimate is about 25 to 30 percent, or at least 50 million persons.

We know that this large group of nondrinkers includes many different subgroups. Some nonconsumers avoid alcohol because they already suffer from an alcohol-related disease. Others abstain because they have a chronic disease and have been advised to avoid alcohol. A third group may have an alcoholic parent and intuitively know they must avoid alcohol. A final group abstains from alcohol because of religious convictions. Clearly, it would be unwise to recommend light or moderate drinking to patients in any of these categories.

What about the residual group of nondrinkers who have no definite reason to avoid alcohol? Would their health improve if they began drinking? To give a thoughtful answer to this important question, we must first review the complex relationship between alcohol and health. What are the detrimental effects of alcohol consumption and what, if any, are its health benefits? This problem has attracted an enormous amount of interest: In the past few years thousands of articles have been published on alcohol and health.

Alcohol consumers are known to have increased risks for many diseases. These include cirrhosis of the liver; digestive-tract diseases such as ulcers or

From Albert B. Lowenfels, "Should Physicians Recommend Alcohol to Their Patients? No," *Priorities,* vol. 8, no. 1 (1996), pp. 25, 27, 29. Copyright © 1996 by The American Council on Science and Health. Reprinted by permission of *Priorities,* a publication of The American Council on Science and Health, 1995 Broadway, 2d Floor, New York, NY 10023-5860. www.acsh.org.

pancreatitis; several painful and often lethal cancers such as throat cancer, esophageal cancer and liver cancer; and certain neurologic disorders such as blackouts and seizures. In addition, all types of accidents, including fatal car crashes, are more frequent in drinkers than in nondrinkers. Finally, fetal alcohol syndrome, now thought to be the most common cause of mental retardation, occurs only in children of alcohol consumers. While it is true that some of these health problems occur primarily in heavy drinkers, any amount of alcohol may be hazardous for other diseases such as fetal alcohol syndrome, for which a safe, lower limit is unknown.

There is only one well-recognized health "benefit" of alcohol consumption: Health professionals now agree that drinking small amounts of alcohol seems to reduce the risk of coronary heart disease. But is this single gain enough to balance the long list of alcohol-associated health problems?

We could find a convincing answer to the overall impact of alcohol on health if we were able to conduct the following experiment, a prospective randomized trial. Nondrinking adults would be randomly assigned to one of two groups: an alcohol-consuming group in which all the participants would be required to drink a daily glass of fruit juice spiked with about an ounce or two of alcohol, and a second "control" group who would drink only fruit juice without alcohol. The two groups would be followed for 10 to 20 years so that we could compare the death rates in alcohol consumers to the rates in nonconsumers.

For various ethical and practical reasons, this experiment—which would give us badly needed information about the potential health benefits of light or moderate drinking—will never be performed. Therefore, to answer the "to drink or not to drink" question, we're forced to rely upon indirect, weaker evidence from nonrandomized trials—retrospective studies that look back at past alcohol exposure and cross-cultural studies that compare drinking levels and health status among different groups. These types of studies can be plagued by confounding and bias.

If we accept the premise that alcohol protects against certain types of heart disease, will we gain or lose by telling our nondrinking patients they should drink? We know that there are already at least 100,000 alcohol-related deaths each year in the United States. It is difficult to predict the number of heart disease deaths caused by alcohol abstinence, but the number has been estimated to be approximately equal to the number of alcohol-related deaths. Thus a health policy of advocating light or moderate drinking for our abstinent patients would be unlikely to save many lives.

According to a report prepared for the Robert Wood Johnson Foundation, the cost of alcohol addiction for the year 1990 in the United States amounted to almost 100 billion dollars—higher than the estimated 67 billion dollars we spend for illicit drugs and the 72 billion dollars we spend for tobacco addiction. An unpredictable number of new alcohol consumers would eventually turn into heavy drinkers or become addicted to alcohol, requiring additional funds to cover the costs of their alcohol-related problems.

Advocates for moderate drinking often speak of the "French paradox." In the southwest of France—despite high consumption of foods rich in cholesterol, such as buttery sauces, various cheeses and goose liver—the risk of heart disease, particularly in men, appears to be lower than expected. According to moderate-drinking advocates, this "paradox" of a high-cholesterol diet and a low risk of heart disease can be explained by the beneficial, protective effect of copious amounts of alcohol—particularly red wine.

But men in France actually die about two years earlier than do men in Sweden or Norway, even though per capita alcohol consumption in Scandinavia is only about one third the consumption in France. Frenchmen, although they may not be dying of heart disease, are dying of other causes. Drinking alcohol does not guarantee longevity—and it certainly does not provide immunity against death!

And what has been the health experience of groups of individuals who have been lifelong abstainers? Do they die prematurely? Do they suffer from excess heart disease or other illnesses? Fortunately, such information is available from many reports reviewing the health of Seventh Day Adventists and Mormons—groups that abstain from alcohol on religious grounds. Their survival rates are generally higher than the American average. Avoiding alcohol does not interfere with an active, prolonged, healthy life.

From available statistics we know that there are more female than male nondrinkers. We also know that women are more likely to develop complications of alcohol, such as liver cirrhosis, at lower levels of alcohol intake than men. We therefore can predict that a policy of telling our nondrinking patients to begin drinking would be likely to yield more alcohol-related complications in women than in men.

There are many readily available nonaddictive drugs that effectively reduce the risk of coronary-artery occlusion. Why, then, should we recommend a drug that we know leads to loss of control or alcohol addiction in about 10 percent of users? It makes little sense to recommend alcohol as a safeguard against coronary heart disease when there are so many much safer drugs already at hand.

As we focus on the problem of alcohol and public health, we can learn a great deal by reviewing recommendations from organizations with recognized expertise in this area.

In 1991 the World Health Organization assembled a special review group to formulate worldwide alcohol policy. The group's conclusion on drinking and heart disease was this: "Any attempt to put across a message which encourages drinking on the basis of hoped-for gains in coronary heart disease prevention would be likely to result in more harm than benefit to the population."

In the United States, the National Institute on Alcohol Abuse and Alcoholism warns us that vulnerability to alcoholism and alcohol-related pathologies varies among individuals and cannot always be predicted before a patient begins to drink.

Finally, the Christopher D. Smithers Foundations, the largest private philanthropic organization devoted to research on alcoholism in America, does not advocate light or moderate drinking as a public health measure.

Over 2,000 years ago Hippocrates, one of our wisest physicians, reminded us, "Above all, do no harm." Let us remember this prudent advice as we decide what we should tell our patients about alcohol and health.

# POSTSCRIPT

## Should Doctors Promote Alcohol for Their Patients?

Approximately 10 percent of adults in the United States are alcoholics. The social and economic burdens placed on society as a result of heavy alcohol use are immense. Heavy drinking leads to increased health care costs, accidents, premature death, and reduced productivity in the workplace. In view of the myriad of problems caused by excessive alcohol use, is it prudent to suggest that moderate alcohol consumption should be promoted?

Experts agree that heavy drinking is a problem in society; however, heart disease is also a grave concern. Numerous public health education programs strive to reduce the risk factors associated with heart disease. If it can be shown that moderate alcohol use lessens that risk, wouldn't it make sense for physicians to advocate moderate consumption?

An important point to consider is the effect of a program that promotes moderate alcohol use. Would such a program result in heavy drinkers' reducing their alcohol consumption? Or would nondrinkers start drinking and people who are predisposed to alcoholism become alcoholic? Peele feels that none of these effects are likely and, moreover, that promoting moderate use, especially among young people, will help them to develop a healthy attitude toward alcohol. Lowenfels questions whether or not nondrinkers would obtain lower rates of heart disease if they started drinking moderately.

There are numerous papers and studies that examine the issue of heart disease and moderate alcohol use. An excellent article by Holger Theobald et al. is "A Moderate Intake of Wine Is Associated With Reduced Mortality From Cardiovascular Disease," *Journal of Studies on Alcohol* (vol. 61, 2000). Two additional good articles are "Some Health Effects of Alcohol," by Beatrice Hunter, *Consumers' Research* (March 1999) and "What Is Moderate Drinking? Defining 'Drinks' and Drinking Levels," by Mary C. Dufour, *Alcohol Research and Health* (Winter 1999). Finally, Jean Kinney warns of the potential dangers of moderate alcohol use in her book *Loosening the Grip: A Handbook of Alcohol Information,* 6th ed. (McGraw-Hill, 2000).

# ISSUE 11

## Do the Consequences of Caffeine Outweigh the Benefits?

**YES: Nell Boyce**, from "Storm in a Coffee Cup," *New Scientist* (January 29, 2000)

**NO: Editors of *Choice***, from "Caffeine Fix?" *Choice* (June 2000)

### ISSUE SUMMARY

**YES:** Writer Nell Boyce states that caffeine is more addictive than most people realize. Boyce maintains that caffeine not only causes dependency but also has a myriad of other effects. Caffeine raises blood pressure, a factor leading to heart disease, and there is also evidence that caffeine consumption during pregnancy involves some risk for the fetus.

**NO:** The editors of *Choice* magazine argue that many of the risks associated with moderate amounts of caffeine are exaggerated. They admit that caffeine produces some mild effects, such as dependence and high blood pressure. However, they maintain that the research showing that moderate caffeine use causes heart disease, osteoporosis, and cancer is inconclusive.

$A$lthough both of the following selections point out the positive and negative effects of caffeine, they differ in terms of what they perceive to be the extent of caffeine's benefit and harm. Caffeine is one of the most widely consumed legal drugs in the world. In the United States, more than 9 out of every 10 people drink some type of caffeinated beverage, mostly for its stimulating effects. Caffeine elevates mood, reduces fatigue, increases work capacity, and stimulates respiration. Caffeine often provides the lift that people need to start the day. Although many people associate caffeine primarily with coffee, caffeine is also found in numerous soft drinks, over-the-counter medications, chocolate, and tea. Because caffeinated drinks are common in society and there are very few legal controls regarding the use of caffeine, its physical and psychological effects are frequently overlooked, ignored, or minimized.

In recent years coffee consumption has declined; however, the amount of caffeine being consumed has not declined appreciably because of the increase in caffeinated soft drink consumption. To reduce their levels of caffeine intake, many people have switched to decaffeinated drinks and coffee. Although this results in less caffeine intake, decaffeinated coffee still contains small amounts of caffeine.

Research studies evaluating the effects of caffeine consumption on personal health date back to the 1960s. In particular, the medical community has conducted numerous studies to determine whether or not there is a relationship between caffeine consumption and cardiovascular disease because heart disease is the leading cause of death in many countries, including the United States. In spite of the many studies on this subject, a clear relationship between heart disease and caffeine is not yet apparent. Studies have yielded conflicting results. Rather than clarifying the debate regarding the consequences of caffeine, research has only added to the confusion. As a result, studies suggesting that there is a connection between caffeine consumption and adverse physical and psychological effects have come under scrutiny by both the general public and health professionals.

One serious limitation of previous research indicating that caffeine does have deleterious effects is that the research focused primarily on coffee use. The problem is that there may be other ingredients in coffee besides caffeine that produce harmful effects. Moreover, an increasing percentage of the caffeine being consumed comes from other sources, such as soft drinks, tea, chocolate, antihistamines, and diet pills. Therefore, caffeine studies involving only coffee are not truly representative of the amount of caffeine that people ingest.

Another important criticism of caffeine research, especially studies that link caffeine use with heart disease, is gender bias. Until recently, research has focused primarily on the caffeine consumption of men. The bias in medical research is not limited to caffeine studies; men have traditionally been the primary group studied regarding many facets of health. This situation is changing, however, and the potential consequences of caffeine use on the fetus and nursing mother is currently being examined.

People who believe that drinking caffeine in moderation does not pose a significant health threat are critical of previous and current studies. This is particularly true of studies that demonstrate a relationship between caffeine and heart disease. Critics contend that it is difficult to establish a definitive relationship between caffeine and heart disease due to a myriad of confounding variables. For example, cardiovascular disease has been linked to family history, a sedentary lifestyle, cigarette smoking, obesity, fat intake, and stress. Many individuals who consume large amounts of coffee also smoke cigarettes, drink alcohol, and are hard-driven. Several factors also affect caffeine's excretion from the body. Cigarette smoking increases caffeine metabolization, while the use of oral contraceptives and pregnancy slow down metabolization. Therefore, determining the extent to which caffeine use causes heart disease while adjusting for the influence of these other factors is difficult.

In the following selections, Nell Boyce cautions readers about the use of caffeine, even in moderate amounts. In contrast, the editors of *Choice* argue that a moderate intake of caffeine should be no cause for concern and may have some health benefits.

Nell Boyce  **YES**

# Storm in a Coffee Cup

The situation was very troubling. Counsellors at the Hazelden Foundation in Center City, Minnesota, a leading drug treatment clinic, had learned that some of the residents were smuggling in an addictive stimulant and sharing it with their friends. This was a clear violation of the rules, but the clinic's staff concluded that they would fight no longer, and rescinded the unpopular ban on coffee.

Some of the staff felt relieved. Why withhold a harmless substance that helped the patients stay off alcohol or crack cocaine? After all, the founder of Alcoholics Anonymous famously drank vast amounts of coffee, and almost all AA meetings take place around a coffee pot. But others were concerned that some patients were drinking so much coffee they weren't getting enough sleep. And there was a principle at stake. They felt that the caffeine in coffee was, quite frankly, an addictive drug.

If that's the case, the whole world is cheerfully addicted. In the US, almost everyone drinks coffee. In Britain and Australia people drink coffee and tea. And for Nigerians there's the cola nut to chew on. People consume vast quantities of caffeine in chocolate and soft drinks, and even in a pure pill form. But is it truly a drug of abuse like cocaine or heroin? And if so, should we kick the habit?

These are remarkably tricky questions. Headlines around the world last year proclaimed that French researchers had proved that caffeine wasn't really addictive. In July, Astrid Nehlig from the Strasbourg laboratory of INSERM, the French National Health and Medical Research Institute, announced that giving rats moderate amounts of caffeine does not promote activity in a brain region called the nucleus accumbens, thought to play a role in addiction (*ChemTech*, vol 29, p 30). Even low doses of cocaine, amphetamines, nicotine and morphine all activate this part of the brain. "The activation of the shell of the nucleus accumbens seems to be one of the key mechanisms of addiction of psychostimulants," Nehlig says.

But what of the other mechanisms and brain structures thought to be involved in drug addiction, such as the dopamine system? Caffeine makes us feel alert because it blocks the receptors for a brain chemical called adenosine, which normally dampens the activity of other neurotransmitters. Blocking adenosine boosts brain activity, and may indirectly boost dopamine levels. Cocaine, alcohol, nicotine and heroin also raise dopamine levels. "Obviously caffeine shares some properties with the drugs of abuse," Nehlig admits.

But she rejects the notion that caffeine could be considered an abused drug. Some scientists think that rises in dopamine levels may be a general plea-sure response, not anything specifically linked to addiction. The main mecha-nisms of action of caffeine and the other drugs are different, Nehlig insists. She points out that with caffeine, "the extent of tolerance, withdrawal, or reinforce-ment is never as dramatic as those observed with the drugs of abuse."

Other researchers don't dismiss these shared properties so lightly. "I usu-ally steer clear of the word addiction because it's loaded with additional bag-gage," says Roland Griffiths, an expert on caffeine at the Johns Hopkins Medical Institutions in Baltimore, Maryland. But he points to the behavioural changes that caffeine can bring about. "Over the last ten years there has been a greater appreciation in the general public that caffeine is a drug and produces with-drawal, but I would guess that caffeine users are unaware of the extent to which their behaviour is controlled by caffeine."

Take, for example, a simple study in which Griffiths gave moderate caf-feine users red or blue capsules containing either a dose of caffeine or an inert powder. On one day everybody got a caffeine pill of one colour, and on the next day they got an inert pill that was the other colour. The following day they got to choose whichever colour they preferred, and 80 per cent of the time they chose the caffeine pill, regardless of whether this was red or blue. He told the participants that they were testing the effects of compounds found in common foods, so they had no idea what they were taking.

People clearly seek out caffeine, and when they can't get it they're not happy. This fact should be obvious to anyone who has ever tried to function in the morning without their usual cuppa, but until recently most researchers assumed that caffeine withdrawal was mild and transient. "There seemed to be an almost flat-out denial on the part of many that this is of any relevance and/or importance," says Griffiths. "Caffeine withdrawal occurs at much lower doses than we had previously recognised."

Withdrawal can occur in people who have as little as 100 milligrams of caffeine a day, about the amount in two cups of tea or one cup of instant coffee. Symptoms include headache, fatigue, difficulty concentrating and drowsiness. The ill effects peak after a day or two without caffeine, and can continue for more than a week. Surprisingly, Griffiths says, withdrawal can be suppressed by rather low levels of caffeine. If you usually imbibe three cups of coffee a day, or around 300 milligrams of caffeine, you can alleviate withdrawal symptoms with as little as 25 milligrams. "There may be lots of people who are dependent who think they are immune to withdrawal," notes Griffiths. Someone who skips their morning coffee and then has a cola with lunch won't suffer as badly.

## Slow Reactions

Some researchers worry that children are especially vulnerable to withdrawal, as they often don't have steady access to caffeine. Gail Bernstein at the University of Minnesota in Minneapolis studied 30 children at times when they were drinking caffeine regularly and during withdrawal periods. She showed that they had slower reactions in tests that required them to watch a computer screen and click a mouse in response to certain images during periods of withdrawal (*Journal of the American Academy of Child & Adolescent Psychiatry*, vol 37, p 858). "It's maybe hard to say what you can transfer from the lab to the real world," she admits, but thinks the issue deserves more study, given the aggressive promotion of soft drinks to children.

Although adults tend to drink the same amount of caffeine from day to day, Griffiths says there is no convincing evidence that people can monitor and regulate their caffeine intake. But in one study he did show that if people are given coffee containing different doses of caffeine, they tend to drink more when the dose is low. He notes that "if you put someone in withdrawal, they're going to head towards caffeinated foods."

Researchers have also found that as people get used to drinking coffee, they acquire tolerance to its effects. In one study, people given 400 milligrams of caffeine a day initially experienced sleep problems. But after a week, their total sleep time, and the number of times they awoke, returned to normal. In another study, people got either caffeine or a placebo for 18 days. The two groups did not differ significantly in ratings of mood, until they were given a 300-milligram dose of caffeine: this made people in the placebo group nervous and jittery, but had no such effect on the group that was chronically exposed to caffeine.

At a biochemical level, caffeine increases levels of catecholamines, the neurotransmitters involved in the fight-or-flight response. So your body reacts in the way it would if you were facing down a lion: your pupils dilate, your breathing tubes open up, and your muscles get ready for action. Individuals differ in their reaction to caffeine. Part of this is down to genes, but there are other influences too. The half-life of caffeine is normally four to six hours, but this doubles in women taking oral contraceptives and is halved in smokers. Smokers are more likely than non-smokers to be coffee drinkers, and ex-smokers consume more coffee than non-smokers but less than smokers. If someone quits smoking but keeps drinking their usual amount of coffee or tea, their caffeine levels can suddenly rise to levels that make most people feel jittery, complicating efforts to stay off the cigarettes.

We all know why people should quit smoking. But does continually drinking coffee or tea have any health risks that might make it worth giving up? Large quantities of caffeine are deadly: tea or coffee could kill you, if you managed to drink between 50 and 100 cups in one go. Your liver treats caffeine like any other poison, and plants produce it to keep pests at bay. Yet evidence for coffee's contribution to common diseases remains far from clear. "You'll find that most people go into hyperbole on one side or the other," says Griffiths.

Health worries have been around since at least 1674, when women in London claimed it made their men impotent, according to Mark Pendergrast's 500-page opus on coffee, *Uncommon Grounds*. The most recent coffee concerns began in the 1970s, when epidemiologists linked coffee consumption to heart disease, pancreatic cancer and reproductive problems. More than twenty years later, these links remain controversial, and scientists have yet to confirm any of them. Several large epidemiological studies have failed to find any association between coffee consumption and heart disease.

James Lane of Duke University Medical Center in Durham, North Carolina, is convinced that there are risks, however. Caffeine raises blood pressure, and so could contribute to heart disease later in life, he says. Over the past ten years Lane has shown that the caffeine in four or five cups of coffee can raise blood pressure by about five points and increase production stress hormones such as cortisol and catecholamines. "People in high-stress jobs become dependent on caffeine. But the caffeine is making the stress in their life worse," says Lane.

Lane believes that we haven't picked up this increase in risk because people don't report their caffeine intake accurately. They just don't realise how much they take in, he says, especially when one cup doesn't always equal another. A large coffee from Starbucks, for example, can contain a whopping half-gram of caffeine, while a small cup of instant may contain less than 100 milligrams (see Figure 1). And consumption isn't necessarily consistent over the years.

There are further complications, too. Coffee and tea are a soup of many chemcals, not just a vehicle for caffeine, says Peter Martin, of Vanderbilt University's new Institute for Coffee Studies in Nashville, Tennessee. Studies by Lane and others that use pure caffeine miss the point, Martin says, because substances such as chlorogenic acids are more abundant in coffee than caffeine. "There may be pharmacological interactions that counteract the effects of caffeine," Martin says. He notes that chlorogenic acids have been shown to affect opiate receptors in the same way as naltrexone, a medication that blocks the "high" feeling that makes people want to use narcotics and alcohol.

Even the way coffee is prepared can create different compounds with effects of their own. In 1996, Dutch investigators reported that unfiltered coffee made in a cafetière or "French press" raised levels of harmful cholesterol by 9 to 14 per cent, while the same amounts of filtered coffee had no effect. The researchers attributed the effect to cafestol and kahweol, alcohols found in coffee oils (*British Medical Journal*, vol 313, p 8). It's perhaps not surprising that there is no clear picture of the effects of caffeine on health.

Mark Klebanoff of the National Institute of Child Health and Human Development near Washington DC decided that rather than relying on his volunteers to report their own caffeine intake, he would look for a metabolite of caffeine called paraxanthine in blood samples to test whether caffeine has any effect on rates of miscarriage. "It's not perfect, but at least it's looking at the issues in another way," says Klebanoff. The study found an increased risk of miscarriage only in women with the very highest levels of paraxanthine, corresponding to more than five cups of coffee a day. Klebanoff views the results as "at least reasonably reassuring for women." Many pregnant women say they quit drinking coffee anyway, because they lose the taste for it.

Brenda Eskenazi of the University of California School of Public Health in Berkeley thinks that women should minimise their caffeine intake during pregnancy just to be safe. She notes that caffeine can cross the placenta, is

*Figure 1*

### What's Your Dose?

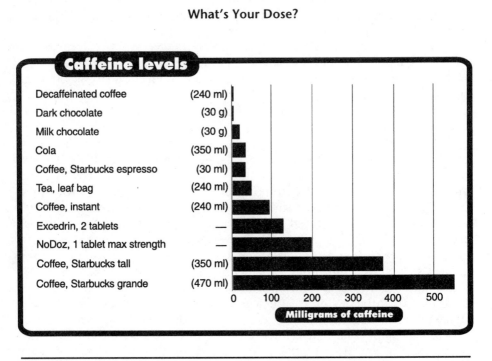

Many people have no idea how much caffeine they consume every day. So the Center for Science in the Public Interest in Washington DC petitioned the US Food and Drug Administration in 1997 to label the caffeine content of various foods. The FDA never took the recommended action, but here are some typical caffeine quantities found in various foods and beverages, according to the CSPI.

present in breast milk, and has a longer half-life in a pregnant woman's body (11 hours compared to 6). Studies have shown that low doses of caffeine can change a fetal heart rate even when the caffeine has no apparent effect on the mother.

The debate over health effects is likely to continue for as long as people keep drinking coffee and tea. But Klebanoff doesn't think we should worry too much about caffeine. "It didn't take us long to figure out that cigarettes were bad for you," he points out. "If there was something terrible that it does to us, we would have found it by now." But caffeine consumption is so widespread that even small risks for individuals could add up to major problems for society as a whole. "It's such a popular drug," says Lane. "I think we really need to have more people investigating it, just for peace of mind."

Most people who come to work in Griffiths's lab decide that they want to give up caffeine, once they see the evidence of their dependence and how it influences their daily life. If you want to quit, Griffiths suggests that you first spend a week keeping a careful log of your intake. Then taper off slowly, rather than quitting cold turkey, to minimise withdrawal symptoms. But be warned: caffeine has a powerful allure. "Without exception, people in time have decided to go back," says Griffiths, who admits to drinking an occasional caffeinated beverage. "If I have a message it's that people should know that caffeine is a drug and that they should treat it with respect."

**NO**

# Caffeine Fix?

During the past few decades we've been told caffeine could cause cancer and heart disease. On the other hand, more recent studies have refuted its harmful health effects, and some even argue that it could be good for us. So what do we really know about caffeine's effects on our health?

In fact we know a lot, because it's one of the most thoroughly studied food ingredients. Over 60 plants contain caffeine in their leaves, seeds and fruits—including the coffee and tea plant species. And it's added to cola and energy drinks because of its stimulant effect.

The Australia New Zealand Food Authority (ANZFA) is currently considering allowing caffeine to be added to any soft drinks, not just cola, as is currently permitted. In the US it's even added to bottled water and fruit juice.

You'll also find caffeine in over-the-counter medications, including some painkillers and cold and flu remedies. In painkillers, it's used to enhance the action of the active ingredient.

It also acts as a mild diuretic, working on the kidneys to decrease the reabsorption of water and salt. While it can make you urinate more frequently, there's debate about whether or not caffeine has a dehydrating effect.

### Caffeine in Your Body

Caffeine is absorbed by the stomach, metabolised by the liver and eliminated from the body within two to 10 hours. Generally, smokers metabolise caffeine more quickly than non-smokers, and pregnant women take longer to metabolise it.

We know it acts on the central nervous system as a mild stimulant, and some studies have argued that this may be beneficial in some circumstances. Drugs known to stimulate the nervous system—appetite suppressants, asthma drugs, thyroid hormones and oral decongestants—can increase the effects of caffeine.

The sedative effect of drugs like Diazepam (Valium) can be reduced by caffeine. If you take certain anti-depressants, like phenelzine sulphate (Nardil) or tranylaypromine sulphate (Parnate), caffeine can trigger high blood pressure or abnormal heart rhythms.

Taking some drugs may make it difficult for the body to get rid of caffeine, including the contraceptive pill and the ulcer or heartburn drugs Cimetidine (Tagamet) and Ranitidine (Zantac). Even low doses of caffeine may cause insomnia, irritability and palpitations if you take those drugs.

### Can You Get Hooked?

There's conflicting evidence on whether caffeine is addictive. Imbibers don't exhibit the signs usually associated with a classic drug dependence, though some people can't do without their daily intake. However, excessive consumption can have physical effects, including sleep difficulties and irritability.

The degree to which you're affected depends on how fast you metabolise caffeine. Too much caffeine may make you feel restless and anxious and make your hands tremble.

If you cut your consumption, these symptoms will disappear, but you can experience withdrawal symptoms if you stop suddenly—for example, tiredness and headaches. If you want to cut back, it's best done gradually to avoid these mild side effects.

### Will It Give Me High Blood Pressure?

The connection between caffeine and cardiovascular disease is quite weak, despite health scares about it causing heart attacks and high blood pressure.

Drinking tea or coffee in moderation generally has little influence on blood pressure. Major studies in Britain and the US concluded that moderate caffeine consumption (for example, up to six cups of coffee each day) wouldn't significantly increase the risk of coronary heart disease or stroke for most people.

If you have high blood pressure it may be worth avoiding caffeine before exercise or if you're under stress. Even moderate caffeine intake has been known to raise blood pressure in those situations.

Coffee brewed in certain ways may raise blood cholesterol levels. Boiled, espresso and plunger coffee (French press) contains compounds called cafestol and kahweol. A 1995 study suggested that these compounds possibly help raise levels of the type of cholesterol that can block your arteries. Instant and drip-filtered coffee don't contain significant levels of these compounds.

### Does It Cause Cancer?

There's little evidence that caffeine causes cancer. Both the American Cancer Society and the World Cancer Research Fund have reported a lack of evidence.

In fact, it's been suggested that caffeine offers protection against the development of colorectal cancer.

### Will It Weaken My Bones?

Caffeine consumption has been linked to osteoporosis but, again, studies have produced conflicting conclusions.

The more caffeine you consume, the more calcium you'll lose in your urine, so there's a concern for those at risk of osteoporosis. But, there seems to be a compensating decrease in the calcium you lose via the gut so, in general, moderate consumption shouldn't increase your vulnerability to osteoporosis.

Postmenopausal women who don't eat much calcium should avoid high levels of caffeine, though. For example, the caffeine in two cups of coffee has been shown to cause bone loss in postmenopausal women with low-calcium diets, or who have other risk factors like a family history of osteoporosis. One authority suggests women drink a cup of milk for every cup of coffee they drink.

### Caffeine and Pregnancy

It's been suggested that caffeine may contribute to problems with fertility, cause miscarriage or have significant effects on the development of the foetus.

In the early 1980s the American Food and Drug Administration (FDA) advised pregnant women to avoid caffeine because animal studies have shown some evidence of birth defects.

More recent research has found that women with a high caffeine intake may have a higher risk of miscarriage and may give birth to underweight babies.

Caffeine can make its way into breast milk, and high doses could make a breast-fed baby jittery.

### Sleep Deprived?

Some people report difficulty getting to sleep if they have caffeine drinks in the evenings. If you're sensitive in this way, you could try decaffeinated drinks.

### Antioxidant Magic

It's been argued that because caffeine is an antioxidant, it may help prevent the development of some types of cancer. Antioxidants are found in many products derived from plants, and it's widely believed that they help protect against diseases such as heart disease, cancer and cataracts.

It's been found that coffee contains flavenoids, which have antioxidant properties. And recent research suggests that the roasting process generates other antioxidant substances.

### Other Health Benefits

Caffeine can help expand airways and is used to treat sleep apnea in newborn babies.

Its role as a stimulant has also been shown to have benefits in specific situations. The amount of caffeine in two cups of coffee has been shown to improve alertness and concentration, and studies have argued it helps some night-shift workers to maintain concentration, potentially reducing the chances of an industrial accident. It may also play a role in reducing driver fatigue and preventing road accidents.

Caffeine may also reduce your chances of getting kidney stones and gallstones. A recent study involving 81,000 women showed drinking coffee reduced the risk of kidney stones by 10% for each 200 mL cup drunk daily. A similar result was found in an earlier study of 45,000 men.

A 1999 study found that it may possibly protect the liver against cell damage due to alcohol.

### *Just How Much Are You Drinking?*
The amount of caffeine in a cup of coffee or tea can vary greatly, depending on the size of the cup, the method of preparation (filtered, percolated, espresso, etc), the strength of the brew and the variety and blend of the coffee or tea. Table 1 shows the approximate amount of caffeine found in common foods, beverages and some painkillers.

*Table 1*

| Caffeine: Average Content in Food and Drugs | |
| --- | --- |
| **In a standard 150 mL cup:** | |
| Roast and ground coffee | 80–90 mg |
| Instant coffee | 60 mg |
| Decaf coffee (roast/ground) | 3 mg |
| Decaf coffee (instant) | 3 mg |
| Tea | 40 mg |
| Hot chocolate | 2–4 mg |
| **In a 330 mL can:** | |
| Standard cola drink | 40 mg (range 11–70 mg) |
| **Per 100 mL:** | |
| Energy drink | 11mg (range 0.05–35 mg) |
| **Per 100 g:** | |
| Milk chocolate | 18 mg |
| Plain chocolate | 75 mg |
| **Per dose:** | |
| Some painkillers | 10–100 mg |

### *Caffeine and Kids*
Children whose diet is high in cola or chocolate can suffer from hyperactivity and anxiety; and if they're used to drinking cola and eating chocolate, they can experience withdrawal symptoms and lack concentration when they stop consuming caffeine.

The Australia New Zealand Food Authority (ANZFA) is currently considering applications to permit the use of caffeine in soft drinks other than cola and to raise the maximum level of caffeine in energy drinks. However, Australia currently has one of the lowest permitted levels of caffeine in cola drinks in the world and ANZFA says it will maintain this maximum level in drinks containing caffeine (145 mg/kg).

ANZFA has established an expert working group to examine the wider aspects of the safety of caffeine and its dietary sources. The group's recommendations will be considered in the assessment of the current applications before ANZFA.

According to ANZFA, the expert working group should help address community concerns about the effects of caffeine, particularly in relation to how it affects children's behaviour.

ANZFA will make a final recommendation to the Australia New Zealand Food Standards Council on both applications after considering the expert working group's findings and other evidence and advice provided by interested groups and individuals.

The Public Health Association of Australia (PHAA) argues that ANZFA's own modelling shows that the proposal could lead to a 45% increase in the total caffeine intake of children and teenagers.

"Given the lack of information relating to the effects of caffeine in children, the PHAA falls to see how the conclusion of unlikely public health and safety effects can be drawn."

However, it can also be argued that such concern could be misplaced, as young children metabolise caffeine faster than adults.

### How Much Is Enough?

The latest research suggests that a moderate intake of caffeine shouldn't do you any harm and may in fact have some health benefits.

But what's meant by 'moderate' intake? About four or five cups of average-strength coffee each day are acceptable. Just remember to include in your calculations the caffeine you consume from other sources like chocolate, tea and soft drinks.

If you have around 1 g of caffeine per day (eight to 10 cups of strong coffee) you may experience the following symptoms and suffer withdrawal if you give up suddenly:

- Jitters, anxiety, agitation.
- Light-headedness.
- Rapid breathing.
- Rapid heartbeat.
- Upset stomach.
- Loose stools.
- Heartburn.
- Headache.

# POSTSCRIPT

## Do the Consequences of Caffeine Outweigh the Benefits?

Although caffeine is consumed by millions of people each day without much regard to its physical and psychological effects, many studies have questioned its safety. However, other studies have reported very few hazards. The basic question is whether or not people who drink several cups of coffee or other caffeinated beverages daily should be more concerned than they are. Are claims of caffeine's benefits or hazards exaggerated?

Determining whether certain foods or beverages promote disease or have health benefits can be trying. Many people become frustrated because quite a few of the things that we eat and drink are suspected of being unhealthy. For example, various reports indicate that the fat in beef is unhealthy, that we should consume less salt and sugar, that processed foods should be avoided, and that whole milk, butter, and margarine should be reduced or eliminated from our diets. If people paid attention to every report about the harmful effects of the foods and beverages that they consume, then they would not be able to eat much at all. What is the average consumer supposed to do?

A legitimate question is whether or not food studies are worth pursuing, considering that so many of the products that are reportedly bad are enjoyed by millions of people. Caffeine is simply one more example of a commonly used product that has come under scrutiny. In addition, although the research is vast, it is inconclusive and contradictory. One study, for instance, linked caffeine to pancreatic cancer; later it was found that the culprit was not caffeine but cigarette smoking. Research on caffeine's effects on cancers of the bladder, urinary tract, and kidney have also proven to be inconsistent and inconclusive. If professional researchers cannot agree as to whether a product is safe or harmful, how can the average person know what to believe?

Boyce contends that caffeine may cause dependence and that it shares some of the characteristics of cocaine, alcohol, and nicotine. The editors of *Choice* assert that caffeine's potential for dependency is overstated. Other articles that examine caffeine's psychological and physical effects are Karen Goldberg Goff's "Studies Bring Good News for Addicted Coffee Fiends," *Insight on the News* (October 4, 1999); Linda Mooney's "Should You Decaf Your Life?" *Prevention* (July 2000); and Laura Goldstein's "Good News About Coffee," *Prevention* (December 2000). Two articles that address caffeine's impact during pregnancy are "Caffeine and Miscarriage Risk," *Family Practice News* (February 1, 2000) and "Caffeine—Filtering the Facts," by Brenda Eskenazi, *The New England Journal of Medicine* (November 25, 1999).

# ISSUE 12

## Are Too Many Children Receiving Ritalin?

**YES: Richard Bromfield**, from "Is Ritalin Overprescribed? Yes," *Priorities* (vol. 8, no. 3, 1996)

**NO: Jerry Wiener**, from "Is Ritalin Overprescribed? No," *Priorities* (vol. 8, no. 3, 1996)

### ISSUE SUMMARY

**YES:** Harvard Medical School professor Richard Bromfield contends that physicians are often too eager to prescribe Ritalin for children with attention deficit/hyperactivity disorder (ADHD). Bromfield is concerned that Ritalin's long-term effects have not been adequately researched and that its overuse may be masking other childhood disorders.

**NO:** George Washington Medical School professor Jerry Wiener maintains that Ritalin has been proven to be safe and effective. Wiener argues that attention deficit/hyperactivity disorder is under-diagnosed in many instances and that children who could benefit from the use of Ritalin often do not receive it.

The number one childhood psychiatric disorder in the United States is attention deficit/hyperactivity disorder, which affects approximately 6–7 percent of all school-age children. The most commonly prescribed drug for ADHD is the stimulant Ritalin (the generic name is methylphenidate). About 2.5 million U.S. children, primarily boys between the ages of 5 and 12, receive Ritalin prescriptions for ADHD. In contrast, only 1 in 200 European children are diagnosed with ADHD. Ritalin is therefore much less likely to be prescribed in Europe. ADHD is characterized by inattentiveness, hyperactivity, and impulsivity. Many children are diagnosed as having only attention deficit disorder (ADD), which is ADHD without the hyperactivity.

The use of stimulants to treat such behavioral disorders dates back to 1937. The practice of prescribing stimulants for behavioral problems increased dramatically beginning in 1970, when it was estimated that 150,000 American children were taking stimulant medications. It seems paradoxical for physicians to be prescribing a stimulant such as Ritalin for a behavioral disorder that already involves hyperactivity. However, Ritalin appears to be effective with many children, as well as with many adults, who suffer from this condition. Looking at this issue from a broader perspective, one needs to ask whether or not behavioral problems should be treated as a disease. Also, does Ritalin really address the problem? Or could it be covering up other maladies that otherwise would be treated?

Ritalin enhances the functioning of the brain's reticular activating system, which helps one to focus attention and to filter out extraneous stimuli. The drug has been shown to improve short-term learning. Ritalin also produces adverse effects such as insomnia, headaches, irritability, nausea, dizziness, weight loss, and growth retardation. Psychological dependence may develop, but physical dependence is unlikely. The effects of long-term Ritalin use are unknown.

Since 1990 the number of children receiving Ritalin has increased 250 percent. This large increase in the number of children diagnosed with ADHD may be attributed to a broader application of the criteria for diagnosing ADHD, heightened public awareness, and changes in American educational policy regarding schools' identifying children with the disorder. Some people feel that the increase in prescriptions for Ritalin reflects an increased effort to satisfy the needs of parents whose children exhibit behavioral problems. Ritalin has been referred to as "mother's little helper." Regardless of the reasons for the increase, many people question whether Ritalin is overprescribed and children are overmedicated or whether Ritalin is a miracle drug.

One problem with the increased prevalence of Ritalin prescriptions is that illegal use of the drug has also risen. There are accounts of some parents getting prescriptions for their children and then selling the drugs illegally. On a number of college campuses there are reports of students using Ritalin to get high or to stay awake in order to study. Historically, illegal use of Ritalin has been minimal, although officials of the Drug Enforcement Administration (DEA) are now concerned that its illegal use is proliferating. Problems with its use are unlikely to rival those of cocaine because Ritalin's effects are more moderate than those of cocaine or amphetamines.

The fact is that children now receive prescriptions for Ritalin rather readily. Frequently, parents will pressure their pediatricians into writing the prescriptions. One survey found that almost one-half of all pediatricians spent less than an hour assessing children before prescribing Ritalin. On the other hand, if there is a medication available that would remedy a problem, shouldn't it be taken? If a child's academic performance can improve through the use of Ritalin, should that child be denied the drug?

In the following selections, Richard Bromfield argues that despite the benefits of Ritalin, too many children are being given it inappropriately and that the long-term consequences of its use are unknown. Jerry Wiener maintains that ADHD is underdiagnosed and that more children should receive Ritalin. Wiener concedes that some children are misdiagnosed, but he argues that the benefits of Ritalin outweigh its risks.

**Richard Bromfield**  **YES**

# Is Ritalin Overprescribed? Yes

Ritalin is being dispensed with a speed and nonchalance compatible with our drive-through culture, yet entirely at odds with good medicine and common sense. The drug does help some people pay attention and function better; some of my own patients have benefited from it. But too many children, and more and more adults, are being given Ritalin inappropriately.

Psychiatry has devised careful guidelines for prescribing and monitoring this sometimes-useful drug. But the dramatic jump in Ritalin use in the past five years clearly suggests that these guidelines are being ignored and that Ritalin is being vastly overprescribed. The problem has finally been recognized by medical groups such as the American Academy of Child and Adolescent Psychiatry, the American Psychiatric Association and the American Academy of Pediatrics, which have written or are developing guidelines for diagnosing ADHD [attention-deficit/hyperactive disorder]; and even by CibaGeneva Pharmaceuticals, the manufacturer of Ritalin, which issued similar guidelines to doctors [recently].

Under the pressure of managed care, physicians are diagnosing ADHD in patients and prescribing them Ritalin after interviews as short as 15 minutes. And given Ritalin's quick action (it can "calm" children within days after treatment starts), some doctors even rely on the drug as a diagnostic tool, interpreting improvements in behavior or attention as proof of an underlying ADHD—and justification for continued drug use.

Studies show that Ritalin prescribing fluctuates dramatically depending on how parents and teachers perceive "misbehavior" and how tolerant they are of it. I know of children who have been given Ritalin more to subdue them than to meet their needs—a practice that recalls the opium syrups used to soothe noisy infants in London a century ago. When a drug can be prescribed because one person is bothering another—a disruptive child upsetting a teacher, for example—there is clearly a danger that the drug will be abused. That danger only increases when the problem being treated is so vaguely defined.

ADHD exists as a disorder primarily because a committee of psychiatrists voted it so. In a valiant effort, they squeezed a laundry list of disparate symptoms into a neat package that can be handled and treated. But while attention is an essential aspect of our functioning, it's certainly not the only one. Why not bestow disorderhood on other problems common to people diagnosed with ADHD, such as Easily Frustrated Disorder (EFD) or Nothing Makes Me Happy Disorder (NMMHD)?

Once known as Minimal Brain Dysfunction and Hyperkinetic Syndrome, ADHD is considered a neurological disorder. Certainly, some people diagnosed with ADHD are neurologically impaired and need medication. But nervous system glitches account for the disruptive behavior of only a small minority of people who are vulnerable to distraction or impulsive behavior—perhaps 1 percent or 2 percent of the general population. Many more people have ADHD symptoms that have nothing to do with their nervous systems and result instead from emotional distress, depression, anxiety, obsessions or learning disabilities.

For these people, who exhibit the symptoms of ADHD but suffer from some other problem, Ritalin will likely be useless as a treatment. Taking it may postpone more effective treatment. And it may even be harmful.

No one knows how Ritalin works. Some miracle drugs, of course, have helped people for decades or even centuries before their mechanisms of action were understood. But we need to know more about the possible effects of a drug used mainly on children.

We're willing to overlook side effects when it comes to treating a life-threatening disease. But with a less weighty disorder like ADHD, therapeutic rewards must be weighed against possible adverse reactions. In a drug targeted at children, there is concern that harmful effects may crop up decades after treatment stops. Since Ritalin is a relatively new drug, in use for about 30 years, we still don't know whether long-term side effects await its young users. But we do know that more immediate problems can occur.

It's already clear that Ritalin can worsen underlying anxiety, depression, psychosis and seizures. More common but milder side effects include nervousness and sleeplessness. Some studies suggest that the drug may interfere with bone growth. And [recently] the United Nation's International Narcotics Control Board reported an increase in teenagers who were inhaling this stimulant drug, which is chemically similar to cocaine but not nearly as potent.

While Ritalin's mode of action isn't clear, the drug is known to affect the brain's most ancient and basic structures, which control arousal and attention. I question the wisdom of tampering with such crucially important parts of the brain, particularly with a drug whose possible long-term side effects remain to be discovered.

The surge in both ADHD diagnoses and Ritalin prescriptions is yet another sign of a society suffering from a colossal lack of personal responsibility. By telling patients that their failures, misbehavior and unhappiness are caused by a disorder, we risk colluding with their all-too-human belief that their actions are beyond their control, and we weaken their motivation to change on their own. And in the many cases where ADHD is misdiagnosed in children, we give parents the illusion that their child's problems have nothing to do with the home environment or with their performance as parents.

It must be true that bad biology accounts for some people's distracted and impulsive lifestyles. But random violence, drugs, alcohol, domestic trauma and (less horrifically) indulgent and chaotic homes are more obvious reasons for the ADHD-like restlessness that plagues America. We urgently need to address *these* problems. To do that, we need legislators who will provide support for good parenting, especially in the early years of childhood when the foundations for handling feelings, self-control and concentration are biologically and psychologically laid down.

Some people who can't concentrate probably do merit the diagnosis of ADHD and a prescription for Ritalin to treat it. But the brain, the neurological seat of the soul and the self must be treated with the utmost respect. With the demand for Ritalin growing, we must be increasingly wary about doling out a drug that can be beneficial but is more often useless or even harmful.

# NO ⬅

## Is Ritalin Overprescribed? No

In defending the current use of Ritalin for treating ADHD [attention-deficit/hyperactive disorder], it's important first to emphasize that the disorder really exists.

Telling whether a child has ADHD is more complicated than a diagnosis of the mumps or chicken pox, but the diagnosis of ADHD can still be as valid as any in medicine. An analogous health problem would be multiple sclerosis: As with ADHD it's a distinct disease, yet we don't know what causes the illness and have no laboratory test for diagnosing it.

Since the 1950s what we now call ADHD has been a well-recognized syndrome involving, as all syndromes do, a group of signs and symptoms that occur together. Years of research have documented that some children differ from their peers in being inattentive and hyperactive as well as impulsive. Extensive field trials and numerous studies have established that hyperactivity and impulsivity are at the core of the diagnosis, with inattention a consequence of the other two, especially in school-age boys.

Adding to the evidence that ADHD is a legitimate clinical problem are recent results of magnetic resonance imaging (MRI) studies showing that children diagnosed with ADHD have subtle but significant anatomical differences in their brains compared with other children. Furthermore, studies of families suggest there is a genetic component for many cases of ADHD. More specifically, recent research has found a possible link between ADHD and three genes that code for receptors (proteins that jut from the surface of cells) that are activated by dopamine, a neurotransmitter (a chemical that conveys messages from one nerve cell to another). Defects in these genes could mean a reduced response to dopamine signals, perhaps accounting for the uninhibited behavior observed in ADHD.

A child suspected of having ADHD should be evaluated by a trained and experienced clinician who takes the time to assess the child's development, family history and behavior at school and at home. The clinician should require that the criteria set forth in the current *Diagnostic and Statistical Manual of Mental Disorders* (DSM-IV) are met before concluding that a child has ADHD.

From Jerry Wiener, "Is Ritalin Overprescribed? No," *Priorities*, vol. 8, no. 3 (1996), pp. 25, 27, 29. Copyright © 1996 by The American Council on Science and Health. Reprinted by permission of *Priorities*, a publication of The American Council on Science and Health, 1995 Broadway, 2d Floor, New York, NY 10023-5860. www.acsh.org.

To receive the diagnosis of ADHD, a child should display a significant number of symptoms and behaviors reflecting hyperactivity, impulsivity and inattention—and the symptoms and behaviors must be more persistent and severe than normally occur in children of that age. In addition and importantly, there must be impaired functioning in school, at home and/or in social relationships.

Are mistakes made in diagnosing ADHD? Of course. They usually occur when the clinician is rushed, inexperienced, untrained, pressured or predisposed either to "find" ADHD or to overlook it. As a result, there is both over- and underdiagnosis of ADHD. The reported fivefold increase in Ritalin prescriptions over the past five years is reason to reflect about possible overusage. However, repeated findings of a three-percent prevalence rate of ADHD among school-age children give as much cause for concern about underdiagnosis as for overusage: At these prevalence rates, up to 30 percent of children with ADHD may not be receiving sufficient treatment.

While there is no cure for ADHD, there is a very effective treatment to minimize its symptoms—through the use of stimulant medications such as Ritalin. Such drugs are by far the most effective treatment for moderating and controlling the disorder's major symptoms—hyperactivity, inattention and impulsivity—in 75 percent to 80 percent of children with this disorder.

The safety and effectiveness of Ritalin and other stimulant drugs, including Dexedrine (dextroamphetamine) and Cylert (pemoline), have been established more firmly than any other treatments in the field of child and adolescent psychiatry. Literally scores of carefully conducted blind and double-blind controlled studies have repeatedly documented the improvement—often dramatic—in symptoms of ADHD following the use of stimulant medication, with Ritalin the most common choice. By contrast, no other treatment, including behavior modification, compares with stimulant medication in efficacy; in fact, no treatment besides these medications has had much success at all in treating ADHD.

Stimulant medication is so effective that a parent with a child diagnosed with ADHD should receive an explanation if the clinician's judgment is *not* to prescribe medication. Appropriate considerations for not opting for Ritalin and similar drugs include a history of tic or Tourette's disorder, the presence of a thought disorder, significant resistance to such medications in the patient or family or insufficient severity of the symptoms or dysfunction. Other classes of drugs, such as antidepressants, can be effective and can be used when there is concern about the use of a stimulant medication or when side effects occur.

The issue should not be whether stimulants are overprescribed but the risk that they may be misprescribed. The most common example: children who are described as overactive or impulsive but who do not meet the criteria for the diagnosis of ADHD. Another example is the use of stimulants as a diagnostic "test" by a rushed or inexperienced clinician who may not realize that a favorable response was due to the placebo effect and therefore mistakenly assumes that the diagnosis of ADHD has been confirmed.

As effective as Ritalin can be for treating the symptoms of ADHD, it should rarely, if ever, be the only treatment for someone with the problem.

The child or adolescent may also benefit from remedial work for any identified learning disability and from family therapy or psychotherapy for problems of self-image, self-esteem, anger and/or depression.

Is Ritalin overprescribed? Not when it's used for children who meet the criteria for the diagnosis of ADHD, including the requirement that the child's ability to function must be "significantly impaired." All too often, the mistakes in prescribing Ritalin are errors of omission, where children who could benefit from the drug never receive it. Instead, they go through school labeled as troublemakers, or as unmotivated or hostile. They'll have missed out on the opportunity for at least a trial on a medication that could have significantly improved their symptoms and allowed for improved academic performance, self-esteem and social interaction.

# POSTSCRIPT

## Are Too Many Children Receiving Ritalin?

To satisfy their own emotional needs, many parents push their physicians into diagnosing their children with ADHD. Parents believe that their children will benefit if they are labeled ADHD. The pressure for children to do well academically in order to get into the right college and graduate school is intense. Some parents feel that if their children are diagnosed with ADHD, then they may be provided special circumstances or allowances such as additional time when taking college entrance examinations. Some parents also realize that if their children are identified as having ADHD, then their children will be eligible for support services in school. In some instances, the only way to receive such extra help is to be labeled with a disorder. Some teachers favor the use of Ritalin to control students' behavior. During the last few years, there has been increasing emphasis on controlling school budgets. The result is larger class sizes and higher student-to-teacher ratios. Thus, it should not be surprising that many teachers welcome the calming effect of Ritalin on students whose hyperactivity is disruptive to the class.

Whether or not drug therapy should be applied to behaviors raises another concern. What is the message that children are receiving about the role of drugs in society? Perhaps children will generalize the benefits of using legal drugs like Ritalin to remedy life's problems to using illegal drugs to deal with other problems that they may be experiencing. Children may find that it is easier to ingest a pill rather than to put the time and effort into resolving personal problems. For many adults, drugs represent a shortcut to correcting life's difficulties. Through its reliance on drugs, is American society creating a wrong impression for its children, an illusion that there is a pill for *every* ill?

When to prescribe Ritalin for children also places physicians in a quandary. They may see the benefit of helping students function more effectively in school. However, are physicians who readily prescribe Ritalin unintentionally promoting an antihumanistic, competitive environment in which performance matters regardless of cost? On the other hand, is it the place of physicians to dictate to parents what is best for their children? In the final analysis, will the increase in prescriptions for Ritalin result in benefits for the child, for the parents, and for society?

One article that questions the validity of attention deficit/hyperactivity disorder is John Breeding's "Does ADHD Even Exist?" *Mothering* (July/August 2000). Another article that examines the role of Ritalin is "Running From Ritalin: Is the Hectic Pace of Contemporary Life Really to Blame for A.D.D.? Not So Fast," by Malcolm Gladwell, *The New Yorker* (February 15, 1999). The social consequences of and reasons for the explosion of Ritalin use in recent years are discussed in Lawrence Diller's article "The Run on Ritalin: Attention Deficit Disorder and Stimulant Treatment in the 1990s," *Hastings Center Report* (March–April 1996). Several articles addressing whether or not Ritalin is overprescribed appear in the March 18, 1996, issue of *Newsweek*. Finally, differences between the United States and Europe in the practice of prescribing Ritalin are described by Dorothy Bonn in "Methylphenidate: U.S. and European Views Converging?" *The Lancet* (July 27, 1996).

# ISSUE 13

## Should Advertisements for Prescription Drugs Be Regulated?

**YES: Matthew F. Hollon**, from "Direct-to-Consumer Marketing of Prescription Drugs: Creating Consumer Demand," *JAMA, The Journal of the American Medical Association* (January 27, 1999)

**NO: Alan F. Holmer**, from "Direct-to-Consumer Prescription Drug Advertising Builds Bridges Between Patients and Physicians," *JAMA, The Journal of the American Medical Association* (January 27, 1999)

### ISSUE SUMMARY

**YES:** Matthew F. Hollon, a physician, maintains that doctors may compromise their judgment when patients insist on being given drugs that they see advertised in the media. He asserts that pharmaceutical manufacturers advertise directly to consumers to increase their profits, not to help patients.

**NO:** Alan F. Holmer, president of Pharmaceutical Research and Manufacturers of America, contends that advertisements for prescription drugs serve to educate the consumer, that such advertisements provide a benefit to the public's health, and that patients are more likely to comply with treatment if they request it.

One of the most lucrative businesses in the world today is the prescription drug business. Billions of dollars are spent every year for prescription drugs in the United States alone. But the only way for consumers to obtain a prescribed drug is through a physician. In the early 1980s drug companies in the United States began to advertise directly to the consumer. It is logical for drug companies to advertise to physicians because they are responsible for writing prescriptions. However, is it logical for pharmaceutical manufacturers to advertise their drugs directly to consumers? Are consumers capable of making informed, rational decisions regarding their pharmaceutical needs? Should there be greater regulation of prescription drug advertising?

An increasing number of individuals are assuming more responsibility for their own health care. In the United States, over one-third of all prescriptions are written at the request of patients. Also, many patients do not take their doctors' prescriptions to pharmacies to be filled. Both of these scenarios raise the question of whether or not consumers are adequately educated to make decisions pertaining to their pharmaceutical needs or to assess risks associated with prescription drugs. Evidence suggests that many are not. Prescription drugs, for example, cause more worksite accidents than illegal drugs do.

Some commentators argue that there are several advantages to directly advertising drugs to consumers. One advantage is that direct advertisements make consumers better informed about the benefits and risks of certain drugs. For example, it is not unusual for a person to experience side effects from a drug without knowing that the drug is responsible for the side effects. Advertisements can provide this information. Another advantage is that consumers can learn about medications that they might not have known existed. Furthermore, advertising lowers the cost of prescription drugs because consumers can ask their physicians to prescribe less expensive drugs than the physician might be inclined to recommend. Finally, prescription drug advertising allows consumers to become more involved in choosing the medications that they need or want.

Critics argue that there are a number of risks associated with the direct advertising of prescription drugs. One concern is with the content of drug advertisements. For example, consumers may not pay enough attention to information detailing a drug's adverse effects. Also, sometimes a drug's benefits are exaggerated. Another problem is that there are many instances in which drugs that have been approved by the Food and Drug Administration (FDA) for one purpose have been promoted for other purposes. Is the average consumer capable of understanding the purposes of the drugs that are being advertised?

Opponents of direct-to-consumer drug advertisements express concern with the way in which the information in the advertisements is presented. Promotions for drugs that appear as objective reports are often actually slick publicity material. In such promotions, medical experts are shown providing testimony regarding a particular drug. Many consumers may not be aware that these physicians have financial ties to the pharmaceutical companies. Celebrities—in whom the public often places its trust despite their lack of medical expertise—are also used to promote drugs. Finally, the cost of the drugs advertised, a major concern to most consumers, is seldom mentioned in the advertisements.

In the following selections, Matthew F. Hollon argues that direct-to-consumer marketing of prescription drugs should be more closely regulated because many drug advertisements are misleading. In addition, some patients who have been influenced by advertising ask their physicians to write prescriptions for drugs that they do not need. Alan F. Holmer contends that advertisements for prescription drugs are beneficial to consumers because they lower the cost of drugs and they effectively inform consumers about the benefits of new drugs. He also indicates that prescription drug companies advertise responsibly and that such advertisements are adequately regulated by the FDA already.

Matthew F. Hollon

 **YES**

# Direct-to-Consumer Marketing of Prescription Drugs: Creating Consumer Demand

In the early 1980s, the pharmaceutical industry began marketing prescription drugs directly to patients. The Food and Drug Administration (FDA) imposed a moratorium on this marketing strategy in 1983 then lifted it in 1985.[1] Since then, the industry has devoted increasing resources to this strategy. In a 1988 editorial on direct-to-consumer (DTC) marketing, Eric P. Cohen, MD, wrote, "Issues of regulation of advertising, cost, competition, public health, and individual well being need to be carefully examined."[2] Examination of these issues in rigorous, independent studies has not occurred. Despite the lack of studies, the FDA has relaxed regulations governing DTC marketing of prescription drugs.[3]

Proponents hypothesize that DTC marketing, by providing educational information, is valuable, notifying consumers of new therapies and motivating them to seek care. However, the pharmaceutical industry, driven in part by financial motives, is providing information of suspect quality and thus minimal benefit. Reckoning the costs, economic and otherwise, the public health value of DTC marketing is negligible. Moreover, the effects of DTC marketing are undesirable. Most important, by creating consumer demand, DTC marketing undermines the protection that is a result of requiring a physician to certify a patient's need for a prescription drug. For the benefit of patients, physicians, and the public's health, the FDA should consider stricter—not more permissive—regulations.

While providing educational information may be one of the industry's motives, the bottom-line desire for profit is undoubtedly another. In this respect, industry efforts have been successful. Advertising nicotine patches directly to consumers turned patches into "an $800 million dollar category."[4] Aggressive marketing of Claritin (Schering-Plough, Madison, NJ) captured 56% of the $1.8 billion nonsedating antihistamine market.[5] In the wake of successes, spending on DTC advertising rocketed from $13.1 million in 1989 to more than $900 million in 1997, double the $438 million spent on advertisements in medical journals.[6,7]

The pharmaceutical industry's interest in the bottom line is legitimate. The industry, which has made important medical contributions, exists because it is profitable. However, as the profit motive can affect the content of information in advertisements, the public health value of DTC marketing should be examined by comparing the benefits the public gains with the costs the public incurs.

The industry is not marketing to consumers in a health information vacuum. A vast amount of health information is accessible to and inundates the public every day.[8,9] Since "almost every drug product has some advantage for some patient," it is anecdotally true that any information the industry provides about a product has some benefit for someone.[10] However, when dumped into the ocean of available information, the sum of these anecdotes does not necessarily equal public health benefit, especially when the quality of the information provided is suspect. If studies of advertising directed at physicians offer a clue, this information, in fact, has minimal educational benefit.

In one study, Wade et al[11] asked pharmaceutical companies to supply their best evidence in support of marketing claims. Of 67 references cited, only 31 contained relevant original data and only 13 were controlled trials. These investigators concluded, "Standards of evidence used to justify advertising claims are inadequate." In a study of advertising in the leading medical journals in 18 countries, Herxheimer et al[12] reported that important warnings and precautions were missing in half of the 6700 advertisements surveyed. In yet another study, Stryer and Bero[13] concluded that advertisements contained a higher proportion of promotional material than educational material, and little of this material contained information about important therapeutic breakthroughs. In 1992, Wilkes et al[14] evaluated 109 pharmaceutical advertisements and found that 57% of these advertisements had little or no educational value.

Recently, *Consumer Reports,* evaluating the accuracy of information in prescription drug advertisements directed at patients, substantiated the conclusions drawn from studies of marketing directed at physicians.[15] Information from marketing has little educational benefit and, in general, its quality is poor. Less than half of DTC advertisements reviewed were candid about efficacy. *Consumer Reports* concluded, "the rules governing prescription drug advertising should not be loosened," and that "[advertisements] are not public service messages—they're meant to move goods."

David A. Kessler, MD, while commissioner of the FDA, wrote in response to the study by Wilkes et al, "[it] serves an important purpose. It heightens awareness of the degree to which misleading information may pervade the 'informational marketplace.'"[16] In his editorial, Kessler documented the subtle techniques used by the pharmaceutical industry to distort information including "data dredging" and making claims of "no difference" from studies with limited statistical power. Providing poor quality information in today's marketplace of health information results in little or no benefit for the public. Considering the costs, providing this information is unlikely to have public health value.

Costs can include an increase in expenditures, improper use of drugs, and harm from adverse events. Unlike many products, the use of prescription drugs can have serious consequences. The improper use of antibiotics in humans is one of the major factors accelerating antimicrobial resistance.[17,18] Prescription drugs can and do cause harm. Consider the recent concern that the use of the combination of anorectic agents, fenfluramine and phentermine, may be associated with valvular heart disease.[19] Consider also benoxaprofen, a prescription nonsteroidal anti-inflammatory agent, launched in 1980 in the United Kingdom and subsequently the United States.[20] The product gained "a major foothold merely on the strength of a well-orchestrated marketing strategy, which included full-page advertisements in the popular press." Sixty-one drug-related deaths occurred during the 2 years in which the drug remained on the market.

Expenditures are also an important consideration. Drugs reduce expenditures by preventing complications from diseases.[21] However, this statement is not axiomatic. Expenditures may increase when marketing of prescription drugs creates need, when disease complications are rare or nonexistent, or when choices of drug therapy for a disease are available. For example, a recent survey of trends in antihypertensive drug use in the United States revealed that despite the recommendations of the Fifth Joint National Committee on the Detection, Evaluation, and Treatment of High Blood Pressure, the use of calcium antagonists and angiotensin-converting enzyme inhibitors has increased.[22] The investigators cite the effectiveness of pharmaceutical promotion practices as one of the possible reasons for this. They note, "the cost implications of these practice patterns are enormous."

If DTC marketing affects physicians' prescribing practices, then DTC marketing has no public health value because the public ostensibly incurs costs that exceed the minimal benefits. Some argue that physicians serve as the system's safety net, preventing the inappropriate use of prescription drugs. This argument, however, rests on a number of questionable assumptions. It assumes that physicians are always rational in prescribing. It assumes that such things as patients' demands do not influence physicians' prescribing practices. It assumes that, at a population level, physicians are nearly infallible. Available evidence casts doubt on these assumptions.

Variability not explained solely by the pharmacological needs of patients exists in physicians' prescribing practices.[23,24] Examining this variability, Schwartz et al[25] identified physicians who prescribed 3 drugs "at a rate far greater than that warranted by scientific evidence of their effectiveness." In this study, patient demand was the most commonly cited motivation for prescribing the target drugs. In a study of antibiotic use for upper respiratory tract infections, Hamm et al[26] documented that the patient's expectation for an antibiotic is an important factor in the decision to prescribe the drug. Moreover, 2 recent studies concur with previous findings that patients who expect a prescription are "many times more likely to receive one."[27] At the population level, Willcox et al[28] found that 23.5% of Americans aged 65 years or older living in the community receive at least 1 of 20 inappropriate drugs. These authors call for broader educational and regulatory initiatives. Finally, preliminary evidence from a study by Hueston et al[29] suggests managed care organizations have not reduced inappropriate prescribing.

The act of issuing a prescription is the culmination of a complex set of decisions; certainly, physicians' decisions can improve. What effect does DTC marketing have on these decisions? Consumer advocates of DTC marketing argue that this strategy, highlighting the evolving relationship between physicians and patients, shifts control over prescription decisions from physicians to patients, giving patients greater command over their health care.[30] In reality, the principal effect of DTC marketing is to create consumer demand, changing the physician-patient relationship to a physician-consumer relationship. The consequences of this change are open for debate, but the impact is noticeable.

In 1992, physicians reported that 88% of patients asked for a drug by brand name, up from 45% in 1989.[6] At the same time, a survey revealed that 63% of consumers do not believe they can tell if they are being misled by advertisements for prescription drugs.[31] An advertising industry executive concludes, "Creating consumer demand [among patients] for prescription pharmaceuticals is now an attainable marketing objective."[32] Physicians' prescribing decisions can improve, but creating consumer demand does not help. Rather, by influencing these decisions, consumer demand undermines the protection that is a result of requiring a physician to consider seriously a patient's need for a drug, then certify that need.

Neither physicians nor patients are immune to the effects of marketing. However, while physicians are not immune, their education and knowledge presumably make them more competent than consumers in interpreting promotional material for prescription drugs. Additionally, unlike consumers who hear of just 1 drug, physicians are capable of offering sound advice to patients about a range of therapeutic options. If the value of DTC marketing is negligible and the primary effect of this strategy is to create consumer demand, then, unlike the truly valuable contributions of the pharmaceutical industry, DTC marketing is not good for patients, physicians, or the public's health.

An industry consultant predicts, "The winners in the prescription drug category are not going to be the ones with the best patents or products, but those that are the best marketers."[5] Currently the industry is pursuing the next steps in DTC marketing, including using broadcast media and the Internet. The industry is moving beyond mass media vehicles to more focused efforts such as direct marketing through databases to targeted consumers.[32] Until well-designed, independent studies based on available observational data prove the information from DTC marketing has public health value and desirable effects, the FDA should consider stricter—not more permissive—regulations.

# References

1. Food and Drug Administration. Direct-to-consumer advertising of prescription drugs: withdrawal of moratorium. Federal Register. September 9, 1985;50:36677–36678.
2. Cohen EP. Direct-to-the-public advertisement of prescription drugs. N Engl J Med. 1988;318:373–376.
3. US Department of Health and Human Services, Public Health Service, Food and Drug Administration. FDA to review standards for all direct-to-consumer

Rx drug promotion. Available at: `http://www.fda.gov/bbs/topics/NEWS/NEW00582.html`. Accessed August 25, 1997.

4. Weber J, Carey J. Drug ads: a prescription for controversy. Business Week. January 18, 1993:S8–S9.
5. Freeman L. Aggressive strategy helps propel Claritin to top slot. Advertising Age. March 16, 1998;69(11):S6–S7.
6. Liebman H. Consumer, heal thyself: ads for prescription drugs are popping up more frequently in consumer media. Mediaweek. July 5, 1993;3(27): 12.
7. Wilke M. Prescription for profit. Advertising Age. March 16, 1998:69(11):S1,S26.
8. Why do Americans resist a healthy lifestyle? USA Today Magazine. October 1994; 123(2593):1–2.
9. Harper J. Information overload may be making some Americans sick. Insight on the News. September 15, 1997;13(34):40–41.
10. Peck CC, Rheinstein PH. FDA regulation of prescription drug advertising. JAMA. 1990;264:2424–2425.
11. Wade VA, Mansfield PR, McDonald PJ. Drug companies' evidence to justify advertising. Lancet. 1989:2:1261–1264.
12. Herxheimer A, Lundborg CS, Westerholm B. Advertisements for medicines in leading medical journals in 18 countries: a 12-month survey of information content and standards. Int J Health Serv. 1993;23:161-172.
13. Stryer D, Bero LA. Characteristics of materials distributed by drug companies. J Gen Intern Med. 1996;11:575–583.
14. Wilkes MS, Doblin BH, Shapiro MF. Pharmaceutical advertisements in leading medical journals: experts' assessments. Ann Intern Med. 1992;116:912–919.
15. Drug advertising: is this good medicine? Consumer Reports. June 1996;61(6): 62–63.
16. Kessler DA. Addressing the problem of misleading advertising. Ann Intern Med. 1992;116:950–951.
17. Williams RJ, Heymann DL. Containment of antibiotic resistance. Science. 1998:279:1153–1154.
18. Low DE, Scheld WM. Strategies for stemming the tide of antimicrobial resistance. JAMA. 1998;279:394–395.
19. Connolly HM, Crary JL, McGoon MD, et al. Valvular heart disease associated with fenfluramine-phentermine. N Engl J Med. 1997;337:581–588.
20. Gerber P. Mass product-liability litigation. Med J Aust. 1988;148:485–488.
21. US Department of Health and Human Services, Public Health Service, Food and Drug Administration. FDA public hearing: direct-to-consumer promotion. Available at: `http://www2.evolvingtech.com/etc/industry/hearings/95N227contents.html`. Accessed June 21, 1997.
22. Siegel D, Lopez J. Trends in antihypertensive drug use in the United States: do the JNCV recommendations affect prescribing? JAMA. 1997:278:1745–1748.
23. Hemminki E. Review of literature on the factors affecting drug prescribing. Soc Sci Med. 1975:9:111–115.
24. Weiss MC, Fitzpatrick R, Scott DK, Goldacre MJ. Pressures on the general practitioner and decisions to prescribe. Fam Pract. 1996:13:432–438.
25. Schwartz RK, Soumerai SB, Avorn J. Physician motivations for nonscientific drug prescribing. Soc Sci Med. 1989:28:577–582.
26. Hamm RM, Hicks RJ, Bemben DA. Antibiotics and respiratory infections: are patients more satisfied when expectations are met? J Fam Pract. 1996:43:56–62.
27. Greenhalgh T, Gill P. Pressure to prescribe. BMJ. 1997:315:1482–1483.
28. Willcox SM, Himmeistein DU, Woolhandler S. Inappropriate drug prescribing for the community-dwelling elderly. JAMA. 1994:272:292–296.
29. Hueston WJ, Mainous AG III, Brauer N, Mercuri J. Evaluation and treatment of respiratory infections: does managed care make a difference? J Fam Pract. 1997:44:572–577.

30. National Consumers League, Golodner LF. Consumer group responds to FDA draft guidance on direct-to-consumer advertising on television. Available at http://www.natlconsumersleague.org/dtcp.htm. Accessed August 26, 1997.
31. Whyte J. Direct consumer advertising of prescription drugs. JAMA. 1993: 269:146,150.
32. Wilke M, Teinowitz I, Kelly KJ. Ad fever sweeps healthcare industry. Advertising Age. January 13, 1997:68:21:1,18–19.

**Alan F. Holmer**

 **NO**

# Direct-to-Consumer Prescription Drug Advertising Builds Bridges Between Patients and Physicians

Direct-to-Consumer (DTC) advertising is an excellent way to meet the growing demand for medical information, empowering consumers by educating them about health conditions and possible treatments. By so doing, it can play an important role in improving public health.

"In health care, there is a general trend toward having consumers more responsible for their own health," according to Linda Golodner, president of the National Consumers League.[1]

The sources of user-accessible information about health care have increased exponentially just in the past few years. More than 50 consumer magazines about health care appear on the newsstands every month. Many television stations have a physician dispensing medical news. Nearly one quarter of the Internet is devoted to health care information[2] the *Physicians' Desk Reference,* once largely confined to physicians' offices, is now available in a consumer edition at pharmacy counters.

Along with these sources, DTC advertising is a key means of informing and empowering patients. *Prevention Magazine,* in a study based on a national survey conducted during the spring of 1998 with technical assistance from the Food and Drug Administration (FDA),[3] found that:

- More than 53 million consumers talked to their physicians about a medicine they saw advertised, and an additional 49 million sought information from another source, such as the Internet.
- Thirty-eight percent of those who talked to their physicians about a medicine they saw advertised sought information about the product from at least 1 other source.
- Direct-to-consumer advertising "encouraged a projected 21.2 million consumers to talk with their doctor about a medical condition or illness they had never talked with their doctor about before seeing an advertisement."

- As many as 12.1 million consumers received a prescribed drug as a direct result of seeing a DTC advertisement.

The *Prevention Magazine* study also found that DTC advertising may improve patient compliance with drug regimens. "Many consumers who have seen advertisements for medicines they are currently taking say the advertising makes them feel better about the medicine they're taking, makes them more likely to take it and reminds them to have their prescriptions refilled," the study stated. The study concluded that DTC advertising "may play a very real role in enhancing public health."

Because DTC advertising is so new, more studies are needed to determine more definitively its cost-effectiveness and its precise impact on improving outcomes and public health. The FDA is planning a survey of consumers who have recently visited a physician to ask their views on prescription drugs they have received and their behavior regarding prescription drug advertising.

Not surprisingly, spending on DTC advertising has accelerated since the FDA changed US guidelines in August 1997 to allow manufacturers who advertise prescription medicines on television more flexibility in providing information about the risks of the drugs. IMS HEALTH, a health care information company in Plymouth Meeting, PA, expects spending on DTC television advertising to more than double in 1998, following a large gain in 1997.

According to IMS HEALTH, spending on DTC advertising increased 46% in 1997 (to $917 million), while spending on promotion directed to physicians was about $4 billion in 1997.[4] In other words, companies spent more than 4 times as much promoting products to physicians as they spent promoting products to consumers.

Direct-to-consumer advertising that encourages millions of Americans to consult their physicians can help to improve public health because a number of leading diseases are underdiagnosed and undertreated. For example:

- An estimated 8 million undiagnosed cases of diabetes exist among adults in the United States.[5]
- Only about 10 million of the 30 million Americans with high cholesterol levels take cholesterol-lowering drugs.[6]
- Only 1 depressed person in 10 receives adequate medical treatment, and one third of people with major depression do not seek treatment.[7]
- Millions of Americans are estimated to have undiagnosed high blood pressure.[8]

For conditions such as these, which can be treated with prescription drugs, the consequences of not seeking appropriate treatment can be dire—for the individual, the family, and society. Untreated diabetes can lead to blindness or limb amputation. Unchecked high cholesterol levels can lead to heart attack or stroke, while cholesterol-lowering drugs can cut this risk by about 30%.[9] Failure to treat depression can result in suicide, and high blood pressure can lead to stroke, heart attacks, and kidney failure.

Conversely, there is a growing body of evidence that increased use of pharmaceuticals will improve public health:

- The Air Force/Texas Coronary Atherosclerosis Prevention Study concluded that use of a cholesterol-lowering drug can lower the risk of heart attacks, chest pain, and cardiac arrest by 37%, even in people with no symptoms of heart disease. The authors of the study estimate that 6 million Americans currently not recommended for this treatment could benefit.[10]
- A study by the Agency for Health Care Policy and Research found that increased use of anticoagulant drugs would prevent 40,000 strokes a year.[11]
- A study conducted at the University of Maryland Medical Center concluded that patients treated with 3-blocker drugs after myocardial infarction were 40% less likely to die than those who do not receive the drug.[12] In a study from the National Cooperative Cardiovascular Project, only half the people who could be helped by a [beta]-blocker following myocardial infarction were taking such a medicine.[13]

Direct-to-consumer advertising is a highly effective way to communicate the availability of treatments to the public. In 1992, the first DTC consumer television advertisement for a nicotine patch aired during the Super Bowl. According to the American Association of Advertising Agencies (AAAA), the public response was so great that, within weeks, demand for the patches exceeded the supply. The product had been available for months, but people who might have been interested in quitting smoking were simply not aware of it.

Advertising promoted widespread awareness overnight, prompted patient-physician conversations, and may have helped many people to stop smoking.[14] John Kamp of the AAAA stated: "Government agencies and medical professionals can use their tools until they're blue in the face and not reach the people who will be reached through television."[1] Similarly, according to data compiled by IMS HEALTH, patient visits to physicians for osteoporosis nearly doubled in the 1-year period following the debut of DTC advertisements for a new drug for the disease. In the fourth quarter of 1995, there were 409,000 visits to physicians for osteoporosis. Advertisements for the new medicine started appearing at the end of 1995. In the fourth quarter of 1996, there were 713,000 physician visits by patients seeking help for osteoporosis.[15]

An advertising campaign for a medicine for genital herpes was launched in 1997. Some 45 million people aged 12 years and older in the United States are infected with the virus that causes this disease. In a survey by the manufacturer of the medicine, 49% of the patients who had called the toll-free telephone number in the advertisement saw their physicians within 3 months after seeing the advertisement. Fifty-one percent of these patients did not receive a prescription for the medicine, indicating that the physician decided a prescription was inappropriate, even though the patient had probably asked for one (Andrew P. Witty, Glaxo Wellcome Inc, Research Triangle Park, NC, unpublished data, December 1998).

Pharmaceutical companies have both a right and a responsibility to inform people about their products under the supervision of the FDA, which regulates prescription drug advertising. Companies are committed to responsible advertising that enhances the patient-physician relationship and encourages the appropriate use of prescription drugs under a physician's supervision. While such advertising prompts more people to seek professional help, it does not dictate the outcome of the physician visit or the kind of help patients eventually receive.

Direct-to-consumer advertising merely motivates patients to learn more about medical conditions and treatment options and to consult their physicians. Once the dialogue is started, the physician's role is preeminent. The patient has been empowered with information, not prescribing authority. In the words of Harvard Medical School Professor Jerry Avorn: "There's no detail man or pharmaceutical company or patient that puts a gun to a doctor's head to write a prescription. Ultimately, it isn't the patient's signature on the prescription—it's the doctor's.[16]

Participatory health care—consumers assuming more responsibility for their own health—is changing the nature of the patient-physician relationship. In a recent survey conducted by Yankelovich Partners, 95% of both physicians and patients described the ideal patient-physician relationship as a mutual partnership.[17] Such a partnership can lead to better health outcomes through appropriate use of safe and effective prescription medicines that save lives, cure disease, and alleviate pain and suffering.

The mortality rate for the acquired immunodeficiency syndrome (AIDS) dropped more than 3-fold from 1995 through 1997, for example, due to the increasing use of combination antiretroviral therapy.[18] Deaths due to heart disease decreased more than 30% during the 1980s, with 50% of the decline attributed to the use of new medicines.[19] Antibiotics and vaccines have virtually wiped out such diseases as diphtheria, syphilis, pertussis, measles, and polio.[20] And there are more than 1000 new medicines in development—for Alzheimer's disease, cancer, heart disease, stroke, infectious diseases, AIDS, arthritis, Parkinson's disease, diabetes, and many other diseases—promising even more effective treatments and better outcomes in the future.[21]

By greatly increasing the likelihood that patients will seek help for their medical problems and receive a safe and effective prescribed medicine, DTC advertising will, as the *Prevention Magazine* study stated, "play a very real role in enhancing public health."

# References

1. Nordenberg T. Direct to you: TV drug ads that make sense. FDA Consumer. January-February 1998:32:7–10.
2. Kodysz M, Bower BA. Medical sites on the Internet continue to proliferate. Mod Med. May 1998;66:56.
3. Prevention Magazine. National Survey of Consumer Reactions to Direct-to-Consumer Advertising. Emmaus, Pa: Rodale Press; 1998.
4. IMS reports pharmaceutical promotions rose 16% in 1997 [press release]. Plymouth Meeting, Pa: IMS HEALTH; March 31, 1998.

5. American Diabetes Association: Clinical Practice Recommendations 1997. Diabetes Care. 1997; 20(suppl 1):S1-S70.
6. Pill pushers. Economist. August 8, 1997;344(8029):58–59.
7. Hirschfeld RM, Keller MB, Panico S, et al. The National Depressive and Manic-Depressive Association consensus statement on the undertreatment of depression. JAMA. 1997:277:333–334.
8. National Health and Nutrition Examination Survey. Washington, DC: National Center for Health Statistics; 1988–1994.
9. Avorn J, Monette J, Lacour A, et al. Persistence of use of lipid-lowering medications: a cross-national study. JAMA. 1998:279:1458–1462.
10. Downs JR, Clearfield M, Weis S, et al. Primary prevention of acute coronary events with lovastatin in men and women with average cholesterol levels: results of AFCAPS/TexCAPS. JAMA. 1998;279:1615–1622.
11. Secondary and Tertiary Prevention of Stroke Patient Outcome Research Team: 9th Progress Report, March 1996. Rockville, Md: Agency for Health Care Policy and Research; 1996.
12. Gottlieb SS, McCarter RJ, Vogel RA. Effect of beta-blockade on mortality among high-risk and low-risk patients after myocardial infarction. N Engl J Med. 1998; 339:489-497.
13. Krumholz HM, Radford MJ, Wang Y, Chen J, Heiat A, Marciniak TA. National use and effectiveness of [beta]-blockers for the treatment of elderly patients after acute myocardial infarction: National Cooperative Cardiovascular Project. JAMA. 1998;280:623-629.
14. DTC ads prompted prescriptions for 7.5 million Americans, AphA/Prevention survey concludes. F-D-C Reports—The Pink Sheet. October 20, 1997;59 (42):9–10.
15. National Disease and Therapeutic Index [database online]. Plymouth Meeting, Pa: IMS HEALTH; 1996.
16. Tanouye E. Drug ads spur patients to demand more prescriptions. Wall Street Journal. December 22, 1997;B1.
17. Executive summary. In: A Survey of the Patient-Physician Relationship to America. Norwalk, Conn: Yankelovich Partners Inc; April 1998:4.
18. Ventura SJ, Anderson RN, Martin JA, Smith BL. Births and Deaths: Preliminary Data for 1997, National Vital Statistics Reports [vol 47, No. 4] Hyattsville, Md: National Center for Health Statistics; 1998:1.
19. Hunink MGM, Goldman L, Tosteson ANA, et al. The recent decline in mortality from coronary heart disease, 1980–1990; the effect of secular trends in risk factors and treatment JAMA. 1997:277:535–542.
20. Peters KD, Kochaneck KD, Murphy SL. Deaths: Final Data for 1996: National Vital Statistics Reports [vol 47, No. 9]. Hyattsville, Md: National Center for Health Statistics, 1998:52.
21. Pharmaceutical Research and Manufacturers of America (PhRMA). New Medicines in Development Database. Available at: http://www.phrma.org/webdb/phrmawdb.html. Accessed December 1, 1998.

# POSTSCRIPT

## Should Advertisements for Prescription Drugs Be Regulated?

Hollon asserts that drug companies' promotions are frequently inaccurate or deceptive. He further maintains that drug companies are more interested in increasing their profits than in truly providing additional benefits to the consumer. Drug companies do not deny that they seek to make profits from their drugs, but they argue that they are offering an important service by educating the public about new drugs through their advertisements.

An important issue is whether or not the average consumer is capable of discerning information distributed by pharmaceutical companies. Are people without a background in medicine, medical terminology, or research methods sufficiently knowledgeable to understand literature disseminated by drug companies? With the help of the Internet and other media, Holmer maintains, the average consumer is indeed capable of understanding information about various drugs.

Some critics argue that restricting drug advertisements is a moot point because consumers cannot obtain prescriptions without the approval of their physicians. Yet physicians frequently acquiesce to the wishes of their patients and write prescriptions upon request. If in this way patients receive prescriptions not appropriate for their needs, who is responsible: the patient, the physician, or the drug manufacturer and advertiser?

When drug manufacturers introduce a new drug, they get a patent on the drug to protect their investment. Drug companies, therefore, receive financial rewards for introducing new drugs. However, some critics maintain that many so-called new drugs are merely "me too" drugs (similar to existing drugs) and that they do not provide any additional benefits.

Two articles that are critical of direct-to-consumer prescription drug advertisements are "Pharmaceutical Advertisements: How They Deceive," by Ashish Chandra and Gary Holt, *Journal of Business Ethics* (February 15, 1999) and "Peddling Pills: The Rise of Direct-to-Consumer Prescription Drug Advertising and the Dangers to Consumers," by Larry Sasich, *Multinational Monitor* (January–February 1999). Tamara Terzian's article "Direct-to-Consumer Prescription Drug Advertising," *American Journal of Law and Medicine* (Spring 1999) examines many facets of this issue. Finally, whether or not Great Britain will allow direct-to-consumer drug advertising is discussed in "Consumer Choice or Chaos?" *Chemist & Druggist* (June 10, 2000).

### CBEL.com: Secondhand Smoke

This site features over 200 links to sites on secondhand smoke. Categories include effects on children, industry actions, organizations, restaurants, and health risks.

http://www.cbel.com/Secondhand_Smoke/

### DARE.com

This is the official Web site of Drug Abuse Resistance Education (DARE).

http://www.dare.com/index_3.htm

### Drug Testing News.com

The purpose of Drug Testing News.com is to provide the most comprehensive source for up-to-date news and information on the drug and alcohol testing industry, including legislation, legal issues, business, technology, prevention, and treatment.

http://www.drugtestingnews.com

### Treatment Improvement Exchange (TIE)

The Treatment Improvement Exchange (TIE) is a resource sponsored by the Division of State and Community Assistance of the Center for Substance Abuse Treatment (CSAT) to provide information exchange between CSAT staff and state and local alcohol and substance abuse agencies.

http://www.treatment.org

### National Youth Anti-Drug Media Campaign

The Office of National Drug Control Policy's National Youth Anti-Drug Media Campaign is a multidimensional effort designed to educate and empower youth to reject illicit drugs. This Web site features progress reports on the campaign's performance, campaign publications, television and print antidrug advertisements, up-to-date news stories, and more.

http://www.mediacampaign.org

# PART 3

# Drug Prevention and Treatment

*I*n spite of their legal consequences and the government's interdiction efforts, drugs are widely available and used. Two common ways of dealing with drug abuse is to incarcerate drug users and to intercept drugs before they enter the country. However, many drug experts believe that more energy should be put into preventing and treating drug abuse. An important step toward prevention and treatment is to find out what contributes to drug abuse and how to nullify these factors.

By educating young people about the potential hazards of drugs and by developing an awareness of social influences that contribute to drug use, many drug-related problems may be averted. The debates in this section focus on different prevention and treatment issues, the value of antidrug public service announcements, and the effectiveness of the most widely employed drug education program—Drug Abuse Resistance Education (DARE).

- Should Nonsmokers Be Concerned About the Effects of Secondhand Smoke?

- Is Total Abstinence the Only Choice for Alcoholics?

- Is Drug Abuse Resistance Education (DARE) an Effective Program?

- Should Employees Be Required to Participate in Drug Testing?

- Does Drug Abuse Treatment Work?

- Are Antidrug Media Campaigns Effective?

# ISSUE 14

## Should Nonsmokers Be Concerned About the Effects of Secondhand Smoke?

**YES: John R. Garrison**, from "Scientific Research Shows Overwhelmingly That Other People's Smoke Can Hurt You," *Insight on the News* (June 16, 1997)

**NO: J. B. Copas and J. Q. Shi**, from "Reanalysis of Epidemiological Evidence on Lung Cancer and Passive Smoking," *British Medical Journal* (February 12, 2000)

### ISSUE SUMMARY

**YES:** John R. Garrison, CEO of the American Lung Association, contends that evidence of adverse effects of secondhand smoke on nonsmokers is strong. He asserts that years of research clearly show that secondhand smoke is a factor in the development of lung cancer, heart disease, asthma, and respiratory infections.

**NO:** Statisticians J. B. Copas and J. Q. Shi argue that research demonstrating that passive smoking is harmful is biased. They argue that many journals are more likely to publish articles if passive smoking is shown to be deleterious and that the findings of many studies exaggerate the adverse effects of passive smoking.

T he movement to restrict secondhand smoke—the smoke that a person breathes in from another person's cigarette, cigar, or pipe—is growing. Smoking is banned on all commercial airplane flights within the continental United States. Canada, Australia, and many other countries have enacted similar bans. Smoking is prohibited or restricted in all federal public areas and workplaces. The right to smoke in public places is quickly being eliminated. Is this fair, considering tobacco's addictive hold over smokers? Former surgeon general C. Everett Koop and many researchers point out that smoking is an addiction that is as difficult to overcome as an addiction to cocaine or heroin. Should smokers be penalized—prevented from smoking or isolated from nonsmokers— for having a nicotine addiction?

Articles describing secondhand smoking, or passive smoking, can be confusing because several terms are frequently used to describe it. *Passive smoking* has been referred to as *involuntary smoking,* and the smoke itself has been identified as both *secondhand smoke* and *environmental tobacco smoke,* or *ETS.* Secondhand smoke can be further broken down into *mainstream smoke* and *sidestream smoke.* Mainstream smoke is the smoke that the smoker exhales. Sidestream smoke is the smoke that comes off the end of the tobacco product as it burns. Sidestream smoke has higher concentrations of carbon monoxide and other gases than mainstream smoke. Scientists also believe that sidestream smoke contains more carcinogens than mainstream smoke.

The issue of passive smoking is extremely divisive. On one side of the debate are the nonsmokers, who strongly believe that their rights to clean air are compromised by smokers. Their objections are based on more than aesthetics; it is not simply a matter of smoke being unsightly, noxious, or inconvenient. Nonsmokers are becoming more concerned about the toxic effects of secondhand smoke. Groups of nonsmokers and numerous health professionals have initiated a massive campaign to educate the public on the array of health-related problems that have been associated with inhaling the smoke generated by those who smoke tobacco products.

On the other side are smokers, who believe that they should have the right to smoke whenever and wherever they wish. This group is backed by the tobacco industry, which has allocated vast sums of money and resources to conduct research studies on the effects of secondhand smoke. Based on the results of these studies, smoking rights groups contend that the health concerns related to secondhand smoke are based on emotion, not scientific evidence. They argue that there are too many variables involved to determine the exact impact of secondhand smoke. For example, to what extent does a polluted environment or a poorly ventilated house contribute to the health problems attributed to secondhand smoke? Isolating the effects of secondhand smoke, these groups maintain, is difficult, and any studies concluding that secondhand smoke is harmful are questionable.

Many smokers who acknowledge that smoking may have adverse effects on health argue that their freedoms should not be limited. They feel that they should have the right to engage in behaviors that affect only themselves, even if those behaviors are unhealthy. Some smokers reason that if smoking behavior is regulated, perhaps other personal behaviors also will become regulated. They fight against the regulation of smoking because they believe that behavior regulation is a potentially harmful trend.

If smoking is restricted, many people employed in the tobacco industry may lose their livelihoods. What may be a health benefit for some people may be detrimental to the economic health of others. Are the people who want to restrict smoking willing to help those individuals who would be economically affected by such a restriction?

In the following selections, John R. Garrison asserts that the dangers associated with secondhand smoke are clear and that even exposure to low doses of secondhand smoke is toxic. J. B. Copas and J. Q. Shi maintain that much of the information about the health hazards of secondhand smoke has been distorted and accepted as fact without adequate critical questioning.

John R. Garrison

# Scientific Research Shows Overwhelmingly That Other People's Smoke Can Hurt You

The toxic effects of secondhand smoke have been so well-documented during the last 25 years that there should be no doubt that smoke emitted from other people's cigarettes is a real and preventable health risk. Secondhand smoke, also known as environmental tobacco smoke, or ETS, passive smoke or sidestream smoke is estimated to cause 53,000 deaths each year among nonsmokers in the United States. The Environmental Protection Agency, or EPA, estimates that secondhand smoke is responsible for about 3,000 lung-cancer deaths each year among nonsmokers; of these, an estimated 800 are due to exposure to second-hand smoke in the home and 2,200 from exposure at work or in social settings. A recent study from Harvard University reports that ETS may even double a person's risk of heart disease.

Unlike the dangers of cigarette use, the threat that secondhand smoke presents is especially insidious because it affects the health of adults and children who cannot always protect themselves: Children do not choose to live in smoke-filled homes, and nonsmoking adults can't control the smoky air they breathe at work.

The scientific community began compiling evidence about the adverse health effects of secondhand smoke as early as 1972, when a report of the surgeon general concluded that "an atmosphere contaminated with tobacco smoke can contribute to the discomfort of many individuals."

Since then, several reports have been released outlining the toxic effects of secondhand smoke. They include the 1986 surgeon general's report which concluded that secondhand smoke can cause lung cancer in healthy nonsmokers and that children whose parents smoke have an increased frequency of respiratory infections and respiratory symptoms compared with children whose parents do not smoke. The National Academy of Sciences and the International Agency for Research on Cancer also issued reports in 1986 that offered similar conclusions.

In 1991, the National Institute for Occupational Safety and Health, or NIOSH, concluded that ETS is a potential occupational carcinogen. NIOSH recommended that employers take measures to reduce their employees' exposure to secondhand smoke by designating a separate area for smoking.

The final breakthrough came in 1993, with the publication of the EPA's definitive report, *Respiratory Health Effects of Passive Smoking: Lung Cancer and Other Disorders*. This report not only supported earlier findings regarding the risks of lung cancer, it also augmented previous reports with an exhaustive review of the health effects of secondhand smoke on children.

The EPA's report classified secondhand smoke as a Group A carcinogen that is responsible for an estimated annual toll of 37,000 heart-disease deaths and 13,000 deaths from other cancers in U.S. nonsmokers. Secondhand smoke was found to be a risk factor for the development of asthma in children. It also was found to worsen asthma symptoms for up to 1 million children already diagnosed with asthma. Annually, an estimated 150,000 to 300,000 cases of lower respiratory-tract infections, such as bronchitis and pneumonia, among children under 18 months of age were linked to secondhand-smoke exposure. The EPA report also concluded that infants and young children exposed to secondhand smoke experience increased cases of ear infection, coughing, wheezing and mucus buildup.

The EPA report was subjected to an extensive open review both by the public and the agency's Science Advisory Board, a panel of independent scientific experts. The board, the Department of Health and Human Services, the National Cancer Institute, the surgeon general and many other major health organizations, including the American Lung Association, have endorsed the EPA's findings.

Despite these endorsements, the tobacco industry continues to question the EPA's conclusions on lung cancer. While the industry neither acknowledges nor disputes EPA's findings on the respiratory effects in children, it continues to argue that the EPA manipulated the lung-cancer data to arrive at a predetermined conclusion. Furthermore, the tobacco industry argues that a nonsmoker's exposure to secondhand smoke is so minimal as to be insignificant.

The EPA's findings that secondhand-smoke exposure causes lung cancer in nonsmoking adults was not based on a single analysis but, rather, on the total weight of all the evidence available at the time. In addition, no claims ever have been made that minimal exposure to secondhand smoke poses a huge individual cancer risk. While the lung-cancer risk from secondhand smoke is relatively small compared with the risk from smoking, exposure to secondhand smoke often is involuntary and varies greatly among exposed individuals. Clearly, those who work or live with smokers experience a greater risk of lung cancer than those who are less exposed.

Several lung-cancer studies published since the release of the EPA report reinforce the link between secondhand-smoke exposure and lung cancer. They include a 1992 study by Stockwell et al., that found a group of Florida women whose husbands smoked experienced a 60 percent increase of lung-cancer risk. A similar study of Missouri women conducted the same year by Brownson et al., found a significant increase in risk among women exposed to high levels of secondhand smoke from their spouses. Finally, a 1994 study by Fontham et al., found significant increases in lung-cancer risk among women in two California and three Southern cities who were exposed to secondhand smoke.

There is no doubt today that smoking by parents is associated with a broad range of adverse effects in children. Tobacco use during pregnancy is responsible for an estimated 20 to 30 percent of low-birthweight babies, up to 14 percent of preterm deliveries and some 10 percent of all infant deaths.

A study reported by the *American Journal of Respiratory and Critical Care Medicine* in 1992 found that even apparently healthy, full-term babies of smokers are born with narrowed airways and impaired lung function. Research released in 1994 found the children of mothers who smoked a half-pack of cigarettes or more during pregnancy had lower IQ scores than children whose mothers had not smoked. Studies also have shown that smoking in pregnancy can lead to delayed physical growth in children.

Clearly, pregnant women who quit smoking can contribute greatly to their child's health and well-being. However, recent findings reveal that quitting smoking may not be enough. Mothers need to protect their unborn children from other people's secondhand smoke as well. A 1995 study of 3,500 pregnant women found that nonsmoking women who were exposed to secondhand smoke during pregnancy had lower-birthweight babies than nonexposed expectant mothers.

Americans most certainly should be worried about the toxic effects of secondhand smoke. What should worry them even more are the proponents of the tobacco industry who continue to deny not only the lethal effects of secondhand smoke but of smoking itself. For years, the tobacco industry has denied the health effects of smoking and secondhand smoke with accusations of poor science, questions about statistical significance and assertions of ignorance.

Perhaps Joseph A. Califano, then secretary of Health, Education and Welfare, responded most aptly to such tactics in his preface to the 1979 *Surgeon General's Report on Smoking and Health:*

"In truth, the attack upon the scientific and medical evidence about smoking is little more than an attack upon the science itself: an attack upon the epidemiological, clinical and experimental research disciplines upon which these conclusions are based. Like every attack upon science by vested interests, from Aristotle's day to Galileo's to our own, these attacks collapse of their own weight."

In 1992, a Gallup survey conducted for the Coalition On Smoking or Health, cofounded by the American Lung Association, found that nine in 10 adults were aware that secondhand smoke is harmful to infants and young children, pregnant women and older healthy adults. Women were more likely than men to believe that secondhand smoke is harmful to all of these groups. Nonsmokers also were more likely than smokers strongly to agree about the harmful effects of secondhand smoke. An important finding was that even eight in 10 smokers know that secondhand smoke is bad for the people around them. The good news is that an increased percentage of those surveyed supported total bans or restrictions on smoking in public places such as restaurants, workplaces, hotels, buses and trains.

Forty-eight states and the District of Columbia have some restriction on smoking in public places. These laws range from designating a separate smoking area in schools to complete bans or restrictions on smoking in areas open to the public, including elevators, public buildings, restaurants, health facilities, public transportation, museums, shopping malls, retail stores and educational facilities. Among the states that limit or ban smoking in public areas, 43 restrict smoking in government workplaces and 23 restrict smoking in private-sector workplaces.

Since early 1990, smoking has been banned from almost all U.S. domestic airline flights. Most of today's travelers can barely remember the days of hazy, smoke-choked air travel. In recent years, many airlines have made some or all of their international flights smoke-free as well.

While progress certainly has been made toward reducing exposure to secondhand smoke, a great deal still needs to be accomplished. Thousands of corporate and restaurant employees throughout the country are exposed to harmful levels of secondhand smoke on a daily basis. In addition, a dangerous new trend in the form of "glamorous" cigar bars is exposing many to the harmful effects of secondhand cigar smoke.

Clearly, all Americans need to recognize and protect themselves and their children from the harmful effects of secondhand smoke. They should encourage the smokers in their lives to quit, and they should encourage their legislators to maintain or strengthen bans on smoking in public places. Only then can we breathe easy, knowing that our lungs and our lives aren't at risk from someone else's smoke.

J. B. Copas and J. Q. Shi

 **NO**

# Reanalysis of Epidemiological Evidence on Lung Cancer and Passive Smoking

**Objective** To assess the epidemiological evidence for an increase in the risk of lung cancer resulting from exposure to environmental tobacco smoke.

**Design** Reanalysis of 37 published epidemiological studies previously included in a meta-analysis allowing for the possibility of publication bias.

**Main outcome measure** Relative risk of lung cancer among female lifelong non-smokers, according to whether her partner was a current smoker or a lifelong non-smoker.

**Results** If it is assumed that all studies that have ever been carried out are included, or that those selected for review are truly representative of all such studies, then the estimated excess risk of lung cancer is 24%, as previously reported (95% confidence interval 13% to 36%, $P < 0.001$). However, a significant correlation between study outcome and study size suggests the presence of publication bias. Adjustment for such bias implies that the risk has been overestimated. For example, if only 60% of studies have been included, the estimate of excess risk falls from 24% to 15%.

**Conclusion** A modest degree of publication bias leads to a substantial reduction in the relative risk and to a weaker level of significance, suggesting that the published estimate of the increased risk of lung cancer associated with environmental tobacco smoke needs to be interpreted with caution.

## Introduction

Exposure to environmental tobacco smoke (passive smoking) is widely accepted to increase the risk of lung cancer, but different epidemiological studies have produced varying estimates of the size of the relative risk. Hackshaw et al reviewed the results of 37 such studies that estimated the relative risk of lung cancer among female lifelong non-smokers, comparing those whose spouses (or partners) were current smokers with those whose spouses had never smoked.[1]

From J. B. Copas and J. Q. Shi, "Reanalysis of Epidemiological Evidence on Lung Cancer and Passive Smoking," *British Medical Journal*, vol. 320 (February 12, 2000). Copyright © 2000 by The BMJ Publishing Group. Reprinted by permission. Notes omitted.

Of the 37 studies, 31 reported an increase in risk, and the increase was significant in seven studies. The remaining six studies reported negative results, but none of these was significant. Pooling these results using a method which allows for statistical heterogeneity between studies, Hackshaw et al concluded that there is an overall excess risk of 24% (95% confidence interval 13% to 36%).[1] This is strong epidemiological evidence for an association between lung cancer and passive smoking (P < 0.001).

The approach used by Hackshaw et al does not allow for the possibility of publication bias—that is, the possibility that published studies, particularly smaller ones, will be biased in favour of more positive results. We reanalysed the results and looked for evidence of publication bias.

## Methods and Results

... [T]he relative risks from the 37 epidemiological studies analysed by Hackshaw et al[1] [were] plotted against a measure of the uncertainty in that relative risk. This uncertainty (s) decreases as the size of the study increases so that large studies are on the left of the plot and small studies on the right. The plot shows a trend for smaller studies to give more positive results than the larger studies (correlation = 0.35, P < 0.05, or P = 0.012 by Egger's test[2]). This graph is similar to the funnel plot used in the meta-analysis of clinical trials, when a trend such as this is interpreted as a sign of publication bias.[3] This bias arises when a study is more likely to be written up and submitted to a journal and more likely to be accepted for publication if it reports positive results than if its results are inconclusive or negative. Since it is reasonable to assume that publication is more likely for larger (small s) than smaller (large s) studies, the problem of publication bias will be most evident among the smaller studies, as suggested by the figure. By "publication" we mean the whole process of selecting a study for review.

We reanalysed the results of the 37 epidemiological studies to allow for the trend evident in the figure. Our method describes the apparent relation between relative risk and study size by a curve. This gives a good fit to the observed points. The basic idea of the method is that there is no real relation between study outcome and study size, the relation that we observe is simply an artefact of the process of selecting these studies.

Our method has been published,[4] and further details are available from us on request. The estimated average relative risk depends on a statistical parameter that can be interpreted as the probability that a paper with a certain value of s is published (publication probability). If the publication probability is 1, all papers are published and so there is no possibility of publication bias; the relative risk is then estimated as 1.24 (24% risk excess), agreeing as expected with Hackshaw et al's result.[1] But smaller values of publication probability give smaller estimates of relative risk. We do not know how many unpublished studies have been carried out. Therefore there is no way of estimating the publication probability from any data: all we know is that there is a significant correlation in the funnel plot, so that some degree of publication bias is needed to explain this trend.

Table 1 gives the estimated relative risk for values of publication probability between 0.6 and 1, together with 95% confidence intervals and P values. The P value is less than 5% only when the publication probability is more than about 0.7. The indirect estimate of 19% excess risk derived from studies on biochemical markers (table 5 of Hackshaw et al's paper[1]) agrees with the epidemiological analysis when the publication probability is about 0.9.

*Table 1*

Estimated Relative Risk and Number of Unpublished Smaller and Larger Studies for Various Values of Publication Probability

| Publication probability | Relative risk (95% CI) | P value | No of unpublished studies (*) | |
| --- | --- | --- | --- | --- |
| | | | Small | Large |
| 0.6 | 1.11 (0.97 to 1.27) | 0.110 | 36 | 24 |
| 0.7 | 1.13 (1.00 to 1.27) | 0.052 | 23 | 15 |
| 0.8 | 1.15 (1.03 to 1.28) | 0.014 | 14 | 9 |
| 0.9 | 1.18 (1.07 to 1.31) | 0.002 | 7 | 4 |
| n | 1.24 (1.13 to 1.36) | <0.001 | 0 | 0 |

(*) Smaller studies s > 0.4; larger studies s [is less than or equal to] 0.4.

For any given value of publication probability it is possible to estimate the number of studies which have been undertaken but not published. This is shown in the final two columns of Table 1. If the publication probability is 0.8 then there are a total of 23 unpublished studies so that the 37 selected ones represent a sample of 37/60 = 62% of all such studies that have been undertaken. If this is the case, then the excess risk is likely to be closer to 15% than 24%. . . .

## Conclusions

Although the trend . . . seems clear, Bero et al suggest that the number of unpublished studies is unlikely to be large,[5] and so the problem of publication bias may be less severe here than in systematic reviews of other aspects of medicine. However, the possibility of publication bias cannot be ruled out altogether, and at least some publication bias is needed to explain the trend we found. Our results show that the publication probability does not have to fall much below 1.0 before there is quite a substantial reduction in the estimated risk.

## References

1. Hackshaw AK, Law MR, Wald NJ. The accumulated evidence on lung cancer and environmental tobacco smoke. BMJ 1997;315:980–988.

2. Egger M, Smith GD, Schneider M, Minder C. Bias in meta-analysis detected by a simple graphical test. BMJ 1997;315:629-634.
3. Egger M, Smith GD. Misleading meta-analysis. BMJ 1995;310:752-754.
4. Copas JB. What works; selectivity models and meta analysis. J R Stat Soc Am 1999; 162:95-109.
5. Bero LA, Glantz SA, Rennie D. Publication bias and public health policy on environmental tobacco smoke. JAMA 1994;272:133-136.

# POSTSCRIPT

## Should Nonsmokers Be Concerned About the Effects of Secondhand Smoke?

In today's health-conscious society, many people seem to be more aware of what they eat, whether or not they get enough exercise, and how much stress they experience. Thus, it is only logical that people are also concerned about possible environmental threats to their health, such as secondhand smoking.

Whether or not secondhand smoke is injurious to nonsmokers is relevant because many businesses have adopted policies and many states have passed laws based on the premise that secondhand smoke is a health risk. A number of states restrict smoking in the workplace; most shopping malls prohibit smoking; the military has banned or restricted smoking in many of its facilities; and numerous restaurants forbid smoking in their establishments. The issue of smoking has also become a point of contention in child custody cases. It has been argued that parents who smoke around their children are unfit parents.

Increasingly, smokers are being isolated in society; they are almost pictured as social outcasts. There is a growing contempt and disdain shown toward smokers. The emotionality of this issue often puts smokers on the defensive. This confrontational stance is not conducive to addressing the issue of smokers' rights in a constructive way.

A report released in 1993 by the Environmental Protection Agency (EPA) links environmental tobacco smoke to lung cancer and heart disease in nonsmokers and to respiratory infections in children. The report states that passive smoking is responsible for an estimated 3,000 lung cancer deaths annually in adults, as many as 300,000 childhood cases of bronchitis and pneumonia, and between 8,000 and 26,000 new cases of asthma in children. Although groups that support restricting environmental tobacco smoke cite the EPA's report as evidence for their position, the report has been criticized for exaggerating and distorting the harmful effects of passive smoke.

An overview of the government's position and that of the tobacco industry on the issue of passive smoking is discussed in Elisa Ong and Stanton Glantz, "Tobacco Industry Efforts Subverting International Agency for Research on Cancer's Second-Hand Smoke Study," *The Lancet* (April 8, 2000). Scott Gottlieb, in "Study Confirms Passive Smoking Increases Coronary Heart Disease," *British Medical Journal* (1999), reviews numerous studies demonstrating that heart disease among nonsmokers is caused by passive smoking. And a thorough examination of secondhand smoke can be found in a report by the California Environmental Protection Agency entitled *Health Effects of Exposure to Environmental Tobacco Smoke* (September 1997).

# ISSUE 15

# Is Total Abstinence the Only Choice for Alcoholics?

**YES: Thomas Byrd**, from *Lives Written in Sand: Addiction Awareness and Recovery Strategies* (Hallum, 1997)

**NO: Joseph Volpicelli and Maia Szalavitz**, from *Recovery Options: The Complete Guide* (John Wiley, 2000)

## ISSUE SUMMARY

**YES:** Professor of health Thomas Byrd maintains that Alcoholics Anonymous (AA) provides more effective treatment for alcoholics than psychiatrists, members of the clergy, or hospital treatment centers. Byrd contends that AA is the most powerful and scientific program, in contrast to all other therapies.

**NO:** Addiction treatment specialist Joseph Volpicelli and journalist Maia Szalavitz advocate a moderate drinking approach for individuals with drinking problems. They support alcohol treatment programs that are tailored to meet the different needs of problem drinkers. Volpicelli and Szalavitz argue that abstinence may be counterproductive for many problem drinkers.

Acccording to government figures, there are an estimated 10 to 20 million alcoholics in the United States. Cocaine addicts number between 250,000 and 1 million. Eating disorders, sexual addictions, compulsive gambling, excessive spending, and compulsive working affect millions more people. Knowing the best way to help people who engage in these compulsive or addictive behaviors is difficult. One way to control addictive behavior is to abstain from it. However, is total abstention, which is promoted by Alcoholics Anonymous (AA), the best or only viable treatment goal?

The concept of helping people with addictions can be approached from opposing perspectives. Some critics take the view that addiction occurs when people lose control over their addictive behavior. Moreover, there is always some kind of reward or payoff that fuels one's addictive behavior. The benefit may be security, sensation, or power, but as long as one or more of these benefits are experienced, people will not stop their behavior. Not everybody needs to abstain from unhealthy behaviors; only those people whose behaviors have reached the addictive stage. With some potentially addictive behaviors, such as eating or working, it is impossible to abstain. However, with behaviors that are not necessary for survival, such as alcohol consumption, abstention is, according to some viewpoints, the only path to follow.

If addiction leaves people powerless, as some professionals maintain, then the only way to gain personal power and control is through abstention. If alcoholics are powerless against alcohol, then they cannot drink simply for the enjoyment of alcohol; they will invariably drink to excess.

The abstinence model is currently the most popular approach for treating addiction. Abstinence is included in the 12-step model promoted by Alcoholics Anonymous and other self-help groups. Elements of this model include admitting to being powerless over one's addiction, accepting a higher power, and restructuring one's life. Opponents of the 12-step approach argue that it is not suitable for everyone and that it has not been proven effective. The idea of placing faith in a higher power, for example, is inconsistent with the values of many people, especially those who do not believe in the concept of a higher power. Another problem is that programs such as AA claim to be effective based on the testimonies of the program participants. However, because of the anonymity of people who attend or have attended AA meetings, follow-up studies are negligible.

A number of studies show that most people who stop addictive behavior do so on their own. Heroin addicts who quit using heroin generally do not go through any type of formal treatment. Likewise, the majority of individuals who quit smoking also stop without an organized program. Factors contributing to spontaneous remission are not well understood. It is believed that people stop self-destructive behaviors once they "hit bottom."

One criticism of the abstinence approach is that it stigmatizes people. The label "alcoholic" may deter people from receiving help because it connotes social deviance. Also, individuals who admit that they cannot control their own behavior are implying that they lack the strength to do so. That is, they are too weak to take care of their problems themselves. This stigma may prevent some people from seeking help.

In recent years alternative self-help groups to Alcoholics Anonymous have appeared. The Secular Organization for Sobriety (SOS) is one such group for alcoholics that does not have the same emphasis on a belief in a higher power. There is also Women for Sobriety/Men for Sobriety, which does not accept AA's disease model of addiction. Abstinence is a prominent aspect of this group, but overcoming alcoholism is based on self-acceptance and the role of love in relationships. Other programs are Rational Recovery (RR) and Moderation Management (MM). Unlike other models, RR and MM incorporate the belief that moderate alcohol use is possible.

In the selections that follow, Thomas Byrd makes the case that the abstinence-only, 12-step AA model is the only viable approach for overcoming alcoholism. Joseph Volpicelli and Maia Szalavitz promote a moderate drinking approach based on specific guidelines for helping problem drinkers.

Thomas Byrd

# Lives Written in Sand: Addiction Awareness and Recovery Strategies

## Alcoholics Anonymous, What Works Best for Most

Finding the words to describe an organization which has saved millions of lives and countless relationships is difficult. Fundamentally, Alcoholics Anonymous provides hope to those in despair. The contents of the "program" focus on feelings, and how to cope with them throughout life. It is not an intellectual program, rather focusing on problem resolution and the subsequent spiritual rewards. The fellowship teaches a philosophy whose rewards are immediate and practical. AA is not a religion where prime benefits may be promised in the afterlife. It is a group of people who share a common problem and experience. Members are committed to living in the solution, not in the problem. Only a distinct minority of alcoholics are able to put their disease in remission and enter recovery. Most alcoholics do not recover. AA is a simple program for complicated people. New members frequently ask "how" does the program work. If you dissect the word, the first letter stands for an honest appraisal of the problem; the second letter refers to being openminded to new concepts from those in recovery; and the third letter stands for a willingness to devote the energy it takes to enter recovery. Members have committed two fundamental crimes. One is against the growth and development of another person. The second transgression is the indifference to the growth and development of self. Members are encouraged to make amends when possible and to carry the message to those still suffering. It is a program of attraction, not of promotion. The only requirement for membership is a desire to quit drinking.

Stopping drinking seems simple. You just don't drink. The problem is that there is a lot of failure. However, many of those who drink again will eventually stop drinking. Family members seem more likely to get their hopes up, only to suffer further discouragement if the alcoholic resumes drinking. The problem drinker seems to be less upset with relapse, probably because drinking has played such a major role in his or her life.

The physician may help identify the problem but is best at tending to physical problems. The alcoholic is generally not a desirable patient in most medical offices. Rejection of prescribed treatment, dishonesty, evasiveness, and rationalization of drinking are typical. Alcoholism is best treated by the specialist, a fellow recovering alcoholic, where there is no barrier of misunderstanding. Fears, guilt and self-condemnation and other psychiatric problems are minimized in this relationship.

Most rehabilitation programs encourage their patients to participate in Alcoholics Anonymous as part of an aftercare program. This organization exists because alcoholics need help and AA is more successful than psychiatry, the clergy, hospitals or jails in providing that needed aid. The organization works one day at a time for anyone who thinks help is needed. Membership is anonymous unless the member desires to drop the anonymity.

Alcoholics Anonymous was founded by two prominent men whose lives had been seriously affected by excessive drinking. They set out simply to survive. What they did was to try anything and everything, keeping what works and rejecting the rest.

John D. Rockefeller made a $5,000 contribution to the co-founders Bill Wilson and Dr. Bob Smith to help the fledging organization. Bill Wilson had grandiose ideas of establishing a network of recovery centers throughout the United States. These plans were stilled by Rockefeller's son. At a dinner presided over by Nelson Rockefeller he declined to make any further family donations to the organization, stating "this is too good to be destroyed by money." This decision ultimately led to the establishment of a non-profit organization, which became self-supporting through their own membership's contributions. Wilson acquiesced to the condition of the one time gift, and the wealthy and visionary New York politician salvaged the organization by replacing profit with humanity.

AA is at the basis of all good treatment simply because it is the most powerful, and because it is the most scientific of all therapies. The first months of membership in Alcoholics Anonymous are most critical. Getting to the first meeting is difficult. Continuing to participate in your own recovery is also difficult. There are erroneously preconceived attitudes that can form barriers to recovery. The alcoholic needs to keep attending until he or she wants to attend. In other words, they need to give it a chance.

Help from another alcoholic is something that can be depended on. Service to others is one of the components of recovery. The drinker is accepted without question into the AA group. The 12 steps of Alcoholics Anonymous constitute a recovery program that begins with the admission that the member is powerless over alcohol and that strength is needed from another source to overcome the problem. A searching, fearless moral self-inventory is also part of the program. Restitution to those who have been harmed gives the alcoholic emotional strength. Knowing there is help if a person wants to stop drinking can be vital.

There are no rules, no dues, and participation is voluntary. It is a fellowship based upon a common problem. Sponsors in the organization are available to give support to the newcomer. Suggestions on how to stay sober are exchanged between members. "Tomorrow may never come, yesterday is a canceled check." The alcoholic can't be cured, but is only an arrested case. If the alcoholic takes a drink again, the problem will surface and the member will be right back in the depths of active alcoholism. The objective is to stay sober today. Alcoholics understand this, simple as it is. Personality reorientation can come later. *The Big Book of Alcoholics Anonymous* is an excellent source of information. The author also recommends another book, authored by Nan Robertson. It's titled, *Getting Better: Inside AA,* published by Fawcett Crest, New York, New York, 1988.

# Actions Among Equals

There are many approaches to the treatment of alcoholism, successful programs involve abstinence by whatever method it is achieved. Yet if one method of approaching a problem yields noticeably better and more striking results than others, then this method must contain some unique factor or factors that set it apart and form the basis of its supremacy.

"Alcoholics Anonymous is a fellowship of men and women who share their experience, strength and hope with each other that they may solve their common problem and help others to recover from alcoholism." The experiences of alcoholics are essentially the same, the theme is always the same: a progressive deterioration of the human personality. What then is the constant factor? What is AA's unique difference? I feel there are four distinctive characteristics that set apart this successful recovery program.

One of the answers lies in the manner in which this experience, strength and hope are shared and who is doing the sharing. Long before the average alcoholic walks through the doors of an AA meeting, help has been offered, in some instances even forced upon them. But these helpers are always superior beings. The moral responsibility of the alcoholic and the moral superiority of the helper, even though unstated, are always clearly understood. The overtone of parental disapproval and discipline in these authority figures is always present. Instead of the menacing, "This is what you should do," there is an instantly recognizable voice saying, "This is what I did." Therefore, one of the constant factors of a premium recovery program is where one alcoholic consciously and deliberately turned to another alcoholic, not to drink with, but to stay sober. I am personally convinced that the basic search of every human being is to find another human being, before whom one can stand completely without pretense or defense, and trust that person not to hurt them, because that person is exposed too. It is self-evident that the newcomer has been invited to share in the experience of recovery.

If the alcoholic responds to this invitation, the member then encounters a second unique factor: AA treats the symptoms first. The conviction that alcoholism is the symptom of deeper troubles. Even the cleverest diagnosis of these troubles is of little benefit if the patient dies. Autopsies do not benefit the persons upon whom they are performed. Total abstinence is the name of the game. Recovery can only begin with a decision to stay away from the first drink. No one can or will make that decision for the ill. In fact, one soon further learns that if he makes the decision, no one can or will force fulfillment of the goal. There are reports of action taken, rather than rules not to be broken. Action is the magic word. There are steps to be taken which are suggested as a program for recovery. Quoting from Chapter Five of the book, *Alcoholics Anonymous: Step One,* "We admitted we were powerless over alcohol, that our lives had become unmanageable." The newcomer finally sees that they must take these Steps before being entitled to report on them. It is important to "utilize, not to analyze."

The desire to make this decision often results from what appears to be a third unique quality: The intuitive understanding the alcoholic receives, while compassionate, is not indulgent. The new member is not asked what they are thinking, rather they are told what they are thinking. The companion "therapists" already have their doctorates in the four fields where the alcoholic reigns supreme: phoniness, self-deception, evasion, and self-pity. There's not much point in trying to fool people who may have invented the game that's being played. In the end, the member begins to achieve honesty by default.

There is a fourth factor which I feel is significant, and that is the recovering alcoholic's infinite willingness to talk about alcoholism. Without the newcomer's ever becoming fully aware of it, the fascination with alcohol is literally talked to death. There is a reversal of form which the educational process takes. The participant is asked, not so much to learn new values, as to unlearn those that brought the seeker to the doors of recovery; not so much to adopt new goals, as to abandon old ones. The real answer is that this unique therapy occurs wherever two alcoholics meet: at home, at lunch, in the street, at work or school, and on the telephone. Members may faithfully attend meetings waiting for "something" to rub off, namely the "miracle of AA." The sad part about it is that "something" is rubbing off on them. Death. The real miracle is simply the willingness to act.

The formless flexibility of AA's principles as interpreted by their different adherents finally pushes the alcoholic into a stance where he must use only himself as a frame of reference for personal actions, and this in turn means there must be a willingness to accept the consequences of those actions. In my viewpoint, that is the definition of emotional maturity. True freedom lies in the realization and calm acceptance of the fact that there may very well be no perfect answer. The search for perfection is the hallmark of the neurotic. In the final analysis, we are all striving to be a better human beings. The future is that time when you will wish that you had used the time that you have now. Live in the present.

Other programs such as Rational Recovery and S.T.A.R.T. emphasize self-management and recovery training. Both programs do not incorporate the "higher power" aspect of the AA program, neither use a 12 Step format, reject the recovering concept, sponsorship, nor a 'one at a time' philosophy.

## Growth, a Day at a Time

Recovering people can become overwhelmed by new responsibilities. Sometimes too, members wonder why we can't ever be finished and just stop for awhile.

Feeling this way can mean it is time to stop and rest. The process of recovery has plateaus and detours along the way, and it's okay at times to take a break. But the "it's too much trouble" feeling also can be a signal that we need to pay more, not less, attention to ourselves and our recovery program.

Just as the chemically dependent person chooses not to drink or use drugs on a daily basis, so must a codependent person choose to continue recovery one day at a time. It is easy to see progress or lack of it in the big choices—to abstain from chemicals, to dissolve destructive relationships, to change careers. Less visible, but at least as important, are the little choices we all make every day.

Recovery means choosing to confront small instances of abusive behavior instead of letting them go. It means choosing to set boundaries to protect your time for recreation and rejuvenation. It means saying "no" to demands you can't meet. It means deciding every day to take care of yourself by paying attention to your needs for sleep, exercise, and healthy diet.

We can let all these choices overwhelm us if we focus on the "every single day for the whole rest of my life" aspect of them. Or we can take them one day at a time, recognizing that some days are easier than others. And we can remember that, as choosing growth becomes a pattern, it gets easier. Each seemingly insignificant daily choice is a separate affirmation that recovery is worth the trouble.

# NO ⬅

Joseph Volpicelli and Maia Szalavitz

# Moderate-Drinking Approaches

T o many, the idea of teaching an alcoholic to drink moderately is as absurd as the idea of toilet training a newborn. While it might be technically possible in a rare few instances, it seems highly unlikely to succeed without causing a great deal of trauma and pain to everyone around. The vehemence with which proponents of abstinence-focused treatment have opposed even discussing the question has made unbiased information about such treatment very difficult to find. Even though AA recommends that people who are not convinced that they are alcoholics try controlled drinking, Minnesota Model treatment providers tend to think that helping people do so is "enabling." The fear is that offering the hope of control will simply make alcoholics unwilling ever to put down the booze.

In this [selection], we look at the research on moderate-drinking programs, people's experiences in them, and the options available in this approach. Despite how it has been demonized, many benefit from it, and you may be surprised at how straightforward and sensible the techniques are.

## Who Can Be Helped by Moderate-Drinking Programs?

Part of the debate about moderate drinking has resulted from difficulties in classifying drinking problems. Because many people define alcoholics as people who can never control their drinking, tautologically, moderation is impossible for such people. However, if you define alcoholism by a certain level of drinking and a certain number of negative events related to drinking, as a psychiatric (Diagnostic and Statistical Manual—DSM) definition does, return to nondestructive drinking becomes at least a possibility. Many opponents of controlled drinking have claimed, however, that if someone manages to moderate, "he or she wasn't *really* an alcoholic," even if he or she drank just as much for just as long as someone who couldn't learn control.

Research on whether those who have had drinking problems can return to normal drinking patterns shows several things. For one, the longer and more problematic the drinking is, the less likely moderation becomes, though even here, there is a tiny minority who do attain it. Second, moderation among

From Joseph Volpicelli and Maia Szalavitz, *Recovery Options: The Complete Guide* (John Wiley & Sons, 2000). Copyright © 2000 by Joseph Volpicelli and Maia Szalavitz. Reprinted by permission of John Wiley & Sons, Inc.

long-term heavy drinkers is more difficult to achieve and maintain than abstinence is. For those whose drinking problems are not the most severe and long-standing, moderate drinking is achieved about as often as complete and lasting abstinence is—that is, among around 15–20% of those who try it at any given time. In the population of heavy drinkers, those on the less severe end of the spectrum outnumber the extremely dependent alcoholics by about 3:1.

How can you determine whether to try for moderation or abstinence for yourself? The worse your drinking is, the less likely it is that you will be able to successfully moderate it, so that is one factor to consider. Also, abstinence is without question the least risky option: If you don't drink, you can't have alcohol-related problems, period. If you are already comfortably abstinent, why take the risk? However, if you are like most people who are currently experiencing serious drinking problems, abstinence may seem like the least appealing choice. If you can't imagine totally quitting drinking and believe that you will be able to achieve and maintain control, a moderate-drinking program may be a good place to start. If you do get a handle on your drinking, the problem is solved—if not, the motivation to become abstinent becomes more compelling. Many alcoholics do not believe that their drinking is harmful and think that they have total control over it. An attempt at moderation with guidance can be the decisive evidence you need to determine for yourself whether drinking is a problem: If you are honest, and you work hard at the program, you will learn whether moderation is possible for you. If not, you will certainly be more aware of your drinking problem and its effects on you and those around you, which is likely to lead you to take further action to deal with it.

## How Do Moderate-Drinking Programs Work?

Currently, there are several moderate-drinking programs available in the United States. Some counselors offer a program called "Drinkwise," developed by Canadian researcher Martha Sanchez-Craig. Others offer other cognitive and behavioral therapies aimed at helping people cut down. There is also a small self-help group called "Moderation Management," which has adopted some of Sanchez-Craig's approach, as well as other techniques that research-based programs found to be helpful. Additionally, there are several self-help books aimed at achieving this outcome. Also, many alcoholism research centers, such as ours at U Penn, will support someone who chooses moderation as a valid treatment option, although abstinence is our primary recommendation.

We know of no inpatient programs aimed at moderate drinking because there would be little sense to them. If a person's problem is severe enough to require inpatient treatment, moderation is an unlikely outcome. Also, how would you practice and monitor your drinking in a hospital? The artificial environment wouldn't teach you much about dealing with your problem in your real life.

Most moderate-drinking programs start with a month-long period of abstinence, to create a transition between the problematic drinking and moderate drinking as well as to break the "habit" aspect of the previous drinking. This

allows a fresh start when drinking is resumed. Also, if you cannot successfully abstain for 30 days, you are extremely unlikely to be able to control your
drinking.

## FOR FAMILY MEMBERS AND OTHER LOVED ONES: SUPPORT HIS OR HER SUCCESSES

W hen people you love drink heavily, you often come to hate the way they
are while drunk, and just the smell of alcohol may become repellent. If your
loved ones decide not to quit, but just to moderate, you may feel betrayed or
that they aren't really trying. If possible, try not to see it this way—try to see
these efforts as a first step. If your loved ones have started treatment because
you have been showing them how drinking is harming their relationships,
try reaching an agreement that if they don't succeed at moderation after a
set period of time, they will enter abstinence-oriented treatment. Three to
six months is typically long enough to tell.

You should see improvements if your loved ones are actually moderating
—and if not, you should try to gently foster recognition that things aren't
getting better. Their therapist and support group will challenge them if
there's no significant progress during the trial period, and this itself should
help prepare them to try for abstinence without constantly thinking, "I
know I could control it, I never even tried to cut back. I don't really have a
problem."

While your loved ones work on moderation, you should try to support
them in their successes and to recognize how hard this type of change can
be. During their 30 days of abstinence, remember how irritable people can
feel when changing major habits, and try to be easy on them. If problems in
your relationship have become tied up with their drinking, you may want
to have some joint counseling to deal with this.

There are currently no support programs that help family members of
those who are trying to moderate. Al-Anon doesn't recognize such efforts as
valid, and attending it may make you feel worse as a result—though some
family members of people who have moderated have reported that they find
it helpful.

You may be asked to help your loved ones remember to take their naltrexone or other medications. To do so, try to make it a part of your morning
or evening routine. Don't ask about it more than once, but if you have
agreed to contact their counselor if they don't take it, be sure you do so, and
don't let them talk you out of it. Setting up a definite system can help keep
everything on track if you both are consistent about it.

—Joe

After this, drinking is permitted, but only within guidelines that are
healthy. For women, they are generally not to exceed 3 standard drinks per
day or 9 drinks per week and not to drink on more than 4 days a week. For
men, the limits tend to be 4 drinks a day, 14 a week and not to drink on more
than 4 days a week. These are maximums—many members actually drink much

less. Guidelines also include such things as never drinking and driving and not drinking to get drunk. Moderation Management's guidelines state, "A moderate drinker considers an occasional drink to be a small, though enjoyable part of life."

Participants are expected to count their drinks and report to the group (or therapist, if they are doing it through individual counseling) about whether they managed to moderate, and if not, what they believe led to the failure. Over time, a lighter drinking pattern becomes established, or if not, people are encouraged to enter abstinence-oriented treatment.

The Moderation Management (MM) program was created in 1995 by Audrey Kishline, a heavy drinker who had been unable to find a program she thought suitable to deal with her own problem. Kishline read the research showing that moderate drinking is as likely an outcome for many problem drinkers as is abstinence. Her book *Moderate Drinking: The Moderation Management Guide* was published by Crown and is a good place to start if you are considering trying the program.

The MM program has nine steps:

1. Attend meetings and learn about the program of Moderation Management.
2. Abstain from alcoholic beverages for 30 days, and complete Steps 3 through 6 during this time.
3. Examine how drinking has affected your life.
4. Write down your life priorities.
5. Take a look at how much, how often, and under what circumstances you used to drink.
6. Learn the MM guidelines and limits for moderate drinking.
7. Set moderate drinking limits, and start weekly "small steps toward balance in other areas of your life.
8. Review your progress, and update your goals.
9. Continue to make positive lifestyle changes and attend meetings for ongoing support and to help newcomers.

## A Return to Social Drinking

Alicia, a 38-year-old actress, successfully moderated her drinking through the Moderation Management program in New York. "In show biz, there's lots of drugs and alcohol," she said. "I was drinking daily. I felt like crap most of the time. A few times a week, I would drink enough that I would feel lousy the next day."

She tried quitting by herself, but, "It was like dieting," she said. Alicia is overweight and still fighting the battle of the bulge. "I just vowed to cut down over and over but never did."

Alicia tried AA, but "detested it," she said. "I didn't feel that my experience matched the stories I was hearing. I am an atheist and didn't agree with the concept of powerlessness." She saw an article in the *New York Times* about Moderation Management and decided to try it.

Alicia began with a month of total abstinence. "The 30 [days] separates the men from the boys," she said. "If someone repeatedly tries but cannot put 30 days together or is consistently drunk, then they urge them to check out abstinence treatment." She herself was able to do it, and then she began keeping a chart of her drinking and reporting on herself at weekly MM meetings.

"The steps are about examining the role of alcohol in your life," said Alicia, who found that for her, alcohol was tied up with her family. "There's alcoholism in my family," she said. "I didn't want to be like that.

"The first year was very tough, but it got progressively easier. When I was having lunch before we met for this interview, I thought, 'Gee, I'd like a glass of wine.' But because I was going to be interviewed, I thought I wouldn't. It's not a huge deal now—it's like not eating dessert. And though I've had a weight problem for years, the alcohol problem was more urgent if less unsightly.

"I'm much happier now. I've not had a drinking problem for two years. I feel like a normal person."

Alicia has, however, lost friends because of her affiliation with MM. "My friends who are in AA cut off contact. They think we give people permission to drink and be in denial."

She has also seen some people in the program fail. "One member came for months and showed no signs of change. I sat down with the group leader to talk about it, and the following week, [the guy's] chart showed that he was triple the weekly limit. But he insisted that that was progress and he was happy —it was half of what he had been drinking before."

Other members said to him, "Normal people can stop drinking for 30 days and can drink within the guidelines." Though he got angry, however, he continued to attend and now is closer to the limits. Some would consider this a successful outcome, but those who believe in the Minnesota Model might be dubious.

"It's easier to be abstinent—we talk about that a lot," said Alicia. "But our basis is individual choice. And for me, once I acknowledged how important drinking was to me, it became progressively less important."

Moderation Management literature says explicitly that it is not for "former dependent drinkers who are now abstaining and want to try drinking again." Nonetheless, Alicia reports that some former AA members have tried MM—some successfully, some not. "They have a lot of guilt," she said.

MM is also exclusively for dealing with alcohol problems—members didn't want the added controversy of trying to help people moderate an illegal habit, and they also wanted to keep the focus on drinking. They have not addressed the question of someone who had a drug problem once and now wants to see whether they can drink safely, although anyone who wants to work on moderate drinking is welcome.

## An Unlikely Success

Gordon's drinking was dramatically reduced at our research program here at U Penn. Many would think him a poor candidate for moderation because his drinking problem was much more serious than that of Alicia, but naltrexone seems to have made the difference for him. He's a 46-year-old loan officer who had applied to take part in a study of this drug and other medication for depression and alcoholism. His marriage was "falling apart," he said. He had been drinking daily for more than 20 years—and had been arrested for DWIs and had caused drunk-driving accidents. He says, "My father drank. I would say there was a good chance he was an alcoholic."

When he didn't qualify for the study he had come in for, I took him on as a patient in my private practice. I told him that the medication we would have used in the study might help him with his goal of regaining control over his drinking.

"I have two kids. I was trying to hold my family together. I was drinking anywhere between 15 and 18 cans of beer a night, 12-ounce cans. The way I used to drink was, once I started, I didn't stop. Now I can have a couple of drinks and I'm fine," he said.

Gordon had never tried treatment previously because he thought it meant going to the hospital or a treatment center, and "I didn't think that those were really pleasant places to be. I didn't think I needed to be there, it's not like I was down and out and laying in the gutter somewhere, or I couldn't function to the point where I was losing my job. I used to see my father-in-law at 5:00 A.M. before he'd go to work wacking down beers or vodka, and he would continue to do that all day long. I never did that. I would work; when I was done working, I would have my few beers and it just got out of control."

He was mandated into counseling after a drunk-driving arrest, but, "It didn't help. You went there and you were in there with a bunch of other people in the same situation, and you were forced to do that, but as far as counseling, the counselor was there collecting his money and you showed up you got credit for your time and you're out the door and that was it."

When he saw our ad in the paper, he told his wife that he was going to try to take part in the study, and that he wanted to deal with his drinking problem. He hadn't known that there was any alternative to complete abstinence. We gave him a medication to help him detoxify from the heavy drinking, and after about 10 days of abstinence, he began taking naltrexone.

Now I can have a couple of drinks and stop and I'm fine. You don't have the euphoric high, you feel more in control, you feel more clear-headed, you don't get drunk. When you drink and you're taking this stuff, I don't know how it works, but my impression is it does something to your brain, and you just don't get that sloppy, you don't want to just keep drinking.

My consumption has decreased by at least two thirds. Now sometimes I'll have four or five drinks in the evening, after work or whatever—and I can stop in the middle of that, it's more controlled. I don't think over the last six months, there's been a time when I've hinged on it—and I used to do that every day.

My wife and I are separated now—I wish we weren't, but what are you going to do, you can't twist someone's arm to love you. She gave me no support in treatment—she was, this is it, it's over. I'm content with where my drinking is at now, and I'm prepared to take this medication for the rest of my life if that's what it takes.

### From "Moderation" to Abstinence

Tim, a 59-year-old lawyer, entered treatment at the request of his new, young wife, who complained that when Tim was at social functions, he made a complete fool of himself. Tim himself admitted that occasionally his drinking might embarrass him but pointed out that, "I drink at least a six-pack every day, and only rarely does drinking get out of hand." Tim was in remarkably good health for someone his age, and he exercised regularly and was successful in his law practice.

It is true that his first wife had been upset about his drinking constantly, but he said, "she complained about everything I did." On further evaluation, Tim also admitted that he was having some difficulty getting and maintaining erections. When it was pointed out that excessive drinking could have this "side effect," he decided to moderate. Although Tim was advised that complete abstinence was probably a better option in his case, he resisted this suggestion. He agreed to not have more than four drinks a day and to maintain a drinking diary. Tim was also given the option of taking naltrexone and attending Moderation-Management meetings, but he said, "I'll do it on my own, Doc."

The first month, Tim showed some improvement. He did have fewer than five drinks per day on 15 days that month. Unfortunately, he also had 15 days in which his drinking exceeded four drinks, often by a great deal. After three months of similar results, Tim decided to change tactics. It probably helped that at this time, his new wife was increasingly concerned that things were not improving in the bedroom.

When a month of abstinence was suggested as a start, Tim now agreed to try it. His wife rolled her eyes in disbelief. Antabuse was recommended, with his wife to monitor him in taking it. When she heard about the bad consequences of drinking on top of Antabuse, she began to smile. "You mean on this pill, he will get violently ill, throw up, and could die if he drinks? I'll be sure to see that he takes it." If Tim refused, she was to call her doctor, but not nag Tim about taking the medication. During the next month, Tim did abstain completely from alcohol, and he remained on Antabuse for the next six months. At that time, Tim reported that he had no desire to drink. His relationship with his wife had never been better, and he smiled, "Doc, things are much better in the bedroom, in fact they are better in the den, the sofa in the living room, and on the chaise lounge on the patio, too. This abstinence is better—and cheaper—than Viagra, and I'm going to keep doing it, a day at a time."

# Research on Moderate-Drinking Programs

The research on moderate drinking is among the most hotly contested in the field. One study, by Mark and Linda Sobell, has been used by both sides of the debate: The authors say it shows that moderate drinking can be achieved even by severe alcoholics; others, who followed up the patients later, say that it demonstrates that moderation is rarely achieved. The controversy over this one study from 1973 continues to this day.

In this [selection], we choose to ignore it and to focus instead on the rest of the literature. Basically, the research finds that people with alcohol problems on the less severe end of the spectrum (with drinking patterns more like Alicia than like Gordon) do as well with moderate-drinking attempts as they do with trying to abstain. One study by Martha Sanchez-Craig randomly assigned such drinkers to either an abstinence-focused program or a controlled-drinking one. After two years follow-up, both groups were doing equally well. Several other researchers replicated these results.

One interesting finding that shows up in many studies is that women are more likely than men to succeed at drinking moderately. This may be due to the fact that cultural notions of masculinity are often tied up with "drinking like a man" and that moderation may be seen as wimpish. For women, excess is more often viewed as taboo—and a drunk woman is seen as immoral. Moderation fits society's female role better than it does the male role, basically.

William Miller has also done numerous studies of moderate drinking, and his research finds that over time, many drinkers who initially choose moderation, decide to abstain. In fact, the research shows that over time, more drinkers who start with a moderation goal wind up abstinent than continue moderation. The success rates are comparable to those for abstinence treatment —so it is not as though moderation treatment convinces people who would have otherwise abstained to keep drinking for longer. It simply helps those who planned on continuing to drink (whether their treatment program offered them a goal of moderation or not) to reduce harmful consequences associated with alcohol use.

## How to Choose a Moderate-Drinking Program

Unfortunately, because moderate drinking is so controversial in the United States, in many regions, you may not have much of a choice if you are interested in moderation. In fact, in some places, there may be no counselors or treatment programs that offer moderate-drinking goals at all. Moderation Management (MM) is still a small program—and even in many cities, there are only one or two groups. Contacting MM is a good place to start. Their website offers online meetings and complete information about the program. Often, local therapists who help patients with moderation refer them to MM, as well—so people at MM can frequently refer you to a supportive therapist.

Another place to check is any nearby university with a center focused on alcohol and other drug problems. Many—such as the University of Pennsylvania, the University of New Mexico, the University of Washington–Seattle, and Rutgers University (New Jersey)—have long researched this area and may offer help with moderate drinking as part of ongoing studies. You may want to call the treatment research center at the closest of these universities to you, even if you don't live near enough to attend treatment there, to see whether they can refer you to someone locally.

Also, if there is no local moderation program, you may want to start your own MM group. While this sounds like a challenging process, it is the people who work hardest at their recovery who tend to do the best. MM's website has information on how to do this and whom to contact.

If you are not this ambitious, however, you may simply want to read the books listed on this subject [elsewhere]. Interestingly, those who used "biblio-therapy," in the form of a guide produced by William Miller, have been studied extensively. The research found that even with almost no counseling, many patients who used the guide did as well as those who received more intensive treatment. There was one important difference, however: Those who received empathetic and supportive counseling did better than those who tried to moderate with minimal support. Also, those whose counselors were not seen as understanding actually did worse than those who had no or little contact with professionals at all! Once again, this confirmed the research showing that people who see counselors who are confrontational and abrasive drink more than those whose counselors are supportive—and they drink even more than those who get no counseling!

Please note: This doesn't mean that an empathetic counselor will avoid issues such as whether you are actually succeeding at moderation and will only say "nice" things. It just means that they will present difficult information when necessary in a sensitive and understanding fashion, rather than trying to pound it into your head.

### Knowledge Is Power

- Because those who do not wish to become abstinent will attempt to control their drinking after abstinence-oriented treatment anyway, research finds that moderate-drinking programs do not make it more likely that someone who should be abstinent will drink longer.
- Those whose drinking problems are on the less severe end of the spectrum—who drink less often, who drink fewer drinks, and who have been having a problem for the shortest periods of time—are most likely to succeed at moderation.
- Women are more likely than men to succeed at controlling their drinking.
- Most moderate-drinking programs begin with at least 30 days of complete abstinence—if you cannot achieve this, moderation is unlikely to be successful for you.
- Naltrexone can be a useful aid for those who wish to moderate their drinking because it cuts craving for the second drink dramatically. However, if you wish to use it this way, you will probably have to continue taking it, so long as you continue to drink moderately because the "anti-second drink" effect works only while you are taking it.
- Empathetic and supportive counselors are very important for those working on moderate drinking; confrontational counselors can actually be worse than no counselor at all.

# POSTSCRIPT

## Is Total Abstinence the Only Choice for Alcoholics?

The fundamental question here is, Must alcoholics totally abstain from alcohol use, or can they benefit from other types of treatment? This issue was initially raised in the 1970s, when Linda and Mark Sobell presented research showing that alcoholics who were taught to drink socially were less likely to relapse than people who were told to abstain from alcohol. (This study was subsequently criticized for its methodology.) In another study supported by the RAND Corporation in the 1970s, it was found that the majority of alcoholics who went through formal treatment were drinking moderately or occasionally up to 18 months after treatment. Most did not resume their abusive use of alcohol. A criticism of this study was that it did not follow those in treatment long enough—a four-year follow-up revealed that many had relapsed.

Many people who attempt to completely stop addictive behaviors fail. If a person tries several times to abstain from drinking alcohol (or other self-destructive behaviors) and cannot stop, perhaps other forms of treatment may be worth pursuing. However, moderation as a treatment goal may not prove to be productive because alcohol—the central element to the addiction—is still present in the alcoholic's life.

Rather than trying to identify the one best type of treatment, it may be better to match people with the type of treatment that is best for them. It may be shortsighted to think that one form of treatment is best for all addicts. Kimberly Walitzer and Gerard Connors review various forms of alcohol treatment in "Treating Problem Drinking," *Alcohol Research and Health* (vol. 23, no. 2, 1999). Keith Humphreys, in "Professional Interventions That Facilitate 12-Step Self-Help Group Involvement," *Alcohol Research and Health* (vol. 23, no. 2, 1999), discusses the benefit of Alcoholics Anonymous when used in conjunction with other types of therapy. Two articles that are critical of Alcoholics Anonymous are Stanton Peele's "All Wet: The Gospel of Abstinence and Twelve-Step, Studies Show, Is Leading American Alcoholics Astray," *The Sciences* (March–April 1998) and Michael Lemanski's "The Tenacity of Error in the Treatment of Addiction," *The Humanist* (May–June 1997).

In "Alcoholics Synonymous: Heavy Drinkers May Get Comparable Help From a Variety of Therapies," *Science* (January 25, 1997), Bruce Bower discusses an ongoing study in which clients are matched to appropriate therapies. An older, excellent essay that reviews the efficacy of alcohol treatment is William Miller and Reid Hester's "The Effectiveness of Alcoholism Treatment: What Research Reveals," in William Miller and Nick Heather, eds., *Treating Addictive Behaviors: Processes of Change* (Plenum Press, 1986).

# ISSUE 16

## Is Drug Abuse Resistance Education (DARE) an Effective Program?

**YES: Michele Alicia Harmon**, from "Reducing the Risk of Drug Involvement Among Early Adolescents: An Evaluation of Drug Abuse Resistance Education (DARE)," *Evaluation Review* (April 1993)

**NO: Richard R. Clayton et al.**, from "DARE (Drug Abuse Resistance Education): Very Popular but Not Very Effective," in Clyde B. McCoy, Lisa R. Metsch, and James A. Inciardi, eds., *Intervening With Drug-Involved Youth* (Sage, 1996)

### ISSUE SUMMARY

**YES:** Researcher Michele Alicia Harmon reports that Drug Abuse Resistance Education (DARE) had a positive impact on fifth-grade students in terms of attitudes against substance abuse, assertiveness, positive peer association, association with drug-using peers, alcohol use within the previous year, and prosocial norms.

**NO:** Drug researchers Richard R. Clayton et al. maintain that despite DARE's popularity, it does not produce less drug use among its participants. They argue that the money that is spent by the federal government to fund DARE could be used for more effective drug prevention programs.

D rug education is arguably one of the most logical ways of dealing with the problems of drugs in American society. Drug-taking behavior has not been significantly affected by attempts to reduce the demand for drugs, and drug prohibition has also failed. One remaining option to explore is drug education. Drug education is not an overnight panacea for eliminating drug problems. Rates of cigarette smoking are much lower than they were in the last four decades, but it took years of public health efforts to achieve this. If drug education is to ultimately prove successful, it too will take years.

Many early drug education programs were misguided. One emphasis was on scare tactics. Experts erroneously believed that if young people saw the horrible consequences of drug use, then they would certainly abstain from drugs. Another faulty assumption was that drug use would be affected by knowledge about drugs, but knowledge is not enough. Over 400,000 people die each year from tobacco use, but 25 percent of adult Americans and increasing numbers of teenagers continue to smoke, even though most know the grim statistics about tobacco. Young people have a hard time relating to potential problems like lung cancer and cirrhosis of the liver (which is caused by long-term alcohol abuse) because these problems take years to develop. If drug education is going to be effective, it will need to deal with the immediate effects of drugs, not the long-term consequences. Another major problem with early drug education is that much of the information that teachers relayed concerning drugs was either incorrect or exaggerated. Teachers were therefore not seen as credible.

There is a lack of consensus as to what a drug education program should encompass. However, there is general agreement among drug prevention experts that drug awareness programs are counterproductive. Many schools conduct drug awareness programs in which, over the course of a week, former drug abusers talk to students about how their lives and families were ruined by drugs, pharmacologists demonstrate the physical effects of drugs, and films are shown that depict the horrors of drugs. These sensationalized programs stimulate curiosity, and it is not unusual for drug use to increase after one of these presentations.

Many drug prevention programs in the 1970s focused on self-esteem and values clarification. If low self-esteem is a factor in drug use, as many believed, then it would make sense to improve self-esteem to reduce drug use. However, self-esteem is not always a good indicator of drug use. Many young people who have good feelings about themselves use drugs. In addition, many believed that if students clarified their values, they would see the folly of using drugs. This approach overlooked the possibility that young people may turn to drugs because they want to be accepted by their peers, because drugs are forbidden, or simply because they enjoy the high that comes from drug use. The values clarification approach has been discarded by most drug educators.

The current emphasis in drug education is on primary prevention. It is easier to have young people not use drugs in the first place than to get them to stop after they have already started using drugs. The Drug Abuse Resistance Education (DARE) program—the subject of this debate—attempts to get upper-elementary students to pledge not to use drugs. The rationale is that putting energy into teaching elementary students about drugs rather than high school students will be more likely to reduce drug use because the latter are more likely to have already begun using drugs. The program focuses mainly on tobacco, alcohol, and marijuana. These are considered to be gateway drugs, which means that students who use other drugs are most likely to have used these first. The longer students delay using tobacco, alcohol, and marijuana, the less likely they will be to use other drugs.

In the following selections, Michele Alicia Harmon points out some of the benefits of Drug Abuse Resistance Education, especially on students' attitudes toward substance abuse, assertiveness, positive peer association, association with drug-using peers, alcohol use, and prosocial norms. Richard R. Clayton et al. seriously challenge the value of the DARE program.

Michele Alicia Harmon

 **YES**

# Reducing the Risk of Drug Involvement Among Early Adolescents

The purpose of the current study is to evaluate the effectiveness of the Drug Abuse Resistance Education (DARE) program in Charleston County, South Carolina. Specific aims of the program include the stated DARE objectives—increasing self-esteem, assertiveness, coping skills, and decreasing positive attitudes toward drugs, actual drug use, and association with drug-using peers. The study also examines the program's effectiveness for reducing other known risk factors associated with adolescent drug use such as social integration, commitment and attachment to school, and rebellious behavior.

Much of what is known about adolescent drug use is a result of the annual High School Survey conducted by the Institute for Social Research at the University of Michigan (Johnston 1973). Data from a recent report examining drug use (Johnston, Bachman, and O'Malley 1991) show 90% of U.S. seniors reported drinking alcohol at some time in the lives, 64% said they had smoked cigarettes, 41% reported smoking marijuana, and 18% had taken stimulants.

High school survey data from Charleston show similar prevalence rates. For example, 77% of Charleston County seniors said they had drunk alcohol at some point in their lives, 47% had smoked cigarettes, and 31% reported smoking marijuana (South Carolina Department of Education and South Carolina Commission on Alcohol and Drug Abuse 1990).

Efforts to combat the drug problem have led to a variety of strategies over the past two decades. The three most widely used attempts to control drug use are supply reduction, treatment, and prevention.

Supply reduction efforts by law enforcement agencies to decrease production, importation, distribution, and retail sales of street drugs appears ineffective in reducing the drug problem. Increased arrests and imprisonment, given our crowded penal institutions, and the ready replacement of suppliers and dealers mitigates the actions of legal authorities.

Similar to supply reduction, millions of dollars are spent every year on treatment as a means of curtailing drug use. Much like supply reduction strategies, treatment also shows little promise for eliminating drug use, particularly among adolescents (Polich et al. 1984; Stein and Davis 1982). Some feel adolescent drug problems stem from youth "life problems," not physiological dependence (Bennett 1983). This implies adolescent drug abusers are treated for the wrong problem. Subsequently, traditional drug treatment programs are often ineffective in treating adolescent clients (Sells and Simpson 1979).

Prevention holds more promise for controlling adolescent drug use than supply reduction or treatment. Reasons for promise include the timing of prevention programs and their focus on "gateway" substances—alcohol, tobacco, and marijuana. National data show youths initiating alcohol use as early as age 11 and marijuana and other illicit drugs at age 12 (Elliot and Huizinga 1984). Because drug use often begins at such an early age, prevention programs must target youths before they come in contact with drugs. Currently, many drug prevention programs (such as DARE) target youths while they are still in elementary school.

Targeting gateway substances is important because early use of such substances often follows a logical progression to experimentation with other drugs (Hamburg, Braemer, and Jahnke 1975; Kandel 1978; Richards 1980).

Prevention efforts have not always been as promising, however. Research clearly demonstrates the "first generation" of drug prevention programs such as information dissemination (stating facts about drugs), affective education (clarifying values and/or increasing self-esteem), and alternative activities to drug use have little or no impact on deterring adolescent drug use (Berberin et al. 1976; Hanson 1980; Kinder, Pape, and Walfish 1980; Schaps et al. 1981). In fact, some of these programs are associated with an increase in drug use (Gordon and McAlister 1982; Swisher and Hoffman 1975).

The "second generation" of drug prevention efforts has proven more effective in reducing adolescent drug use. This generation includes programs that focus on increasing general personal and social skills such as problem solving, decision making, coping, resisting peer pressure, and assertiveness through skill acquisition (Botvin and Dusenbury 1987; Schinke and Gilchrist 1985; Hansen et al. 1988; Telch et al. 1982).

# DARE (Drug Abuse Resistance Education)

DARE is a drug abuse prevention program that focuses on teaching students skills for recognizing and resisting social pressures to use drugs. DARE lessons also focus on the development of self-esteem, coping, assertiveness, communications skills, risk assessment and decision-making skills, and the identification of positive alternatives to drug use.

Taught by a uniformed police officer, the program consists of 17 lessons offered once a week for 45 to 50 minutes. The DARE curriculum can be taught only by police officers who attend an intensive two-week, 80-hour training. The DARE program calls for a wide range of teaching activities including question and answer sessions, group discussion, role play, and workbook exercises.

The DARE curriculum was created by Dr. Ruth Rich, a curriculum specialist with the Los Angeles Unified School District, from a second-generation curriculum known as Project SMART (Self-Management and Resistance Training) (Hansen et al. 1988).

DARE is one of, if not the most, widespread drug prevention programs in the United States. In 1989, over 3 million children in 80,000 classrooms were exposed to DARE ("Project DARE" 1990). Currently, there are DARE programs in every state in the United States and some counties have mandated DARE as part of the school health curriculum. It has also been implemented in several other countries including Canada, England, Australia, and New Zealand. In addition, it has been adopted by many reservation schools operated by the Bureau of Indian Affairs, and by the worldwide network of U.S. Defense Department schools for children of military personnel. There is a Spanish version and a Braille translation of the student workbook. Efforts are also under way to develop strategies for teaching DARE to hearing-impaired and other special-needs students.

## Prior DARE Evaluations

Several DARE evaluations have been conducted over the past 9 years. Some show positive results, some show negative results, and most have serious methodological flaws. Recent DARE evaluations demonstrate an improvement in methodology over earlier studies. Initially, most of the DARE studies concluded that DARE was a "success." For these evaluations, success often meant students responded that they liked the DARE program. Still others claimed success if teachers and students rated DARE as "useful" or "valuable." For the most part success is based on the finding that students are more able to generate "appropriate" responses to a widely used 19-item questionnaire about drug facts and attitudes after the DARE program than before. In these last instances, almost all had no control group.

Many DARE studies contain such severe methodology problems that the results should be questioned. Methodological flaws contained in the evaluations include one or more of the following problems: (1) no control group, (2) small sample size, (3) posttest only, (4) poorly operationalized measures, (5) low alpha levels for scales ($< .50$), (6) no statistical tests performed, and (7) pretreatment differences not taken into account. Despite the lack of methodological rigor among most of these studies, three used rigorous methodology and should be mentioned because they have corrected many of the cited weaknesses.

The three studies are similar with respect to their evaluation designs but different in terms of their results. All three evaluations used adequate sample sizes and employed both pre- and posttest measures. They also randomly assigned schools to receive the DARE program or serve as controls.

Controlling on pretreatment differences, the dependent variable at Time 1 (pretest), and school type, Ringwalt, Ennett, and Holt (1991) in North Carolina reported significant differences in the expected direction for general attitudes toward drugs, attitudes toward specific drugs (beer, wine coolers, wine, cigarettes, and inhalants), perceptions of peers' attitudes toward drug use, assertiveness, recognizing media influences to use drugs, and the costs associated with drug use. However, no statistically significant effects were found for self-reported drug use, future intentions to use drugs, perceived benefits of drug use (alcohol and cigarettes), or self-esteem.

In Frankfort, Kentucky, Faine and Bohlander (1988) compared DARE to control students and found significant differences favoring the DARE students on all outcome measures, which include self-esteem, attitudes toward the police, knowledge of drugs, attitudes toward drugs, perceived external locus of control, and peer resistance scores.

The third DARE study worth mentioning took place in Lexington, Kentucky (Clayton, Cattarello, Day, and Walden 1991). The authors used analysis of variance to compare the treatment and control group outcomes. However, they only controlled on race despite other pretreatment differences. Statistically significant differences between the treatment and control group were found for general drug attitudes, negative attitudes toward specific drugs (cigarettes, alcohol, and marijuana), and peer relationships (interpreted as DARE students self-reporting more popularity among their peers). Differences were not observed for self-esteem, peer pressure resistance, or self-reported drug use.

A 2-year follow-up study (Clayton, Cattarello, and Walden 1991) examined the same cohort of sixth-grade students using two follow-up questionnaires (1 year apart) after the initial posttest. The only statistically significant difference occurred at the first follow-up for last-year marijuana use. Unfortunately, this finding occurred in the opposite direction than that expected. Significantly more marijuana use was reported by the *DARE students* than non-DARE students. Otherwise, no significant effects were found at any other time for any other drug type.

The only common outcome measures of the three studies mentioned are drug attitudes, self-esteem, and peer resistance (assertiveness). Inconsistent results were reported with respect to self-esteem and peer resistance (assertiveness) but the three evaluations agree that those in the DARE group had significantly less positive attitudes toward drug use compared to the control group.

Although some long-term studies have been attempted, the only one demonstrating adequate methodology is the Lexington, Kentucky study (Clayton, Cattarello, and Walden 1991) and the results do not warrant program success.

In short, studies of the DARE program have produced mixed results and DARE evaluations up to this point are inconclusive. Further replications are necessary in order to make more confident conclusions about the effects of the DARE program.

## DARE Compared to Most Promising Prevention Approach

Several aspects of the DARE program make it a likely candidate for success. First, the program is offered to students just before the age when they are likely to experiment with drugs. Second, although there is little research on the effectiveness of law enforcement personnel as classroom instructors, uniformed police officers serve as teachers of the DARE curriculum in hopes of increasing favorable attitudes toward the law and law enforcement personnel. Third, the DARE program seeks to prevent the use of "gateway drugs" (i.e., alcohol, cigarettes, and marijuana), thereby decreasing the probability of subsequent heavier, more serious, drug use. Fourth, the DARE program draws on several aspects of effective drug prevention efforts from the second generation such as the development and practice of life skills (coping, assertiveness, and decision making).

Although DARE shows promise as a drug prevention strategy, more evaluation efforts need to take place before forming an overall conclusion about the program. This is especially important considering the fact that millions of government dollars are spent on this one particular drug prevention program every year and its dissemination continues to spread rapidly throughout the United States.

# Methods

### Research Design

The current study used a nonequivalent control group quasi-experimental design (Campbell and Stanley 1963) to determine if participating in the DARE program had any effect on the measured outcome variables compared to a similar group that did not receive the program.

The 17-week DARE program took place during the fall and spring semesters of the 1989–1990 school year. A student self-report questionnaire was used to measure the outcome variables and all pre- and posttests were administered approximately 20 weeks apart.

The survey administration was conducted by the school alcohol and drug contact person. The administration was conducted in such a way as to preserve the confidentiality of the students. All students were assigned identification numbers prior to the time of the pretest. The identification number was used to link the pre- and posttest questionnaire responses. A questionnaire was distributed in an envelope with the student's name in the top right-hand corner. Each name was printed on a removable label that the students tore off and threw away. The administrator read the cover page of the survey informing the students there was a number on the survey booklet that may be used to match their responses with questions asked later. The administrator also informed the students they had the right not to answer any or all the questions.

Response rates for the sample were high. The average pretest response rate was 93.5% for the DARE students and 93.7% for the comparison students. An average of 90% of the DARE students and 86.4% of the comparison students completed the posttest. The pre- and posttest (combined) response rates were similar for both groups; 86.5% (295) of the treatment and 83.7% (307) of the comparison students completed both surveys.

Analysis of variance procedures were employed to examine the differences between the DARE and non-DARE students at the time of the pretest. Controlling for any pretreatment differences between the two groups and the measured dependent variable on the pretest, analysis of covariance was used to detect significant differences at the time of the posttest.

## Sample

From 11 elementary schools in Charleston County, South Carolina, 708 fifth-grade students participated in the present study. Students came from five schools receiving the DARE program and six that did not. Of the 708 students involved in the study, 341 received the treatment (DARE), and 367 served as comparison students. The students came from schools representing a cross section of those found in the Charleston County School District. Three schools were urban, six suburban, and two rural.

Each of the DARE schools were paired with a comparison school based on the following characteristics: number of students, percentage of students receiving free or reduced lunch, percentage white, percentage male, percentage never retained, and percentage meeting BSAP (Basic Skills Assessment Program) reading and math standards....

In summary, the evidence shows DARE students had more beliefs in prosocial norms, more attitudes against substance use, more assertiveness, and more positive peer associations than the comparison group. The DARE students also reported less association with drug-using peers and less alcohol use in the last year. However, the DARE students were equivalent to the non-DARE students on social integration, commitment and attachment to school, rebellious behavior, coping strategies, attitudes about the police, self-esteem, and last-year and last-month drug use (with the exception of last-year alcohol use).

## Current Findings and Comparisons

The current DARE evaluation demonstrates the program's effectiveness on some of the measured outcome variables but not on others. The current study shows DARE does have an impact on several of the program objectives. Among these are attitudes against substance use, assertiveness, positive peer association, association with drug-using peers, and alcohol use within the last year.

It should be noted that several of the variables showing no difference between the treatment and control groups are not specifically targeted by DARE (although they are shown to be correlated with adolescent drug use). Among these are social integration, attachment and commitment to school and rebellious behavior. It could also be argued that the DARE program does not specifically aim to change attitudes toward police officers, although this may be a tacit objective. Because the program does not target these outcomes specifically, it may not be surprising there were no differences found between the DARE and non-DARE groups. It was hypothesized that the DARE program may impact factors relating to later adolescent drug use, even if those factors were not specific aims of the program but this hypothesis did not hold true. In a sense this is evidence that helps to reject the selection argument. If the positive results were due to selection, they would not be found only for the outcomes targeted by DARE.

Much like the three previously reviewed DARE evaluations, the current study adds to the mixed results produced thus far with one exception. Across all studies using a pre-post comparison group design, DARE students' attitudes against drug use have consistently been shown to increase and differ significantly from the control students. Because favorable attitudes toward drug use have been shown to predict or correlate with later adolescent drug use (Kandel, Kessler, and Margulies 1978), this finding provides some of the most convincing evidence that DARE shows promise as a drug prevention strategy.

On the other hand, there are no other consistent findings for assertiveness (resisting peer pressure), self-esteem, or attitudes toward police. The current study found an increase in assertiveness among the DARE students as compared to the non-DARE students. Ringwalt et al. (1991) and Faine and Bohlander (1988) also found this to be true but Clayton, Cattarello, Day, and Walden (1991) did not. Effects on self-esteem were not demonstrated in the present DARE evaluation nor were they in Clayton's (Clayton, Cattarello, Day, and Walden 1991) or Ringwalt's (Ringwalt et al. 1991). However, significant differences in self-esteem were seen for the DARE participants over the controls in Faine and Bohlander's (1988) study. Thus the Charleston study helps to increase the consistency of the assertiveness and self-esteem results.

Faine and Bohlander's (1988) study also showed that positive attitudes toward police were significantly greater for the treatment group than the control group but the present study did not replicate such findings. However, the difference found between these two studies may be due to the measures used. The current DARE study uses only two single-item questions to assess students' attitudes about the police, whereas Faine and Bohlander (1988) used an 11-item scale that is likely to be more valid.

With reference to drug use, all of the stronger DARE evaluations found no effects with the exception of the current study, which found a significant difference on last-year alcohol use. Clayton's follow-up evaluation showed only one significant difference in the wrong direction on the first of two follow-up posttests (Clayton, Cattarello, and Walden 1991). As Clayton, Cattarello, and Walden (1991) point out, the lack of short-term drug use differences may be due to low base rates and thus should not be interpreted to mean DARE has no effect on adolescent drug involvement.

## Recommendations

Replication studies of the evaluation of the DARE program should be continued because mixed evidence exists about the program's overall effectiveness. Conducting randomized experiments would certainly be best for drawing more confident conclusions about DARE program outcomes. Longitudinal studies would also aid in assessing the long-term program goal of deterring adolescent drug use.

There is one large problem with recommending a long-term study on a drug prevention program that is conducted in schools in the United States. The problem involves finding a true "no treatment" control group. Almost every school in the nation has some type of drug education component embodied in the school curriculum that is often mandated by the state. Therefore, it is likely the control group will receive some form of drug education. This problem has been documented as Clayton's (Clayton, Cattarello, and Walden 1991) study used a comparison group that received the school drug education unit and the ETI (Evaluation and Training Institute) had to discontinue their 5-year longitudinal study because the entire control group has essentially become a treatment group (Criminal Justice Statistics Association 1990).

In the future, it may be possible only to compare students' receiving some specificed drug prevention program with the school system's drug education unit. However, this appears acceptable if the school system simply requires a unit session on factual drug information or a similar low-level intervention because prevention efforts such as these have consistently been shown to have no positive effects (Berberin et al. 1976; Kinder, Pape, and Walfish 1980; Schaps et al. 1981; Tobler 1986).

Should evaluations of the DARE program continue, it is suggested one national survey instrument be developed and used for all outcome evaluations. Currently, it is difficult to assess whether or not DARE is actually a success because different researchers use different survey instruments to examine a variety of outcome measures. Measuring DARE program objectives and other risk factors associated with later drug use with one survey would enable researchers to compare results across evaluations conducted in U.S. cities and other parts of the world.

Additional recommendations include employing peer leaders (i.e., high school students) as instructors instead of police officers. There are two reasons for this suggestion. First, it has not been consistently demonstrated that attitudes toward police become more positive upon receiving the DARE program, and second, there has been some evidence supporting the use of peer leaders as primary program providers (Botvin and Eng 1982; Botvin et al. 1984; Perry et al. 1980).

It would be not only interesting, but informative, to compare DARE program outcomes using peer leaders versus police officers as instructors. Should peer leaders provide equal or better outcomes, DARE programming costs would be considerably less and police officers would be more readily available to respond to citizen calls.

It is further recommended that DARE be restructured to incorporate components shown more consistently to be effective such as those found in second-generation approaches. Although DARE aims to increase resistance skills, coping, and decision making, the lessons specifically targeting these factors do so in the context of drug use only. Adolescents engaging in drug use behavior are often involved in other problem behaviors (Jessor and Jessor 1977). It would seem most practical and beneficial to target all of these behaviors using one program as Botvin (1982) and Swisher (1979) have suggested. The DARE program could serve as this one program, assuming several changes were implemented.

First, existing components would have to be expanded and additional components added in order to target more broad-based adolescent life problems such as family struggles, peer acceptance, sexual involvement, intimate relationships, and effective communication (expressing ideas, listening). Additional sessions should include components from second-generation programs such as setting goals, solving problems, and anticipating obstacles (Botvin, Renick, and Baker 1983; Schinke and Gilchrist 1985).

Second, skill acquisition is said to come about only through practice and reinforcement (Bandura 1977). It is proposed that any new skills taught, such as problem solving, be reinforced with "real life" homework where students practice these skills in the context of the "real world" rather than simply role playing them in the classroom.

The last recommendation is applicable not only to the DARE program but any drug prevention effort. It involves the addition of booster sessions following the prevention program. Because adolescence is a time of growth, individual attitudes and behaviors may continue to change and develop as the youth is maturing. Although short-term evidence of program effectiveness is encouraging, there is no guarantee a youth will continue to practice those same behaviors or hold those same beliefs years, or even months, after the program has ended. In fact, follow-up studies have documented the eroding effects of drug prevention programs (Botvin and Eng 1980, 1982) and the superior effects of booster sessions (Botvin, Renick, and Baker 1983; Botvin et al. 1984). For these reasons, DARE, or any other drug prevention program targeting adolescents, should include a series of follow-up sessions in order to increase the likelihood of sustaining any positive effects.

# NO

**Richard R. Clayton et al.**

# DARE: Very Popular but Not Very Effective

The purpose of this [selection] is to review and examine what is known about the most widely distributed school-based drug abuse prevention program in the world, DARE (Drug Abuse Resistance Education). It is likely that you know about DARE; you have seen the T-shirts, the bumper stickers, floats in Independence Day parades, DARE cars, and the hundreds of other ways that this program has been marketed. Perhaps you yourself were in a class or school that received the DARE curriculum in the fifth or sixth grade.

DARE is a social phenomenon (Wyson, 1993). In the 1983–84 school year, it was delivered to about 8,000 elementary school students in Los Angeles. Today, DARE is found in more than one half of all school districts in the United states and reaches at least 25 million students each year (Ennet, Tobler, Ringwalt, & Flewelling, 1994). Although the numbers are difficult to confirm, it is estimated that $750 million is spent on DARE each year in the United States. DARE can also be found in Australia, Canada, Mexico, New Zealand, Norway, and Sweden.

## The DARE Program

DARE began in Los Angeles in 1983–84 as a school-based drug prevention program. The curriculum is a result of the joint efforts of the Los Angeles Police Department and the Los Angeles Unified School District, one of the country's largest.

Unlike most other school-based prevention programs, which are taught by teachers, DARE is taught by uniformed police officers who must undergo 80 hours of rigorous training before they can teach the program (Falco, 1989).

The stated purpose of DARE is to "prevent substance abuse among school children." The principal way it seeks to achieve this goal is to teach students the skills for recognizing and resisting social pressures to experiment with tobacco, alcohol, and other drugs. The 17 DARE lessons also focus on enhancing students' self-esteem, decision making, coping, assertiveness, and communication skills and on teaching positive alternatives to substance use. The curriculum and basic goals and structure of the DARE program have remained essentially the same since its beginnings. However, in 1992–94, additional lessons were added to place greater emphasis on the prevention of tobacco use and a new and enhanced focus was placed on violence prevention and conflict resolution. In addition, the actual classroom style became more "interactive" rather than one-directional from officer to student. The revisions were phased in during 1993–94, and beginning January 1, 1995, all DARE officers were required to use the "new" program.

The original DARE program was targeted at students in the fifth or sixth grade, preferably the grade immediately prior to entering junior high or middle school. Now there are DARE programs for kindergarten through third-grade students, middle-school students, and high school students (Kochis, 1995).

## Being at the Right Place at the Right Time

National political interest in the drug problem was focused in 1986 with President Reagan's "War on Drugs" address to the nation. This led to broad support from both the Democratic and Republican parties and the passage of the Anti-Drug Abuse Act of 1986 (Falco, 1989). In both the Bush and the Clinton administrations, there was increasing recognition of the complexity of the problem and the requirements that law enforcement/supply reduction and prevention-treatment/demand reduction efforts be coordinated. The Office of National Drug Control Policy (ONDCP) is responsible for this coordination and has placed increasingly strong emphasis on prevention and drug education programs. In fact, federal spending for all "educational" prevention activities rose from $230 million in 1988 to $660 million in 1995.

DARE was at the right place at the right time, with just the right types of political support to become what the Justice Department called the "long term solution to the drug problem." In fact, the congressional testimony of Los Angeles Police Chief Daryl Gates and support from powerful members of Congress and President Bush led in 1990 to an amendment to the 1986 funding for DARE. The Drug Free Schools Act divided money given to the states into two parts: 70% of the money went to the departments of education in the states, and 30% went to the governor. The amendment required that 10% of the governor's portion be used to fund programs such as Project Drug Abuse Resistance Education (DARE). In fact, DARE was the only school-based prevention program singled out for mandated funding.

Congressional and other support for DARE continued into the mid-1990s, when it was again singled out for federal funding through a renewed commitment in Congress to what was now called the "Safe and Drug Free Schools and Communities Act."

## DARE: More Than Just a Drug Prevention Program

One of the reasons DARE has been so successful in spreading across the country is organizational. DARE America is a private, nonprofit corporation organized in 1987 with a goal of getting the program into all states and communities, developing and supporting a national DARE instructor training program, and getting funding nationally.

## Training

The Bureau of Justice Assistance (BJA) within the Department of Justice started funding DARE in 1986 with a BJA grant of $140,000. In the late 1980s, BJA funded five regional DARE training centers. As part of the funding agreement, BJA appoints 5 of the 15 members of the DARE training center policy advisory board.

## Additional Funding and Support

DARE America has been successful in attracting major corporate sponsors such as Bayliner, Herbalife, Kentucky Fried Chicken, Kimberly-Clark, McDonalds, Packard Bell, Security Pacific National Bank, and Warner Brothers. At the local and state level, there are thousands of large and small firms contributing to the program.

# Inconsistency: DARE's Popularity and Its Effectiveness

The principal purpose of DARE is to reduce substance abuse among school children. About the only way to determine if DARE has achieved success (i.e., "works") is to conduct research on students who receive DARE and those who do not receive DARE. Both the experimental group (received DARE) and the control group should be examined prior to the start of the prevention effort and followed for 1 to 5 years to see if differences persist. DARE is the most widely research-evaluated school-based prevention program in the United States. There have been at least 15 evaluation studies conducted (Ennett et al., 1994), several of which followed DARE and non-DARE students for up to 4 or 5 years (Clayton, Cattarello, & Johnstone, 1996). Although the results from various studies differ somewhat, all studies are consistent in finding that DARE does not have long-term effects on drug use (Kochis, 1995). It does seem to have some effects on knowledge and attitudes toward drugs, but even these effects diminish over time. In fact, two long-term follow-up studies show that after 3 or more years, students who received DARE do not even have more positive attitudes toward the police than students who did not receive DARE (Clayton et al., 1996; Wysong, Aniskiewicz, & Wright, 1994).

# Why Is DARE So Popular If It Is Not Effective?

This is an important question because it reveals so much about the United States and its approach to social problems (Aniskiewicz & Wysong, 1990).

## Police

DARE is popular among police for two reasons. First, it puts police officers into community institutions previously "off limits" to them. Before the advent of DARE, there was a widespread and deep-seated mistrust of police officers by school officials. In fact, police were seen by many community members and organizations as generally less educated and brutish. By entering school systems to teach DARE, police can change these stereotypes. Second, it allows police officers to do things that are seen as "positive." In most police departments prior to the mid-1980s, absolutely the worst assignment was what was then called "community relations." No police officer wanted that assignment. Now police officers are standing in line for an opportunity to be a DARE officer. Police officers perceive a different response to them from the public if they are involved with DARE. In fact, it could be said that DARE has had a major effect on the relationship between police departments and other community-based organizations. Police are now active players in a wide variety of positive community projects and initiatives.

## Parents

DARE is popular among parents for at least two reasons. First, they are extremely concerned about drug abuse and violence, and most feel helpless in dealing with either. Therefore, if there is a police officer in the school teaching the DARE program, it might protect their child from being victimized by violent predators or by drug dealers. Second, most Americans have a naive and false sense of confidence in the power of "education." It is the panacea brought out to "solve" all our problems: If people just know the "facts," they will make rational choices. The DARE officer represents authority, and parents have faith that children will listen to and heed the advice of an authority. Besides, the prevailing orientation to drugs in this society is primarily concerned with legality/illegality—a law enforcement perspective. The DARE officer represents the prevailing perspective held by parents.

## Teachers

DARE is also quite popular among teachers, and for two very good reasons. First, teachers, just like the parents, perceive the school to be a safer place when DARE officers are in the school. Second, the DARE officer teaches the drug prevention curriculum, which means that the teachers do not have to teach the lessons. In fact, although the teachers are required to be "in the classroom" during the drug prevention lessons, they get a respite from their work, a break of sorts. This second reason is very important as an unintended consequence of how far and how quicly DARE has diffused across the country. At present, no colleges of education require preparation of teachers to deliver substance abuse prevention curricula. Even so, a significant proportion of fifth- and sixth-grade teachers in the United States could probably teach the DARE curriculum because they have seen and heard it taught one or more times. If the education establishment had been called on to provide 80 hours of training to teach a drug prevention curriculum such as DARE, it would have cost billions of dollars. Instead, such a curriculum has been provided at no cost to the education establishment in the course of the spread of DARE across America.

## Administrators

School administrators, the principals and superintendents, seem to like DARE because it provides a sense of extra security at the school, it provides a respite for the teachers which makes them happy, it is generally very popular among parents and gets them more involved with the school than would otherwise be likely, and it links the school with another important institution of the community, the police department. A number of principals regularly request that the DARE officer be in the school on Mondays because attendance is noticeably higher when the DARE officer is in the school (Clayton, Cattarello, Day, & Walden, 1991).

# The "Feel-Good" Approach to Drug Prevention

Someone might wonder: If everybody likes DARE and it makes students, teachers, administrators, parents, police, and politicians "feel good" because something is being done about drug abuse, why should we be worried by lack of evidence that it delays the onset or inhibits the continuance of drug use by adolescents? The answer to this question is quite simple and has three parts. First, publicly funded programs should be accountable for what they achieve. If they do not achieve their states goal (in this instance, a reduction in drug use), how can further expenditure of public funds be justified? Second, other similar programs consistently show some effects in the desired direction, although the effects are not huge (Botvin, Dusenbury, Botvin, & Diaz, 1995). Why should the American public pay for a program that has proven to be ineffective when programs that have proven to be successful exist? Third, a principal reason for evaluation research is to examine the effectiveness of public programming that may seem sound on the surface but is unsound in practice. The evidence for the lack of sustained effectiveness of DARE is strong, consistent, and impressive.

Why, then, the continued strong support of DARE? The answer to this question must be: Because it makes all the important groups (parents, teachers, administrators, police, politicians) "feel good." It is sad to say, but an overwhelming majority of people in the United States have a rather naive view of the world and how to solve social problems such as drug use and abuse by adolescents. DARE seems to reflect most of these naive notions and in some ways to exploit them.

Drug use is *not* a simple phenomenon. It will not be solved by simple slogans and bumper stickers and T-shirts and a bunch of people believing that DARE is "the" answer to drug abuse in America. If anyone really and truly believes this is true, we have some swamp land in Florida we would like for them to buy.

The "scientific" research on the effectiveness of DARE is clear. DARE does not produce sustained effects on drug use or on even attitudes toward police

(Clayton et al., 1996). Furthermore, the most recent data suggest that drug use (marijuana, inhalants, LSD, stimulants, cigarettes) began to rise significantly among 8th, 10th, and 12th graders beginning in 1992 and continuing through 1994. The cohorts in which drug use began to rise for the first time since 1979 would have been 6th graders in 1990, 8th graders in 1992, and 10th graders in 1994. If we assumed that DARE had spread all across America by 1990, these would be the students who would have been most affected by the diffusion of DARE.

To be fair, DARE could not be expected to produce miracles and wipe out drug use among adolescents entirely. Many forces in society promote drug use or dilute efforts to fight drug use among adolescents. However, DARE could be expected to produce some reduction in drug use, or at the very least positive and sustained effects on attitudes toward drug use by adolescents. Instead, as has been shown, there are *no* sustained effects from the DARE program on attitudes or behavior. In fact, it is probably naive to think that any *universal* (one size fitting all students) type of school-based, curriculum-driven drug prevention program could exert enough influence to counter the forces driving youth toward experimentation with various drugs. These types of programs are simply not powerful enough, do not provide enough exposures to the intervention, and may not even directly address the primary causes of drug use by youth. For example, one entire lesson in the DARE curriculum is designed to heighten self-esteem. However, the extensive research literature on the relationship between self-esteem and drug use among adolescents indicates very little correlation between drug use and self-esteem. Therefore, even if the lesson helped to improve self-esteem for some of the students, that improvement would probably not be translated into a lower probability of drug use. So although DARE is very popular, it is not very effective. Therefore we as a nation should be ready to accept that fact and deal with its implications if we *really* want to have an effect on drug use among youth.

# References

Aniskiewicz, R., & Wysong, E. (1990). Evaluating DARE: Drug education and the multiple meanings of success. *Policy Studies Review, 9,* 727–747.

Botvin, G. J., Dusenbury, L., Botvin, E. M., & Diaz, T. (1995). Long term follow-up results of a randomized drug abuse trial in a white middle class population. *Journal of the American Medical Association, 273,* 1106–1112.

Clayton, R. R., Cattarello, L., Day. E., & Walden, K. P. (1991). Persuasive communication and drug prevention: An evaluation of the DARE program. In H. Sypher, L. Donohew, & W. Bukoski (Eds.), *Persuasive communication and drug abuse prevention.* Hillsdale, NJ: Lawrence Erlbaum.

Clayton, R. R., Cattarello, A. M., & Johnstone, B. M. (in press). The effectiveness of Drug Abuse Resistance Education (Project DARE): Five year follow-up results. *Preventive Medicine.*

Ennett, S., Tobler, N., Ringwalt, C., & Flewelling, R. (1994). How effective is Drug Abuse Resistance Education? A meta-analysis of Project DARE outcome evaluations. *American Journal of Public Health, 84,* 1394–1401.

Falco, M. (1989). *Winning the drug war: A national strategy.* New York: Priority.

Kochis, D. S. (1995). The effectiveness of Project DARE: Does it work? *Journal of Alcohol and Drug Education, 40,* 40–47.

Wysong, E. (1993, October). *The frontier of drug education: D.A.R.E. as a social movement.* Paper presented at the annual meeting of the Indiana Academy of Social Sciences, Hanover College, Hanover, IN.

Wysong, E., Aniskiewicz, R., & Wright, D. (1994). Truth and DARE: Tracking drug education to graduation and as symbolic politics. *Social Problems, 41,* 448–473.

# POSTSCRIPT

## Is Drug Abuse Resistance Education (DARE) an Effective Program?

**B**efore the effectiveness of drug education programs can be determined, it is necessary to define the goals of drug education. Are the goals of drug education to prevent drug use from starting? To prevent drug abuse? To prevent drug dependency? Perhaps the goal of drug education is to teach young people how to protect themselves and others from harm *if* they are going to use drugs. Without a clear understanding of the goals one wants to achieve in teaching about drugs, it is impossible to determine the effectiveness of drug education.

Before a drug education program can be designed, questions regarding what to include in the drug education curriculum need to be addressed. Should the primary focus be on teaching abstinence or responsible use? Is it feasible to teach abstinence from some drugs and responsible use of other drugs? Almost 90 percent of high school students have drunk alcohol; should they be taught they should not drink at all, or should they be taught how to use alcohol responsibly? Does the age of the children make a difference in what is taught? Do elementary students have the reasoning skills of high school students? Should the goal be for students to engage in a decision-making process or simply to adopt certain behaviors?

In the 1980s there was a significant reduction in drug use among high school seniors in the United States, although drug use has climbed since the early 1990s. How much of the reduction in the 1980s was due to drug education, and how much was due to other factors? Throughout American history drug use has been cyclical—perhaps the United States was in a down cycle in the 1980s and is currently in an up cycle in terms of drug use.

If drug prevention programs such as DARE are going to be effective in reducing drug use, schools and other institutions will need to work together. Many young people drop out of school or simply do not attend, so community agencies and religious institutions need to become involved. The media have a large impact on young people. What is the best way to incorporate the media in the effort to reduce drug use? Are antidrug commercial spots shown during programs aimed at teenage audiences effective?

An article that sheds a positive light on DARE is "The Minnesota DARE PLUS Project: Creating Community Partnerships to Prevent Drug Use and Violence," by Cheryl Perry et al., *Journal of School Health* (March 2000). Articles that are critical of DARE include Ryan Sager's "Teach Them Well: Drug Talk That Fails," *National Review* (May 1, 2000); "Project DARE: No Effects at 10-Year Follow-Up," by Donald Lyman et al., *Journal of Consulting and Clinical Psychology* (August 1999); and Dennis Rosenbaum's "Assessing the Effects of School-Based Drug Education: A Six-Year Multilevel Analysis of Project D.A.R.E.," *Journal of Research in Crime and Delinquency* (November 1998). Another perspective on teaching about drugs is provided by Gail Milgram in "Responsible Decision Making Regarding Alcohol: A Re-Emerging Prevention/Education Strategy for the 1990s," *Journal of Drug Education* (vol. 26, 1996).

# ISSUE 17

## Should Employees Be Required to Participate in Drug Testing?

**YES: Gillian Flynn**, from "How to Prescribe Drug Testing," *Workforce* (January 1999)

**NO: Leslie Kean and Dennis Bernstein**, from "More Than a Hair Off," *The Progressive* (May 1999)

### ISSUE SUMMARY

**YES:** Gillian Flynn, a contributing editor to *Workforce,* argues that workplace drug testing has proven to be beneficial to companies with such a policy because the number of workers who test positive for drug use has declined. She also maintains that many accidents that occur at the workplace can be prevented if drug testing is implemented.

**NO:** Authors Leslie Kean and Dennis Bernstein oppose drug testing because many employees, especially African Americans, falsely test positive for drugs. As a result, too many employees with false positive findings are unfairly discharged.

In 1986 President Ronald Reagan first called for a drug-free federal workplace, ordering all federal employees in "sensitive" jobs to submit to random drug testing. The goals were to begin attacking the drug problem by reducing the demand for drugs and by involving all employees, both public and private, in the fight against drugs. Today, an overwhelming percentage of major corporations in the United States require drug testing as a condition of employment. In addition, government agencies, including the military, have adopted the practice of random urine testing to screen its personnel for illicit drugs.

One event that served as a springboard for random drug testing was a 1987 collision between an Amtrak train and a Conrail train near Baltimore, Maryland, that killed 16 people. Because the Conrail engineer and brakeman had both used marijuana just prior to the wreck, the cause of the crash was immediately tied to drug use, even though the warning indicators on the Conrail train were malfunctioning at the time. This accident was a strong indication to many people that drug testing was necessary—if not for the sake of deterring employees from using illicit drugs for their own well-being, then to ensure the safety of others.

The Fourth Amendment of the U.S. Constitution guarantees citizens the right to be protected from unreasonable searches and seizures. With regard to drug testing, the Fourth Amendment protects citizens from being tested unless probable cause, or a reason to suppose that an individual is engaged in criminal behavior, is shown. Many people feel that random drug testing is unreasonable because it involves testing even those employees who are not drug users and who have shown no cause to be tested. On the other hand, if one is not using drugs, then one should not have to worry about drug testing.

One problem with a positive drug test result is that it may not clearly differentiate between on-the-job drug use and off-the-job drug use. Many people contend that an infringement of personal liberties and an unwarranted invasion of privacy for the sake of the government's drug battle agenda are at stake. However, should companies be required to keep employees if those employees use drugs while off the job?

One could argue that all people are affected by individuals' use of illicit drugs. For example, the public pays higher prices due to lost productivity from work-related accidents and job absenteeism caused by drug use. Also, innocent people are often directly victimized by individuals on drugs who inadvertently make dangerous mistakes. From this perspective, random drug tests are not unreasonable searches. Proponents of drug testing contend that the inherent dangers of drug use, particularly while on the job, necessitate drug testing. Accidents and deaths can and do occur because of drug-induced losses of awareness and judgment. The fact that a majority of Americans who use illicit drugs are employed has convinced many that random drug testing at the workplace should be mandatory.

In the following selections, Gillian Flynn argues that the benefits of drug testing outweigh its drawbacks. She contends that drug testing discourages drug use and that workplace safety should take precedence over the concern that someone's right to privacy might be violated. Leslie Kean and Dennis Bernstein argue that drug testing is subject to too many errors and that people are unfairly dismissed because of these errors. They also say that drug testing is prejudicial in that it may be biased against African Americans. Thus, although drug use is a problem in society, drug testing is not the fairest and most efficient way of dealing with the problem.

**Gillian Flynn**

 **YES**

# How to Prescribe Drug Testing

Few things are more potentially devastating to a workplace than an employee with a drug or alcohol problem—and few things are more difficult to prove. With the heightened awareness of privacy issues, instituting a drug-testing policy can land a company on shaky legal ground. Yet such a policy can be useful. Many experts consider the decrease in positive employment-related drug test results as a sign that employees take testing seriously. If your company does drug testing, or wants to implement a program, Nancy Bertrando, chair of the employment law department for Greenberg Glusker Fields Claman & Machtinger LLP in Los Angeles, offers some rules.

*How common is drug use in the workplace?*

SmithKline Beecham Corp., one of the primary testing agencies based in Philadelphia, has an interesting study. In 1987, its statistical information showed that in employment-related testing, 18.1 percent of those tested showed positive drug use. In 1997, only 5 percent of approximately 5 million employment-related tests came back positive. I think, in part, that's a sign that drug-testing programs are working.

Almost 98 percent of Fortune 200 companies have drug-testing policies. As more employers implement drug-testing policies, it seems to have an effect on drug use in the workplace. As far as the drugs of choice in these tests, according to SmithKline, 60 percent of positive tests are for marijuana, 16 percent of positive tests are for cocaine, and opiates make up 9 to 10 percent.

*How difficult is it to conduct legally defensible drug testing?*

A lot of it depends on the state. In California, for example, there's tension between privacy rights of employees and rights of employers to test. The California state constitution contains an individual right to privacy which has been applied fairly rigorously to drug testing, so it's hard to implement random testing in California. Unless it's a safety position or there are some real signs that drug use is going on, employers in that state don't have the right to test current employees. Random testing is a risk in many states [for similar reasons]. Even if a company already has a drug-testing policy, HR [human resources] should look at the state law—especially if it's an employer that has multiple state offices. Make sure the state supports random testing. And be cognizant of state laws concerning privacy.

*What does a good drug policy have?*

At a minimum, a policy should prohibit the use, possession, sale or transfer of illegal drugs in the workplace. Most employers have that. It doesn't say drug testing may be implemented, but it says drugs and alcohol won't be permitted and no one is allowed to work under the influence. More detailed policies are going to prohibit the use, possession, sale or transfer of illegal drugs on or off company time. That kind of policy brings privacy issues into play.

In certain jurisdictions, you have to be very careful of a policy that's going to regulate your employees' time away from the company. The conflict is privacy—regulating off-duty hours that don't affect the workplace. There's going to be a conflict created by that. Somebody terminated because of off-premises drug use that doesn't affect the workplace may well have a claim for invasion of privacy. California's privacy consideration is unique in that it's part of the constitution, but even if other states don't have constitutional privacy rights, they will have common-law developments that deal with the same issues.

*How do you decide which side wins in drug testing vs. privacy?*

In any of these balancing acts, you'll look at workplace safety vs. employee privacy, and if you have safety or security issues, you'll have much more latitude implementing drug testing with those types of employees—a forklift driver versus an accountant, for example. Also, prohibiting work under the influence of drugs or alcohol, even if the employee didn't use it on company property, is a valuable and enforceable policy in any jurisdiction. But with those policies, employers must be cognizant of their obligations under the Americans with Disabilities Act (ADA), which, although it doesn't protect employees from use of illegal drugs, it does protect them from discrimination once they've been rehabilitated.

*Is an employee protected by the ADA if he or she hasn't been rehabilitated?*

The ADA will only protect them in instances in which they've been rehabilitated. The ADA has specific qualifiers that current users of drugs aren't protected, but former users of drugs—individuals participating in or completing drug programs—are a different story.

Let's talk about different types of drug testing policies, starting with pre-employment. Many employers have drug testing as a condition of employment. Done properly, that type of testing will be allowed. So a lot of employment applications say that hiring will be effective upon completion of a drug test. If you're going to do pre-employment testing, employers want to be sure prospective employees have been given notice of this, that all applicants are treated similarly, and that testing is conducted by a reputable lab that respects each individual's rights of privacy. The applicant should have the opportunity to explain positive test results. Generally, these tests will be upheld if they're done right.

*What about random drug testing?*

In safety-sensitive environments, random drug testing will be upheld. Random drug testing for companies that aren't safety-sensitive, like accounting, is going to be much more difficult because there's the argument that the employer has violated the right to privacy. It's the biggest area of vulnerability to employers. If your industry is covered by federal regulations that provide for drug testing, or if an employee is in a sensitive position or in a position in which use could result in the employee's death or death of others, random testing will probably be OK. But this is a risky area for employers.

*What about testing for "reasonable suspicion?"*

When a supervisor determines an employee is acting improperly and elects to implement drug testing, that's liable to be challenged based on privacy. According to SmithKline, last year, 73 percent of employees sent to them for "reasonable-suspicion" testing were clean. All those employees have cases for invasion of privacy, infliction of emotional distress and so on.

It's particularly important in reasonable-suspicion testing to make sure managers are well trained to understand signs of potential drug abuse: bloodshot eyes, frequent sniffling, tremors, sunglasses worn indoors, profuse perspiration, appearing confused, refusing to talk, talking too loudly, mood swings, lack of coordination, aggressive or violent behavior, frequent unreported absences, unexplained disappearances during work time, difficulty remembering tasks and lapses in concentration. But managers need to be trained to look for all these signs, things that taken together would give reasonable suspicion of drug use. The more objective information you have to support a drug test, the better off you'll be in defending a challenge to it. Also, always put employees on notice—don't just tell them one day that they seem like they're on drugs. They have to be tested.

*What if a drug test shows up positive for prescribed legal drugs, but drugs that can affect performance, like sedatives?*

Drugs for depression or other mental conditions get into some more of the ADA issues. Employers can't discriminate against an employee for taking a medically prescribed drug for a condition. And once the employer has knowledge of that condition, the employer has to worry about potentially violating the ADA if the company takes action. Mental illnesses like depression are covered under the ADA. Employers need to be cognizant of their obligations under the ADA. So only certain banned substances should be looked at.

*How do new state laws that allow marijuana use for certain conditions fit in here?*

For those laws in California and Arizona [that support] medical-need marijuana use, the ADA comes into play. If the person is in a safety-sensitive position and marijuana use could hurt the employee or others, there's no obligation to reasonably accommodate.

*For employers currently implementing a policy, how much warning should they give employees?*

If the testing isn't based on a particular incident, they can implement today and start testing within a month or two. If it's a particular individual you want to test, first objectively document the information that supports testing. Make sure the proper homework is done. Then send the employee to a reputable lab—hopefully with he or she having been on warning already. Also, don't tell anyone that doesn't have to know about the employee being tested.

*And if the results are positive?*

The employee should have the ability to explain any positive results. For current drug use, the ADA isn't going to prohibit you from terminating somebody if you feel that it's warranted under the circumstances. Some states require employers to accommodate an employee's request for unpaid time off for rehab. If an employee requests time off, the best thing is to work with that employee. If the employee isn't willing to face the issue, then you may have no option but to terminate. But from various perspectives, it may be in everyone's best interest to allow an employee time for rehabilitation because if a good employee is saved, everyone benefits.

**Leslie Kean and Dennis Bernstein**

# More Than a Hair Off

Althea Jones, an African-American mother of two, always wanted to go to police school. "It was my lifelong dream to be a police officer, ever since I was a little girl," she says. When she applied for admission to the Chicago Police Academy, it requested a sample of her hair, which it sent to Psychemedics, the largest hair-testing company in the country. The results came back positive for drug use.

"I was shocked. I couldn't believe it," says Jones. "I don't even smoke or drink. I was heartbroken by this." She was denied admission to the academy and is now a criminal justice major at Chicago State University.

Adrian McClure, an African-American woman, was also keen on a career with the Chicago police department. When she was a senior in college in 1997, she submitted a hair sample to the academy, which sent it to the Psychemedics Corporation. Her test came back positive, too. She says she tried to explain that it was an error and requested a new test, but was rebuffed. "Everybody knows I don't use drugs," McClure says. "This thing has a hold of me. They have shattered me."

Last August, Althea Jones and Adrian McClure, along with six other Chicago African-Americans who say they received erroneous hair test results when applying for the Police Academy, filed complaints of racial discrimination with the Equal Employment Opportunity Commission. The complaints are currently under investigation, and the group is considering suing both the city of Chicago and Psychemedics.

Jones and McClure are just two of many who have lost out as a result of hair testing. Numerous scientific studies have shown hair testing to be inaccurate and unreliable. And the procedure appears to give false positives disproportionately to African-Americans. Nevertheless, use of hair tests is expanding nationwide. Psychemedics reports that business is booming. The Cambridge, Massachusetts, firm more than doubled sales of its hair test between 1993 and 1997, and in 1997 *The Boston Globe* named Psychemedics one of the "Top Fifty Growth Companies" of Massachusetts. "The total annual market for drug testing in the United States has been estimated at between $500 and $600 million, and is growing fast," says Psychemedics CEO Raymond C. Kubacki Jr.

Psychemedics services 1,400 businesses that use hair testing on their employees and job applicants. These include General Motors, Anheuser Busch, BMW, Rubbermaid, and Steelcase Corporation. The company is also conducting hair tests for forty to fifty schools, five Federal Reserve banks, and the police departments of New York City, Chicago, Boston, and San Francisco.

Whites and blacks have complained about the tests.

Three Police Academy members were given hair tests in New York City as part of their application to the police department. The three Caucasian men claim that they did not take drugs and that the test was flawed. Two of the men had clean urine tests within months prior to the New York police department test. To bolster their assertions, these two men sent hair samples off for a second test to Laboratory Corporation of America and Metropolitan Drug Screening. According to Peter Coddington, an attorney retained by the Patrolmen's Benevolent Association to represent the men, the tests from the other labs produced opposite results. "They were clean," he said.

"It is quite clear that the police got the wrong results, either through the mishandling of the samples or through the laboratory techniques," says Coddington. "My clients should be reinstated, based on the contradictory tests." Coddington says that the men's lives have been devastated. "There is no question that they don't use drugs. They are three clean-cut, all-American boys. It was their lifetime goal to become police officers, and two of them are from police families. Now their whole lives are on hold."

New York attorney Regina Felton is representing a group of nine police officers, all African-American, dismissed in 1996 due to a positive Psychemedics hair test. All nine had random urinalysis tests throughout their two-year probationary period, which were negative. According to court transcripts, one of Felton's clients sent her hair to National Medical Services within three weeks after the New York Police Department sent her hair sample to Psychemedics. As in the Patrolmen's Benevolent Association cases, the test came back positive from Psychemedics and negative from National Medical Services.

Felton's clients appeared at hearings to seek unemployment compensation from the New York Department of Labor.

Ann Marie Gordon, the Director of Quality Assurance from Psychemedics, testified in each case as the expert on the accuracy of hair testing. As a result, the dismissed officers are not receiving any unemployment compensation. "The person who testified as the expert actually has a proprietary interest in Psychemedics," says Felton. "This person works for Psychemedics, and if she doesn't testify appropriately, she may not have a job."

◦◦◦

The Food and Drug Administration (FDA), the Department of Transportation, the National Institute of Drug Abuse, and the Society of Forensic Toxicologists (the preeminent professional association in the field of drug testing) all raise serious questions about the accuracy of hair testing. "The consensus of scientific opinion is that there are still too many unanswered questions for [hair analysis] to be used in employment situations," said Edward Cone, the National Institute of Drug Abuse's leading researcher on the test, in June 1998. In a recent interview, Cone said that hair testing "is not ready for use yet, where people's lives are at stake."

The Society of Forensic Toxicologists stands by its 1990 report, which said: "The use of hair analysis for employees and pre-employment drug testing is premature and cannot be supported by the current information on hair analysis for drugs of abuse."

According to a 1996 letter from Secretary of Health and Human Services Donna Shalala to the U.S. Senate, her agency "has not approved the use of hair testing for drugs of abuse." Shalala stated that "the available research suggests there are significant scientific and procedural concerns that must be addressed," and that these problems "make it impossible for us to recommend at this time its use in the federal program."

D. Bruce Burlington, a medical doctor who is director of the FDA's Center for Devices and Radiological Health, spoke before the House Committee on Commerce on July 23, 1998. "Many scientific questions remain ... about the effectiveness of hair testing for detecting drug use," he said. "The agency [FDA] has not been presented with adequate independent data on the effectiveness of such tests."

Some of the tests appear to give false positives to people who don't consume drugs. More disturbing yet, test results appear to vary according to ethnicity. "Dark hair, blond hair, and dyed hair react differently [from each other], thus creating questions of equity among ethnic groups and genders," Burlington testified.

A U.S. Navy study released by the National Institute of Drug Abuse in 1995 shows that the dark, coarse hair of many African-Americans, Hispanics, and Asians is more likely to retain external contamination, such as drug residues absorbed from the environment. Since these residues can be absorbed into hair even when they are not ingested, these groups could face a greater chance of error when subjected to the test. The issue of external contamination is particularly serious for police officers, who may be exposed to drugs during day-to-day law-enforcement operations.

A 1997 study by the National Institute of Drug Abuse supports the Navy's study, stating that "significantly greater nonspecific and specific radioligand binding occurred in dark colored hair compared to light hair." It concludes: "There may be significant ethnic bias in hair testing for cocaine." National Institute of Drug Abuse scientists showed in May 1998 that melanin is the most likely binding site for cocaine in human hair. The study found that cocaine binding was greater "in male Africoid hair than in female Africoid hair and in all Caucasoid hair types."

More recently, Douglas Rollins, director of the Center for Human Toxicology at the University of Utah, gave equal amounts of drugs to rats with black hair and white hair. He found that the black hair retained the drugs at a rate up to fifty times higher than the white hair. He is beginning comparable studies on humans.

William Minot, director of marketing communications at Psychemedics Corporation, says his company is "very conscious" about concerns that a person's race may affect the outcome of the test. The current test, he says, is "fail-proof" because Psychemedics extracts all the melanin from the hair before testing it. Minot says that hair samples are washed thoroughly to remove the hair surface, a procedure that also totally removes any external environmental contaminants before testing.

But the March/April 1998 issue of the *Journal of Analytical Toxicology* reported that scientists studied the effect on the hair of cocaine users when the melanin was removed. By measuring the cocaine content of the hair both with and without the melanin, the scientists observed that "removal of melanin from hair digests by centrifugation does not eliminate hair color bias when interpreting cocaine concentrations."

Psychemedics's corporate profile claims that its "no-nonsense" hair test is "five to ten times more effective at detecting drug abusers than urinalysis." But Psychemedics, like other hair-testing companies, provides little in the way of hard evidence to support such assertions.

Psychemedics has refused to disclose its testing and analysis procedures to the scientific community, says Leo Cangianelli, who headed the U.S. Navy drug testing division from 1980 to 1990 and is currently vice president of the Walsh Group, a research firm that studies drug and alcohol testing. This makes the hair test difficult for scientists to replicate and makes it almost impossible to establish a system of quality assurance for hair testing, Cangianelli says. And no hair testing labs have been federally certified, according to Burlington.

·◦⟨◉⟩◦·

Sergeant Duane Adens, an African-American father of five, was a fourteen-year employee of the Pentagon. Adens was less than six years away from retirement and had received the highest possible rating for overall performance in his last job evaluation when his life was turned upside down by a drug test.

In October 1996, two agents from the Army's Criminal Investigation Division called Adens to a meeting and asked him to testify against an associate of his, who the agents said was stealing and selling computers. Adens says he told them he could not do this, since he had no knowledge of the crimes. "The agent told me that I was obstructing justice and they would play hardball with me," recalls Adens. He says one of the agents then accused him of using drugs and threatened him with the loss of his Pentagon job. At that point, the agent asked Adens to provide him with a sample of his body hair, which he intended to have tested for drugs. Adens refused to provide the hair, and following the suggestion of his commander, the Army conducted a urine test on him the next day. That test came back negative.

In January 1997, two new agents came to Adens's home. "They told me they had a warrant," says Adens. This time, Adens's attorney advised him to provide the hair. They took Adens to a hospital and laid him on a table. One of the agents asked him if he would prefer the hair to be taken from his head or his pubic area. When Adens requested that it be taken from his head, the agent "said he would take it from my pubic area anyway so as not to mess up my haircut," says Adens, who believes the agent intended to humiliate him. A medical doctor removed the pubic hair, which the agent put in a small box in his pocket. After a delay of twenty days and without Adens signing off on the hair to identify it as his own—in violation of custody regulations—the hair was sent to National Medical Services in Willowborough, Pennsylvania. The results came back positive.

Adens was stunned. He says he does not use drugs and had not been exposed to environmental contaminants. Seven urinalysis tests he had taken over the course of a year and a half—most of them random tests required by the military—all came back negative. Adens took these tests between October 1996 and May 1998. He also did more tests once he knew the Army's Criminal Investigation Division was after him and can document the negative results.

Adens was brought before an Army court martial. He and his new attorney, Charles Gittins, requested a DNA test to verify the identity of the hair, which Adens believes was not even his. The U.S. Army denied his request. Because of the hair-test results, Sergeant Adens received a bad conduct discharge in July 1998.

❧

Representative Cynthia McKinney, Democrat of Georgia, has taken up the issue. In a July 22, 1998, letter to Secretary of Defense William Cohen, McKinney told the Secretary that the case of Sergeant Adens "has the potential to trigger hearings before the House National Security Committee" and that she is "exploring a possible legislative remedy to prohibit human hair testing for drugs in the military" until guidelines are established. "Hair testing has been proven by forensic toxicologists to be racially biased," she wrote.

McKinney received a response to her inquiry from Under Secretary of Defense Rudy de Leon on October 1. He reported that the Army had "contracted for hair analysis in six cases in the last two years involving five African-American subjects." In response to McKinney's letter, de Leon responded, "I understand your concern that hair color and other factors may affect hair absorption and extraction rates, and the ability of the test to detect the presence of illegal drugs. While this does not invalidate test results, DOD does not plan to use these tests in administrative drug testing programs until this matter is thoroughly studied and adequately addressed."

Representative Charles Rangel, Democrat of New York, wrote to the Army in behalf of Adens in September. Rangel's personal assistant Albert Becker wrote to Lieutenant Colonel Aaron B. Hayes: "Something is wrong with our military system of equal justice when an individual can pass all the required blood tests on Monday and fail the same procedure on Tuesday using a method that has not been approved by a branch of the federal government (the FDA). For a soldier to lose his self-esteem, family and military respect is a bit too much based on the strength of a body hair." Deputy Under Secretary of Defense Jeanne Fites declined to comment on the specifics of the Adens case.

The issue of hair testing has recently been brought to the House Judiciary Committee through the office of ranking committee member John Conyers,

Democrat of Michigan. Conyers is concerned about the ethnic bias of the hair test, and Judiciary Committee staff members are looking into it.

⋅≪◉≫⋅

Adens was removed from his position at the Pentagon at the beginning of his ordeal. He says he has been demoted to "doing odds and ends jobs like driving for people, filing, office work.... I've tried through my contacts to get some other jobs in the military, but they don't want to touch me at this point." Since his removal, Adens has missed out on two promotions that would have increased his income substantially. As soon as the Army approves the transcript of his case, he will be put on involuntary leave, which means he will lose his job and his government-subsidized home.

"One of the things that really, really bothers me is that this is a federal conviction," says Adens. "I will never be able to get a good job. I lose my voting rights. Something I worked hard at for fourteen years is all going to be taken away from me—for no reason at all."

# POSTSCRIPT

## Should Employees Be Required to Participate in Drug Testing?

As a follow-up to the discussion of whether or not employees should be required to submit to drug testing, one needs to ask what should be done with people who test positive for drugs. Should they be dismissed, or should they be treated? Is the purpose of drug testing to eliminate workers who use drugs or to help them? Do companies have the right to punish workers for activities that they engage in away from work?

Many questions surround the legalities of drug testing. Over the past two decades the courts have been divided over whether or not drug testing is reasonable and whether or not it constitutes a search under the Fourth Amendment. Most courts have concluded that a mandatory urine, blood, breath, and hair test can be considered a search under the Fourth Amendment; the focus now is on the extent to which drug searches may be reasonable.

Advocates of random drug testing argue that testing at the workplace will prevent illicit drug use and problems that are associated with drug use. Proponents believe that it is not a violation of civil rights when the government acts to protect all citizens from the problems of illicit drug use. However, drug tests are not always accurate. To avoid a positive result, some drug users submit another person's urine or put salt and detergent in their own samples, which affect the accuracy of the test. People on both sides of the argument contend that more reliable tests and better handling by laboratory workers are needed if drug testing is to be allowed.

Drug testing raises other questions: How should confidentiality of drug test results be maintained? Should drug testing be implemented at the worksite or at a neutral location? Who should be allowed access to employees' files regarding drug test results? How could employees be assured of their privacy? In addition, will job discrimination or employee stigmatization come about from positive test results?

Two articles that examine the advantages and disadvantages of drug testing are Kathy Koch, "Is Workplace Drug Testing Effective?" *CQ Researcher* (November 20, 1998) and Chris Penttila, "Testy, Testy," in *Entrepreneur* (June 2000). In "Bad Hair Days: Hair Follicle Testing Offers an Alternative to Traditional Drug Tests," *Management Review* (February 1997), Teresa Brady contends that hair testing is more reliable than urine testing. Criticisms of employee drug testing can be found in Jacob Sullum's "Pissing Contest," *Reason* (January 2000) and in Lee Fletcher's "Employer Drug Testing Has Pitfalls," *Business Insurance* (October 23, 2000).

# ISSUE 18

## Does Drug Abuse Treatment Work?

**YES: John B. Murray**, from "Effectiveness of Methadone Maintenance for Heroin Addiction," *Psychological Reports* (vol. 83, 1998)

**NO: Robert Apsler**, from "Is Drug Abuse Treatment Effective?" *The
American Enterprise* (March/April 1994)

### ISSUE SUMMARY

**YES:** Psychology professor John B. Murray contends that drug abuse
treatment, especially methadone maintenance, has been shown to
reduce illegal opiate use, curtail criminal activity, and lower rates of
HIV infection.

**NO:** Assistant professor of psychology Robert Apsler questions the
effectiveness of drug abuse treatment and whether or not drug addicts would go for treatment if services were expanded.

N umerous drug experts feel that more funding should go toward preventing
drug use from starting or escalating and toward treating individuals who are
dependent on drugs. Today, when budget battles loom and taxpayers dispute
how their tax monies are spent, the question of whether or not government
funds should be used to treat people who abuse drugs is especially relevant.
Questions surrounding this debate include: Does drug abuse treatment reduce
criminal activity associated with drugs? Will drug addicts stop their abusive
behavior if they enter treatment? Will more drug addicts receive treatment than
currently do if services are expanded? and, Will the availability and demand for
illegal drugs decline?

The research on the effectiveness of drug treatment is mixed. In *The
Effectiveness of Treatment for Drug Abusers Under Criminal Justice Supervision*
(National Institute of Justice, 1995), Douglas S. Lipton states that drug abuse
treatment not only reduces the rate of arrests but also reduces crime and lowers the cost to taxpayers over the long run. Also, it has been shown that illicit
drug use is curtailed by drug abuse treatment and that treated drug addicts are
better able to function in society and to maintain employment. Perhaps most
important, drug treatment may prove beneficial in curbing the escalation of
HIV (human immunodeficiency virus), the virus that causes AIDS. The logic

here is that when drug users (a high-risk population for HIV) enter treatment, they can be advised about the behaviors that lead to HIV transmission. Drug treatment is less costly than hospitalization and incarceration.

Some experts contend that reports regarding the effectiveness of drug treatment are not always accurate and that research on drug abuse has not been subjected to rigorous standards. Some question how effectiveness should be determined. If a person relapses after one year, should the treatment be considered ineffective? Would a reduction in an individual's illegal drug use indicate that the treatment was effective, or would an addict have to maintain complete abstinence? Also, if illegal drug use and criminal activity decline after treatment, it is possible that these results would have occurred anyway, regardless of whether or not the individual had been treated.

There are a variety of drug treatment programs. One type of treatment program developed in the 1960s is *therapeutic communities*. Therapeutic communities are usually residential facilities staffed by former drug addicts. Although there is no standard definition of what constitutes a therapeutic community, the program generally involves task assignments for residents (the addicts undergoing treatment), group intervention techniques, vocational and educational counseling, and personal skill development. Inpatient treatment facilities, such as the Betty Ford Center, are the most expensive type of treatment and are often based on a hospital model. These programs are very structured and include highly regimented schedules, demanding rules of conduct, and individual and group counseling.

Outpatient treatment, the most common type of drug treatment, is less expensive, less stigmatizing, and less disruptive to the abuser's family than other forms of treatment. Vocational, educational, and social counseling is provided. Outpatient treatment is often used after an addict leaves an inpatient program. One type of treatment that has proliferated in recent years is the self-help group. Members of self-help groups are bound by a common denominator, whether it is alcohol, cocaine, or narcotics. Due to the anonymous and confidential nature of self-help groups, however, it is difficult to conduct follow-up research to determine their effectiveness.

Individuals who are addicted to narcotics are often referred to methadone maintenance programs. Methadone is a synthetic narcotic that prevents narcotic addicts from getting high and eliminates withdrawal symptoms. Because methadone's effects last about 24 hours, addicts need to receive treatment daily. Unfortunately, the relapse rate is high once addicts stop treatment. Because there is much demand for methadone maintenance in some areas, there are lengthy waiting lists.

In the following selections, John B. Murray examines methadone maintenance programs and finds that such drug treatment programs effectively curtail illegal drug use and reduce criminality and the spread of AIDS. Robert Apsler contends that the benefits of drug treatment are not as significant as proponents of drug treatment profess.

John B. Murray

 **YES**

# Effectiveness of Methadone Maintenance for Heroin Addiction

*Summary.*—Methadone maintenance programs have effectively reduced heroin dependency and are available in most countries affected by heroin addiction. Methadone, developed in Germany during World War II as a pain killer, does not have the euphoric effects of heroin and the goal of treatment is to substitute methadone for heroin use. Recidivism is probably a life-long risk. Methadone maintenance programs began in the 1960s in the United States in New York City. Once tolerance is developed, it may be used continually without harmful side effects. Dosage is important for effectiveness as are counseling, rehabilitation services, and employment support. Reduction in criminality and AIDS has been associated with methadone maintenance programs.

Many reports in the past few decades have documented the effectiveness of methadone maintenance treatment for heroin addicts (Newman, 1995). This treatment is most often used for opiate addiction and has been the first outpatient treatment that heroin patients would attend reliably (Sorenson, 1996). It began after World War II in community-based programs and now exists in most countries where there is heroin addiction (Ball, Lange, Myers, & Friedman, 1988; Digiusto, Seres, Bibby, & Batey, 1996). Worldwide 250,000 heroin addicts are being treated in such programs (Farrell, Ward, Mattick, Hall, Stimson, Des Jarlais, Gossop, & Strang, 1994). Reviewed here are research on the effectiveness of methadone maintenance for heroin addiction as well as studies indicating contribution to employment, reduction in criminal activity, and improved life style.

Methadone hydrochloride, which has a pharmacological profile similar to morphine, is an opioid developed during World War II in Germany as a substitute pain-killer (Blaine & Renault, 1976). It does not produce euphoria in those who develop tolerance and metabolizes to inactive substances more slowly than morphine thereby extending its action to 24 hours and permitting a dosage per day. The effectiveness of methadone maintenance in reducing use of opiates was first reported in the United States by Dole and Nyswander (1965) and Dole, Nyswander, and Warner (1968) in research at Rockefeller University

From John B. Murray, "Effectiveness of Methadone Maintenance for Heroin Addiction," *Psychological Reports*, no. 83 (1998), pp. 295-300. Copyright © 1998 by *Psychological Reports*. Reprinted by permission of the author and publisher. References omitted.

and Beth Israel Medical Center in New York City. Methadone maintenance can be continued indefinitely on a single dose administered daily without harmful effects (Cushman, 1977; Dole & Nyswander, 1965). Fatal overdose of methadone has occurred more often in those who did not have a prescription and obtained methadone from others (Bell, Digiusto, & Byth, 1992; Cairns, Roberts, & Benbow, 1996).

Methadone maintenance has been extensively evaluated (Dole, 1988; Farrell, *et al.*, 1994; Kirn, 1988; Public Policy, 1991). Many well controlled studies, conducted mostly in the United States, have compared groups on methadone maintenance with control groups over a year or more of treatment and have shown the programs' superiority in reducing, although not always eliminating, use of opiates (Sorenson, 1996). However, evaluations of these programs go beyond reduction of heroin dependency (Ball, *et al.*, 1988; Newman, 1987). Observational studies have indicated that they have an influence in reducing criminal activity of participants (Bell, Hall, & Byth, 1992; Cushman, Trussel, Gollance, Newman, & Bihari, 1976; Dole, *et al.*, 1968; Sechrest, 1979). Those with good psychosocial adjustment more often benefit but also many who come from populations lacking strong social support and from lower social economic status (Sorenson, 1996; Vaillant, 1988). Research has indicated a high incidence of coexisting mental disorders in the patients treated, particularly depression, alcoholism, and antisocial personality disorder (Kosten & Rounsaville, 1986; Milby, Sims, Kauder, Schumacher, Huggins, McLellan, Woody, & Haas, 1996).

Because methadone treatment is effective in reducing needle use, the program has contributed to reducing the risk of HIV infection (Ball, *et al.*, 1988; Brown, Burkett, & Primm, 1988; Cooper, 1989; Katz, Galanter, Lifshutz, & Maslansky, 1995; Public Policy, 1991; Stimmel, 1993). Methadone maintenance does not significantly impair the immune system and it is safe for those with HIV (Wodak, Capelhorn, & Crofts, 1995). It does not complicate pregnancy for the mothers who are in the programs (Blinick, Wallach, Jerez, & Ackerman, 1976; Nadelmann & McNeely, 1996). Effective counseling, rehabilitation services, and employment support are components of effective methadone programs (Farrell, *et al.*, 1994; Sechrest, 1979).

Programs in the United States have focused on long-term use of methadone. The programs aim at voluntary rehabilitation of hard-core addicts who are motivated to escape heroin and its debilitating effect on their health and lifestyle (Alexander & Hadaway, 1982; Belding, Iguchi, Lamb, Lakin, & Terry, 1995, 1996; Bellis, 1993). As they progress in treatment, clients are encouraged to undertake more difficult rehabilitation steps to move away from street drug subcultures in favor of a more stable life style (Cushman, 1977).

These programs are not panaceas and always have been controversial (Dole, 1995; Kirn, 1988; Sorenson, 1996). Patients are often disadvantaged, and rehabilitation may be long with relapses (Sechrest, 1979). The criteria for eligibility vary and often are controlled by government agencies at different levels (Bell, *et al.*, 1992). Some long-term drug abusers do well when methadone is terminated but the majority experience a return of symptoms so recidivism is a life-long risk (Dole, 1988; Newman, 1987). Approximately 70% of the patients may relapse within one year after they are discharged and with relapse, criminal activities and sharing needle injections may reoccur (Zanis, McLellan, Alterman, & Cnaan, 1996). The programs are designed for maintenance of heroin addicts in a manner similar to that of chemotherapy for other chronic illnesses (Des Jarlais, Joseph, Dole, & Nyswander, 1985).

Since patients often are polydrug users, one particular problem is that others for whom methadone was not prescribed may obtain it from patients (Grapendaal, 1992). Where the programs are well supervised, diversion of methadone to others is less likely (Sorenson, 1996), but the hazards of diversion appear to have been overestimated since methadone is readily available on the black market (Dole, 1995). The demand for illicit methadone results in part from its limited legal availability.

## Structure and Regulation of Methadone Maintenance Programs

Methadone maintenance programs may vary in the structure of their treatment (Ball, *et al.*, 1988; Bell, Hall, & Byth, 1992; Bellis, 1993). Length of time in the program varies although it has been significantly related to improvement. Longer stays in treatment have been associated with better outcomes (Farrell, *et al.*, 1994; Stimmel, 1993). French, Zarkin, Hubbard, and Rachal (1993) who interviewed 11,000 addicts in a long-term follow-up of drug abusers in North Carolina reported that time in treatment was negatively and significantly related to outcome variables and appeared to have a stabilizing effect. The programs were concerned with reducing the use of heroin but patients' polydrug abuse may confound estimates of effectiveness (Belding, *et al.*, 1995). For example, use of cocaine correlated highly with incident of criminality in a study wherein 65% to 70% of 150 drug users were clients in methadone clinics (Grapendaal, 1992).

Dosage is an important factor in effectiveness of the programs (Caplehorn, Bell, Kleinbaum, & Gebski, 1993; Cooper, 1992). Because these treatment programs vary in organization and practices, dosage may vary in different studies (Ball, *et al.*, 1988; Dole, Nyswander, Des Jarlais, & Herman, 1982; Farrell, *et al.*, 1994; Fisher & Anglin, 1987). Dosage in many programs was stabilized at 40 mg despite research data over 15 years indicating that this should be individualized, and that the most effective daily dosage is between 50 and 100 mg (D'Aunno & Vaughn, 1992; Nadelmann & McNeely, 1996). In early research heroin addicts accepted into the programs began as inpatients, and the methadone dosage administered every day began with 10 mg a day and was gradually increased to a tolerance level (Dole & Nyswander, 1965; Dole, *et al.*, 1968). Once the methadone tolerance level was reached patients could be shifted to outpatient status and maintained on a daily dose of methadone between 50 mg and 100 mg. If taken by someone who has not developed tolerance, a dosage of 70 mg to 75 mg can be fatal. Flexible dosage according to need has been associated with longer stays in treatment.

When supervised by a nurse or medical doctor, administration of methadone is less subject to abuse (Des Jarlais, *et al.*, 1985). In most research methadone has been taken in pill or liquid form. Injections may be preferred by patients but it is more likely to be abused if patients are also using cocaine.

In a national mail survey of 25% randomly sampled community pharmacies in England and Wales almost 80% of patients used the oral liquid form and 11% used pills (Strang, Sheridan, & Barber, 1996). In one program patients received a daily cup of orange juice in which a methadone diskette was dissolved (Kirn, 1988). The use of injections also may encourage needle sharing and reduce any benefits of methadone maintenance of HIV. Daily visits to the clinic for medication and frequent checks by urinalysis reduce diversion of methadone to others. When patients have proven themselves, take-home medication may be allowed one day or more weekly (Ball, *et al.*, 1988).

Urinalysis is a regular part of the programs as well as a way of monitoring the patients' progress in treatment. In a study of 341 heroin addicts who were applying for acceptance into four clinics in Sydney, Australia, concordance between self-reported use of drugs and the results of urinalysis was acceptably close (Digiusto, *et al.*, 1996). Agreement between self-report and urinalysis was better for heroin than for psychostimulants. Magura, Goldsmith, Casriel, Goldstein, and Lipton (1987) checked the validity of self-reports of drug use against the urinalysis readings in 248 methadone maintenance patients. The two methods complemented each other in that self-reports indicated drug users' problems which were not detected in patients through urinalysis. Self-reports tended to be more accurate for older patients.

Counseling, psychosocial services, and rehabilitation facilities are components of many effective programs (Public Policy, 1991). Employment and employment counseling contribute to the effectiveness of treatment because patients who are without jobs are more likely to slip back into the lifestyle of the drug culture (Platt & Metzger, 1985; Vaillant, 1988). However, psychosocial components may not be the important factors in the effectiveness of programs, and controlled provision of methadone alone may be effective. Because waiting lists were so long, 301 addicts in 22 units sponsored by New York City, who were unable to get into the regular program, were assigned randomly to either an experimental or a control group (Yancovitz, Des Jarlais, Peyser, Drew, Friedmann, Trigg, & Robinson, 1991). Waiting time for an opening in a regular clinic was three months. Both groups received initial medical evaluation. The experimental group received education on the dangers of AIDS and methadone treatment beginning at 20 to 30 mg a day increasing gradually to 80 mg daily but received no counseling or vocational rehabilitation. Urinalysis was used once a month to check on possible use of opiates and indicated there was significant reduction in heroin use for the experimental group versus the control group. The two groups were equivalent in their initial drug use. A higher percentage of the experimental group entered the regular program when an opening occurred.

McClellan, Arndt, Metzger, Woody, and O'Brien (1993) studied the cost-effectiveness of psychosocial services in methadone maintenance programs. In a veterans hospital 92 opiate addicts were randomly assigned to one of three groups who differed in the available psychosocial services. One group received only methadone; in the second group counseling was added to methadone; and the third group received methadone, counseling, family therapy, as well as medical and psychiatric assistance on site. The second and third groups showed significantly more improvement than the first group. The two groups receiving psychosocial assistance showed significant reduction in opiate use and illegal activity, and more of them stayed longer in the program. Minimum treatment with methadone alone appeared effective only for a minority of eligible addicts.

Kraft, Rothbard, Hadley, McLellan, and Asch (1997) also addressed the question of the cost-effectiveness of psychosocial support services in programs. They compared three groups of patients receiving methadone for treatment of opiate addiction, with 100 patients randomly assigned to each of three groups during a 24-wk. clinical trial. One group received only methadone, the second group received methadone along with counseling, and the third group received methadone along with extensive counseling that included family therapy and employment services. Analysis of data at 6 months follow-up showed that the group with extensive counseling had the highest rates of abstinence but their treatment was not as cost-effective as that for a second group, a combination of methadone and moderate amounts of counseling. Methadone alone also was less cost effective as measured by fewer abstinent patients. Cost-effectiveness appeared to be best with the moderate counseling and methadone treatment group but the authors pointed out that there is a level of support below which supplemental services should not fall.

## Discussion

Methadone maintenance has demonstrated effectiveness in reducing opiate use in many controlled studies. In addition, reduced criminal activity has been reported and psychosocial adjustment improved in those who remain in the programs. Recently the programs have been credited with reducing HIV on the basis of reduction of patients' opiate use and less frequent sharing of needles.

Methadone maintenance is expensive. Estimates of annual cost per patient vary with the amount of supplemental support offered. This outlay can be considered to be offset somewhat by lower costs in reduced criminal activity, increased employment, and reduction in public assistance. These trade-offs, along with reduction in hospitalization for comorbidity, have not been computed but are involved in estimates of the real cost of methadone maintenance.

The consensus that methadone maintenance is helpful in preventing HIV transmission is encouraging. It is discouraging that many, even most patients, in these programs do not overcome their addiction and must continue in treatment indefinitely, perhaps because methadone reinforces associated physiological and behavioral habits. Better counseling methods may improve the chances of complete recovery and decrease likelihood of relapse. However, details of psychotherapeutic interventions have not been included in reports on these programs so it would be difficult to know how counseling might be introduced or improved. Figures or percentages of vocational rehabilitation have rarely been reported.

To be effective methadone maintenance programs should be oriented towards encouraging participants to remain in treatment. This is not only useful for their health but retention in maintenance programs may be a key to reduced criminal involvement of addicts. Methadone maintenance has provided an alternative to life-long heroin addiction. Success in these programs has grown to include not only reduced opiate use but also less crime in the community, social and vocational rehabilitation, and improved general health. In sum, many realize a more productive and socially acceptable life style. Social stability, especially stable employment, is an effective predictor of long-term outcome.

A major concern for research will be identifying the possible specific deficiency in heroin dependency and what to do. Discovery of the process by which methadone blocks the euphoric effects of heroin might be translated into a means of reversing dependency on heroin as well as on cocaine and alcohol. Differences in dosage of methadone might be resolved into minimum and maximum doses with range in between being important for effective treatment. Finally, one more issue addressed in research on the program's effectiveness would be the necessity for total abstinence from all opiates. Those structuring treatment for alcoholism have wrestled with this issue of partial versus total abstinence but it has not been given attention in current research.

**Robert Apsler**

 **NO**

# Is Drug Abuse Treatment Effective?

In early February [1994], the Clinton administration spelled out its national antidrug strategy. Much of the debate over the new program will turn on how much federal support should be made available for treating drug addicts. The administration plans to spend $355 million in new grants for the states to use to treat hard-core drug users, while cutting funds for interdiction. Many years of massive federal investment in interdiction—including involvement of the U.S. military—have failed to reduce the availability of low-cost street drugs. And the policy momentum is now toward shifting federal funds from supply reduction to demand reduction, a move that would benefit treatment and prevention programs. Also, news stories about the administration's deliberations often report on drug treatment programs with long waits for new admissions. What is implied if not stated is that the size of the country's drug abusing population, estimated by the Institute of Medicine to be 5.5 million people, would be significantly reduced if more money were spent for drug abuse treatment.

But missing from the news stories and analyses of proposed antidrug strategies is any frank discussion of the underlying assumption that drug abuse treatment is effective. This assumption is based largely on reports from clinicians and recovered drug addicts. It is encouraged by a growing drug treatment industry and accepted by a public that wishes for a solution to the drug problem. The premise may be accurate, but it is not yet supported by hard evidence. We do not know that drug abuse treatment is effective. Clinicians' reports in other areas have not always been reliable. For example, many medical procedures developed through clinical experience alone have been abandoned when researchers showed, through carefully controlled comparisons, that placebos or other alternatives matched their effectiveness.

With a few exceptions, drug abuse treatment has not been subjected to rigorous tests for effectiveness. Good research doesn't exist for a number of reasons. Researchers are hampered by fundamental conceptual issues. Even defining basic ideas is difficult. There are significant practical obstacles that make conducting research difficult as well, and little federal support for drug treatment research has been available for over a decade.

# What Is "Drug Abuse Treatment"?

One of the conceptual and practical problems of research is the simple fact that no one process or combination of procedures comprises "drug abuse treatment." Nor do the various types of drug programs have much in common beyond the shared objective of reducing drug abuse.

There are four major types of drug treatment. *Residential therapeutic communities* are highly structured residential settings for drug addicts and typically employ a mixture of psychological and behavioral therapies. Duration of treatment varies widely among these programs. *Inpatient/outpatient chemical dependency treatment* begins with a three- to six-week residential stay in a clinic or hospital that uses the Alcoholics Anonymous philosophy. These clients are then encouraged to attend self-help groups for the rest of their lives. A third type, *outpatient methadone maintenance programs,* involves supervised addiction to methadone hydrochloride as a substitute for addiction to other narcotics, such as heroin. Programs may include counseling and other social services for clients. The fourth category, *outpatient nonmethadone treatment,* joins many different types of programs whose main similarity is that they tend not to treat individuals who are dependent on opiates such as heroin, morphine, and codeine.

This four-group classification is crude because the programs within each category differ markedly from each other. For example, methadone maintenance programs differ in the size of the methadone dose, the number and type of additional services provided, the frequency of urine testing, the strictness of program regulation enforcement, and whether clients are permitted to take their methadone dose home. Some programs focus on illicit drug use and criminal activity, while others target the overall functioning of clients. Some demand abstinence from all illicit drugs; others help clients gain control over their drug use. They differ in whether they concentrate on a particular drug and, if they do, on which drug. Some programs rely heavily on professional practitioners; others employ nonprofessionals, often ex-addicts, as counselors. Programs also differ in the clients they serve: those in the private sector cater mainly to employed drug abusers, whose care is covered by health insurance. The public sector programs serve large numbers of indigent clients.

The differences within each of the four major categories of drug programs are so great that information about the effectiveness of one program in a particular category tells us little about the effectiveness of other programs in the same category. In fact, some differences among programs within a classification group may prove to be more important than the differences among the four groups of programs. For example, new evidence shows that the sheer quantity of treatment provided to clients is crucial to a program's effectiveness. Thus, the amount of counseling and auxiliary services provided by a program may be a more important defining characteristic with respect to efficacy than the types of drug abuse it treats, its treatment philosophy, or whether it operates through a residential or outpatient setting.

# What Is "Effective" Treatment?

Just as there is no simple answer to what comprises drug abuse treatment, neither is there an agreed-upon definition of what constitutes *effective* drug abuse treatment. Definitions clash in two important ways. First, strongly held views divide the treatment community on whether abstinence from illicit drug use is necessary. One position holds that successful treatment is synonymous with total abstinence from illicit drugs. The other position holds that treatment is successful if it ends clients' *dependence* on drugs. Continued, moderate drug use is accepted for those clients able to gain control over their drug use and prevent it from interfering with their daily functioning.

Definitions of effectiveness also differ in the number of behaviors they measure. The most common view of effectiveness judges treatment by its ability to reduce the two behaviors most responsible for society's strong reaction against drug abuse: illicit drug use and criminal activity. Others argue that a broader definition of effectiveness is necessary to describe treatment accurately. Advocates of the broader definition believe that treatment should not be considered effective if it can only demonstrate reductions in drug use and illegal activity, since these changes are likely to dissipate rapidly unless clients undergo additional changes. Returning clients who have completed treatment to their previous drug using environment, it is argued, subjects them to the same social and economic forces that contributed to their drug use. According to this view, sustained changes occur only when clients are willing and able to survive and prosper in new environments. To do so, clients must first develop the necessary employment, social, and other skills. Broad definitions of effectiveness usually include: (1) drug abuse, (2) illegal activities, (3) employment, (4) length of stay in treatment, (5) social functioning, (6) intrapersonal functioning, and (7) physical health and longevity.

# Motivation and Crisis

Without having resolved even basic definitions about drug abuse treatment, the administration is nevertheless proceeding on the assumption that more money for treatment will mean more help. Doing so ignores the fact that we don't know very much in this area and also ignores the little we do know. We don't know much about client differences, for instance. But we do know that a drug addict's motivation for seeking treatment is crucial. Most clinicians believe that successful treatment is impossible if a client does not want help. Addicts must admit the existence of a serious problem and sincerely want to do something about it. Only then will they accept the assistance of clinicians. However, most experts in the drug abuse field reluctantly acknowledge that almost no drug abusers actually *want* treatment. The news reports implying that thousands of needy addicts would enter treatment and soon be on their way to recovery if the country were willing to spend more money and increase the number of drug programs are inaccurate. While waiting lists exist for some programs, others have trouble attracting addicts.

Furthermore, most drug abusers enter treatment when faced with a crisis, such as threats by a judge, employer, or spouse, or a combination of the three. As a result, the drug abuser's objective may be limited to overcoming the current problem. When the crisis has abated, patients often admit they do not intend all drug use to stop. A national survey of admissions to public drug programs from 1979 to 1981 found that pressure from the criminal justice system was the strongest motivation for seeking treatment. Thus, the existence of long waiting lists may tell us more about judges' efforts to find alternatives to incarceration in overcrowded jails than about the actual intentions of drug abusers or the effectiveness of treatment programs.

The assumption that drug addicts enter treatment at a crisis point has another important ramification for interpreting research on the effectiveness of treatment programs. Studies of treatment effectiveness typically measure clients at least twice: when they enter a program and when they complete treatment. If the first measurement occurs during a time of crisis, it will reflect clients' negative circumstances by showing high levels of drug use, criminal behavior, unemployment, and so on. The second measure of clients, taken at the conclusion of treatment, will likely occur after the precipitating crisis has passed or at least lessened. Consequently, a comparison of the measurements taken at the beginning and end of treatment will show significant improvement for many clients. Is this improvement evidence of effective treatment? Or does it merely reflect the natural cycle of a passing crisis? The main problem is that the research designs used in nearly all drug treatment research cannot separate the effects of treatment from other factors such as these.

## Research Problems

Questions about drug treatment effectiveness must be answered the same way as similar questions about treatments for the common cold, AIDS, or other ailments, that is, by obtaining evidence that compares the outcomes of treated and untreated individuals. While this may seem obvious, most drug treatment research has neither compared the necessary groups of drug users nor employed the types of research designs capable of producing strong conclusions. In addition, serious measurement and attrition problems weaken the conclusions of most studies of drug treatment effectiveness.

*Research design.* Comparisons between drug users who receive treatment and others who do not are almost nonexistent. Researchers study only treated drug users. Yet the observed behavior of drug users who do not enter drug programs reinforces the need for researchers to include untreated addicts in their studies. We have known for years, for instance, that some drug abusers, including heroin addicts, end drug use largely on their own. Researchers have also observed large reductions in drug use among drug abusers waiting for, but not yet receiving, treatment for cocaine abuse.

The phenomenon of people ending their use of highly addictive *legal* substances on their own is well documented. For example, there is mounting evidence that smokers quit on their own at about the same rate as those attending smoking treatment programs. Estimates of remission from alcoholism and alcohol problems without formal treatment range from 45 to 70 percent. No comparable estimate is available for the number of drug users who quit on their own. Until we know the recovery rates for untreated drug abusers, it is impossible to claim that treatment is more effective than the absence of treatment.

Furthermore, the research designs and methods employed in most drug treatment research are so seriously flawed that the results can be considered no more than suggestive. Many investigations study a single group of treated clients and attempt to draw conclusions without a comparison group. Other investigations compare different groups of clients receiving different treatments. In nearly all such cases, the types of clients differ from group to group. Consequently, it is impossible to distinguish between effects caused by treatment differences and effects caused by client differences.

*Measuring the outcomes of treatment.*   One major need in drug treatment research is for an objective, reliable, and inexpensive method for measuring treatment outcomes. Presently most treatment researchers rely entirely on clients' own reports of past and current behavior. Much of the behavior that clients are asked about is illegal, occurred while they were intoxicated, and may have taken place months, and even years, earlier. As one would expect, clients underreport their drug use and other illegal activities. Yet the drug treatment field continues to rely heavily on these dubious reports because there are no suitable alternatives. Chemical tests, such as urine and hair testing, are important adjuncts for validating clients' reports. But at best these tests confirm use or abstinence; they do not indicate anything about quantity or intervals of use. So they are crude measures that cannot easily track patterns of drug use over long periods after a client leaves a treatment program.

Many treatment studies measure clients at the beginning and end of treatment because it is so difficult and expensive to keep track of them after they have completed a program. Some studies do attempt to assess the impact of treatment six months, a year, or even longer after completion. But investigators can seldom locate more than 70 percent of clients, if that. Clients who cannot be contacted are often deceased, in prison, unemployed, and/or homeless. Leaving them out of the studies may skew the findings, making the conclusions appear more positive than is warranted.

*Length of treatment.*   The length of drug abuse treatment is a complex and confusing element in the overall picture of treatment effectiveness. To begin with, simply keeping clients in treatment is a major challenge for many drug programs. Most clients are forced into treatment. And many leave shortly thereafter. Therefore, merely remaining in treatment has become a widely accepted measure of treatment effectiveness. While it makes sense that clients can only benefit from treatment if they remain in a program, there is the risk of confusing happenstance for cause and effect.

Addicts who truly want to change their lifestyles are likely to make many changes. Such changes include entering and remaining in a treatment program, reducing drug use, holding a steady job, eschewing illegal activities, and so on. Other individuals not willing to change their lifestyles are more likely to drop out of treatment after being forced into a drug program. They continue using drugs, do not hold steady jobs, engage in illegal activities, and so on. Thus, to prove that drug programs are effective, researchers must show that (1) drug programs help addicts commit to changing their lifestyles, and/or that (2) the resulting improvement among treated clients is greater than the improvement expected anyway from individuals who have already chosen to change their lifestyles.

Another challenge is determining the length of an optimum stay in a drug treatment program. Most private chemical dependency residential programs used to run for 28 days, though cost-reduction pressures have shortened this time. Outpatient nonmethadone treatment averages roughly six months of once-or-twice-a-week counseling sessions. Some therapeutic communities provide treatment for a year or more, while methadone maintenance programs may involve lifetime participation for clients. How much treatment is enough? Some research shows that methadone clients remain in treatment for an unnecessarily long time. This may mean that programs with waiting lists should consider ending treatment for long-term clients to make room for new ones. The impact of treatment may be much greater on someone receiving treatment for the first time than on an individual who has been on methadone for years.

The complex treatment histories of many drug addicts increase the difficulty of judging treatment effectiveness. Over the course of their addiction careers, typical drug addicts enter several different treatment programs. They may enter the same programs on different occasions for different lengths of time. At any point during this involved treatment history, addicts may find themselves participating in a study of treatment effectiveness. However, that study is likely to examine only the most recent treatment episode without taking into account previous treatment stays. Perhaps even small amounts of treatment accumulate over time until they influence an individual. Some drug addicts may try different forms of treatment until they find a type of treatment or a particular counselor that helps them. However, existing treatment research cannot disentangle the effects of multiple treatment episodes in different types of drug programs that last for varying amounts of time.

## What We Know About Treatment Programs

Because of research problems, very little is known about the effectiveness of three out of the four categories of drug abuse treatment identified earlier in this article—*residential therapeutic communities, inpatient/outpatient chemical dependency treatment,* and *outpatient nonmethadone maintenance programs.* Surveys of *residential therapeutic communities* have produced promising results, but important questions remain unanswered. Two longitudinal studies of many drug treatment programs reported reductions in drug use and criminal activity among therapeutic community clients who remained in treatment for at least several months. But therapeutic communities are highly selective in at least two ways. First, they appeal only to clients willing to enter a long-term residential setting. Second, most addicts who enter therapeutic communities quickly drop out. Thus, therapeutic communities may influence the drug addiction of only a small and select group of individuals. Furthermore, there is almost no research about the factors that affect success and failure in therapeutic communities.

As for the other two, almost nothing reliable has been produced on *inpatient/outpatient chemical dependency treatment,* though it has become the dominant approach of privately financed inpatient programs. Nor are there reliable findings on *outpatient/nonmethadone treatment.*

The strongest evidence that drug abuse treatment can be effective comes from randomized clinical trials of the remaining category of treatment programs, *methadone maintenance treatment* programs. Randomized clinical trials are powerful studies that randomly assign a pool of subjects to different conditions, such as different types of treatment; researchers are able to conclude that if some groups of subjects improve more than others, the improvement is probably due to the treatment condition, not to preexisting differences among the individuals. The first of three rigorous trials of methadone treatment, a U.S. study conducted in the late 1960s, randomly assigned highly motivated criminal addicts to either a methadone program or a waiting-list group that received no treatment. All 16 addicts on the waiting list quickly became readdicted to heroin, as did 4 addicts in the treatment group who refused treatment. Eighteen of the 20 untreated individuals who became readdicted returned to prison within 1 to 10 months. Only 3 of the 12 addicts who received treatment returned to prison during this period, and their heroin use decreased.

A test in 1984 of a methadone maintenance program in Sweden provides further evidence of treatment effectiveness, though the stringent client selection criteria make it difficult to generalize the findings. Heroin addicts became eligible for this study only after (1) a history of long-term compulsive abuse, and (2) repeated failures to stop, despite documented serious attempts to do so. Thirty-four addicts meeting these eligibility requirements were randomly assigned to either treatment or no-treatment. Two years later, 12 of the 17 drug addicts assigned to treatment had abandoned drug use and started work or studies. The remaining 5 still had drug problems, and 2 had been expelled from the program. Conversely, only 1 of the 17 addicts in the no-treatment group became drug free; 2 were in prison, 2 were dead, and the rest were still abusing heroin.

A very recent randomized clinical trial in the United States compared three levels of methadone treatment: (1) methadone alone without other services, (2) methadone plus counseling, and (3) methadone plus counseling and on-site medical/psychiatric, employment, and family therapy. The results showed that methadone alone was, at most, helpful to only a few clients. The results for clients who received methadone plus counseling were better, and clients who received additional professional services improved most of all. In sum, these three studies demonstrate that methadone treatment has the potential to reduce illicit narcotics use and criminal behavior among narcotics addicts.

To what extent do these findings apply to methadone maintenance programs in general? We do not know, and we must remain skeptical about the level of effectiveness of most methadone programs; their results could be quite different. For example, two of the three studies described above restricted their research to clients who were highly motivated to end their addiction. But methadone programs in this country typically treat individuals who are forced into treatment, many of whom exhibit little desire to change their addict lifestyles. The third study did not restrict the research to highly motivated clients. However, the study took place in a well-funded, stable, hospital-based, university-affiliated setting. Most methadone programs operate on small budgets that severely restrict their ability to provide services and hire qualified staff. Therefore they differ in important ways from the study program.

To learn about the impact of less extraordinary methadone programs, a U.S. General Accounting Office study examined the efficacy of 15 methadone programs in a five-state survey. The survey found that (1) the current use of heroin and other opiates ranged from 2 to 47 percent of clients enrolled in the clinics, (2) many clients had serious alcohol problems, (3) clients received few comprehensive services despite high rates of unemployment, and (4) clinics did not know if clients used the services to which they were referred. Other research has shown that many methadone programs administer doses of methadone smaller than those known to be effective. In sum, typical methadone programs differ significantly from the methadone programs evaluated in the randomized clinical trials discussed above, and they may be less effective.

## Conclusions

Drug abuse treatment features prominently in discussions of how the Clinton administration should respond to the country's concern about drug abuse. Yet little hard evidence documents the effectiveness of treatment. Almost nothing is known about (1) the effectiveness of three of the four major treatment modalities, (2) the relative effectiveness of different versions of each major treatment modality, and (3) the prognosis for different types of drug abusers. Instead of answering questions, drug treatment research raises troublesome issues for policymakers. How can treatment work when clinicians claim that success depends on clients wanting help, and we know that most clients are forced into treatment? What happens to drug abusers who never seek treatment?

What can be said with some certainty is that (1) methadone maintenance programs can help clients who are highly motivated to end their drug abuse, and (2) a model program that provides counseling along with methadone has been able to help less well-motivated clients. But there is little good news here since most drug addicts do not want to end their drug use, and typical methadone maintenance programs may not possess the resources to duplicate the impact of the model program.

The absence of convincing evidence about the effectiveness of drug abuse treatment results from the lack of rigorous evaluations. Only a handful of randomized clinical trials have been conducted to date. More need to be done, and valid and comprehensive measures of treatment effectiveness need to be employed in these studies in order to end the reliance of treatment researchers on clients' self-reports of sensitive behaviors. Treatment research also needs more post-treatment follow-ups to show that treatment effects persist once clients leave their programs.

Finally, researchers must learn what happens to untreated drug abusers. Past and current research focuses almost exclusively on drug abusers who enter treatment. This research does not make comparisons between treated and untreated drug abusers and cannot answer the most fundamental question of all: is treatment more cost-effective than no treatment?

# POSTSCRIPT

## Does Drug Abuse Treatment Work?

**M**uch of the research on drug treatment effectiveness is inconclusive; furthermore, researchers do not agree on what the best way is to measure effectiveness. Determining the effectiveness of drug treatment is extremely important because the federal government and a number of state governments are now contemplating increasing the amount of funding allocated to drug treatment. Many experts in the drug field agree that much of the money that has been used to deal with problems related to drugs has not been wisely spent. To prevent further waste of taxpayer funds, it is essential to find out if drug treatment works before funding for it is increased.

Another concern related to this issue is that addicts who wish to receive treatment often face many barriers. One of the most serious barriers is that there is a lack of available treatment facilities. In *Improving Drug Abuse Treatment,* NIDA Research Monograph No. 106 (1991), C. L. Veatch states that there are an estimated 291,000 drug abusers in California but fewer than 15,000 licensed treatment slots for methadone patients. Compounding the problem is the fact that many communities resist the idea of having a drug treatment center in the neighborhood, even though there is little research on the effects of treatment facilities on property values and neighborhood crime rates. Another barrier to treatment is cost, which, with the exception of self-help groups, is high. Furthermore, some addicts avoid organized treatment altogether for fear that if they go for treatment, they will be identified as drug abusers by law enforcement agencies.

Many addicts in treatment are there because they are given a choice of entering either prison or treatment. Are people who are required to enter treatment more or less likely to succeed than people who enter treatment voluntarily? Early studies showed that treatment was more effective for voluntary clients. However, a study conducted by the federal government of 12,000 clients enrolled in 41 publicly funded treatment centers found that clients referred by the criminal justice system fared as well as if not better than voluntary clients in terms of reduced criminal activity and drug use.

Two articles that look at the effectiveness of methadone maintenance programs are "Methadone Maintenance and HIV Prevention: A Cost-Effectiveness Analysis," by Gregory Zaric, Margaret Brandeau, and Paul Barnett, *Management Science* (August 2000) and "Revisiting the Effectiveness of Methadone Treatment on Crime Reduction in the 1990s," by Aileen Rothbard et al., *Journal of Substance Abuse Treatment* (June 1999). A national poll by Peter Hart Research Associates found that more people support drug treatment over drug interdiction. See "Survey Finds Public Support for Treatment Over Interdiction," *Alcoholism and Drug Abuse Weekly* (July 24, 2000).

# ISSUE 19

## Are Antidrug Media Campaigns Effective?

**YES: Barry R. McCaffrey**, from *Investing in Our Nation's Youth: National Youth Anti-Drug Media Campaign: Phase II (Final Report)* (U.S. Government Printing Office, 1999)

**NO: David R. Buchanan and Lawrence Wallack**, from "This Is the Partnership for a Drug-Free America: Any Questions?" *Journal of Drug Issues* (Spring 1998)

### ISSUE SUMMARY

**YES:** Barry R. McCaffrey, former director of the Office of National Drug Control Policy (ONDCP), argues that the attitudes and behaviors of young people regarding drug use are affected by antidrug media campaigns. He therefore supports the federal government's spending millions of dollars for antidrug public service announcements.

**NO:** David R. Buchanan, an assistant professor of community health studies, and professor of health education Lawrence Wallack argue that antidrug media campaigns are not only ineffective but may result in a backlash. They maintain that many drug-prevention messages are inaccurate, and they question the value of the scare tactics that are part of most antidrug announcements.

There has been a significant proliferation in drug use by young people since the beginning of the 1990s. Because drug use can have a negative effect on one's health, interpersonal relationships, emotional and social development, family relations, and academic success, most people would agree that reducing drug use is a desirable, if not necessary, goal. However, what is the best strategy for achieving this goal? Experts disagree on the best course of action to take to decrease drug taking. Some experts feel that more effort should be put into enforcing laws against drug use. Others believe that the federal government should make a greater commitment to stopping drugs from entering the country. Still others maintain that more money should be used for drug education.

Among the different approaches being explored for curtailing drug use by young people is the use of antidrug public service announcements. The question being debated in this issue is whether or not antidrug public service announcements affect drug-taking behavior. Do young people who watch announcements that denounce and ridicule drug use alter their drug-taking behavior? Moreover, should the federal government spend millions of taxpayer dollars on antidrug public service announcements, especially if it is unclear that they have any effect?

Assessing the effectiveness of antidrug public service announcements is problematic. Many young people seem to scoff at antidrug advertisements. Yet could these advertisements have a subtle effect on their attitudes? Teenagers may laugh at the advertisements, but the idea that drug use is harmful might be planted in the heads of these young people. Also, although antidrug announcements appear to be aimed at teenagers, preteens could also be affected by these messages.

According to the researchers for the annual Monitoring the Future Survey of drug use by 8th-, 10th-, and 12th-grade students, one of the several factors behind the increase in drug use by young people in the 1990s was the lack of attention in the media to the detrimental effects of drugs. News accounts and stories detailing the physical, emotional, and social problems caused by drugs were shown less frequently. Consequently, say the researchers, many young people became less concerned and aware of the potential problems of using drugs. To combat this previous neglect by the media, public service messages highlighting what problems may occur because of drug use were aired.

Supporters of the antidrug media campaign acknowledge that this is just one element of a much larger effort to halt drug use by young people. They affirm that community-based prevention activities and school-based drug education programs need to be continued. Supporters of reducing drug use through media campaigns also feel that the media *promote* drugs in various ways. For example, a number of musical groups appear to advocate drug use through their songs. Also, although movies such as *Trainspotting* and *The Basketball Diaries* illustrate the personal problems that can result from drug use, others show drug use in a matter-of-fact way. Hence, some young people may discount the potential hazards of drug use.

Critics of antidrug public service announcements feel that these messages are not effective because many young people do not view them seriously. It is also argued that these announcements sometimes lack credibility because the effects of drugs are exaggerated. Therefore, many public service announcements are disregarded by young people who have used drugs without experiencing the problems that are depicted.

In the following selections, Barry R. McCaffrey argues in favor of the federal government's spending millions of dollars on antidrug media messages because he feels that they may have a positive effect on the attitudes and behaviors of young people toward drug use. David R. Buchanan and Lawrence Wallack maintain that antidrug media campaigns are not only ineffective but may result in increased drug use because the messages are based on scare tactics and inaccuracies.

**Barry R. McCaffrey**

 **YES**

# Investing in Our Nation's Youth

## Introduction

This report presents findings from the evaluation of Phase II of the National Youth Anti-Drug Media Campaign (the Media Campaign) sponsored by the Office of National Drug Control Policy (ONDCP). The largest and most comprehensive anti-drug media campaign ever undertaken by the Federal Government, the Media Campaign features paid advertising.

The Media Campaign is being implemented in three phases, with an evaluation of each phase. Phase I was a pilot test of the campaign intervention in 12 target sites matched with 12 comparison sites. Phase II expanded the Phase I intervention to the national level and used additional media as new creatives became available (e.g., Internet banners). Phase II included 82 different advertisements that were presented through a range of media, including television, radio, newspapers, magazines, school book covers, movie theaters, and the Internet. The national media buy will continue in Phase III and other elements of the campaign will be fully underway, including additional partnerships with the media, entertainment, and sports industries, as well as civic, professional, and community groups. In each phase of the campaign, every media outlet that accepts the campaign's paid advertising has been required to match the government's purchase with an equal value of public service in the form of public service announcement (PSA) time or space, or other programs or activities related to youth substance abuse prevention. This public service time is shared with other organizations to promote anti-drug related messages, such as mentoring, underage alcohol and tobacco use, early childhood development, teen volunteering, crime prevention, and after-school activities. Media outlets can also provide in-kind contributions for local community events, and other unique activities.

For Phase II, the overall communication objective was to reach 90 percent of the target audience with 4 to 7 anti-drug messages each week. The specific goals for the paid campaign component were to reach 90 percent of the teen audience with 4 messages a week across all media (360 total gross rating points [GRPs]), 66 percent of youth aged 9 to 14 with 3 messages per week (198 GRPs), and 74 percent of adults aged 25 to 54 with 3.5 messages per week (259 GRPs).

From Barry R. McCaffrey, *Investing in Our Nation's Youth: National Youth Anti-Drug Media Campaign: Phase II (Final Report)* (1999). Washington, D.C.: U.S. Government Printing Office, 1999.

Parents and other adult influencers were to be the focus of approximately 40 percent of the messages and youth aged 9 to 18 were the emphasis of 60 percent of the intervention, prioritized as follows: young teens 11 to 13 years of age, teens 14 to 18 years of age, and youth 9 to 10 years of age.

This report on the evaluation of Phase II focuses on the effect of the paid television advertising on awareness of anti-drug messages among youth, teens, and parents of school-age children.

The major findings of the evaluation are as follows:

The findings from national school-based surveys of youth and teens, national telephone surveys with parents, and site visits in twelve sites indicate that the paid placement of anti-drug advertisements resulted in significant increases in awareness of anti-drug ads and messages among all three target groups.

- For all three paid ads included on the youth survey instrument, there were significant increases in awareness from baseline to followup, with substantial differences ranging from 7 to 10 percentage points.
- For all four of the paid ads included on the teen survey instrument, there were increases in the percentage who reported seeing the ads "often"; for three of the ads the difference was substantial, ranging from 5 to 14 percentage points.
- For three of the four ads included on the parent survey instrument, there were statistically significant increases in the percentage who reported seeing the ads "often"; the increase was substantial for two of the ads, with changes of 8 and 9 percentage points.

Quantitative data also show that the ads were effective among youth:

- The percentage of youth who agreed that the ads make them "stay away from drugs" increased a substantial 8 percentage points between baseline and followup; and
- The percentage of youth who agreed that the ads tell them something they didn't know about drugs increased 5 percentage points between baseline and followup.

Teen questionnaire data show that the ads were also effective among that group at the national level:

- From baseline to followup, there was a significant increase of 13 percentage points among teens who "agree a lot" that *Frying Pan* made them less likely to try or use drugs (from 23 to 36%);
- From baseline to followup, there was a significant increase of 7 percentage points among teens who "agree a lot" that *Alex Straight A's* made them less likely to try or use drugs (from 12 to 19%);
- From baseline to followup, there was a significant increase of 6 percentage points among teens who "agree a lot" that *Rite of Passage* made them less likely to try or use drugs (from 10 to 16%);

- From baseline to followup, there was a significant increase of 8 percentage points among teens who "don't agree at all" that *Frying Pan* exaggerated the risks or dangers of drugs (from 16 to 24%);
- From baseline to followup, there was a significant increase of 7 percentage points among teens who "don't agree at all" that *Alex Straight A's* exaggerated the risks or dangers of drugs (from 13 to 20%); and
- From baseline to followup, there was a significant increase of 6 percentage points among teens who "don't agree at all" that *Rite of Passage* exaggerated the risks or dangers of drugs (from 9 to 15%).

Television commercials were an important source of information about the risks and dangers of drugs; there was a significant increase in the percentage of youth who said they learned "a lot" from TV commercials that "drugs are bad," from 44 to 52 percent between baseline and followup, and there was a significant increase in the percentage of teens who learned "a lot" from TV commercials about the "risks of drugs," from 25 to 30 percent between baseline and followup.

The major findings on awareness and effectiveness of the ads are consistent in almost every instance across demographic variables, i.e., grade in school, gender, and race/ethnicity for youth and teens, and gender, race/ethnicity, age group, income level, and education level for parents.

## The Media Campaign Design

The number one goal of *The National Drug Control Strategy* is to "Educate and enable America's youth to reject illegal drugs as well as alcohol and tobacco." Objectives in support of that goal include "Pursue a vigorous advertising and public communications program dealing with the dangers of drug, alcohol, and tobacco use by youth." The President's drug control budget for FY 1998 included proposed funding for a Media Campaign, which received bipartisan support in Congress. Under the Treasury-Postal Appropriations Act, 1998, the House and Senate approved funding (P.L. 105–6 1) for "a national media campaign to reduce and prevent drug use among young Americans."

Planning for the Media Campaign began in early 1997. ONDCP initiated a collaboration with the Partnership for a Drug-Free America (PDFA), which provided the creative advertising for the Media Campaign through their existing pro bono relationship with leading American advertising companies.

The Media Campaign has three goals:

- Educate and enable America's youth to reject illegal drugs;
- Prevent youth from initiating use of drugs, especially marijuana and inhalants; and
- Convince occasional users of these and other drugs to stop using drugs.

Through realistic portrayals, the Media Campaign is designed to show the harmful effects of drugs and the benefits of a drug-free lifestyle, "denormalize" drug use by reminding people that most youth do not use drugs, and empower parents with information and strategies to prevent their children from using drugs.

The three phases of the Media Campaign are progressively more sophisticated:

- *Phase I* was a 26-week pilot test that ran from January through June 1998 in 12 metropolitan areas across the country. Because the time-frame for launching the first phase did not allow the development of new advertisements, television, radio, newspaper, and outdoor advertisements that had already been produced by PDFA were used and were placed in paid spots, with a pro bono match requirement.
- *Phase II* was the initial nationwide advertising phase. It began in July 1998 and ran into early 1999. Expanded to a national audience, Phase II included advertising through such outlets as television, radio, newspapers, magazines, movie theaters, and the Internet. Television advertising included national network and cable stations as well as local stations and in-school Channel One. As in Phase I, the Media Campaign purchased time slots for broadcasting television and radio ads to ensure that the ads reached their target audiences. Stations agreed to provide pro bono, one-to-one matching time for other advertisements or in-kind programming. Some of the ads used in Phase I were also used in Phase II, but new ads were also introduced.
- *Phase III* will mark full implementation of the Media Campaign, beginning in 1999 and running for four years. Phase III will disseminate new advertisements developed specifically for the Media Campaign. A key feature of the Phase III effort is to build partnerships with community-based and national anti-drug groups, local and State governments, industry, private businesses, and professional sports teams. For the most part, those partners will play various non-advertising roles....

# Lessons Learned

Based on analysis of Phase II data, certain themes and issues emerged. Lessons learned support conclusions about the effectiveness of the Phase II Campaign and the formulation of recommendations that may support Phase III of the Campaign.

## Lesson 1: Phase II Resulted in Increased Awareness of Anti-Drug Advertisements at the National Level

The major objective of the Phase II Campaign was to increase awareness at the national level of anti-drug ads paid for by the Campaign. This was important in order to provide guidance to the Phase III national Campaign in terms of baseline assessments and the design and implementation of the larger evaluation.

Comparisons of baseline and followup survey data clearly indicate that youth, teens, and parents saw or heard significantly more anti-drug ads at followup than at baseline. Youth were more aware of three ads—*Long Way Home, Girlfriend,* and *Drowning.* Teens indicated greater recall of four ads—*Alex Straight A's, Frying Pan, Layla/Old Friends,* and *Rite of Passage.* And, parents were more aware of three ads—*Girl Interview, O'Connor,* and *Under Your Nose.* Given these findings, the following conclusions can be drawn about the impact of the Phase II Campaign on its audiences:

- Repeated broadcasts of individual advertisements on drug use dangers raised viewer awareness of anti-drug ads at the national level, regardless of the viewer's age; and
- The content of drug-specific ads was appropriately matched with the audiences targeted through national and local television buys (e.g., inhalants with youth).

Two recommendations are pertinent here:

- Survey questions should be expanded in the future to include other media used (e.g., radio, newspaper, magazine, theater) so that the Media Campaign can assess the effectiveness of components other than television; and
- In all age groups, awareness of specific ads increased among some ethnic groups significantly more than other ethnic groups. Both the content and the language (English or Spanish) of these ads should be examined for clues as how best to target and develop ads for areas with appreciable ethnic populations. Phase III will include ads in 11 languages other than English.

## Lesson 2: TV Commercials and Other Media Are Key Information Sources on Drug Use Dangers for Youth and Teens

Youth and teens were asked how much they learned about the dangers of drugs from a variety of media and nonmedia sources that included school classes; their parents/grandparents; siblings; friends; television commercials; television shows, news, or movies; radio; and the street. The most statistically significant increase over the Phase II Media Campaign evaluation period was in the percentage of young persons reporting TV commercials as a source of information about the dangers of drugs. This holds true across demographic variables. Furthermore, for youth and teens, the use of television is associated with the Media Campaign because the percentage of youth who said they had actually seen the anti-drug ads on television increased significantly over the Phase II Campaign evaluation period.

Additionally, over the course of the evaluation period, there was a significant increase in the percentages of both youth and teens who perceived that

TV shows, news, and movies were important sources of anti-drug information. Also the percentage of youth and teens who reported they had seen anti-drug ads on billboards and posters on buses, bus stops or subways increased significantly over the course of the evaluation period. And, the percentage of teens who learned about drug risks from newspapers or magazines increased from baseline to followup.

The conclusions that can be drawn from these findings include:

- The use of paid television ads as a source of anti-drug information for youth and teens was effective in reaching these target groups; and
- The use of TV shows, news, and movies; outside billboards; and posters on buses, bus stops and subways are effective ways of reaching youth and teens with anti-drug messages.

### Lesson 3: Parents, Youth, and Teens Perceived Phase II Ads to Be Effective

From baseline to followup, there was a significant increase in the percentage of all age groups who perceived the anti-drug ads to be effective. Youth indicated that the ads told them something about drugs that they did not already know, encouraged them to stay away from drugs, and made them aware of the dangers of drugs. Teens said that the four ads targeted to their age group made them less likely to try or use drugs. And, parents stated that the ads provided them with new information or told them things that they did not know or that the ads made them aware that America's drug problem could affect their children. This indicates that all age groups perceived some benefits from the anti-drug messages.

Furthermore, from the baseline to the followup periods, the percentage of youth and teens who viewed the ads as lying about the dangerousness of drugs or exaggerating the risks of drug use decreased significantly. These findings support the following recommendation:

- Ads that present negative consequences of drug use and that target parents, youth, and teens should be continued as the Media Campaign progresses.

### Lesson 4: Teens and Parents Did Learn Some New Facts About the Risks of Using Drugs

While the major expectation of the Phase II Campaign was to increase awareness of the anti-drug ads shown, a secondary objective was to begin to change attitudes and perceptions about the harmfulness and risks of illegal drug use. Findings indicate that increased frequency of drug-specific ads led to greater recognition of the drug risks and dangers addressed by those ads. Survey findings indicated that from baseline to followup, teens showed an increase in awareness about the risks associated with using marijuana "once or twice" or "occasionally." This is important because we know from the Phase I evaluation that some teens view marijuana as acceptable and as one of their drugs of choice. Also, the percentage of parents who recognized the risks involved with using methamphetamine regularly increased significantly from baseline to followup.

Given these findings, the following conclusions can be made about the impact of the Phase II Campaign on increasing knowledge about the risks associated with using drugs:

- The Phase III Media campaign should continue to target teens with anti-marijuana messages; and
- Future campaigns should continue to target parents with anti-drug messages on drugs that they lack information about rather than those that are commonly understood to be risky. Future campaigns should provide guidance to parents on how to talk to their children about the dangers of drugs.

## Lesson 5: The Media Campaign Changed Some Attitudes Toward Drug Use

There were a few findings suggesting that even the short period examined has resulted in some inroads to changing youth and teen attitudes toward drug use.

The percentage of youth who said they were scared of taking drugs increased during the Phase II Campaign evaluation period.

The Campaign also had some success in changing teens' attitudes about drug use. For example, the percentage of teens who said that taking drugs scares them, who said they did not want to hang around anyone who used marijuana, and who perceived great risk in using methamphetamine regularly increased from the baseline to the followup periods.

Additionally, teens were asked specific questions pertaining to their attitudes about marijuana. Over the course of the Campaign evaluation period, the percentage of teens who understood specific negative consequences of marijuana increased significantly. For example, they increasingly understood the negative effects of marijuana: use would most likely lead to harder drugs; use would lead to doing worse at school, work or sports; or that one could mess up one's life or miss out on the good things in life. The fact that the teens experienced attitude changes in a positive direction about marijuana is important because we know that this a commonly accepted drug among this age group.

Additionally, survey findings revealed that the disapproval of close friends is important to teens. For example, there was a significant increase from the baseline to followup periods in the percentage of teens who believed that their close friends would strongly disapprove of them trying marijuana once or twice, occasionally, or regularly, or trying methamphetamine once or twice. These findings highlight the substantial influence that teens can have on one another.

The following conclusions are supported by these findings:

- Drug-specific ads targeted at teens were effective in increasing negative attitudes about marijuana and methamphetamines; and

- Ads targeted to teens should build on the influence of peer relationships, especially with regard to using teen disapproval to facilitate positive attitudes and behaviors.

## Lesson 6: Parents Are Key Sources of Information and Influence Regarding Drug Use

Survey results indicated that parents were a key information source about the risks of drugs for both youth and teens. However, survey data also show serious discrepancies in parents' claims about their drug-related communication with their children. The percentage of parents who stated that they had ever talked with their child about drugs or that that they talked to their child about drugs during the past year did not increase significantly over the course of the Phase II Campaign. We know from the Phase I Media Campaign findings that many parents do not talk with their children because of their own past or present drug use, lack of information about drugs, concern over how or when to present information to their children, denial that the problem could affect their children, or acceptance of the youth drug culture.

Additionally, teens clearly indicated that they thought their parents would strongly disapprove of many types of drug use. For example, there were significant increases over time in the percentage of teens who believed that their parents would strongly disapprove of trying marijuana once or twice, occasionally, or regularly; of trying methamphetamine once or twice; taking crack/cocaine once or twice or occasionally; or of taking heroin once or twice or occasionally. These findings appear to indicate that the views of parents matter to teens and influence them.

In light of these findings, the following recommendations are offered:

- Parents urgently need to know more about drugs, their risks, what they look like, and how young people gain access to them;
- A significant portion of the Phase III Campaign ads should be devoted to the improvement of communication between parents and their children on the subject of drug use;
- Ads on parent-child communication should point out the possible discrepancies between young people's knowledge and experience with drugs and parents' perceptions about how much their children know; and
- Ads on improving parent-child communication should move beyond stressing the general importance of parent-child communication and present specific methods to parents that can be expected to be effective in communicating dangers of drug use to their children.

(All of these recommendations are being incorporated in the Phase III design.)

### Lesson 7: Surveying Students in School Settings Is Problematic

In attempting to survey students in school settings, many barriers are encountered. The in-school surveys cannot take place if the school or school district refuses entry. Some schools experience difficulty obtaining signed parent consent forms or do not gain approval from their Institutional Review Board in time for the survey. Also, unrelated legal issues may result in last-minute refusals to participate. Thus, the following recommendation is made:

- Future on-site research should not rely on in-school surveys. The issue of gaining parental consent is only one of the problems encountered on conducting school-based research. The methodological issues regarding parental consent in school-based research have been the subject of a number of recent reviews (e.g., Anderman et al., 1995; Dent et al., 1993). These two studies concur on several findings of relevance to this report. First, students with and without active parental consent have different demographic characteristics (including SES [socioeconomic status] and ethnicity), thus leading to potential sample bias. Second, teenagers without active parental consent are higher in risk taking and in marijuana use, thus reducing the generalizability of the results. Third, teenagers with active consent are more likely to have seen information on alcohol, tobacco, and drug use—again with implications for valid interpretations of survey findings.

### Lesson 8: Media Monitoring and Media Buy Data Are Essential in the Interpretation of Media Campaign Findings

Media monitoring and media buy data are vital in the evaluation of media campaigns because they support, validate, and help to interpret the quantitative survey findings. These data are necessary because they clearly spell out the nature of the intervention (e.g., the specific ads broadcast, daypart, show, gross rating points, reach, frequency, and cost of ads). Such information allows for a comparison of the effectiveness of different ads and media approaches. Media buy data can also be used to do cost-benefit analyses for each ad by comparing its rate of exposure to its payment rate. And, finally, media monitoring data serve as a verification that the ads that were purchased were actually broadcast. Recognition of these strengths of media monitoring data lead to the recommendation that media monitoring data should include information about all types of media used in the intervention because this enables a comparison of the effectiveness of different types of media (e.g., broadcast versus cable television, radio versus television).

## Summary

The findings from the national survey of youth and teens clearly indicate that television, and particularly anti-drug ads, are an important source of information about the risks of drugs. Awareness of specific youth, teen, and adult anti-drug ads that were part of the National Youth Anti-Drug Media Campaign increased over the period examined, indicating the tremendous potential of the campaign to reach parents, youth, and teens with vital anti-drug messages. The quantitative and qualitative data gathered from parents demonstrate the need to increase the reach and frequency of ads targeting adults as well as to develop new creatives focusing on parent-child communication skills and the facts about the dangers of drug use. The lessons learned via the implementation and evaluation of Phases I and II have strengthened the design of Phase III. The implementation and evaluation of Phases I and II demonstrate that these efforts did meet their goal of increased awareness and also found changes in some attitudes—a positive indicator that the Phase III campaign will meet its goals of sustaining long-term anti-drug attitudes and reducing drug use among youth.

David R. Buchanan and
Lawrence Wallack

# This Is the Partnership for a Drug-Free America: Any Questions?

The paper examines the impact and possible unintended side effects of the privately sponsored Partnership for a Drug-Free America (PDFA) media campaign to reduce illicit drug abuse. The paper describes the history, goals, organization, production processes, and process and outcome evaluations of the PDFA advertising campaign. It also reviews major criticisms that have been leveled at the PDFA campaign, including its dissemination of false information, the narrow scope of its message, a number of unintended iatrogenic side-effects, potential conflicts of interest arising from the sources of its funding, and the agenda-setting function of the PDFA campaign in defining which drugs are dangerous and how the attendant problems should be addressed.

## Introduction

There is a prevailing belief in American society—perhaps more a desperate wish —that information is the "magic bullet" to solve our drug problems. If we could just get the right information to the right people in the right way for the right number of times, then seemingly dangerous or unhealthy behaviors could be eliminated. There is no clearer manifestation of this belief than the Partnership for a Drug-Free America (PDFA). For more than a decade, the PDFA has sought to generate a $1-million-a-day media campaign, creatively packaged by seasoned advertisers, to deliver the right message to the American public.

Politically, the PDFA media campaign is the perfect strategy in many respects. It capitalizes on our belief in education (although 30-second, fear-oriented media spots might not reasonably be considered serious education). It reinforces the notion that America's drug problems can be resolved through changing individual attitudes, without addressing fundamental social conditions such as poverty and discrimination. And it takes the heat off of legal— and widely advertised—drugs such as alcohol and tobacco, which are far more dangerous and costly to society. To wit, according to the most authoritative estimates, cigarette smoking causes 320,000 premature deaths annually, alcohol another 200,000 premature deaths every year, yet according to the federal

Office of National Drug Control Policy (ONDCP), the total number of deaths for all illegal drugs combined *rose* to a total of 14,000 in 1994 (ONDCP 1997; Surgeon General 1991; Ravenholt 1984; Trebach 1987).

This paper examines the work of the PDFA. It raises practical questions about its effectiveness and ethical questions about its strategy and implications. It challenges the work of the PDFA by bringing to light the implicit assumptions of their mass mediated messages. Fundamental to the analysis is the question of whose interests are being served by PDFA's approach. "Unselling drugs," as the PDFA attempts to do, is a laudable enterprise and on the surface a seemingly significant public service. But the relationship of the PDFA to alcohol, tobacco, pharmaceutical, advertising, and mass-media industries confounds their intents and provokes unavoidable questions about the differences between public versus private interests and public health versus public relations.

The article begins with a brief description of the PDFA, its history, goals, organization, production process, output, and evaluations of its effectiveness. We then review the major concerns raised by critics of the PDFA. Supporters of the PDFA see it as the quintessential example of the American spirit of voluntarism and service to the country, successfully harnessed to the discipline of free market principles. Critics see the PDFA as a self-serving front for the advertising industry and other private corporations, deflecting both attention and material resources from more serious responses to America's alcohol and other drug problems. This paper reviews and discusses these competing claims.

# Description of the Partnership for a Drug-Free America

## History

People may be surprised to learn that the PDFA is an entirely privately funded mass-media campaign created by professional marketing personnel, with no other organizational base or purpose. It is financed entirely through donations from large corporations, advertising agencies, and private foundations.

Started in 1986, the PDFA is the brainchild of Phil Joanou, then chairman of the Los Angeles advertising agency, Daley & Associates. Joanou introduced the idea of creating the PDFA at the 1986 annual meeting of the American Association of Advertising Agencies (AAAA).

To put this occasion in context, 1986 was the year that college basketball star Len Bias (University of Maryland) and pro football star Don Rogers (Cleveland Browns) died within 8 days of each other from cocaine overdoses, the use of crack cocaine had become much more widespread, and President and Mrs. Reagan launched a new War on Drugs. Media coverage of America's drug problems leaped from obscurity to front-page headlines (Merriam 1989). The Washington *Post* had seven stories on drugs in 1985, but over 400 stories on drugs in 1986 (Boldt 1992). *Newsweek* ran an unprecedented six front-page cover stories on drugs in 1986. On television, we saw such widely viewed news programs as CBS's "48 Hours on Crack Street" (one of the most widely watched news documentaries in television history, with more than 15 million viewers),

ABC's "A Plague Upon the Land," and NBC's "One Nation, Under Siege." The nation was aroused. President Reagan signed the Omnibus Anti-Drug Abuse Act in 1986, which has since become the vehicle for more than a 10-fold increase in federal funding for anti-drug efforts.

Against this backdrop, Joanou asked the AAAA for a $300,000 grant of seed money to launch what was originally called the Media-Advertising Partnership for a Drug-Free America. Based on discussions with leading advertising agencies and campaign consultants, the PDFA was originally conceived as a temporary 3-year effort that would require $1.5 billion worth of advertising to achieve success in "unselling drugs" (Alter 1987; Colford 1988a). With money from the AAAA, the PDFA shortly thereafter set up its offices in New York City and hired its first Chief Executive Officer, Dick Reilly, and president, Tom Hedrick. After a series of minor delays (Alter 1987), the first PDFA ads were aired on April 13, 1987 (Associated Press 1992).

During the first 3 years, the PDFA generated about $150 million worth of donated advertising placements each year, for a total of $434 million over the 3-year period (PDFA 1992). Although this amount was far short of their original, ambitious $1.5 billion goal, it is nonetheless impressive. Since then, the directors of the PDFA have set their expectations on the current goal of attaining $1 million worth of advertising every day, or $365 million over the course of 1 year (see figure 1). In response to recent increases in drug use among youth, Disney's ABC-TV gave the PDFA $100 million worth of airtime in 1 month alone—one ad per hour during the entire month of March 1997—as part of a concerted 'march against drugs' media effort (Goldman 1997).

## Goals

The goals for the PDFA have been variously stated. In their campaign literature the PDFA has identified three major objectives: (1) to reduce demand for drugs by changing attitudes through media communications, (2) to track changes in attitudes toward illegal drugs, and (3) to evaluate the impact of PDFA messages on attitude changes (PDFA 1992). In a personal interview with PDFA President Tom Hedrick, ... he stated that the most clearly defined objective for the PDFA is in management terms: to attain $1 million worth of advertising every day. They project that this level of advertising will ensure that every single American receives at least one anti-drug message every single day (Colford 1989b).

One million dollars a day is a staggering sum. In relative terms, the PDFA is now the second largest advertiser in America, second only to McDonald's, which spends approximately $450 million per year (Levine 1991). The PDFA's corner on media space is about five times that spent selling Coca-Cola™ (Levine 1991).

Beyond monetary goals, the PDFA proclaims that its mission is to unsell drugs. This theme has been variously stated as:

- "to produce a fundamental reshaping of social attitudes toward the use of illegal drugs;
- to make drug use socially unacceptable;

*Figure 1*

**Partnership for a Drug-Free America Annual and Cumulative Media Values**

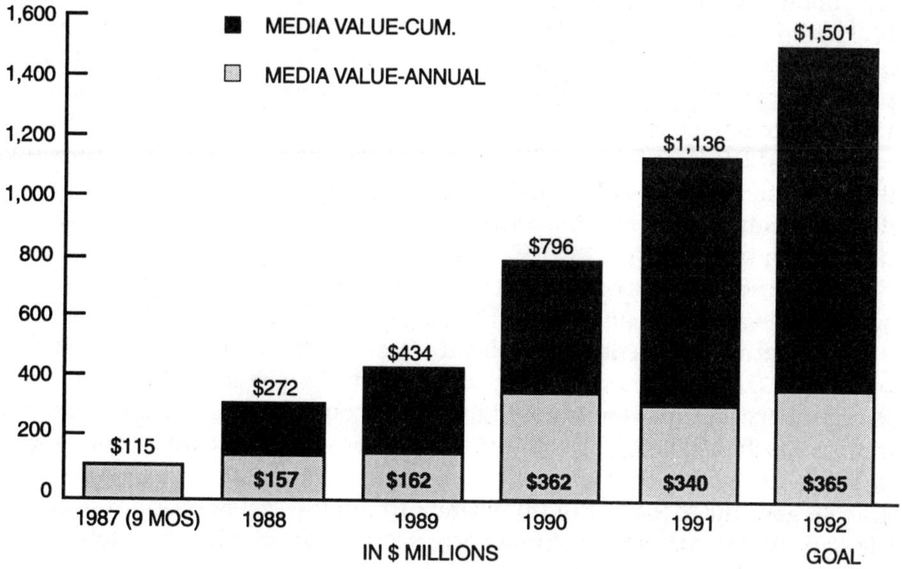

- to accelerate trends in decreasing drug use;
- to push the public's leanings further and faster;
- focused primarily on reducing the number of people trying drugs for the first time, with messages aimed at those who might influence those decisions;" and, more typical of their genre,
- "to compete with drug pushers for the market share of non-users."

In an oft-repeated phrase of their own making, their goal is to "denormalize" drug use. The current CEO, Jim Burke, states that the purpose of the PDFA is to bring America "closer to the day when not one more child tries an illegal drug" (PDFA n.d.).

## Organizational Operations

The PDFA is headed by Jim Burke. A man well connected among America's corporate executives and prominent politicians, Burke retired from his position as Chairman of the Johnson & Johnson Corporation to come to the PDFA. When asked about whether the marketing efforts of the $8 billion Johnson & Johnson Corporation—manufacturer of products including Valium™, Librium™, Tylenol-3™ with codeine, and numerous over-the-counter painkillers

—might inure the public to the idea that drugs are a solution to life's problems, Burke replied,

> "I worry about that. I agree we are a society... that believes if you have a pain, take a pill. That can contribute to the problem" (Colford 1989b).

Upon leaving Johnson & Johnson, Burke obtained a $3 million grant for the PDFA from the Robert Wood Johnson (RWJ) Foundation, a large private foundation whose endowment derives from the profits of the Johnson & Johnson Corporation. In 1994, PDFA was awarded another $7.5 million from RWJ (Health Care Financing Review 1994). As another indication of his—and by extension the PDFA's—influence, Burke chaired the President's Council on Drug Abuse during the Bush administration. During the 1992 electoral debates, President Bush singled out Mr. Burke by name to applaud his spirit of voluntarism in service to the country.

The PDFA operates on about a $3-million annual budget, of which almost two-thirds is spent on support for the approximately 30 full-time employees. This amount is consistent with its labor-intensive operations, as indicated below. The PDFA is staffed by career corporate marketers and sales personnel. Their primary job function is to sell the PDFA, constantly, year in and year out. They must sell the PDFA to: (a) corporate sponsors, (b) advertising agencies, and (c) media executives.

Because the PDFA is funded entirely through private donations, the first sales task for the staff is to persuade the top 100 corporate advertisers to make financial contributions to underwrite the campaign. Each year the PDFA staff ask those corporations with the largest advertising accounts to donate a percentage of their marketing budget to support the PDFA. Based on tax records uncovered by Cynthia Cotts (1992), a reporter for the *Nation,* the major contributors to the PDFA at that time were the leading pharmaceutical, alcohol, and tobacco companies (see table 1). We will return to this point [later].

After soliciting corporate donations, the next major sales assignment targets the advertising agencies. The PDFA staff must convince America's leading advertising agencies—from Ogilvy and Mather to Daley & Associates—to donate *pro bono* staff time and resources to develop the ads themselves. Except for minority ad agencies, all "copy" for the PDFA campaign is developed through *pro bono* contributions.

Finally, the staff must sell the idea of airing or running the ads to the networks, local television stations, newspapers, and magazines. Many of the charts in this paper are drawn from the materials used in presentations to corporate clients. In reviewing these materials, the sales pitch appears to cover the major points typical of any marketing presentation (e.g., themes from formative research with focus groups representative of different market segments).

Given the labor-intensive nature of its operations, more than two-thirds of the PDFA's operating budget is thus spent supporting staff making these sales presentations to potential corporate sponsors, advertising agencies, and media outlets. Only a small portion (< 25%) is spent on the actual production or distribution of materials. This amount is disbursed mainly to smaller, minority advertising agencies who can not afford major *pro bono* work....

*Table 1*

### Corporate Contributors, 1991

| Contributor | Amount |
|---|---|
| Robert Wood Johnson (RWJ) Foundation | $3 million |
| J. Seward Johnson, Sr., Charitable Trust | $1.1 million |
| Dupont | $150,000 |
| Proctor & Gamble | $120,000 |
| Bristol-Meyers Squibb | $110,000 |
| SmithKline-Beecham | $100,000 |
| Merck Foundation | $75,000 |
| Hoffman-LaRoche | $50,000 |
| Phillip Morris | $150,000 |
| Anheuser-Busch | $150,000 |
| R. J. Reynolds | $150,000 |
| American Brands | $100,000 |
| Total (less the RWJ grant) | $2.25 million |

*Note:* adapted from Cotts 1992.

## Inaccuracies

There are now several ads known to contain inaccuracies or falsehoods for which the PDFA has been reproached. The first such ad to receive national notoriety was the "If you're using marijuana, you are not using your brain" ad. As mentioned earlier, this ad created the impression that the electroencephalogram shown was that of someone who was high on marijuana, when in fact it was the ECG of someone in a coma. The discrepancy was first called to the nation's attention by Dr. Donald Blum of the UCLA medical school and later reported in the *Journal of the American Medical Association* (JAMA) (Dubay 1992).

The next major error concerned figures about the consequences of cocaine use in ads appearing in medical journals, which claimed one-third of users, 5 million people, require medical help. These figures are mistaken—the true figure is closer to 1 in 10, similar to rates of alcohol abuse—and were first challenged in an article in *Scientific American* (Horgan 1990). Other similar sorts of misinformation include: reports on the symptoms of marijuana use that are extremely rare (Dubay 1992), reports on the effects of cocaine extrapolated studies of monkeys in cages reinforced under an operant conditioning paradigm (Waldorf et al. 1991), and ads suggesting marijuana use lowers one's sperm count.

## Narrow Message

The PDFA has also been criticized for offering an exceedingly narrow range of messages regarding America's drug problems, relying primarily on fear arousal as the basis for motivating change. PDFA messages have been characterized by journalists in the advertising industry as "the hard sell, equating drugs and death," which "invoke hard-hitting images of death, dependency, mental and physical destruction and wasted lives," guaranteed to "make the mind reel with [their] depiction of horror and waste" (Alter 1987; Reed 1988). For example, one ad equates marijuana use with Russian roulette. In another, "A Sleep Over Date Run Amok" aimed at 6 to 8 years olds, a little boy, after agreeing to spend the night at a friend's house, is greeted by an ambulance conveying the friend's older brother who has just died of an overdose. In a more recent effort, a gunman approaches a drug dealer in his car with his girlfriend and their baby; while watching the unfolding scene through the pistol's sight, the viewer then sees the trigger being pulled just as the baby comes into sight.

The resort to fear tactics is further compounded by the gatekeeping function of local media outlets, who have shown an unwavering preference for the more sensationalistic ads over milder alternatives. Critics raise three points here. There is a long history of communication studies on fear appeals and it is well known that fear-oriented messages work only under very limited conditions. Unless recipients are provided with a clear, viable means for reducing their fears, this type of message has consistently been shown to be ineffective in producing behavior change (McGuire 1985; Severin and Tankard 1988; Soames 1988). Other than "just say no," PDFA ads rarely depict viable outlets to reduce one's fears.

Second, despite the promotional hyperbole about the potent fear quotient in PDFA ads, they are on the whole relatively tame, especially in comparison with the current genre of horror and action films to which adolescents flock. It is unlikely that anyone is really shocked or frightened by their content. Third, PDFA ads have never presented the dangers of alcohol, tobacco, or prescription drugs, which constitute a far greater risk to society (U.S. Surgeon General 1991).

In a comprehensive review of substance-abuse prevention messages, De-Jong and Winsten (1990) conclude that more effective messages include positive portrayals that model how one might handle an offer to try drugs and ones that depict pro-social alternatives, such as active, healthy lifestyles. With few exceptions, the PDFA has failed to deploy such alternative approaches.

## Side Effects

The errors in presentation and resort to scare tactics create the potential for backlash against drug-prevention messages. Just as teens in the 1960s discovered marijuana was not the "killer weed" their parents and teachers said, so the PDFA's current efforts threaten to destroy the credibility of any anti-drug campaign. What happens when the young people find out that smoking marijuana is really not like playing Russian roulette? How will they then react to messages about other more dangerous drugs?

Other potential side-effects from the campaign include the reinforcement of negative stereotypical images. In a relatively new campaign against heroin use, one PDFA ad features a young addict describing how, after losing his job, he had to "have sex with men for money to support his habit." As the Gay and Lesbian Alliance against Defamation noted, the commercials suggest that homosexuality "is merely an extreme reaction made by young people in life-threatening situations" and that "if there is one thing worse than being an addict, it's being a homosexual" (Elliott 1996). Like the ECG ad, the PDFA pulled this ad only in response to the ensuing public outcry (Levere 1996).

Similarly, the PDFA ads may serve to harden public sympathies toward drug treatment, and more specifically, toward the location and expansion of drug-treatment centers. The PDFA campaign sets out explicitly to portray drug users as "aggressive, depressed losers." (These terms are taken from items used to measure changes in attitudes in the mall intercept tracking surveys, i.e., a measure of success of the campaign is the extent to which it makes an increasing number of people think drug users are aggressive, depressed losers.) When drug users are perceived to be highly aggressive types, people become (more) concerned about locating treatment facilities in their neighborhood. Vilifying drug abusers as pariahs makes it harder for people to see that they are not all that different from the rest of us, perhaps just people in need of a better set of coping skills. By the same token, these ads serve to legitimate the criminal justice response to America's drug problems, in lieu of alternatives such as treatment and education.

Another side effect is that air time for PDFA ads has come at the cost of displacing other worthy causes. There has not been an increase in time allocated to PSAs since 1986 (on the contrary, the deregulatory mood has eased pressure on broadcasters), so other public service concerns have been sacrificed. Finally, there is evidence that the PDFA is crowding out other approaches to drug prevention, too. For example, in 1989 and 1990, the 10 largest foundation grants for alcohol and substance abuse prevention totaled $12.4 million. Of that sum, the PDFA took $4.7 million, or 38% of the total.

Other people worry that the hypocrisy of advertisers and the media can only reinforce public cynicism. ABC-TV offers the PDFA $100 million worth of airtime, while at the same time accepting $626 million in ads to push beer sales, which has consistently been demonstrated to be the "gateway" to further involvement with drugs (Scheer 1997). The ads aired during the march against drugs campaign in March 1997 were developed by the Omnicom Group advertising agency, the same agency that handles a $156 million Anheuser-Busch account (Scheer 1997). The lack of integrity adds to public distrust and jaded withdrawal, fueling feelings of suspicion that undermine the message of the ads.

## Conflicts of Interest

As indicated in table 1, the PDFA receives major contributions from the pharmaceutical, alcohol, and tobacco industries. In a written response to Cotts's article (1992) in the *Nation*, PDFA President Hedrick stated that contributions from these industries amount to less than 3% of their total revenues. But if one totals the contributions from these three industries, they come to $2.25 million, which is 75% of the PDFA's stated annual operating budget. When asked during an interview for this [selection], Hedrick refused to be drawn into trying to reconcile the discrepancy.

Further, when questioned about whether they would consider foregoing these funds, Hedrick has responded with increasing irritation to questions about their acceptance. He contends:

> "We've been called a front for the alcohol industry. We take contributions from cigarette and alcohol companies. I have no apologies whatsoever. Anheuser-Busch, R. J. Reynolds are top 100 advertisers. Now am I going to turn down $100,000 or $50,000 from them? Absolutely not! Are they impacting what I'm doing, do I run a different creative? Absolutely not! What is it W. C. Fields said, 'No good deed goes unpunished'" (Associated Press 1992).

... Hedrick indicated that the only problem he saw with their funding might be if large numbers of people learned about it, which could then undermine the PDFA's credibility. Barring this, the omission of alcohol, tobacco, and other legal drugs was justifiable on the eminently plausible grounds that the PDFA could not take on everything. However, after receiving a large $7.5 million grant from the RWJ Foundation in 1994, the PDFA ceased soliciting donations from the alcohol and tobacco industries, albeit they steadfastly defend their on-going acceptance of funding from the pharmaceutical industry.

The absence of alcohol, tobacco, and other legal drugs in PDFA materials constitutes one of its major agenda-setting functions. Whenever anyone thinks about America's drug problems, the polished, professionally crafted images conceived by the PDFA invoke images of marijuana and cocaine, not Budweiser™, Marlboro™, or Valium™. By setting the national tone, the ability of public health professionals to call attention to the health consequences of alcohol and tobacco use is constantly compromised.

Another agenda item for the PDFA is to keep advertising *per se* out of public discussions about the causes of America's social problems. As the war on drugs began to unfold back in 1986, there was tremendous public concern and debate about the effects of the mass media in promoting an irresponsible, hedonistic way of life in America. When the Reagans started criticizing the Hollywood film industry, advertisers were aware of the potential for broadening the debate to include the role of advertising. Thus, the PDFA was conceived at a time when it was important for the advertising industry to appear as much as possible as good, positive, benevolent, responsible corporate citizens. But a couple of examples will serve to illustrate the less than altruistic motives behind this part of the PDFA's agenda.

In a first example, paired editorials ran in the industry's leading trade journal, *Advertising Age,* on November 13, 1989. The lead editorial, titled "Thank you Mr. President," applauds President Bush for his prominent public support on behalf of the PDFA. The editorial immediately below the lead is titled "New Risks in the Courts." It cautions the readership to be vigilant about new efforts to hold advertisers—not just manufacturers—legally accountable in product liability suits. The political agenda is clear.

In another example, the legislature in Florida was considering a new tax on advertising in 1991. Recognizing both the threat and an opportunity, the PDFA introduced a stepped up effort to assist local communities in designing drug-prevention media materials. The result? From an article appearing in *Advertising Age:*

> "I suspect there is another benefit as well. State and local governments share the public's concerns over drug abuse and the terrible financial burden it creates. These are the same governments that are often ignorant and critical of advertising. A positive industry response to a critical public concern could help create a more favorable climate and attitude for advertising that it deserves but rarely achieves. In Florida, where the threat of an ad tax has resurfaced, the governor recently held a special reception to personally thank everyone involved in the Florida Partnership" (Bell 1992).

Finally, although the voluntary *pro bono* nature of the enterprise is intended to demonstrate good corporate citizenship, the work may be undertaken for less altruistic motives. Many agencies are more interested in winning prestigious advertising awards than solving social problems. Cliff Freeman, for example, submitted one of their ads, "Lenny," developed for the PDFA, to the Andy Awards (where it won a silver award). For many, the work was an entirely self-serving act. "It's completely scandalous what they did," says copywriter Richard Yelland of Kirshenbaum Bond. "They just did it for the award—it was all about publicity for Tony Kaye and Cliff Freeman" (Cooper 1996).

## Ideological Implications

The final criticism raised about the PDFA concerns its larger ideological implications. Beyond an agenda-setting function that defines which drugs are—and are not—considered social problems and which industries are—and are not—legitimate targets of reform, there are other, even more disturbing repercussions from the PDFA campaign. In the final analysis, the PDFA has a deeply political message.

The PDFA's model regarding the causes of substance abuse is not objective, neutral, nor reflective of research on its etiology. The PDFA propagates a particular point of view regarding the causes of America's drug problems, which, by the power of its reach, thereby marginalizes and delegitimates other perspectives. The model promoted by the PDFA is that problems like drug abuse are best understood to be the result of individual choices.

In the PDFA perspective, drug abuse is like any other consumer behavior. Individuals enter the marketplace and make free and unfettered choices in pursuit of their own self-interests. Following this premise, the PDFA campaign is designed wholly around the idea of making abstinence the more attractive, preferred consumer choice. The solution to America's drug problem lies in stimulating each and every individual to reappraise his/her self-interests in light of the PDFA message.

But when decisions about drugs are equated with consumer preferences, then the causes of substance abuse must be located within the individual's mental calculus, presumably ill-informed in those who choose to try drugs. As the PDFA pushes this individual consumer behavior model, the effects of social, political, and environmental factors are not afforded the same level of visibility and consideration. Questions about the role and responsibility of private corporations, for instance, in generating and/or resolving social problems are never raised, let alone made part of everyday public discourse. Questions about the justice and consequences of the current distribution of wealth and power in America are relegated to marginal, quirky interjections outside the mainstream. When a model that locates responsibility for resolving America's drug problems within the individual is zealously promoted, the feasibility and truth value of other perspectives are diminished in the public eye. By framing the issue in these terms, the PDFA makes serious consideration of the need for other approaches, such as changes in socioeconomic conditions, more distant and removed. As such, the PDFA message is promoting a particular point of view, and a particularly conservative point of view: The problem is solely the property of individuals, and has nothing to do with society, the social structure, poverty, unemployment, discrimination in opportunities for advancement, etc.

The conservative slant of the PDFA's message is further compounded by the limitations of the medium. When solutions to social problems are packaged in 30-second sound bites, they have to convey a very simple message. The medium does not allow for more complex discussions. The impact of this constraint became apparent in discussions with the PDFA leadership.

When discussing the relative consequences of alcohol versus marijuana use, Hedrick and colleagues repeatedly referred to people who wanted to include alcohol among America's drug problems as "prohibitionists" and those who questioned the dangerousness of marijuana as "legalizers." The PDFA did not want to take on alcohol problems because, among other things, the message would be too complicated. Similarly, to suggest that some illegal drugs might not be as bad as others would muddy the waters in ways that cannot be accommodated in 30-second solutions.

Given this mindset, the PDFA is not equipped to help the public grapple with the idea that our drug problems may be more complex than the labels, legalizer and prohibitionist. The public is not becoming better educated nor more perceptive in its deliberations about our drug problems as a result of their campaign. In this sense, the PDFA may be contributing more to the problem than to the solution.

Finally, one of the more intriguing questions concerning the ideological interests of the PDFA goes back to their resistance to public funding. Wouldn't it be easier for the PDFA to accept a stable, guaranteed level of funding from government coffers, rather than having to hustle donations year after year? There are many reasons for their aversion.

As mentioned earlier, the heads of the PDFA prefer private control over message content. Absent public interference, they are free to pursue their creative muse, accountable only to themselves and their corporate sponsors. In addition, the advertising industry itself has self-interested concerns in protecting alcohol, tobacco and pharmaceutical industries from counter-ads that might run if a publicly financed, publicly controlled media campaign was initiated. The tobacco industry withdrew their ads from television in 1971 after the initiation of a publicly mandated counter-ad campaign, at great loss to the myriad of advertising agencies on contract. But perhaps even more intriguing is the role the PDFA would like to play in demonstrating the effectiveness of private market solutions to social problems.

In meeting with the staff of the PDFA, there is no question that they are sincere in their desire to see the PDFA campaign be successful, to see lives saved, and needless suffering stopped. Many of them have been touched personally by the tragedy of substance abuse. But it became clear that they also want to be able to show that the recourse for government programs may be unnecessary and unwarranted. The private market can provide everything a society needs, and better.

In one of the more eye-opening exchanges in the interview, one of the authors described current public health knowledge about risk factors that make substance abuse problems more likely in populations.... When asked if the PDFA tried to address these known risk factors, Hedrick responded that he thought that this approach was what was wrong with the field of public health, and why the PDFA had a better program. In his mind, there is nothing one could do about changing "any of the classic, stereotypical environmental factors." Notions of improving schools, strengthening families, and providing programs to enhance students' social and academic skills are infeasible and misguided.

As he continued, his "fear ... of taking the broader public health point of view" is that public health looks to "institutional solutions for individual problems." But, for Hedrick and the PDFA, one cannot change the way things are. All anyone can do is get people to "buy into" the idea of "why they shouldn't be into the drug business." It is the free market mentality—people are self-interest maximizers freely choosing in a marketplace devoid of other considerations. According to Hedrick, attitudes toward drug use are "much more important" than the effects of poverty or broken families. The "two most important things" are telling every kid "stay in school and stay off drugs." If successful, the PDFA can show the world that all these other issues really are irrelevant.

# Conclusion

There is a general agreement that public information campaigns can be an important adjunct in promoting public health. But they are not synonymous with effective prevention. Public health agencies learned a long time ago that you cannot "unsell" unhealthy behaviors through advertising alone (Wallack 1989; Wallack et al. 1983). This has been the lesson of the Stanford Heart Disease Prevention Program and many other comprehensive efforts to change behavior and improve public health. We have long known that, without local interpersonal involvement and participation, behavior change interventions are destined for failure.

Advertisers, too, know that advertising by itself does not produce change. That is why private corporations use advertising as only one part of a comprehensive marketing approach, distilled in its most basic terms in the 'four Ps': product, price, place, and promotion. Successful marketing campaigns incorporate all four elements, at a minimum, delivering local tie-ins, widespread product availability, attractive pricing, and products that promise personal and immediate gratification. As an advertising campaign, the PDFA fails on most counts applied in their own circles.

But more importantly, not only has the PDFA been ineffective, it has neglected America's more serious drug problems—alcohol and tobacco. Alcohol and tobacco, in terms of years of potential life lost and total number of deaths, do far more to destroy individual opportunity and family well-being than the illicit drugs targeted by the PDFA (Ravenholt 1984). By defining America's drug problem as marijuana, cocaine and heroin, the PDFA is not providing a public service. It deflects attention away from corporate behavior that affects millions —to focus on individual behavior. It deflects attention away from social issues that must be addressed—to point to individual failures that ultimately lead to blaming the victim.

Public health concerns have a clear message: social and environmental changes are necessary to improve health. Education may be necessary and good, but it is not sufficient to change health behavior. History has shown that significant improvements in the health of the public come about only when the underlying socioeconomic conditions correlated with poor health are ameliorated (McKinlay and McKinlay 1977). By conveying the false sense that something adequate and successful is being done, the PDFA may well be "enabling" our drug problems, rather than contributing to their solution.

In the end, we need to ask whose interests are served by the PDFA. Even with the best of intentions, they may also serve to divert us from more important goals and more effective strategies. It may well be that we continue to turn to—and be impressed by—media strategies because we feel the need to do something, even when it is something merely comfortable and easy. The PDFA does not ask anything of us collectively, what we might do as a society to address our social problems. It lets each of us off the hook. Drug abuse is their problem, the ones who make those foolish decisions. But at some point, we will reap the results of our actions and inactions. At some point, America must come to terms with questions about the kind of society we want to create. The problems are not going away. At some point, we need to do what is right, not what is expedient.

# POSTSCRIPT

## Are Antidrug Media Campaigns Effective?

In the United States, companies spend large sums of money on advertising because it is an effective way to promote the use of their products. Thus, one could argue that it is logical to try to curtail drug use by young people by advertising through the media. That is, if advertisements can promote desirable behaviors, then they should be able to discourage undesirable behaviors.

One concern about antidrug announcements is that they may bring the issue of drugs to the attention of youngsters who had previously never considered using drugs. McCaffrey contends that if the media focus a great deal on the effects of drugs, then young people who have had little interest in trying drugs may become more curious and experiment with them. At what point do warnings against drugs become invitations to use drugs?

One organization that is devoted to antidrug advertisements is the Partnership for a Drug-Free America (PDFA). Although the Office of National Drug Control Policy provides funding to the PDFA, it is a private organization that receives money from charitable organizations as well as from pharmaceutical companies, beer manufacturers, and tobacco companies. One criticism of PDFA advertisements is that they do not address cigarette and alcohol use by young people because the organization is afraid of losing income from the beer and tobacco companies.

Buchanan and Wallack assert that PDFA advertisements contain inaccuracies about the effects of drugs and statistics on drug addicts. They also indicate that PDFA advertisements have been criticized for utilizing primary fear arousal techniques. At best, Buchanan and Wallack argue, fear arousal has short-term benefits. Buchanan and Wallack maintain that depicting prosocial alternatives, such as a healthy lifestyle, is a more effective strategy. Furthermore, they are concerned that the misleading advertisements from the PDFA may create a backlash against antidrug messages.

Two articles that examine the effects of drug messages are "Evaluation of Antismoking Advertising Campaigns," by Lisa Goldman and Stanton Glantz, *Journal of the American Medical Association* (March 11, 1998) and "Male Adolescents' Reactions to TV Beer Advertisements: The Effects of Sports Content and Programming Context," by Michael Slater et al., *Journal of Studies on Alcohol* (vol. 57, 1996), pp. 425–432. An interesting article that looks at how music videos depict tobacco and alcohol is "Tobacco and Alcohol Use Behaviors Portrayed in Music Videos: A Content Analysis," by Robert DuRant et al., *American Journal of Public Health* (July 1997).

# Contributors to This Volume

## EDITOR

**RAYMOND GOLDBERG** is a professor of health education at the State University of New York College at Cortland. Since 1977 he has served as coordinator for graduate programs in the School of Professional Studies. He received a B.S. in health and physical education from the University of North Carolina at Pembroke in 1969, an M.Ed. in health education from the University of South Carolina in 1971, and a Ph.D. in health education from the University of Toledo in 1981. He is the author of *Drugs Across the Spectrum*, 3rd ed. (Morton, 2000) and the author or coauthor of many articles on health-related issues, and he has made many presentations on the topic of drug education. He has received over $750,000 in grants for his research in health and drug education.

## STAFF

Theodore Knight   List Manager

David Brackley   Senior Developmental Editor

Juliana Gribbins   Developmental Editor

Rose Gleich   Administrative Assistant

Brenda S. Filley   Director of Production/Design

Juliana Arbo   Typesetting Supervisor

Diane Barker   Proofreader

Richard Tietjen   Publishing Systems Manager

Larry Killian   Copier Coordinator

# AUTHORS

**ROBERT APSLER** is an assistant professor of psychology in the Department of Psychiatry at Harvard Medical School in Boston, Massachusetts, and president of Social Science Research and Evaluation, Inc.

**DENNIS BERNSTEIN** is an investigative reporter, a radio host, a human rights advocate, and a poet. He is a regular contributor to Pacifica's *Democracy Now* and an associate editor for Pacific News Service. Also, he is currently cohost and associate producer of KPFA's *Flashpoints News Magazine,* and he is a frequent commentator on WBAI airwaves. His articles have appeared in numerous publications, including *The Nation, Mother Jones,* and *The Progressive,* and he is coauthor, with Leslie Kean, of *Henry Hyde's Moral Universe: Where More Than Space and Time Are Warped* (Common Courage Press, 1999).

**NELL BOYCE,** formerly a Washington correspondent for the London-based weekly *New Scientist,* is now an associate editor for *U.S. News & World Report,* where she covers biomedicine, genetics, and other scientific topics. She was awarded the Evert Clark/Seth Payne Award in 1998.

**RICHARD BROMFIELD** is a clinical instructor in psychology in the Department of Psychiatry at Harvard Medical School in Boston, Massachusetts. He is the author of *Doing Child and Adolescent Psychotherapy: The Ways and Whys* (Jason Aronson Publishers, 1999).

**DAVID R. BUCHANAN** is an assistant professor of community health studies in the School of Public Health at the University of Massachusetts–Amherst.

**THOMAS BYRD** is a professor of health at De Anza College in Cupertino, California.

**RICHARD R. CLAYTON** is a professor of psychology at the University of Kentucky in Lexington, Kentucky, and chair of the Tobacco Etiology Research Network. He was a coprincipal investigator for the 1985 National Household Survey on Drug Abuse, and he has been director of the Center for Prevention Research at the University of Kentucky since 1987.

**J. B. COPAS** is a professor in the Department of Statistics at the University of Warwick in Coventry, United Kingdom.

**MATHEA FALCO** is president of Drug Strategies, a nonprofit policy institute in Washington, D.C. He was also assistant secretary of state for international narcotics matters from 1977 to 1981. He is the author of *Making a Drug-Free America* (Times Books, 1994).

**GILLIAN FLYNN** is a contributing editor for *Workforce,* where she writes about a myriad of legal and other issues. She won the Jesse H. Neal award in 1996 for her article "Warning: Your Best Ideas May Work Against You."

**JOHN R. GARRISON** is chief executive officer of the American Lung Association, which he has been leading since 1990, and cochair of the National Coalition to Eliminate Tuberculosis and Lung Disease. He is also a former chairman of the National Health Council and a former president of the National Easter Seals Society. He holds an M.A. in public administration.

GENERAL ACCOUNTING OFFICE (GAO) is the investigative arm of the U.S. Congress. The GAO examines the use of public funds, evaluates federal programs and activities, and provides analyses, options, recommendations, and other assistance to help Congress make effective oversight, policy, and funding decisions.

STEPHEN GOODE is senior writer for *Insight on the News.*

LESTER GRINSPOON is chair of the board of directors for the National Organization for the Reform of Marijuana Laws. He is also executive director of the Massachusetts Mental Health Research Corporation and an associate professor of psychiatry at the Harvard Medical School in Boston, Massachusetts. He has been involved in marijuana research for over 20 years, and he received the Norman E. Zinberg Award for marijuana research in 1990.

MICHELE ALICIA HARMON is a former faculty research associate in the Department of Criminology and Criminal Justice at the University of Maryland in College Park. She also did research at the Urban Institute, a nonprofit policy research organization in Washington, D.C.

TIMOTHY HEEREN is a professor of biostatistics in the School of Public Health at Boston University, where he earned his Ph.D. in mathematics. His interests are in applied statistics, and his current research focuses on traffic safety research, specifically the effects of drinking and driving legislation on drinking and driving behavior and traffic crashes; the consequences of in-utero cocaine exposure on child development through the early school years; and the causes and consequences of Gulf War Syndrome.

RALPH W. HINGSON is a professor in and chairman of the Department of Social and Behavioral Sciences in the School of Public Health at Boston University.

MATTHEW F. HOLLON is a physician and an acting instructor of medicine at the University of Washington in Seattle, Washington. He earned his M.D. in 1994 and his M.P.H. in 1999 from the University of Washington. He was the recipient of the National Institute of Health's National Research Service Award in 1997, and his current research interests include direct-to-consumer marketing of prescription drugs, Western culture and medicine, and prostate cancer screening.

ALAN F. HOLMER is president of Pharmaceutical Research and Manufacturers of America in Washington, D.C.

DREW HUMPHRIES is a professor of sociology in the Department of Sociology, Anthropology, and Criminal Justice at Rutgers University, where she is director of the Criminal Justice Program. She teaches a variety of criminal justice courses, including police, deviance, gender and crime, domestic violence, and drugs and society. She is also coeditor of *Women, Violence, and the Media,* a special issue of *Violence Against Women.*

BENJAMIN JUNGE is senior research coordinator with the Department of Epidemiology at the Johns Hopkins School of Hygiene and Public Health. He is also evaluation director for the Baltimore Needle Exchange Program.

**LESLIE KEAN,** formally the full-time director of the Burma Project USA, a human rights and media advocacy group, is now an investigative journalist and associate producer of KPFA's *Flashpoints News Magazine.* Her articles have appeared in numerous publications, including the *Boston Globe, The Kyoto Journal,* and *The Progressive,* and she is coauthor, with Dennis Bernstein, of *Henry Hyde's Moral Universe: Where More Than Space and Time Are Warped* (Common Courage Press, 1999).

**PAUL A. LOGLI** is state's attorney for Winnebago County, Illinois, and a lecturer at the National College of District Attorneys. A member of the Illinois State Bar since 1974, he is a nationally recognized advocate for prosecutorial involvement in the issue of substance-abused infants. He received a J.D. from the University of Illinois.

**ALBERT B. LOWENFELS** is a professor of surgery at New York Medical College.

**ROBERT J. MACCOUN** is a professor of public policy at the University of California, Berkeley, and a consultant to the RAND Corporation in Santa Monica, California. He is also a member of the editorial advisory board of *Law and Society Review* and a member of the National Consortium on Violence Research. He is coauthor, with Peter Reuter and Mathea Falco, of *Comparing Western European and North American Drug Policies: An International Conference Report* (RAND Corporation, 1993).

**BARRY R. McCAFFREY** is former director of the Office of National Drug Control Policy at the White House, where he served as the senior drug policy official in the executive branch and as the president's chief drug policy spokesman. He is also a member of the National Security Council. Upon his retirement from the U.S. Army, he was the most highly decorated officer and the youngest four-star general.

**JAMES R. McDONOUGH** is director of the Florida Office of Drug Control. From 1996 to 1999, he was director of strategy for the Office of National Drug Control Policy, and he was also an officer in the U.S. Army. In addition, he has served as an associate professor of political science and international affairs at the United States Military Academy, as an analyst with the Defense Nuclear Agency, and as a detailee to the U.S. State Department. His publications include *Platoon Leader* (Presidio Press, 1996).

**JOHN B. MURRAY** is a distinguished professor in the Department of Psychology at St. John's University in Jamaica, New York.

**ETHAN A. NADELMANN** is director of the Lindesmith Center, a New York–based drug-policy research institute, and an assistant professor of politics and public affairs in the Woodrow Wilson School of Public and International Affairs at Princeton University in Princeton, New Jersey. He was the founding coordinator of the Harvard Study Group on Organized Crime, and he has been a consultant to the Department of State's Bureau of International Narcotics Matters. He is also an assistant editor of the *Journal of Drug Issues* and a contributing editor of the *International Journal on Drug Policy.*

**OFFICE OF NATIONAL DRUG CONTROL POLICY** (ONDCP) was created by the Anti-Drug Abuse Act of 1988 to advise the president on a national drug control strategy, a consolidated drug control budget, and other management and organizational issues. The principal purpose of the ONDCP is to establish policies, priorities, and objectives for the nation's drug control program, with the overall goal of significantly reducing the production, availability, and use of illegal drugs both in the United States and abroad.

**STANTON PEELE** is a social and clinical psychologist who has taught at Harvard University, Columbia University, and the University of California. He has authored or coauthored several highly influential books on the nature of addiction and on treatment efficacy and social policy with respect to substance abuse, including *Love and Addiction* (Taplinger, 1975), *The Meaning of Addiction* (Lexington Books, 1985), and *Diseasing of America* (Lexington Books, 1989). The author of numerous journal articles that have challenged and helped redirect mainstream thinking about addiction, he was awarded the Mark Keller Award by the *Journal of Studies on Alcohol.*

**JEFFREY A. SCHALER** has been a psychologist and therapist in private practice since 1973. He is also an adjunct professor of justice, law, and society at American University's School of Public Affairs, where he has taught courses on drugs, psychiatry, liberty, justice, law, and public policy since 1990. He writes a regular column for *The Interpsych Newsletter,* and he is the author of *Smoking: Who Has the Right?* (Prometheus Books, 1998).

**J. Q. SHI** is a research associate for the Mining and Environmental Research Group in the T. H. Huxley School of Environment, Earth Sciences and Engineering at Imperial College of Science, Technology and Medicine in London, United Kingdom. In addition to publishing a number of research papers, he is coauthor, with B. C. Wei and G. P. Lu, of *Introduction of Statistical Diagnostics* (Southeast University Press, 1991). He earned his Ph.D. from the University of Southampton.

**MAIA SZALAVITZ** is a journalist who has written for *New York Magazine,* the *New York Times,* the *Washington Post, Newsday,* the *Village Voice,* and other major publications.

**DAVID VLAHOV** is a professor of epidemiology and medicine at the Johns Hopkins School of Hygiene and Public Health. He is also principal investigator of the evaluation of the Baltimore Needle Exchange Program.

**JOSEPH VOLPICELLI** is on the faculty of the Department of Psychology at the University of Pennsylvania. His research interests include the biological basis of substance abuse and animal models of rehabilitation.

**ERIC A. VOTH** is chairman of the International Drug Strategy Institute and a clinical assistant professor with the Department of Medicine at the University of Kansas School of Medicine. He is also medical director of Chemical Dependency Services at St. Francis Hospital in Topeka, Kansas. He has testified for the Drug Enforcement Administration in opposition to legalizing marijuana, and he is recognized as an international authority on drug abuse.

**LAWRENCE WALLACK** is a professor of public health at the University of California, Berkeley, and codirector of the Berkeley Media Studies Group, an organization that conducts research and training in the use of the media to advance public health policies. He has published extensively and lectures frequently on policy issues related to health promotion. He is the recipient of several awards, including the Beryl Roberts Prize in Health Education (1980). He is the principal author of *Media Advocacy and Public Health* (Sage Publications, 1993) and coeditor, with Charles K. Atkin, of *Mass Media and Public Health: Complexities and Conflicts* (Sage Publications, 1990).

**JERRY WIENER** is on the faculty of George Washington University Medical School in Washington, D.C.

**MICHAEL R. WINTER** is a statistical coordinator for the SPH Data Coordinating Center in Boston University's School of Public Health.

**WORLD HEALTH ORGANIZATION** (WHO) is an international organization dedicated to the attainment by all peoples of the highest possible level of health, as defined in the WHO Constitution. Among other functions, the WHO proposes conventions, agreements, and regulations, and makes recommendations about international nomenclature of diseases, causes of death, and public health practices. Dr. Gro Harlem Brundtland took office as director-general on July 21, 1998. Her term of office is five years.

**ALICE M. YOUNG** is a professor of psychology and of psychiatry and behavioral neurosciences at Wayne State University, where she also serves as associate dean of the College of Science. Her research interests include behavioral and brain processes involved in opioid tolerance and dependence.

**GRAZYNA ZAJDOW** is senior lecturer in the School of Social Inquiry at Deakin University in Australia. She is a member of the Australian Sociological Association, and her research interests include women with drug and alcohol problems and self-help groups.

# Index

marijuana: and controversy over employee drug testing, 283; and controversy over legalizing drugs, 4–9; controversy over legalizing, for medicinal purposes, 158–175; drug trafficking and, 31–32, 33
Marijuana Tax Act, 158–159
Martin, Peter, 193
McCaffrey, Barry R.: on antidrug media campaigns, 312–321; on stopping the importation of drugs, 18–27
McClure, Adrian, 284
McDonough, James R., on legalizing marijuana for medical purposes, 166–175
McKinney, Cynthia, 288
media campaigns, controversy over antidrug, 312–334
Medical University of South Carolina (MUSC), prosecution of pregnant drug users and, 90–94
medicalization of marijuana, 8, 13; controversy over, 158–175; controversy over employee drug testing and, 283
memory, the nature of drug addiction and, 108–109
methadone maintenance programs, 135–136; effectiveness of, 294–299, 301, 305–306
Mexico, drug trafficking and, 19–20, 24, 25–26, 27, 29, 31, 32, 35
micro harm reduction, 117, 121–122
Miller, William, 254, 255
minimum legal drinking age (MLDA), and controversy over lowering the blood alcohol level for drunk driving, 43–44, 45–47
Minot, William, 286–287
*Moderate Drinking: The Moderation Management Guide* (Kishline), 250
moderate-drinking programs, 126–127; and controversy over total abstinence for alcoholics, 247–255
Moderation Management (MM), 248, 250, 254
Moscone Act, 5
Mugford, Stephen, 137
Murray, John B., on drug abuse treatment, 294–299

Nadelmann, Ethan A., 11, on legalizing drugs, 4–9
naltrexone, 251–252
National District Attorneys Association (NDAA), prosecution of pregnant drug users and, 94–95
National Highway Traffic Safety Administration (NHTSA), and controversy over lowering the blood alcohol level for drunk driving, 48–49, 53–54
National Institute of Drug Abuse, 286
National Institutes of Health (NIH), on medicalization of marijuana, 167, 169
National Security Council (NSC), drug trafficking and, 30

National Youth Anti-Drug Media Campaign, controversy over, 312–334
needle exchange programs, 118, 120, 124–125, 127; controversy over, 58–74
Nehlig, Astrid, 190–191
Netherlands: legalization of drugs in, 6, 8; needle exchange programs and, 13, 71
neurotransmitters: caffeine and, 190–191, 192; and controversy over the nature of drug addiction, 109–110
New Haven, Connecticut, Health Department, needle exchange program of, 58–59, 68–70
nicotine patch, 222
Nixon, Richard, 29
non-steroidal antiinflammatory drugs (NSAIDs), 159
norepinephrine, drug use and, 109
North American Free Trade Agreement (NAFTA), drug trafficking and, 35
nosology, and controversy over the nature of drug addiction, 103
nucleus accumbens, drug use and, 110

Office of National Drug Control Policy (ONDCP), 30; controversy over antidrug media campaigns of, 312–314; on needle exchange programs, 65–74
*O'Neill v. Morse*, 81
opioid neurotransmitters, drug use and, 109
organic disorders, 104
O'Shaughnessy, W. B., 158
osteoporosis, caffeine and, 197–198
outpatient methadone maintenance programs, 301, 305–306. *See also* methadone maintenance programs
outpatient nonmethadone treatment programs, 301, 305–306. *See also* methadone maintenance programs
outreach programs, 72–73

Pakistan, drug trafficking and, 27, 29, 32
Papandreou, George, 8
paraxanthine, 193
Partnership for a Drug-Free America (PDFA), controversy over antidrug media campaign of, 312–334
passive smoke. *See* secondhand smoke
Pastrana, Andres, 23
pathology, and controversy over the nature of drug addiction, 103
Peele, Stanton, on doctors promoting alcohol for their patients, 180–183
*People v. Bolar*, 80–81
*People v. Jennifer Clarise Johnson*, 80
*People v. Melanie Green*, 79–80, 88–90, 94
peripheral-route processing, and controversy over the nature of drug addiction, 101–102
Peru, drug trafficking and, 22, 23, 25, 30, 31